D1327492

Looking South

SOUTHERN DISSENT

UNIVERSITY PRESS OF FLORIDA

Florida A&M University, Tallahassee
Florida Atlantic University, Boca Raton
Florida Gulf Coast University, Ft. Myers
Florida International University, Miami
Florida State University, Tallahassee
New College of Florida, Sarasota
University of Central Florida, Orlando
University of Florida, Gainesville
University of North Florida, Jacksonville
University of South Florida, Tampa
University of West Florida, Pensacola

This book is dedicated to my mother, Ruth Evans Frederickson, who encouraged my *Looking South* from an early age, and to the memory of Mary Evans Goodman (1886–1971), lovingly known as Auntie Wee.

Contents

Figures

Foreword

One of the persistent problems in writing about the South is the tendency to assume that this American region stood alone and unique in history. Scholars and "South-watchers" too often look only inward rather than outward to understand the character and extent of a supposed southern exceptionalism. Even when they set up a comparative framework, they confine themselves to an examination of the differences between the southern and northern sections of the United States. As the story often goes, the South developed its "peculiar" society, economy, and culture principally from slavery and a staple-crop economy. Then, after the Civil War and through much of the twentieth century, southern reliance on cheap, oppressed labor trapped in farm tenancy or textile mill isolation, and a strict code of racial segregation and suppression, perpetuated distinctiveness. Class, race, rural life, old-time religion, and (of course) male dominance controlled human relations and public life. Such an understanding of the South is not wrong. But it limits our approach to the region because peculiarities in economic, political, racial, and gender relationships are best understood in a framework that transcends not only the South but also the United States.

Mary Frederickson offers such a wide-angle approach by placing the South in a global context. She also looks closely at developments within the factories, mill towns, churches, households, and labor organizations that made up the so-called New South. She demonstrates how the forces that shaped them are now being replicated in Latin America and Asia. She shows that looking south from a northern, or an American, perspective reveals the ways industries have moved their operations southward in a constant search for cheap labor, low taxes, friendly governments, and racial and/or ethnic tensions that discourage working people from uniting in their common interest. Policies designed initially for the American South now flourish in the Global South.

By looking at the American South from outside the United States, Frederickson places southern exceptionalism in a new light. She shows that the same siren song that, during the late nineteenth and early twentieth centuries, lured textile and other low-skill, cost-sensitive industries to the South has more recently drawn such industries away from the South to developing nations. Workers in the American South did not acquiesce to employers' demands for compliance. They resisted state governments' "right-to-work" laws and other anti-labor policies. Women, in particular, challenged the patriarchal world of industrial capitalism and mill town life. They joined their male comrades in organizing labor on behalf of fair wages and better working conditions. They resisted onerous work rules that threatened families. But the successes of southern workers in gaining some control over their jobs and improvement in their wages became a rationale for manufacturers to move operations overseas, where a boosterism reminiscent of the New South echoes today, amid oppression.

Within this global context, Frederickson provides new insight into the American South. She investigates the supposedly racially exclusive industrial work world that characterized the region during most of the twentieth century. She demonstrates that the color line did not hold so rigidly in textile mills as has been thought. Class interest sometimes superseded racial identity. She also demonstrates (as have others) that southern churches served not only as places of worship and fellowship but also as staging areas for protest. Frederickson's South is full of dissent and movement. In recent years, for example, newcomers such as Latinos have redrawn the cultural profile of southern towns.

Frederickson's exploration of southern patterns of resistance and their impact across three continents and two centuries reveals a great deal. Exceptional as it may have been in important ways, the New South and all the "Souths" it has spawned have suffered from, nourished, and inadvertently helped export one of America's principal products—exploitative industries. Ironically, southern workers who dissented from the false god of "progress at any price" and demanded a fair share of the wealth they created contributed to decisions that have affected millions in the Global South. In revealing these patterns, Frederickson revises our understanding of the New South and its legacy. She does the same for the meaning of southern dissent, which hereafter may be assessed from global perspectives.

Stanley Harrold and Randall M. Miller
Series Editors

Preface

I have spent the past two decades living in Cincinnati, a place that is neither East nor West, North nor South. People living elsewhere position Cincinnati in ways I find fascinating. My relatives in the South think I live in the boundary waters close to the Canadian border; friends in the East put Cincinnati in the same geographical category as Kansas, Nebraska, and Idaho. My cousins in California refer to me as living "back East." And colleagues in Cleveland *know* that Cincinnati is a southern city—why else would you be able to get good barbeque and a glass of sweet tea there?

The division of the United States into North and South has shaped my own life. My parents, a self-supporting southern belle from the Deep South and the son of dairy farmers from Wisconsin, met in Atlanta during World War II. They married after the war and began moving around the country, returning to Atlanta twenty years later. By the time I was eleven years old I had lived in Wisconsin, Washington, D.C., Iowa City, Seattle, and twice in Kansas City. We moved from there to Atlanta the year I turned sixteen. Going south because of my father's work, we entered a region in the throes of change. From the streets of Atlanta to the small towns of Waynesboro, Hephzibah, and West Point, Georgia, the civil rights movement was redressing the boundaries between black and white, seeking justice long overdue, and, in Biblical terms, making "the crooked places straight," "break[ing] in pieces the gates of brass and cut[ting] asunder the bars of iron." Social justice certainly had not been achieved by the mid-1960s and few of the crooked places had been straightened, but the society my white relatives had known all their lives was changing in unmistakable ways.

I went south to the land of my mother's people as an outsider. My claim to connection came through these relatives and the lifelong lessons in southern history I received from my mother and Auntie Wee, the beloved great-aunt who made regular visits to see us when we lived outside the South. After a few years, I was able to pass as southern, but having been born in Wisconsin, my regional identity remained fluid. I became an avid fan of Lillian Smith, reading *Killers of the Dream* so many times that the book, purchased in 1966, the year after we moved to Atlanta, fell apart. Tethered with a rubber band, it still sits on a shelf beside me.

Lillian Smith's description of the southern world she knew made sense of aspects of southern life that I had real trouble understanding. Written in 1949 and reissued in 1961, Smith's memoir opened the field of southern history to new ways of thinking about culture, life stories, and gender, race, and class. Reading *Killers of the Dream* as a high school student in the late 1960s shaped my ideas about the past and present and provided an introduction to economics and social theory. For a girl from Kansas, the book made the Atlanta of those years seem as vivid as Oz. The southern spring dazzled as the flowering quince, forsythia, redbuds, and dogwoods gave way to wisteria, honeysuckle, and roses. The city teemed with life, from the red dirt roads on the edge of downtown to the skyscrapers going up on Peachtree Street. Crowds of people thronged the sidewalks as young African American boys sold newspapers in the streets, hawking dailies as they walked between the cars at busy intersections. Almost half the city's population worked for less than a dollar an hour. Women always earned less than men; black Atlantans always brought home lower wages than their white co-workers, even if they did the same jobs, which they usually didn't.

A few years later, studying southern history as a graduate student, I experienced firsthand the connections between self and society and the working out of the economic conundrums that Smith had articulated so well. I lived in Durham, ten miles northeast of Chapel Hill but a world away, at a time when the smell of tobacco still permeated the humid air, wafting from the L&M factory in the heart of the city out to the Erwin Mills in West Durham, just around the corner from Duke University. You could still hear the clickety-clack of "Mr. Erwin's" looms in those days when textiles and tobacco dominated the local economy and thousands of factory workers called Durham home. I wrote my dissertation at the University of North Carolina at Chapel Hill, that "southern part of heaven" where historians and sociologists had worked since the 1920s to unravel the tangled paradoxes of southern life.

On the other side of Chapel Hill, the town of Carrboro was full of former textile workers, and tobacco farmers south and west of town still tended state-allocated plots passed down from generation to generation, some no bigger than half an acre. Seventy-five miles further west in Burlington, once home to the largest textile mill in the world, unemployment reached 20 percent in the late 1970s, while Winston-Salem, the only town in the United States to supply the name for two cigarette brands, held on as the nation's tobacco capital. Labor issues and the echoes of decades of economic struggle permeated all of these communities. Labor dissent was everywhere, in the struggles for women to get equal pay for equal work and in bitter fights for union representation. Hope remained strong as workers organized at Duke University in Durham and further east in Roanoke Rapids, where the Amalgamated Clothing and Textile Workers took on textile giant J. P. Stevens & Co. It became clear in those days in North Carolina that historical networks of resistance could be reconstructed; the past, as Faulkner put it, "was not even past."

My interest in the topics addressed in this volume has its roots in this milieu. I became a historian because it was the only way that I could make sense of my own crazy-quilt life history and begin to understand the disparate places that I have called home. In that foreign land that is the past, historians are outsiders who work hard to become locals. Although we do our best, we can only partially know the lives and cultures of those whose old mail we read as eagerly as if it had just been delivered to our door. The essays that follow in *Looking South* bring together my work in labor and women's history in an attempt to better understand the complex historical landscape of the American South and its role in shaping the twenty-first century world in which we live.

Acknowledgments

I want to thank my colleagues at Miami University in the Department of History and the Programs in American Studies, Black World Studies, and Women's Studies for their encouragement over the years. Dean Karen M. Schilling of the College of Arts and Science has been particularly helpful, and I thank her and Associate Dean Phyllis Callahan for their support. The College generously provided two semester research leaves, the first to begin this work and the second to complete it. Allan Winkler, Charlotte Goldy, and Mary Cayton have chaired a vibrant and engaging history department. For many years, Michael O'Brien and Jack Kirby made Miami University a premier place to do southern history north of the Ohio River; I am grateful to them for being such exceptional colleagues. Lively conversations with Jeffrey Kimball, Drew Cayton, Judith Zinsser, Robert Thurston, Yihong Pan, Steve Norris, Carla Pestana, Dan Cobb, Kimberly Hamlin, Nishani Frazier, Curt Ellison, Rick Momeyer, and Mark McPhail have enriched my understanding of history and culture in multiple contexts.

This book took shape as I worked with the Wilks Leadership Institute at Miami University to enhance student civic engagement and as a Fulbright Scholar on the Havighurst Silk Road Project. I thank Peggy Shaffer for her leadership and Sheila Croucher, Shelly Jarrett Bromberg, Tom Klak, Tom Dutton, Charlie Stevens, and Nick Longo for their insights. Shelly Bromberg generously answered a number of questions at an important juncture. Havighurst Center Director Karen Dawisha and the other intrepid Silk Road travelers made an 8,000-mile trek on the other side of the world an incredible experience. As we traversed a large swath of the Global South, I learned a tremendous amount from Steve Nimis, Elizabeth Wilson, Afsaneh Ardehali, Gülen Çevik, Rick Colby, Yildirim Dilek, Scott Kenwothy, Sante Matteo, Yihong Pan, Judith Sessions, Gulnaz

Sharafutdinova, Ben Sutcliffe, and Stan Toops. Mary Jane Berman of the Center for American and World Cultures endorsed this project, as she has the work of so many faculty and students at Miami. Jenny Presnell and the staff at King Library make doing research there a pleasure. Jeri Schaner performs a miracle or two each day in the history department office, and I remain grateful to her and to Elizabeth Smith for helping to move my work along. The graduate and undergraduate students I have had the privilege of teaching over many years have also taught me a great deal. I particularly want to thank Timothy Lynch, Corinna Hörst, Susan Eacker, Kristen Reichart, and Kate Volkman. I continue to appreciate my mentors and colleagues at the University of North Carolina at Chapel Hill, especially Donald Mathews, Joel Williamson, John Kasson, Joy Kasson, Jacquelyn Hall, and the staff of the Southern Oral History Program, as well as Harry Watson, Robert Korstadt, and those in the Chapel Hill diaspora, including Betsy Jacoway, Brent Glass, Allan Tullos, Charles Eagles, Gaines Foster, Scott Strickland, and Cliff Kuhn. From Duke University, Anne Scott, Peter Wood, and Bill Chafe always offered encouragement and support. At the University of Alabama in Birmingham, Blaine Brownell, Tennant McWilliams, and especially Virginia Hamilton, Sherry Sullivan, and Judith L. King sustained my work.

I am pleased to have the opportunity to thank those who offered their expertise, critiques, and suggestions for revising this work in various formats over the years. Tom Dublin and Larry Gross helped enormously in identifying the looms discussed in chapter 8. Judith Smith offered her insights and ideas as I worked on an earlier version of chapter 6. Nancy Hewitt and Suzanne Lebsock gave wonderful feedback as they prepared *Visible Women,* where part of chapter 3 first appeared. Bob Zieger did the same as he edited *Organized Labor in the Twentieth Century South,* where a previous version of chapter 4 was published. Michelle Gillespie and Catherine Clinton affirmed my work on southern women workers as they edited *Taking Off the White Gloves.* Michelle Gillespie and Louis Kyriakoudes offered helpful comments on the Global South material in chapter 8 at the Southern Association of Women Historians in June 2009. Thanks to Joan Johnson and Francesca Morgan, coordinators of the Newberry Library Seminar on Women and Gender, for inviting me to share this work-in-progress in September 2008 to a lively group of discussants there in Chicago. Special thanks to Susan Levine of the University of Illinois–Chicago, who served as commentator. My thoughts on connecting the

"New South" and the "Global South" developed first in a paper presented at the Women and Globalization Conference at the Center for Global Justice, San Miguel de Allende, Mexico, in 2005. There, I was grateful for the interest and encouragement of Erica Polakoff, Ligaya Lindio-McGovern, and Mary Margaret Fonow. I much appreciate the criticism and feedback of those who read the entire manuscript and those who weighed in on specific chapters or sections, including Judith Zinsser, Robert Thurston, Jeffrey and Linda Kimball, Yihong Pan, Timothy Lynch, Nishani Frazier, Nancy Robertson, Dan La Botz, and Derry Graves. Thanks to Richard Greenwald, who reviewed the book for the University Press of Florida, and to an anonymous reviewer whose comments and suggestions greatly improved the manuscript.

Those I met along the way and interviewed specifically for this project changed the way I viewed the world and taught me a tremendous amount: long-time textile workers in Troup County, Georgia, labor leaders and activists throughout the South, Ella May Wiggins' daughter Mrs. Merritt Wandell, Dorothy Markey (Myra Page) and Lois MacDonald, and the women in the Margilan Silk Mill, who showed me their looms and reached out across a formidable language barrier to explain their work and their lives. The generosity of these women and men in sharing their life stories seemed boundless, and I was honored to listen.

Archivists, librarians, editors, and others across the country have helped with this project in many ways. My thanks to Betsy Rix and Melanie Stephan at the Atlanta Historical Society; Harry McKown and Jason Tomberlin at the North Carolina Collection; Jessica Desany Ganong at the Peabody Museum at Harvard; Kristen Marangoni and Marc Carlson in Special Collections at the McFarlin Library at the University of Tulsa; Linda De Loach of the George Meany Memorial Archives; Ann Y. Evans of the William Elliott White Homestead Archives; the staff of the North Carolina Room at the New Hanover County Library in New Bern, North Carolina. I thank Anthony Clark for his editorial assistance, and Sue Rossi for her careful design work. Jean Hamilton's skill and expertise advanced my work in important ways. I really appreciate the willingness of my friend, photographer Diane Schneiderman, to climb to the top of the Carew Tower in Cincinnati on Labor Day weekend 2009 to take the cover photograph. Susan Boydston has been a great writing partner. Jane Schulz's overlapping interests in southern history have sustained me for a long time. Nancy Schick's enthusiasm, friendship, and early editing work on this project made a tremendous difference. Evan Joiner provided invaluable research assistance and historical perspective at several key junctures. Jeanne Barker-Nunn brought her sharp eye and breadth of knowledge to the project toward the end and greatly improved the final version. I am fortunate to have had the privilege of working with Randall Miller and Stanley Harrold at the University Press of Florida, the best series editors ever. Director Meredith Babb has been supportive of this project from the beginning and has expertly seen it through to publication. It has been a pleasure to work with her and others at the press, including Gillian Hillis and Marthe Walters. Dennis Lloyd, Ale Gasso, and Heather Turci provided expert help. Jesse Arost did a wonderful job with the images, and I am grateful to Penelope Cray for copyediting changes that improved the clarity of the text.

Insights from my collaboration with Delores M. Walters on another project have spilled over and influenced this one as well. Susan Porter Benson remains an important inspiration, and I miss her voice enormously. I've benefitted from the intellectual energy that Judith Smith and Sonya Michel bring to every project. Marion Roydhouse and Brigid O'Farrell have been great colleagues and boon companions since graduate school and right after, and our continuing friendship is a real joy. Both of you know how important your support has been to *Looking South*. Leon Fink and Susan Levine are the kind of friends and colleagues who come along once in a lifetime, and I have been truly fortunate to share work and friendship with four generations of their family.

My own family has provided various kinds of support and encouragement over many years. My thanks go to Ed and Helen Frederickson, and also to Patricia Frederickson, Rebecca Partridge, Christine Swiggum, Kelly Campion, and all of my wonderful Lloyd-Jones cousins. I especially appreciate the interest in my work that Elizabeth Wright Ingraham, Jean Lloyd-Jones, and Robert and Derry Graves have demonstrated. A bevy of southern aunts and uncles showered me with love and helped me understand my own history. I especially want to thank Leck and Ann Murphey, who always welcome me back to Georgia with open arms. Sarah Knox has listened carefully for a long time now. Friend and kin Carol Willis has supported me in a thousand ways. This brings me to my beloveds, Megan, Evan, Anthony, and Clint, who have done so much, individually and collectively, to help me finish *Looking South* that I will never be able to finish thanking them. Megan and Evan have crafted wonderful lives of their own making, and I am extremely proud of their choices. Anthony is a great person to have as part of our family. And as for Clint Joiner, a southerner by birth who I met in Atlanta, Georgia, many moons ago—his love has grounded my life.

Introduction

Labor Transformation and Networks of Resistance

When W. E. B. Du Bois left Fisk University in Nashville, Tennessee, at the end of his sophomore year in 1886, he walked to the Lebanon Teachers' Institute in Wilson County, where he took and passed the exam to become an elementary school teacher. Continuing east along the Lebanon Pike Road, the eighteen-year-old Du Bois came to the sleepy small town of Alexandria, Tennessee, where he spent the summer teaching students between the ages of six and twenty. There, just fifty miles outside of Nashville, he entered "a zone where time had stopped the day after the day of Jubilee." In a place where slavery and segregation had cast deep shadows, his classroom was a windowless storage barn built of logs. Two decades after the end of the Civil War, Du Bois saw agricultural peonage in the making: the uneasy symbiosis of white farmers and black laborers trapped in a one-crop economy, the "pythian madness" of prayers and "sorrow songs" released in "jerry-built tabernacles," and the futility of book learning in the face of the "rebuked destinies" of a freed people who came out of slavery "singing, praying, and aspiring" only to have their ambition derailed and dreams buried in what Du Bois's Wilson County landlady referred to a decade later as "a heap of trouble."[1]

The political and social negotiations that took place at the end of the Civil War transformed the United States from a slaveholding nation to one with the democratic possibility of universal citizenship. During the paradox that was Reconstruction, state and federal governments made forays in that direction, but then reversed course. The dream of citizenship for all became the nightmare of a citizenry fragmented by race, ethnicity, and gender. Civil liberties afforded former slaves in the aftermath of war were gradually withdrawn, one set of rights after another: voting and access to public transportation, education, housing, and interracial marriage. The list of rights denied grew only longer in the forty years between the end of Reconstruction and the beginning of the "Great War," a conflict the United States entered to make the world safe for democracy, a form of government that remained distorted and unrealized inside its own national borders. That said, extraordinary transformations took place in the years following the Civil War. In every way possible, from the remarkable to the ordinary, freedmen and freedwomen across the South infused liberty with meaning as they reshaped their lives in the turbulent wake of slavery's passing. While a student at Fisk, Du Bois prophesied for African Americans an "early arrival in the Promised Land." Writing about those years in *Darkwater*, a collection of essays and short fiction published in 1920, he remembered believing that "through the leadership of men like myself and my fellows, we were going to have these enslaved Israelites out of the still enduring bondage in short order."[2]

That optimism gained traction as men and women claimed freedom in the late-nineteenth-century South, a process that varied dramatically from the rice fields of the South Carolina Low Country to the Port of New Orleans; from the rebuilt city of Atlanta to the cotton fields of Burke County, Georgia; from the New South city of Durham to the textile communities of Gastonia and Danville to the streets of Nashville that surrounded Fisk University. The difficult work of becoming wageworkers and owners of land and businesses was exacerbated by the arduous and often circuitous routes to citizenship that African Americans were forced to follow. The struggle to establish schools and churches paralleled the enormous effort to achieve political representation. Despite all the barriers they faced, those first generations of freedmen and freedwomen changed the post-war southern world in previously unimaginable ways, carving out the economic and social space necessary to become citizens. Their work can be measured in tangible material, political, and cultural successes as well as in the virulently negative responses of many white Southerners to those very accomplishments.

Looking South underscores the importance of the South in American labor history and the centrality of dissent within the South. It begins with the transformation of the southern economy and labor system at the end of the nineteenth century as the region industrialized in the wake of Emancipation and concludes at the beginning of the twenty-first century with the major economic and cultural conversions brought about by glo-balization. These two paradigm shifts in southern labor history bookend the volume and frame a re-examination of southern dissent that focuses on the intersections of race, class, and gender. The book weaves together the complex histories of women and men involved in labor resistance throughout the region and uncovers networks of dissent that shaped the lives of workers and activists and influenced the New South labor systems established in the late nineteenth and early twentieth centuries. Those sys-tems, forged by manufacturers, workers, and reformers, remained intact for over a hundred years and became the model for industries throughout the United States. After World War II, these New South systems began to be exported abroad, and in the twenty-first century, this prototype of industrialization—dependent upon cheap labor, anti-unionism, and oc-cupational segregation by race and gender—has been transformed again and taken worldwide.

The Global South, which refers collectively to the nations of Central and Latin America and most of Asia and Africa, is a massive region that faces a plethora of serious challenges, including poverty, human and civil rights abuses, ethnic conflicts, and the mass displacement of refugees. At the same time, Global South nations constitute enormous emerging markets for economic growth, natural resources, and workers, just as the Ameri-can South had in the last century. Although New South industrialization presaged much of what we are witnessing in the Global South, the scale and scope of recent industrial development around the world has been unprecedented. Unlike earlier models of industrialization in the United Kingdom and New England, in which regulatory laws, worker guilds, and unionization restrained the power of manufacturers, New South indus-trialization, now the model for expansion in the Global South, sustained and fostered persistent patterns of corporate control, low wages, and an anti-union climate reinforced by state and local governments.

The essays in *Looking South* consider southern labor and gender history from a broadly conceived but carefully focused perspective, grounded in a range of source materials from oral histories collected by the author to the detailed minutes of reform meetings and labor union conventions held during the nineteenth and twentieth centuries. Each essay forms a com-plete text, allowing readers to focus on one aspect of the complex history of southern life. Taken as a whole, however, *Looking South* tells a compel-ling story of resistance that moves across time and place, from the chaotic and transformative years that followed the Civil War through New South industrialization and on to the turbulent decades of economic depression, post-war growth, racial integration, and unprecedented immigration as the twentieth century unfolded. The book's narrative sweep concludes in the early years of the twenty-first century with an examination of the seemingly new but strikingly familiar economic and labor transformations taking place throughout the Global South. The final chapter argues that the New South model of industrialization that developed in the decades after Reconstruction became the prototype used by U.S. companies as they expanded globally in the twentieth century. This expansion has had mixed effects in both the American South and the Global South, on the one hand raising the standard of living for millions of new factory workers coming to manufacturing areas from impoverished rural farms, on the other perpetuating substandard wages and dangerous work situations. For workers in the United States, cheap products made by and for cheap labor are being purchased by women and men who have watched their own wages decline and jobs disappear.

These essays address issues of race, gender, and class within a southern labor movement that includes organized and unorganized workers, labor reform initiatives, workers' education programs, and more traditional analyses of strikes and unionization drives. Looking at generations of black and white activists who worked for over a century to reshape the social and economic systems that dominated the South, they examine the different roles played by women and men within the labor movement, religious organizations, and other groups offering blueprints for an alternative South and broaden our understanding of southern movements for social and economic change that worked within and across the barriers of race, class, and gender. *Looking South* emphasizes economic development in the decades following Emancipation while revealing continuities across regional boundaries, especially in terms of models of industrial development, the work of activists, social reforms, labor organizing, and workers' initiatives to improve their own lives.

Part I of *Looking South* takes a close look at the revolutionary ways in which African American men and women claimed social and economic space within the South in the aftermath of slavery and then refracts those victories through the lens of white southern resistance. The hard-won successes of these men and women, many of whom were not two generations past enslavement, proved enormously threatening to white southerners trying to regain political and economic dominance after Reconstruction. For some southerners, black and white, interracial alliances offered a viable alternative to racial division. For others, there was no more highly charged flashpoint than the specter of southerners uniting across racial lines. Chapter 1, "Labor, Race, and Homer Plessy's Freedom Claim," examines interracial organizing in New Orleans in the decades after 1865 and places labor actions in that city, especially the General Strike of 1892, in the larger context of national confrontations between labor and capital, including the Homestead Strike. The Louisiana racial segregation case that became *Plessy v. Ferguson* was decided in this milieu in a courtroom where Judge John H. Ferguson, a white Massachusetts-born southerner deeply fearful of social disorder, was challenged by Homer Plessy, a mixed-race shoemaker from the Faubourg Tremé neighborhood of New Orleans who had been arrested for refusing to leave the whites-only train car on the East Louisiana Railroad. One-eighth African American, Plessy believed in racial egalitarianism and unification; Ferguson, of abolitionist heritage, sought stability and order. Ferguson saw racial segregation laws as essential in restraining labor's power, in the South and the nation. His conviction of Homer Plessy set in motion the U.S. Supreme Court case that would institute the policy of "separate but equal" and shape American labor and race relations for over half a century. The second chapter in Part I, "Transformation and Resistance: A War of Images in the Post-*Plessy* South," begins after racial segregation had become the law of the land and focuses on the color line that W. E. B. Du Bois saw as the central challenge of the twentieth century. At the 1900 Paris *l'Exposition Universelle*, Du Bois fired a major salvo in what became a war of images over the representation of African American life in the United States. For the Paris exposition, Du Bois chose to exhibit photographs and portraits of achievement, success, and well being, images that contrasted sharply with the drawings on racist trading cards and postcard pictures of lynched bodies and burned-out black neighborhoods circulated by those opposed to full and equal citizenship for African Americans. In the decades that followed, proponents of racial equality squared off against white resisters determined to push back the progress made by upwardly mobile black entrepreneurs, professionals, and skilled workers. Using artists' renderings, photographs, newspaper illustrations, postcards, and film, each group waged fierce battles over the dominant image of black life in the United States.

The essays in Part II focus on women activists and reformers who worked through churches, secular organizations, and the labor movement to resist the barriers of race and class and shape their own claim to freedom. Chapter 3, "I Got So Mad, I Just Had to Get Something Off My Chest," theorizes the complex reform strategies adopted by black and white women on issues ranging from working conditions to collective organizing, public health, education, immigration, and women's rights. Frequently working through their churches, women gently but firmly restructured regional race relations and forged a southern social gospel that drew national attention and became the basis for reform efforts across the region for half a century. This chapter carefully examines the work of activist women in the South as increasing numbers of working-class white and African American women joined women-centered organizations in the early twentieth century. Class and racial tensions simmered, often below the surface, as women negotiated the contested terrain of economic needs and community concerns in a society marked by racial and economic segregation. This chapter looks closely at YWCA industrial clubs, church groups, trade unions, and the Southern Summer School for Women Workers, organizations that constructed their identities by supporting women's activism in the changing cultural and political milieu of the New South.

The second chapter in Part II, "Beyond Heroines and Girl Strikers: Gender and Organized Labor in the South," examines representations of southern women within labor history. For many generations, southern labor history focused on two primary groups of women: "heroines," individual women who performed extraordinary feats, and "girl strikers," women whose protests were both collective and public. These stereotypes framed popular and academic histories of southern women and the labor movement and resonated profoundly in southern culture. This chapter compares these mythical images with the reality of southern women's lives as workers and with their roles as labor activists. Challenging these enduring stereotypes helps expand our historical understanding of the full range of southern women's involvement in the labor movement and other networks of dissent.

Part III of *Looking South* shifts focus to investigate the efforts of the labor movement to organize workers in the rapidly industrializing American South. Chapter 5, "Labor Looks South: Theory and Practice in Southern Organizing," examines the theoretical analysis organized labor developed in its efforts to unionize southern workers, particularly in the textile industry, the region's prototype for industrial development. Focusing on the infamous southern labor strikes in the first years of the Great Depression reveals the historical moment when the nation's union leadership, faced with dwindling ranks, realized that the survival of the labor movement itself depended on the organization of southern workers in every American industry. This essay explores the discrepancies between theory and practice that loomed large as unions under the American Federation of Labor (AFL) refused to pay attention to "organizing the unorganized" in the rapidly expanding southern textile industry. Few labor leaders heeded the alarm of one activist that "this southern task . . . looms as a giant" until the militant actions of southern workers themselves paved the way for a new form of industrial organizing that underscored the importance of the South in determining the future of the American labor movement.[3]

The second essay in Part III, "'Living in Two Worlds': Civil Rights and Southern Textiles," places race at the center of an analysis of textile employment patterns across the twentieth century. Based on interviews with African American textile workers at a specific historical moment, namely, the years immediately after the legal consequences of *Plessy v. Ferguson* were overturned, this chapter argues that the participation of black workers in southern industry has long been underestimated. It uncovers evidence of interracial workforces in southern mills and a sub rosa work system that operated inside southern mills and factories in which black workers were paid directly by white employees to complete jobs that included spinning and operating looms. This system continued into the 1970s and 1980s, even after the southern industrial workforce became less overtly segregated by race and gender. Using the textile industry as the prototype of southern industrialization, this chapter calls for further study of racialized hiring patterns in the southern industrial workforce.

Part IV of *Looking South* emphasizes the connections across time and space between the New South and what has come to be called the Global South. These last two chapters look at the latest wave of Latino immigration into the U.S. South, which began in the mid-1990s in the wake of the North American Free Trade Agreement (NAFTA). Chapter 7, "Transformation and Resistance in the Nuevo New South," analyzes the demographic shift that has brought the Latino population of the region to over 11 million, with 10 million Latinos living in Texas and Florida and 1.6 million relatively new immigrants settling in Georgia, North Carolina,

South Carolina, Virginia, West Virginia, Kentucky, Arkansas, Mississippi, and Louisiana. This in-migration changed the biracial workforce of the South for the first time since Reconstruction. Traditional southern culture, black and white, is changing as well. Spanish is heard on streets from suburban Atlanta to Siler City, North Carolina. The religious life of the South has become more diverse as Catholic congregations have expanded and evangelical churches have welcomed new members. A transnational South holds possibility and promise even as it challenges the region's ability to extend democracy to new groups of southerners.

The final chapter, "Back to the Future: Mapping Workers across the Global South," begins with a visit to a weave room in Uzbekistan filled with cast-iron looms from Carolina textile plants of the 1920s. The story of how these looms ended up in Uzbekistan is not a straightforward tale of southern deindustrialization and expanding Asian labor markets. As the chapter maps the movement of workers into factories across what is now called the Global South, the discussion returns to the New South paradigm that became the archetype for labor relations in twentieth-century America to show how it has now also become the model for industrialization throughout the Global South, transforming that vast swath of the world into another "New South" and now writ large on the world stage.

The essays in *Looking South* thereby trace the transformation of southern society through stories of resistance: the freedom claims of African Americans who worked to shape a new society after the Civil War, the work of women who surmounted barriers of class and race to gain dignity and respect as workers and as citizens, the struggle of contemporary workers across the Global South to call attention to the human costs of industrial capitalism. All are narratives of change that explore different ways of understanding the South in the context of American and now world history.

I

CLAIMING FREEDOM

1

. . . .

Labor, Race, and
Homer Plessy's Freedom Claim

Claiming freedom in the aftermath of slavery was a complex process that involved acquiring citizenship, mastering new jobs, establishing churches, and building schools. This effort defined the lives of the first generations of formerly enslaved men and women in the American South and reconfigured the experiences of southerners who had lived as free people of color. The rapid ascension of this cohort of new citizens engendered both astonishment and fear among white southerners, who in reaction worked to reassert their own economic, political, and social dominance in the wake of Reconstruction. Transformation met resistance when twenty-nine-year-old Homer Plessy, a politically active New Orleans craftsman, tested the legality of the Separate Car Act, a segregation law passed by the Louisiana legislature in 1890.

The *Plessy* case unfolded in the midst of two major confrontations between labor and capital: the Homestead Strike and the New Orleans General Strike, both of 1892. As we shall see, in moving racial segregation to the top of the national agenda, *Plessy* also undercut the potential of interracial labor organization within the South and the nation. Judge John H. Ferguson's original ruling in *The State of Louisiana v. Homer Adolph Plessy* reflected his desire to impose order on what he considered "a state of confusion and lawlessness" caused by the interracial organization of workers participating in the 1892 New Orleans general strike, underlain by a deeper concern over the stability of capitalism.[1] The economic and political changes in the post-war South yielded a new labor paradigm based on racial segregation, low wages, persistent worker indebtedness, and opposition to unions. This transformation would set the stage for the confrontations American workers faced in the twentieth century and presaged, in ways few could have expected, the difficult challenges of twenty-first-century global capitalism.

Under Their Own "Vine and Fig Tree"

On January 1, 1863, freedom came to the South like rain on parched land. President Lincoln's Emancipation Proclamation liberated enslaved men, women, and children in Confederate-held areas, ushering in what African American citizens in Harrisburg, Pennsylvania, called "a new era in our country's history." Looking south, the black men and women of Harrisburg saw "a day from which the enfranchised will be able to look forward into the future with the full assurance that they will be able to sit down under their own 'vine and fig tree, with none to molest them or make them afraid.'" As the word spread to Virginia, the mother of seven-year-old Booker T. Washington "leaned over and kissed her children, while tears of joy ran down her cheeks." Anna Woods reported from Texas that "the soldiers marched in to tell us that we was free. . . . I remembers one woman, she jumped up on a barrel and she shouted. She jumped off and she shouted. She jumped back on again and shouted some more. She kept that up for a long time, just jumping on a barrel and back off again."[2] The process of claiming freedom began on that first day of Jubilee.

As Union forces made increasing inroads into the South, labor issues became paramount among those formerly enslaved and those who fought for the Confederacy alike, foreshadowing the transformation about to come. By the end of the war in April 1865, amidst the material and emotional wreckage of the South, one-fifth of the population lay dead. Those who survived faced the overwhelming work of rebuilding. Two-thirds of the South's assets had vanished during the war. The region had no railroad service or commerce, and civil authority was in short supply. Refugees, black and white, filled the roads. Everyone lined up for Federal rations.[3] The turbulent era of Reconstruction that followed presented a paradox for black Americans. On the one hand, Reconstruction legislation aimed to dismantle the old order and realize equality and opportunity for former slaves; on the other, reactionary white forces undercut black freedom by minimizing social and political change and instituting a crop-lien system built on debt and restraint.[4]

The Congressional Compromise of 1877 that resolved the disputed election between Rutherford B. Hayes and Samuel J. Tilden sanctioned the nation's circumvention of the Reconstruction Amendments and delivered the White House to the Republicans in a Faustian bargain that hinged on returning Federal troops to their barracks, thereby removing them as an enforcement factor in the South. The promise of freedom, citizenship, and the right to vote made in the aftermath of war was denied in the agreement that ended Reconstruction.[5] Labor issues permeated the Compromise of 1877 in what historian Barry Goldberg has described as "one of the most dramatic conjunctures in American history." The federal government stopped using its military power to protect freedmen's citizenship rights in the South and instead mobilized troops to protect capital from white labor in the North, leaving black and white workers during a period of escalating labor conflict to face what W. E. B. Du Bois called "the counter revolution of property."[6]

After 1877, in the midst of the post-Reconstruction alignment of white northern priorities, the American Federation of Labor (AFL) gradually accommodated segregation, a disastrous decision that excluded and economically marginalized black workers. This policy directly contributed to the willingness of black southerners to break strikes called by the craft unions. In post–Civil War America, business owners and employers, despite the rhetoric of a free-labor system, perfected the use of race and ethnicity as tools to divide the workforce, separate workers, and pit one group of employees against the other. The iron and steel industry, for instance, developed multi-tiered job structures and pay scales based on ethnic and racial categories: Irish foremen supervised skilled crews of Italian immigrants, Slavic workers earned less as unskilled laborers, and the most grueling and low-paying jobs in the mills were filled by African Americans.

The New South that developed at this time emulated this model as regional leaders, elected officials, and businessmen worked to erase the Mason-Dixon Line, replace plantation agriculture with industrialization, and improve race relations to the extent that blacks would be at least junior partners in economic development. But despite the success of the New South framework, places remained that did not fit the mold. One of these places was New Orleans, where the city's docks had become a center of interracial unionism during Reconstruction. There, in the South's most interracial city, eighteen hundred Creole, black, and white citizens had effectively organized across racial lines in 1873 to support a Unification Platform calling for racial equality. This bold and ambitious movement called for political equality and racial unity in its "Appeal for the Unification of the People of Louisiana."[7] Within a few years, the Unification Movement's commitment to interracial organizing would collide with the renewed power of southern white Democrats and the withdrawal of Federal troops that resulted from the Compromise of 1877. The Unification Movement itself, however, remained a powerful template for future generations, and New Orleans, that city on the southernmost margin of the American South, became the site of the landmark *Plessy v. Ferguson* case that would make the complex process of claiming freedom even more arduous.

When Reconstruction ended, a wave of newly written laws slowly constricted the lives of African Americans. Restrictions on voting effectively disenfranchised blacks. Miscegenation laws prohibited racial intermarriage. In 1887, Florida adopted the first "Jim Crow" law applied to railroads. Between 1888 and 1900, ten southern states, including Louisiana, passed similar legislation.[8] One after another, newly acquired rights vanished: the right to vote; the right to hold public office; the right of access to public transportation, public schools, and housing. At the same time, a complicated set of legal restrictions and unwritten racial codes developed throughout the South.[9] Locally determined, these laws varied from place to place, shifted constantly, and were often improvised and retrofitted in ways that kept black citizens constantly off balance and on edge.

In 1896, the United States Supreme Court ruling in *Plessy v. Ferguson* codified what came to be called the "separate but equal" doctrine: that separate facilities for blacks and whites were constitutional if those facilities were also equal. Although *Plessy v. Ferguson* is usually viewed from a national perspective, the original case and 1892 decision of *The State of Louisiana v. Homer Adolph Plessy* arose out of the interracial, multi-ethnic, and heavily unionized context of New Orleans. Historians rightly emphasize the role of *Plessy v. Ferguson* in condoning racial segregation throughout the nation by establishing that racial segregation did not violate the Constitution. But context is crucial, and timing is everything. Reading the *Plessy* case from a labor perspective transforms the story in important ways, throws Homer Plessy's freedom claim into sharp relief, and turns the kaleidoscope of history to reveal some previously unseen patterns.

Homer Plessy, Faubourg Tremé, New Orleans, Louisiana

Plessy was born Homère Patris Plessy not quite three months after the Emancipation Proclamation into a family that had lived for generations as free people of color within the Faubourg Tremé, the city's well-established Creole community. Homer Plessy was a man of faith, though his Catholicism ran counter to the mainstream movement of black religion in the New South. He married and worshipped in St. Augustine's, an interracial Catholic congregation that had included, since its founding in 1842, free people of color as well as slaves. Plessy's life was ordinary enough on the surface, but his narrative unfolded in ways that were anything but commonplace. As a result, he occupies a unique place in American history as one of the first to legally challenge segregation in the South. A Janus-faced symbol of race relations, Plessy is synonymous with both the law he had the courage to challenge and with legal segregation itself. The cruel irony of the *Plessy* decision is that in stepping up to fight racial segregation in one southern state, Plessy brought forward a case that legalized discrimination across the entire country.

Plessy's commitment to activism ran deep. When he was four years old, in 1867, the city of New Orleans painted large black stars on one-third of the city's mule-powered streetcars. Whites and black Union soldiers could ride in their choice of cars, but the majority of black residents had to wait for a "star car." This toxic combination of humiliation and inconvenience led to a citywide sit-in as black men and women protested the policy by taking seats in white-only cars. One of the leaders, Joseph Guillaume, led a group of residents down the street a block from the Plessy home and boarded a non-starred streetcar, No. 148. Guillaume argued with the driver who, as instructed by the streetcar company, refused to move with a black passenger on board. Defiant, Guillaume literally as well as figuratively "took the reins in his own hands." A few days later, another star-car protest drew a crowd of over five hundred to Congo Square, long a site of public gatherings in the Faubourg Tremé, among slaves in the early nineteenth century and freedmen and freedwomen in the years after Emancipation. Victory came a day later when the streetcar company gave in and abolished the star-car system. An edict issued by the police read: "Have no interference with negroes riding in cars of any kind. No passenger has a right to reject any other passenger, no matter what his color. If he does so, he is liable to arrest for assault, or breech of the peace."[10]

When Homer Plessy was seven years old, his father, Adolphe, died. In 1871, his mother, Rosa Debergue Plessy, a seamstress, married Victor M. Dupart, a member of a politically active New Orleans family. Dupart, a clerk for the U.S. Post Office, supplemented his income by making shoes and later trained his stepson in the business. When Homer Plessy was ten years old, his stepfather began participating in the Unification Movement, joining that interracial statewide effort of Republicans and Democrats, ex-Confederate and Union soldiers, and Jews, Catholics, and Protestants to advocate "the equal and impartial exercise by every citizen of Louisiana of every civil and political right guaranteed by the constitution and laws of the United States." The nonviolent removal of racial barriers from public education, modes of transport, banks, and employment topped the list of Unification priorities. Victor Dupart's name was printed in the *New Orleans Times* as one of eight hundred supporters of the Unification Platform.[11]

In mid-July 1873, Unification members met in New Orleans' Exposition Hall under the banner "Equal Rights, One Flag, One Country, One People" to ratify their manifesto "to recognize all citizens of the United States as equals before the law." Unification supporters envisioned their resolutions giving birth to a new era "not only in our own state but through the length and breadth of our entire land." Although the Unification Movement fired the hopes of interracialists locally and nationally, it succumbed to a lethal combination of political infighting and the violent strategies of New Orleans white supremacists. In 1874, members of the White League assaulted and murdered eleven members of the city's integrated police force and urged white students "to forcibly remove their black classmates from the schools." This terrorism, followed in 1877 by the rollback of Reconstruction, crippled the movement's capacity to organize and effect change. Nevertheless, participants saw the Unification Movement as "a vision of America's best future," as contemporary activist Rodolphe Desdunes put it, and the historical memory of Unification passed to the next generation and became a template for the political organization that emerged almost a generation later.[12]

During his twenties, Plessy worked at Patricio Brito's shoemaking business on Dumaine Street near North Rampart.[13] When he turned twenty-five, he married nineteen-year-old Louise Bordenave, daughter of Oscar Bordenave and Madonna Labranche and the love of his life. The young couple settled in the Faubourg Tremé neighborhood, a rich mélange of families the census recorded as "white, black, colored, and mulatto," with birthplaces that included Santo Domingo, France, Spain, Ireland, Italy, Germany, and New Orleans. The Plessys rented a house at 1108 North Claiborne Avenue, and Homer Plessy registered to vote in the Sixth Ward's Third Precinct. The house on Claiborne Avenue, Brito's shop a third of a mile to the south, and St. Augustine's Catholic Church in the center of the Faubourg Tremé formed the triangle that delineated his world.

For Homer Plessy, potent memories of the non-violent star-car protests and the movement for racial unification sparked the trajectory of his life as he came of age in the rising tide of racism and segregation that swept the nation in the years after the Compromise of 1877. Surrounded by well-educated and financially secure local leaders in the Creole Faubourg Tremé, Plessy and his neighbors drew on strong traditions of political activism and became even more focused in their opposition to white supremacy in the 1880s and 1890s. As a young man in his early twenties, Plessy became an officer in the Justice, Protective, Educational, and Social Club, a local group committed to reforming public education in New Orleans. And when a Comité de Citoyens (Citizens' Committee), led by a powerful contingent of men twice his age, formed to protest Louisiana's 1890 Separate Car Law aimed at segregating black and white train passengers, Plessy joined.

The Comité de Citoyens

Senior members of the Comité de Citoyens included Radical Republicans Aristide Mary and Laurent Auguste; writer Rodolphe Desdunes, who repeatedly articulated the need for a confident Negro self-identity; and editor and founder of the *Crusader* Louis Martinet, who in 1889 founded the Republican journal with a commitment to labor and civil rights reflected in its masthead: "A Free Vote and Fair Count, Free Schools, Fair Wages, Justice and Equal Rights." For these men, the Separate Car Act revived demeaning memories of previous moves by the white majority to segregate free people of color and African Americans. They saw the 1890 law as a throwback to slavery and the pre-1865 restrictions that discriminated against free blacks. These rules had included having to obtain a permit to leave the city, form a benevolent society, attend a horserace, sell liquor, or even walk the street.[14] Several Comité leaders had been stalwarts in the Unification Movement of 1874 and in 1891 joined the National Citizens

Rights Association formed by Albion Tourgeé, an Ohio-born writer, judge, and activist for civil rights, to oppose the Separate Car Act and deliver to the capital in Baton Rouge what the *Crusader* called a "manly protest" against state-mandated segregation.

In February 1892, the Comité organized the first test of the Separate Car Act. Daniel Desdunes, a member of the Comité and son of Rodolphe Desdunes, boarded the Louisville & Nashville Railroad to Mobile and took a seat in the white coach. Arrested and charged with violating the Separate Car Act, his trial was to take place in the courtroom of Judge John H. Ferguson in July 1892. His defense would be based on the assertion that applying the Act to interstate trains was unconstitutional.

In the meantime, the Comité planned its challenge of the application of the Separate Car Act to intrastate travel. One of the youngest members of the Comité, Homer Plessy was a craftsman in the company of Paris-educated men with law degrees from Straight College Law School. Nevertheless, when the Comité asked for a member who could pass for white and was willing to challenge the Separate Car Law, Plessy, then twenty-nine years old, stepped forward. On the morning of June 7, 1892, according to a plan put together by the Comité, Plessy purchased a first-class ticket on the East Louisiana Railroad to travel from New Orleans to Covington, the seat of St. Tammany Parish. He boarded the train dressed in a suit and cravat, like any other New Orleans gentleman, and sat down in his upholstered seat in the "whites only" car. When the conductor came to collect his ticket, Plessy informed him that although he was one-eighth "colored," he refused to sit in the train's "colored" car.[15] One can imagine the conductor's momentary confusion; it was counterintuitive that the ostensibly white gentleman who sat calmly in the first-class car was *ex situ*. The Comité, intent on Plessy's being arrested, had made sure that a detective was at the station. Captain C. C. Cain entered the car and, according to the *Crusader*, "told Plessy that if he was a colored man, he would have to go to the colored coach." When Plessy refused, he was arrested, taken off the train, and charged with breaking the Separate Car Law. The Comité had a case and were on their way to challenging a railroad conductor's ability to classify passengers by race. Plessy's act of civil disobedience set in motion the long legal process of testing the Separate Car Act and all that it represented. After spending the night in jail, he was released on five hundred dollars bond paid by the Comité and returned home to the Faubourg Tremé to await his trial in criminal court.

In July 1892, newly appointed Judge John Ferguson bolstered the cause of those committed to withstanding the pressures of white segregationists when he threw out the charges against Daniel Desdunes. The Comité relished the victory. Louis Martinet, writing in the *Crusader*, declared, "The Jim Crow car is ditched and will remain in the ditch." Praising Ferguson's decision to render the Separate Car Act unconstitutional when applied to interstate passengers as a triumph for interracial equality and the Comité, Martinet also congratulated Desdunes "on the manly assertion of his right."[16] Optimism reigned as the Comité learned that Ferguson would also preside over Plessy's case. But no one could have foreseen how dramatically the events of the ensuing three months before the trial would change the social and political atmosphere in New Orleans.

A Manly Assertion of Rights

In 1892, the workers of New Orleans were under increasing pressure from industrialization and a local (and national) economy that grew worse by the day en route to the Panic of 1893. Although he continued making and selling shoes, Plessy himself experienced a threat to his livelihood by mechanization in the shoe industry. The same forces that were destroying Plessy's shoe business affected workers throughout the city of New Orleans, and many responded with increased labor organization. Early in 1892, three months before Plessy boarded the first-class car on the East Louisiana Railroad, the city's streetcar conductors had won a contract for a ten-hour day and a union shop. Encouraged by that success, New Orleans labor leaders sought help from the American Federation of Labor and organized thirty new unions across the city. In August 1892, two months after Plessy's civil disobedience, almost fifty unions in New Orleans joined to establish the Workingmen's Amalgamated Council, a group with over twenty-five thousand members and a strong commitment to interracial solidarity. Their model of interracial unionism based on parity directly challenged the prevailing norms of a divided labor movement, discriminatory hiring practices, and the public advocacy of segregation.

Tensions between interracialists based in New Orleans and segregationists who had been gaining power in Louisiana since 1877 became more pronounced after the election of Murphy J. Foster as governor in May 1892. Foster strongly supported the Separate Car Act and no doubt regretted Ferguson's ruling in the Desdunes case. The Comité was naturally aligned against Foster and his allies, whose white supremacist agenda mirrored the country's post-1877 rout of African American civil liberties. The Separate Car Act became the focal point of this ideological schism. In October 1892 the Comité's fight for equality, justice, and fair wages converged with the Workingmen's Amalgamated Council's power struggle against the New Orleans Board of Trade. The interracial Workingmen's Amalgamated Council threatened to call a general strike in support of three local unions—the black majority Teamsters and the white majority Scalesmen and Packers—that were collectively referred to as the "Triple Alliance." At the heart of both of these struggles was a commitment to racial equality.[17]

The Separate Car Act and Interracial Unionism

Meanwhile, Homer Plessy and his lawyer had been waiting for a trial date for over three months. The notice of arraignment came on October 11, and two days later in St. Patrick's Hall in Lafayette Square, Judge John Ferguson called forward the parties in Criminal Court *Case No. 19117 The State of Louisiana v. Homer Adolph Plessy*. Plessy, a French-speaking Creole man whose ancestry spanned the globe, faced a judge whose Puritan roots ran deep. Ferguson, a scion of Massachusetts with an abolitionist legacy, had grown up on Martha's Vineyard, where he was exposed to a multiracial population from the Caribbean, the Cape Verde Islands, Asia, South America, and Europe.[18] Educated in Boston, he had come south in the wake of the Civil War, drawn by reports of economic opportunities brought back to Massachusetts by Union soldiers who had occupied New Orleans. After settling in the city, Ferguson married Virginia Earhart, the daughter of attorney Thomas J. Earhart, a staunch New Orleans unionist who hated slavery and the Confederacy. Earhart had declared in 1863 that "man is man, be the shade of his skin white, green, or black" and was affiliated with the Workingmen's National Union League of Louisiana, a movement of workingmen "asserting the dignity of labor over the pretensions of capital."[19]

A Yankee at heart, Ferguson sought to infuse his adopted city with Puritan values. He supported temperance and worked to stop gambling. His anti-gambling stance allied him with Governor Murphy J. Foster, who opposed the Louisiana Lottery Company, and Ferguson gradually succumbed to the political trade-offs demanded in the post-Reconstruction South. He campaigned extensively for the segregationist Foster, who won his race for governor in 1892. Shortly after his election, Foster appointed Ferguson to a vacant judgeship in New Orleans. Ferguson felt pressured to remain loyal to the governor's office but maintained his own sense of integrity and independence. He was sworn in on July 5, 1892, less than a month after Plessy's arrest and only four days before he had to rule on the Desdunes case. His decision to dismiss that case and rule against the Separate Car Act reflected his abolitionist legacy and aligned him ideologically with his unionist father-in-law and against his patron Foster.

A great deal was at stake in this period as Jim Crow laws spread across the New South. Florida, Mississippi, and Texas had already passed laws requiring railroads to segregate black passengers in separate cars or behind partitions.[20] In New Orleans, the accelerating momentum of white supremacy was kept at bay by the Comité, led by men and women whose genealogies defied racial categorization, and by interracial labor unions like those of the Triple Alliance and the Workingmen's Amalgamated Council. Encouraged by Ferguson's ruling in the Desdunes case, members of the Comité accompanied Plessy to Lafayette Square in mid-October, optimistic that they could obtain a ruling against the Separate Car Act that this time would also apply to intrastate travel. Plessy's lawyer, New Orleans Creole James C. Walker, stood before Judge Ferguson and requested that the charges against Plessy be dismissed on the grounds that the Separate Car Act was unconstitutional, whether applied to inter- or intrastate travel.[21] Walker argued that passengers who were subject to the Separate Car Act and to being labeled criminal if they did not comply faced "invidious distinction and discrimination based on race which is obnoxious to the fundamental principles of national citizenship."[22] Walker requested a delay in the proceedings so that the constitutionality of the Separate Car Act could be considered. Ferguson agreed and set another court date for October 28.

Before Plessy could return to court, the Workingmen's Amalgamated Council's commitment to interracial solidarity was severely tested when, on October 24, the largely African American Triple Alliance went on strike to win a ten-hour day, overtime pay, and a preferential union shop. In response, the New Orleans Board of Trade allied with the city's four main railroads and the cotton, sugar, and rice exchanges to break the strike. The board lost no time calling for support from the state militia and initiating a press campaign to generate public hysteria. The city's major newspapers fell in line, reporting false accounts of "mobs of brutal Negro strikers" charging through the streets and black unionists "beating up all who attempted to interfere with them." The Workingmen's Amalgamated Council, despite intense fear-mongering by the press, stood firmly behind the Triple Alliance and refused to break ranks along racial lines. Nonetheless, the strike called by the Triple Alliance heightened racial tensions across the city. For some, it raised concerns about the potential of interracial cooperation; for others, it revived memories of the Unification Movement's equal rights agenda. When Plessy and Walker returned to court on October 28, Walker argued again that Plessy should go free, while Lionel Adams, the assistant district attorney, defended the right of states to set their own "guidelines of racial association." After both sides had presented their cases, Ferguson congratulated Plessy's counsel for his "great research, learning and ability" and adjourned the court so he could consider the two arguments.[23]

Ferguson found himself on the horns of a legal, political, and personal dilemma. He himself had established the legal precedent in the Desdunes case, ruling that the Fourteenth Amendment made the Separate Car Act illegal in the context of interstate travel. Yet ruling in favor of Plessy would undercut Ferguson's allegiance to the governor who had appointed him. His political alliances demanded that he rule against Plessy in order to bolster the segregationists and defend states' rights. The Plessy case threw different aspects of Ferguson's personal heritage into conflict—his abolitionist and Union background were on Plessy's side and his father-in-law's commitment to "man . . . white, green, or black" must have weighed heavily on him, even as his Puritanical quest for order would soon demand that he close the door on interracial democracy.[24]

A week after Plessy's October 28 court appearance, and while Ferguson continued to consider the constitutionality of the Separate Car Act, the Workingmen's Amalgamated Council ended their deliberations and called for a general strike. On the morning of the strike, November 5, 1892, the *Times-Picayune*, the city's politically moderate newspaper, sounded the alarm: "The Amalgamated Council Finally Decides Upon the Step and Orders the Arm of Labor to Become Inert at Noon."[25] In an interracial turnout of unprecedented proportions, twenty-five thousand New Orleans workers, half of the city's workforce, walked off the job, united in their demands for the ten-hour day, overtime pay, the preferential union shop, and recognition of the predominantly black unions that composed the Triple Alliance. An editorial underscored the dangers of such a move. "The *Picayune* does not propose to forebode evil," it claimed, "but it would be the height of folly not to provide for every possible emergency."[26] Thousands of men freed from daily labor and "condemned to idleness" will prepare the way, the editorial argued, for "more or less disorder, and most probably a vast amount of it." The following day the headline shouted the news: "The Blow is Struck."[27] The strike drew the attention of newspapers as far away as Baltimore; Knoxville; Dallas; Duluth, Minnesota; Springfield, Massachusetts; Boise, Idaho; and Aberdeen, South Dakota.[28] The gas and electric workers and the railroad freight handlers joined the strike on the second day in a move that reinforced labor's success, hit the city hard, and put railroads and industrialists throughout the United States on high alert. Over the following week, even more unions joined the strike: the typographers, shoe clerks, dry-goods clerks, paper-hangers, undertakers, sugar workers, grain shovelers, bricklayers, and carriage drivers.

The General Strike

The general strike organized by New Orleans' Workingmen's Amalgamated Council shut down the city and unleashed fears that had been stirred by incendiary newspaper reports during the Triple Alliance strike in late October. Trade declined, the price of cotton, sugar, and rice dropped, orders fell off, and the inability to move goods stopped sales. Merchants feared that trade sent to other cities "will be permanently diverted." The metaphor of race reverberated in repeated references to lightness and darkness, danger and protection.[29] When the gas and electric workers joined the strike, fears mounted that the city would be "plunged into darkness" and face "a situation dangerous in the extreme." Using apocalyptic language, The *Times-Picayune* warned, "If there is any way to prevent such an eclipse of our public lights it ought to be done at any cost. Light is a most important factor in the protection of the city and its people." City authorities turned to Governor Foster, who reached the city on the second day of the strike. "The situation is one of great seriousness," the *Picayune* warned public authorities, one that demanded "patriotism and devotion to duty in the highest degree."[30]

As the strike entered its third day, white officials feared that "the absorbing interest felt in the strike by every class of the community" would seriously affect the turnout for the presidential election on November 8, an election they deemed "one of the most important that has called for the suffrages of citizens in many years." Concerns mounted that with attention diverted to the strike, the election would be "almost totally lost sight of." The *Picayune* criticized "the merchants and the white men . . . commonly too taken up with their private business to vote" and warned that "this is an election in which the negroes of this city will poll a full vote." They are on strike, warned even this moderate newspaper, "with complete leisure on their hands, and they will go to the voting precincts and put in their ballots for the national and local Republican tickets."[31] Because of these concerns, merchants and laborers called for "a day of peace" for the election, and the worries of New Orleans Democrats eased somewhat. While the city's citizens were voting, striking railroad freight handlers temporarily stopped freight traffic on the Illinois Central-Mississippi Valley, Louisville and Nashville, Texas and Pacific, and Southern Pacific lines, leaving New Orleans merchants "with a great deal of perishable goods on their hands." After the polls closed, two thousand members of the Railway Freight Handlers held a special meeting and amidst "frequent cheers" decided to continue the strike.[32]

Four days into the general strike, the *Picayune* declared that the action of labor in New Orleans amounted "almost to a revolution"[33] and reported that Judge J. H. Ferguson in Section A, criminal court, had called a grand jury together. Drawing on his Puritan heritage, Ferguson issued a special charge to this jury:

> Never before in the history of Louisiana was there as imperative a necessity for prompt and vigorous action on your part as at present. There exists in our midst such a state of confusion and lawlessness that the peace of the city cannot be maintained by the present constituted authorities. Outrages have been and are being committed throughout the city in violation of the criminal laws of the State, property has been destroyed, innocent men are daily assaulted without provocation, and a number of men seriously hurt. It is your sworn duty to investigate immediately every act of violence that

comes to your attention or of which either of you have personal knowledge, and speedily bring the offenders to justice, thereby vindicating the majesty of the law.

Ferguson recommended that the grand jury remain in session "until the present labor troubles are at an end" and meet daily "until the crisis is past."[34]

Ferguson's charge to the New Orleans grand jury echoed one given a month earlier to a grand jury in Homestead, Pennsylvania. Just before the Triple Alliance went on strike in New Orleans, the *Picayune*, under the headline "IS IT TREASON?" reported that the chief justice of the Pennsylvania Supreme Court had, in a courtroom "crowded almost to suffocation," asked jurors to determine "what constitutes treason against the state, in the cases against the members of the Homestead strikers advisory committee." The justice set the parameters for their decision by defining treason as "the organization of a large number of men in a common purpose to defy the law, resist its officers and to deprive any portion of their fellow citizens of their rights." The attention of New Orleans readers fearing an imminent strike by the Triple Alliance was undoubtedly captured by the Pennsylvania chief justice's claim that "it is a state of war when business has to be surrounded by the army of the state to protect it from unlawful violence at the hands of former employees." The press report from Homestead, published in the *Picayune* two days before Homer Plessy's first appearance in court, ended with a caveat that foreshadowed Ferguson's final judgment in the case: "We have reached the point in history where there are two roads for us to pursue: the one leads to order and good government, the other leads to anarchy. The one great question which concerns the people of this country is the enforcement of the law and the preservation of order."[35]

As the general strike continued in New Orleans, the *Times Picayune* reported on November 9, 1892 that Governor Foster, headquartered at the St. Charles Hotel, had "taken measures to meet on its first appearance any show of extensive disorder and lawlessness in the city." Ferguson's charge to the grand jury belied the fact that there had been few reports of disorder or violence, and while several arrests had been made, even the *Picayune* conceded that "the high character of the workingman of New Orleans is involved in this great movement." The Amalgamated Council, willing to settle on wages and hours, refused to submit to arbitration on the issue of the union shop. As the *Picayune* described the council's position, "the question of the domination of the Unions in the employment of labor . . . would be insisted on unconditionally."[36] The "cry of unionism," wrote a reporter from the *Trenton (N. J.) Evening Times* regarding New Orleans, "is the rallying cause of the labor bodies."[37]

A letter from a Cincinnati manufacturer published in the *Picayune* on November 10 reflected national anxieties about labor's power: "NEW ORLEANS SELECTED FOR THE SCENE OF A LABOR WAR," the heading read. "We do not understand," the letter began, "why it was that your city was picked out by the Grand Council, to open the war, all along the line, but we presume that you will have to bear the brunt of the entire attack."[38] Fears of a "Labor War" erupting across the country had suffused the nation since early June when the Homestead strike dominated the headlines of local papers from New Orleans to New York: "Blood Flows," read a *Picayune* headline on June 7, 1892, with "Winchesters, Cannon, Dynamite and Burning Oil" called into use.[39] As union workers at the Carnegie Works outside Pittsburgh fought the private Pinkerton forces hired to quell their strike, Pennsylvania governor Robert Emory Pattison refused to intervene until the county had exhausted its own resources. A prolonged and bloody battle ensued as Homestead workers held off Carnegie's men. The people of New Orleans looked on anxiously.

All through the summer and fall of 1892, the Homestead strike captured headlines in the city's major papers. "A Flag of Truce Repeatedly Shot Down by the Maddened Laborers," reported one *Picayune* headline.[40] By the time the Triple Alliance struck in late October, the fear that armed conflict like that at Homestead would erupt in New Orleans had reached a fever pitch. In sharp contrast to the wait-and-see attitude of the Pennsylvania governor, Governor Murphy Foster threatened to deploy the state militia immediately to break the Triple Alliance strike. The tragedy in Homestead had not yet resolved when the Workingmen's Amalgamated Council called the general strike in support of the Triple Alliance on November 5. As union workers shut down the city, Louisiana authorities saw Homestead as a model of what they wanted to avoid in New Orleans. Judge Ferguson issued his charge to the grand jury and implored them to meet daily, while Governor Foster vowed to remain in the city for the duration of the strike. Foster requested "all peaceable citizens not to congregate in crowds . . . and to discountenance all undue excitement and acts of violence" and pledged to preserve the peace, declaring "that the people of this city must and shall be protected in the full enjoyment of all their constitutional rights and privileges."[41]

To maintain good order and protect the lives and property of citizens, Foster worked on three fronts. First he prepared the militia and doubled the armed guard at the city's armories "in case trouble ensued." Then he also encouraged negotiations between the Amalgamated Council and an executive committee representing the Board of Trade and New Orleans' merchants, meeting with both sides around the clock in "Parlor L" of the St. Charles Hotel; and, in what the *Picayune* called the "unlooked-for end-ing of the strike,"[42] he used the power of the courts to urge two legal actions. First, he supported the filing of a suit "similar to the one filed against the leaders of the Homestead strikers" against the New Orleans Workingman's Amalgamated Association and the presidents of the strik-ing unions. Second, U.S. Attorney Ferdinand Earhart, Judge Ferguson's brother-in-law and the son of Thomas J. Earhart, filed a writ of injunction to restrain the strikers "from attempting to interfere with the trade or commerce of the city." U.S. Circuit Court Judge Edward C. Billings, found at home late on the night of November 10, the sixth day of the general strike, was asked to invoke the federal laws on conspiracy and to issue an order "enjoining the defendants from interfering with the business of the city." Violations of this order were defined as "committing assaults, or by threatening personal violence to the men at work, or by assembling in unlawful gatherings." The *Picayune* reported that word of the suit "speed-ily reached Exchange alley," the site of the Amalgamated Workingman's Council headquarters and "the leaders of the strike were soon gathered in knots . . . very much agitated over the matter" and "anxious to devise some method of clearing themselves." Charged with violation of the federal act, as many as forty-five strike leaders suddenly faced fines of as much as $5,000 and imprisonment for up to six years.[43]

The lawsuit succeeded in driving union leaders to settle almost over-night. On November 11, the headline of the *Picayune* reported "Yesterday Forenoon the Rupture Seemed Wide as Ever"; one day later, the headline read, "Labor Side Listens to Peaceful Counsel."[44] By 2:00 that afternoon, the final agreement had been signed. The Workingmen's Amalgamated Council gained their ten-hour day and overtime pay, but had to relin-quish their demand for the preferential union shop and that the Board of Trade negotiate in good faith with Triple Alliance unions—the strike's two most crucial issues. Yet the Workingmen's Amalgamated Council had maintained its interracial coalition as dozens of unions with a combined membership of 25,000, in a city with a workforce of 50,000, had united to bring New Orleans to a halt. Samuel Gompers praised the strike's success as a "very bright ray of hope for the future of organized labor," writing that "with one fell swoop the economic barrier of color was broken down." By all accounts, the result was a compromise that had not destroyed interracial unionization.[45]

To Vindicate the Majesty of the Law

One week after the general strike ended, Ferguson called Plessy back to the courtroom in Lafayette Square. Over the previous year, Ferguson, who was staunchly opposed to gambling and drinking, had grown increasingly uncomfortable with the mélange of race, class, and culture that was New Orleans. He had moved his family to the outskirts of the city, a quieter area upriver that was a good distance geographically and culturally from the political ferment of the Faubourg Tremé. Extralegal racial violence had increased dramatically over the course of the previous year, lynching was at an all-time high, and while the overwhelming majority of those violently murdered were African American, a huge New Orleans mob had also brutally killed and lynched eleven Italian workers on the streets of the city.[46] Ferguson's decision to render the Separate Car Act unconstitutional in the Desdunes case six months earlier seemed but a distant memory in the aftermath of the strikes that had seized New Orleans that fall. Likewise, the force of the arguments presented by Plessy's lawyer, based, as Ferguson had noted, on "great research, learning and ability," faded in the chaos of the general strike. The labor unrest that rocked the city had seriously disrupted the order, stability, and peace that Ferguson craved.

On November 18, Judge Ferguson entered his courtroom in St. Patrick's Hall, called the Criminal Court of the Parish of New Orleans to order, and prepared to hand down his decision in *The State of Louisiana vs. Homer A. Plessy*. From his perspective, striking down the Separate Car Law to rule in Plessy's favor would encourage black resistance to segregation, directly support the Comite's agenda of racial equality, and send a powerful message to the interracial unions that had just held the entire city of New Orleans hostage to their demands. A ruling that supported the right of Plessy or anyone else, regardless of race or ethnicity, to buy whatever train ticket they could afford and sit wherever they wanted would remove racial barriers, not only on the railroads, but also in the workplace. The subversive potential of labor, so recently and dramatically demonstrated in New Orleans, undoubtedly loomed large in his thinking. On the other hand, a negative decision in the *Plessy* case would give Governor Foster and the segregationists what they wanted in terms of circumventing both the spirit and the letter of Reconstruction. A ruling that upheld the constitutionality of the Separate Car Act would deter integration in the workplace, undercut interracial unionism, and make it easier for employers to reap the economic benefits of an occupationally segregated workforce with a wage and salary scale stratified by race.

Which side was he on? The decision was Judge Ferguson's to make, and in the quiet that pervaded the courtroom after the pounding of his gavel, he announced his ruling in the *Plessy* case without hesitation: "the state of Louisiana," he began, "had the power to set the rules that regulated railroad business within the state." Concise, understated, and devastatingly brief. Ferguson declared that "there is no pretense that [Plessy] was not provided with equal accommodations with the white passengers. He was simply deprived of the liberty of doing as he pleased, and of violating a penal statute with impunity." This dispassionately delivered ruling ushered in an era of legalized segregation that would shape American political, economic, and social life for over a century. The decision set back interracial unionism and upended black-white parity in the workplace. *Plessy* solidified the framework of southern "Redemption," the restoration of white supremacy in the South marked by Hayes's inauguration and the end of Reconstruction, and united North and South under the banner of legalized racial segregation.[47]

The Comité's case essentially ended on that November afternoon in Lafayette Square. Before Ferguson could declare Plessy guilty at a later court date, the Comité's legal team appealed to the State Supreme Court to stop the trial. The court initially issued an order to end the proceedings but then sided with Ferguson, whose name became affixed to the case when Plessy appealed to the U.S. Supreme Court on January 5, 1893. Although the case would go on to be heard by the highest court in the land in 1896, none of those involved—neither Plessy, the Comité de Citoyens, nor lawyers James C. Walker in New Orleans or Albion W. Tourgée in New York—believed there was a way to win the suit in a higher court. Tourgée, considered the country's "most persistent and vociferous white champion of full racial equality," had offered his legal expertise to the

Comité pro bono and committed himself to defending Plessy before the Supreme Court. Everyone involved had planned, strategized, prepared, played their best cards, and lost. The makeup of the Supreme Court also changed dramatically between 1892, when the *Plessy* case originated, and 1896, when the final decision came down. Benjamin Harrison had nominated three judges to the court, including Henry Billings Brown, who wrote the majority decision in the *Plessy* case. In late 1893, Tourgeé wrote to Louis A. Martinet, editor of the *Crusader,* that "when we started the fight there was a fair show of favor with the Justices of the Supreme Court," but now "of the whole number of Justices there is but one who is known to favor the view we must stand on." Tourgée clearly knew what was at stake in appealing the decision to the high court: "It is of the utmost consequence that we should not have a decision *against* us as it is a matter of boast with the court that it has *never reversed itself* on a *constitutional* question." He feared that with the new justices seated on the Court, taking the case forward would invite a negative decision that could do more damage to the cause of interracial equality than would leaving it at the state level. And in the end he was right. Those fighting for racial equality in Louisiana in the early 1890s were caught in a horrible perversion of justice that had serious ramifications for the nation as a whole.[48]

Deprived of the Liberty

The New Orleans general strike, then, was the watershed event between the Desdunes case and *The State of Louisiana v. Plessy*. Through the bloody lens of the Homestead strike, Ferguson's reaction to the chaos of having the city "plunged into darkness," the fear of violence, and the political effects of "negroes with the leisure to go to the polls" was to put aside the issues of equality and justice that had guided his ruling in the Desdunes case and, in the *Plessy* case, used race as a tool to leverage order and control. While ostensibly about transportation, the *Plessy* case was really about much more: mobility, unionism, and interracial solidarity. Mobility represented power, exemplified in the South by the restraints of slavery and the freedom of movement so prized after Emancipation. From the hated star cars of the 1870s to the Separate Car Act of 1890, racially segregated transportation struck at the core of the "privileges and immunities of citizens" defined in the Fourteenth Amendment. From the docks of New Orleans to the steel mills of Birmingham and Pittsburgh, the issues of unionism and interracial solidarity dominated headlines across the United States in 1892, the lowest point in American race relations and a period of repeated strikes and intense resistance to the labor movement. Employers everywhere feared interracial labor power, rank and file militancy, and strikes—three powerful components at play in New Orleans in 1892. The *Plessy* decision arose out of the localized circumstances of the New Orleans general strike and turned on the intermingled issues of labor rights, racial equality, and unionism. Applied nationally, *Plessy v. Ferguson* curtailed the possibility of interracial democracy for generations of Americans. The case, stamped with the imprimatur of the United States Supreme Court, dictated the means by which race could be used to control class by disrupting natural class formation, the process at work in New Orleans when the Board of Trade tested the resolve of the predominantly white Workingman's Amalgamated Council to support the interracial Triple Alliance.

The train itself, the site of Homer Plessy's legal violation and a place where white women and black men might meet in a first-class car, became a powerful metaphor and potent symbol for industrialization and modernization in the late nineteenth century. Racial and class segregation on the trains became the template for a new order within both the workplace and American society as a whole. Judge John Ferguson and Governor Murphy Foster helped secure this order in their handling of the general strike, Ferguson by his charge to the grand jury and Foster by his tripartite effort to defeat the interracial power of the Workingmen's Amalgamated Council in its effort to unionize the New Orleans workforce. In the view of men like Ferguson and Foster, the majesty of the law was that it could be used to impose order. If that involved denying a man like Homer Plessy the "liberty of doing as he pleased," whether that be riding in the first-class coach from New Orleans to Covington or, as would be the case in Louisiana within the decade, marrying across racial lines, attending interracial schools, living in integrated neighborhoods, or riding in the "white section" of the streetcar, then so be it.

In bringing the *Plessy* case, the Comité's leaders knew that a positive ruling would open, or keep open, the doors to economic, social, and geographic mobility in modern America: industrial jobs, equal pay, access to transportation and education. They were perversely proved correct when the *Plessy* decision in fact closed each of those doors. The ruling in effect left Homer Plessy and men and women like him—those with even "one drop" of African blood—unable to get on the train to modernity, condemning them instead to a nineteenth-century world marked by perpetual debt, unending menial labor, and backbreaking work in the fields of the South.[49]

Race and labor in the South are inextricably bound, and this holds true for the rest of the nation. The *Times-Picayune*'s apocalyptic language and racial innuendo conflated the issues of race and labor and cast the resistance represented by the strike as a threat to the very survival of civilization. Lest we forget, the origin of the *Plessy* case was the power of the state to override interracial democracy. As the class war in the nation during that period demonstrates, the ideology of race in the United States has been consistently labor-based. Headlines about war and treason hit a nerve because they were true. In New Orleans in 1892, major issues were being worked out in a dramatic tragedy in which Ferguson represented the corrupted North; Plessy stood for the hope of interracial democracy; and New Orleans, with its multi-ethnic, mixed-race population, symbolized America, with its population of white, black, Indian, immigrant, Protestant, and Catholic. The final scene in the courtroom in Lafayette Square ended when Ferguson allowed race to divide the populace in the service of maximizing capital's power. In the aftermath of Homestead and the general strike, he saw this move as essential to keeping order in the city, the state, and the nation. His act affirmed the authority of those designated as "white" throughout the United States and thereby greatly diminished the possibility of interracial alliances in the workplace, the neighborhood, and the nation.

Plessy's undeniably pernicious racial ramifications have largely masked its significance as a labor case. The context and timing of the decision Ferguson issued from the bench of the New Orleans Criminal Court just one week after the general strike ended has been obscured by the issue of "separate but equal" that dominated the case when it moved to the United State Supreme Court in Washington. Only Justice John M. Harlan, the lone dissenting member of the white male Court, spoke of *Plessy v. Ferguson* in terms that alluded to the commitment of the Comité and the Workingmen's Amalgamated Council to interracial equality and justice in the workplace. "In the eye of the law," wrote Harlan, the son of a Kentucky slave owner, "there is in this country no superior, dominant, ruling class of citizens. There is no caste here. Our constitution is color-blind, and neither knows nor tolerates classes among citizens. In respect of civil rights, all citizens are equal before the law."[50] Harlan's insight came at least in part through his interracial kinship to his "black" half-brother, Robert Harlan of Cincinnati. Over half a century later, Harlan's eloquent dissent would become the blueprint used by attorney Thurgood Marshall in *Brown v. Board of Education*, the landmark 1954 decision in which the court's nine white male justices unanimously overthrew *Plessy*. In declaring that "separate educational facilities are inherently unequal," the Court paved the way for the civil rights movement and the dismantling of the system of legal segregation that had been the law of the land since 1896.[51]

Homer Plessy died on March 1, 1925. The brief notice in the *New Orleans Times Picayune* read simply, "Homer A. Plessy, at 63 years, beloved husband of Louise Bordenave." Long after being denied the right to board an integrated train car, Plessy was laid to rest in the Debergue-Blanco family tomb, the burial site of his wife's mixed-race family in St. Louis Cemetery #1 in the Faubourg Tremé. Given that the name Plessy had become synonymous with efforts to challenge segregation, the front page headline on the day of Plessy's funeral was tragically ironic: "Supreme Court Puts Approval on Segregation: Separate Residential Areas for Negroes and Whites Declared Legal." A quarter century later, in a case that closely mirrored Plessy's, the state supreme court approved a city "segregation ordinance" that would restrain "negroes from establishing their residence in white residential neighborhoods." Abiding by the "separate but equal" doctrine that *Plessy v. Ferguson* established, whites were also "forbidden to establish their residences in negro neighborhoods." The ruling was expected to have "far-reaching influences on construction by negroes . . . in certain uptown and downtown neighborhoods." Bringing the similarities to the *Plessy* decision full circle, the *Picayune* also reported that "Negro benevolent and 'social' circles," successors to the Unification Movement and the Comité de Citoyens, were raising $40,000 to take the case to the United States Supreme Court in a determined attempt to carry on the fight for racial equality.[52]

Indeed, what Du Bois's landlady called a "heap of trouble" had met those who came out of slavery seeking work and citizenship, establishing schools and churches, and making the dream of an interracial, egalitarian society into a reality that could have been the New South. What they had wanted, one journalist argued in the *Tribune*, the first black daily newspaper in the United States founded in New Orleans in 1864, was simply for whites to "deal justly by us, respect our humanity, honor our aspirations, throw open to us the avenues of life."[53] Freedom claims made in the years after Jubilee demonstrated the possibility and material reality of building a society in which people could grow and flourish, regardless of race, class, or gender. But too many in the South in those years wanted to return to what Du Bois referred to as "the day before the day of Jubilee," and for a long time they succeeded. The "Goddess of Liberty, decked with the jewels of justice," who the African American citizens in Harrisburg, Pennsylvania, had thought would usher in "a new era in our country's history," still eluded the African American sons and daughters of the South. In 1911, when Rodolphe Desdunes, the member of the Comité de Citoyens whose son Daniel had successfully challenged the Separate Car Act in the case decided by Ferguson in the months before the New Orleans general strike, published his history of these years, *Nos Hommes et Notre Histoire*, he wrote of the Unification Movement that "the movement failed but we have retained the memory of it." The historical memory of thousands and thousands of freedom claims made in the years after slavery preserved a vision of the South's best future, sustained African American men and women as they resisted the horrors of "The Nadir," and eventually became part of a vision for transforming the South and the nation when African American citizens fighting for full civil rights and racial equality once again ushered in a "new era in our country's history."[54]

2

· · · · · · · · ·

Transformation and Resistance

A War of Images in the Post-*Plessy* South

The 1896 Supreme Court case of *Plessy v. Ferguson* ushered in a new era in American life, one shaped in direct opposition to that envisioned by African Americans as they fought for full civil rights and racial equality in the decades after Emancipation. The *Plessy* case upheld the constitutionality of racial segregation and established the doctrine of "separate but equal," whereby public accommodations could legally be separated by race provided they were of equal quality. *Plessy* condensed the broad spectrum of racial and ethnic identity in the United States into the two supposedly exclusive categories of "black" and "white" and set in motion the process of delineating the color line that W. E. B. Du Bois would declare at the 1900 Paris *l'Exposition Universelle* "the problem of the twentieth century."[1]

This dichotomization of race played an integral role in creating and sustaining the post-slave New South, a region ostensibly reshaped after the Civil War according to the precepts of modernity: technology, science, and the law. In reality, the forces driving the transformation of the South generated multiple eddy currents: industrial and technological development provided progressive momentum in one direction, while a strong undertow of resistance used a mix of law, science, and religion to reinforce the racial dominance of whites over blacks. There were different ways of "knowing," and many southerners relied heavily on religion as the only meaningful source of "truth." Throughout the region, the forces of religion and modernity weighed heavily in the minds of those making policy as well as those pounding pulpits.

Aware of the growing modern obsession with evidence and proof, early in 1900 W. E. B. Du Bois and his colleagues assembled hundreds of photographs, charts, books, and pamphlets to create an Exhibition of American

Negroes for the Paris *l'Exposition Universelle*, an extraordinary world's fair, with fifty-eight nations participating and over fifty million visitors attending between April 15 and November 12. The Exhibition of American Negroes, which was later shown in the United States at the Pan-American Exposition in Buffalo, New York, in 1901 and again at the South Carolina Interstate and West Indian Exhibit in Charleston in 1901-02, gave momentum to what became competing efforts to visually characterize the lives of African Americans in the post-*Plessy* South.[2]

The camera's eye, that mechanical lens combining technology, science, and art, was extensively used by African American scholars and educators such as W. E. B. Du Bois, Booker T. Washington, Nannie Burroughs, and Mary McLeod Bethune to record the transformation of life in the wake of slavery and to annotate the progress of black Americans as new citizens and respectable and industrious members of society. During the same period, the camera also became a tool for those who opposed black progress and endorsed an agenda of racial segregation and white supremacy. The images produced by this group ranged from racially stereotyped drawings and comic postcards depicting African Americans with exaggerated physical features and captions such as "coon," "darkie," or "colored cannibal" to photographs of African American businesses and homes destroyed by white mobs and gruesome pictures of public lynchings that provided intimidating evidence of white power.[3] These divergent representations of transformation and resistance, those affirming black progress and those denying it, became imprinted in the minds of black and white Americans alike as tens of thousands of photographs were made into postcards and mailed through the U.S. Post Office. Powerful images of black educational achievement, commercial success, and prosperity conflicted with a potent visual counter-narrative of lynchings and destruction left in the wake of riots that tore through black communities in the early decades of the twentieth century. This war of images would rage for nearly half a century.

A Metaphysics of Color

In Paris, the Exhibition of American Negroes was displayed in the Palace of Social Economy, a large, Louis XVI–style, white wooden building on the banks of the Seine that housed, in Du Bois's words, "the world's ideas of sociology." Based on his own training in the new social sciences, Du Bois found "little here of the 'science of society.'" The one exception, he argued, was his own exhibit, which he believed to be "sociological in the larger sense of the term . . . an attempt to give, in as systematic and compact a form as possible, the history and present condition of a large group of human beings." The Exhibition of American Negroes, designed by Du Bois and collected and installed under the direction of the U.S. government's "Negro special agent," lawyer Thomas J. Calloway, was intended to be a comprehensive, evidence-based compilation of the post-Emancipation social and political achievements of African Americans. Du Bois reported that the exhibit illustrated in "a series of striking models" the "progress of the colored people, beginning with the homeless freedman and ending with the modern brick schoolhouse and its teachers." Paris Exposition judges awarded the Exhibition of American Negroes a Grand Prix, its highest honor. Thomas Calloway, as compiler, and his collaborator W. E. B. Du Bois, as "compiler of [the] Georgia Negro Exhibit," each received a Gold Medal.[4]

The Exhibition of American Negroes focused international attention on the false dichotomy of the black and white racial divide by visually demonstrating its meaninglessness in photographic images of "American Negroes" who, much like Homer Plessy, or for that matter, W. E. B. Du Bois himself, defied such classification. Du Bois created the exhibit in part to play with and mock the artificially constructed racial categories used to enforce the new system of racial segregation established by *Plessy*. In the visual spaces of the Exhibition of American Negroes, blackness and whiteness merged, divided, and united again. Those who looked closely at the photographs could watch the concept of race change before their eyes. Images of African American men, women, and children ranging in skin tone from dark to fair recorded an equally broad range of occupational signifiers, from "medal-of-honor men in the army and navy" to college students, law professors, business entrepreneurs, farmers, and industrial workers.[5]

This exhibit's treatment of racial categories in the post-*Plessy* years prefigured Toni Morrison's arguments in *Playing in the Dark* a century later. Morrison, critiquing what she terms a "metaphysics of color" within traditional discussions of American literature and history, argues that racialist literary critics either grossly misrepresented or completely ignored the essential Africanist presence in works by Melville, Poe, Twain, Cather, and Hemingway, just as historians wrote about the American past without addressing the fundamental impact of race in shaping the historical narrative.[6] The data and photographs Du Bois presented in Paris defiantly and scientifically affirmed the black presence in American life. At the same time, the exhibit questioned and critiqued in particularly intriguing ways the new categories of blackness and whiteness defined and reconfigured by *Plessy v. Ferguson.*

The *Plessy* case effectively drew a color line across the United States and erected a barricade to full citizenship that viciously divided American society. Nowhere was this more evident than in Homer Plessy's New Orleans, where a range of self-defined racial and cultural categories that included "colored," "Negro," "black," "African," "Africo-American," and "Creole" reflected a long and rich cultural heritage. The large numbers of Italians, Spanish, and Portuguese who had settled in the city had had contact with Africans for centuries; many of the "whites" who had come to New Orleans from the West Indies, the Caribbean, and Latin America had African ancestors as well.[7] While the cultural complexity of New Orleans was not replicated in the rest of the South, centuries of settlement had left layer upon layer of cultural traces from the Seminole, Creek, Lumbee, and Cherokee; from sixteenth- and seventeenth-century Spaniards, Mexicans, Mexican-Indians, Caribbean Indians, and Africans as well as the British, Dutch, and French; from eighteenth-century Scotch-Irish, Irish, English, and West Africans; and from nineteenth-century Germans, Russians, Poles, and Italians. Some of the most important cultural work of the post-*Plessy* years involved collapsing these longstanding cultural and racial signifiers into just two categories: black and white.[8]

Resisting this enterprise, the Exhibition of American Negroes displayed hundreds of formal individual and group portraits of men, women, and children who mirrored the full range of African American racial and ethnic origins: African, European, Indian, and Asian.[9] Du Bois and his assistants provided the names of only a few of the individuals; most are identified simply by gender (male or female), age (man, woman, girl, boy), and by race (African American). Du Bois used formal poses (half-length and head-and-shoulder portraits) and descriptors (right profile, facing left, facing slightly right) that put the collection in eerie dialogue with a set of daguerreotypes that the Harvard professor Louis Agassiz had commissioned fifty years earlier.

Louis Agassiz and his protégé Nathaniel Southgate Shaler, one of Du Bois's professors at Harvard, had laid the intellectual groundwork for the ideology of racial dehumanization that permeated the academy

Figure 2.1. J. T. Zealy, "Portrait of Renty, African-born slave." Quarter Plate daguerreotype, March 1850, Photo T, 1867. By permission of the Peabody Museum, Harvard University.

throughout the second half of the nineteenth century and well into the twentieth, in disciplines from anthropology to zoology. Agassiz had commissioned photographer J. T. Zealy to produce the daguerreotypes as scientific visual evidence of the superiority of the white race and of "separate creation," his theory that each race "originated as a separate species." Agassiz's collection included one series of fully nude images showing front, side, and rear views and a second series that focused on heads and torsos. The "Portrait of Renty," a photograph taken in 1850 of an African-born enslaved man on a South Carolina plantation, typifies the content and format of the Agassiz archive.[10]

The Paris exhibit, so similar in form but so different in content, answered Agassiz and Shaler with carefully amassed data collected by professionals trained in the very disciplines these men had helped create. Drawing on decades of African American achievement, Du Bois, in the midst of what his younger disciples would call "The Nadir"—those tidal years of "disfranchisement and victimization" to which *Plessy* belonged— powerfully countered the visual evidence used by an earlier generation of scholars to prove white superiority.[11] At the same time, Du Bois used the collections of photographs he assembled for the Paris exhibit to undermine Agassiz's theory of separate creation by presenting visual evidence of blurred racial lines and the reality of thriving communities that had transcended color, of people who had lived beyond race, both before and after the Emancipation Proclamation.

Always sensitive to what scholar Nicole Waligora-Davis calls "the labor performed by race," Du Bois used the cosmopolitan environment of *l'Exposition Universelle* to lift the veil that obscured the true identity of black men and women as American citizens.[12] Du Bois and his colleagues deftly demonstrated the fluidity of racial categories as they exhibited photographic images that defied race: the individual portraits of light- and dark-complected black and white African American men and women directly challenge the false dichotomy of race. As seen in figures 2.2–2.5, each of these images also captures a specific cultural milieu and physical evidence of the historical identity of the subjects.

Figure 2.2. W. E. B. Du Bois, *Types of American Negroes, Georgia, U.S.A.* (1900), vol. 1, no. 18. Title: "African American boy, head-and-shoulders portrait, facing right." Reproduced from the Daniel Murray Collection, Library of Congress, Washington, D.C.

Figure 2.3. W. E. B. Du Bois, *Types of American Negroes, Georgia, U.S.A.* (1900), vol. 2, no. 138. Title: "African American man, half-length portrait, left profile." Reproduced from the Daniel Murray Collection, Library of Congress, Washington, D.C.

Figure 2.4. W. E. B. Du Bois, *Types of American Negroes, Georgia, U.S.A.* (1900), vol. 2, no. 152. Title: "African American woman, half-length portrait, facing right." Reproduced from the Daniel Murray Collection, Library of Congress, Washington, D.C.

Figure 2.5. W. E. B. Du Bois, *Types of American Negroes, Georgia, U.S.A.* (1900), vol. 3, no. 203. Title: "African American woman, head-and-shoulders portrait, facing left." Reproduced from the Daniel Murray Collection, Library of Congress, Washington, D.C.

In the final photograph shown here, taken by the Atlanta photographer Thomas E. Askew, the image of the pale, blond, curly-haired "African American girl, full-length portrait, seated on stool, facing slightly right" forcefully underscores, as did the *Plessy* case, the arbitrary nature of racial classifications. In the same way that the New Orleans Comité des Citoyens that brought forward Homer Plessy's case had wanted a "black" man in a "white" body to challenge the Separate Car Act, this fair-skinned African American child on display in Paris in 1900 allowed Du Bois, as literary scholar Ann duCille has argued, "to insinuate into the consciousness of white readers the humanity of a people they otherwise constructed as subhuman—beyond the pale of white comprehension."[13]

White viewers saw images of themselves when they looked into the faces of those who Shawn Michelle Smith describes as "white-looking African Americans in a 'Negro' archive." As Smith points out, this identification between the viewer and the viewed was "bridged by visual signs

Figure 2.6. Photograph by Thomas E. Askew. W. E. B. Du Bois, *Types of American Negroes, Georgia, U.S.A.* (1900), vol. 1, no. 59. Title: "African American girl, full-length portrait, seated on stool, facing slightly right." Reproduced from the Daniel Murray Collection, Library of Congress, Washington, D.C.

of similarity," which included not only skin color, but also the cultural markers of Victorian society: the starched dress and the ruffles, hat, and exquisite leather shoes. Smith argues that such images would suggest to white viewers that "self and other were very much the same."[14] "African American girl, full-length portrait, seated on stool, facing slightly right" powerfully demonstrates the enigmatic nature of blackness and whiteness and dramatically signifies the indisputable and continuous history of interracial sexual contact. As reframed by Du Bois, the violent record of forced racial mixing during slavery stands in sharp contrast to the demeanor of the female subject shown here, an innocent small child of mixed parentage sitting next to a Victorian lace curtain, a piece of fabric that signifies both a refined social class and the metaphor of the veil that Du Bois would argue in *The Souls of Black Folk* (1903) screened the unseen history of African American life in the United States.

Spectators who toured the American Negroes archive in Paris experienced the cognitive dissonance of seeing visual signs of similarity and identification, on the one hand, and the indisputable physical consequences of white violence against and desire for the black body, on the other. Homer Plessy's ancestry, like that of many men, women, and children featured in the Exhibition of American Negroes, defied racial categorization. His pale skin meant he could pass for white; his heritage as the descendant of free people of color firmly grounded him in the cultural milieu of the Faubourg Tremé. A French- and English-speaking Catholic man, married to a biracial woman, Plessy embodied the unfixed nature of racial classifications. Stark evidence of this can be seen in his shifting designation in the federal census: "M" (mulatto) in 1880, "B" (black) in 1900, "W" (white) in 1920.[15] Plessy's indeterminate racial classification and the Exhibition of American Negroes both demonstrated the arbitrary nature of these racial categories. The *Plessy* decision did so by establishing the "separate but equal" doctrine in a landmark segregation case brought by a "black" man with white skin. The exhibition, by its very nature a display, a show, a performance, deconstructed the conceptual framework of existing theories regarding the separate nature of blackness and whiteness to reveal images of Americans whose lives affirmed a different metaphysics of color.[16]

The Age of Miracles

As such a performance, the Exhibition of Negroes painted a brilliant picture of African American success in the post-Emancipation period, years that Du Bois referred to as the "Age of Miracles." Evidence of this remarkable period of transformation could be found across the South in the rapidly growing black communities where the children and grandchildren of formerly enslaved men and women had built churches, schools, and homes at an unprecedented rate. By 1900, these black communities had become a focal point of pride for African Americans. The Paris exhibit represented the collective work of claiming freedom in the years after slavery. Documenting and cataloging the economic and social transformation of black southerners, the photographs and data that Du Bois compiled comprehensively analyzed the social and political achievements of African Americans in the United States, with an emphasis on the South and a specific focus on the state of Georgia.

Individual and group portraits accounted for 245 of the 482 photographs that Du Bois and his colleagues assembled for the Exhibit of American Negroes. The other 237 images were of schools, churches, homes, and places of work. Of those, fifty-eight were pictures of schools, with forty-one depicting professional education, eleven industrial training, four domestic training, one agricultural training, and one elementary education. Of the sixty-one images related to labor, thirty were of black-owned businesses, eleven of rural agricultural labor, ten of industrial labor, and nine of professional work. Du Bois also included eighty-five images of homes and twenty-six images of churches. Seventeen photographs documented African Americans in the military, five were of social organizations such as the Women's League and the Odd Fellows, and four were images of trade unions. These portraits of teachers, students, ministers, churchgoers, and workers, from farmhands to bankers, recorded the broad range of success achieved by men and women not two generations out of slavery.[17]

Point by point, Du Bois's work in the Exhibition of American Negroes also engaged the thinking of his nemesis Booker T. Washington, who championed vocational training and accommodation to segregation as the route to equality. Du Bois's exhibit set up a counter-argument that drove home his belief that black Americans could best achieve social change by investing in higher education and supporting those college-educated African Americans who could go head to head with whites in any field of endeavor. This perspective reflected Du Bois's own elitism and his abhorrence of servitude in any guise. At the same time, the Paris exhibit celebrated labor and work of all kinds—from field to factory, from the university to the courtroom, from the household to the public square. The exhibit highlighted middle-class accomplishments even as it simultaneously embraced the hard work and material prosperity emphasized in the industrial, craft, and agricultural education endorsed by Washington. This, then, was a portrait drawn in inverse relationship to the statistics of black life in the South in 1900, where elementary schools vastly outnumbered professional schools and rural agricultural laborers deeply enmeshed in the crop lien system numerically outranked black business owners by many orders of magnitude. By focusing on men and women whose achievements could be readily observed in portraits and detailed statistics, Du Bois argued that the stylish suits and ties of the men, the elegant hats of the women, and the studio portraits of exquisitely dressed children in the exhibit "hardly square with conventional American ideas"

Figure 2.7. Displayed as part of the American Negro exhibit at the Paris Exposition of 1900. Title: "Portrait group of African American Bricklayers Union, Jacksonville, Florida." Reproduced from the Library of Congress, Washington, D.C.

Figure 2.8. Displayed as part of the American Negro exhibit at the Paris Exposition of 1900. Title: "Sisters of the Holy Family, New Orleans, Louisiana, [1899?]." Reproduced from the Library of Congress, Washington, D.C.

Figure 2.9. From African American Photographs Assembled for 1900 Paris Exposition. Title: "Law graduating class at Howard University, Washington, D.C." Reproduced from the Library of Congress, Washington, D.C.

about African Americans. Photographs of African American nuns, textile manufacturers, teachers, lawyers, dentists, carpenters, and painters documented the range of accomplishments of men and women who had taken advantage of post-Emancipation opportunities in work, education, professional training, and business. Group pictures of the members of the African American Carpenters Union and Bricklayers Union in Jacksonville, Florida, and of the Waiters Union in Georgia captured the rise of trade unionism among African American workers.[18]

The photographs Du Bois exhibited in Paris provide a powerful narrative of triumph over tragedy in which, despite formidable barriers, the first generations of freedmen and freedwomen shaped the postwar southern world in new and significant ways. In image after image, from the remarkable to the ordinary, freedmen and freedwomen across the region are seen infusing liberty with meaning as they organized their lives in the turbulent wake of slavery's passing and carved out the economic and social space necessary to become citizens. The exhibit clearly illustrated that, in the face of constant pressure to restrict citizenship and control movement, extraordinary transformations had taken place. Optimism gained traction as men and women claimed freedom, from the streets of New Orleans to the rice fields of the South Carolina low country to the rebuilt city of Atlanta. The struggle to establish schools and churches paralleled the enormous effort to achieve political representation. The number of new buildings erected in black communities—churches, schools, and homes designed for worship, education, and domestic life—solidly measured the tangible material, social, and cultural successes of African Americans in the post-war South.

Figure 2.10. W. E. B. Du Bois, *Negro Life in Georgia, U.S.A.* (1900), vol. 4, no. 355. Title: "Exterior view of brick church [Georgia]." Reproduced from the Daniel Murray Collection, Library of Congress, Washington, D.C.

Figure 2.11. Displayed as part of the American Negro exhibit at the Paris Exposition of 1900. Title: "Group of children from the Model School, Fisk University, Nashville, Tennessee." Reproduced from the Library of Congress, Washington, D.C.

Figure 2.12. Displayed as part of the American Negro exhibit at the Paris Exposition of 1900. Title: "Negro homes—homes of poorer classes, Chattanooga, Tennessee." Reproduced from the Library of Congress, Washington, D.C.

The Paris exhibit featured twenty-six images of black churches with steeples that graced the landscape of the post-Emancipation South, reflecting Du Bois's belief that the black church served not only as a "spiritual agency, but also [as] a social, intellectual, and economic center."[19] Formerly enslaved men and women across the region had negotiated the intricacies of church polity at the regional and national level, organized self-sustaining and self-governing churches, staffed them with ministers, and drawn hundreds of thousands of parishioners to services. Early on, even before Emancipation, slaves had attended their own separate Baptist churches. After the war, in 1871 the Colored Methodist Episcopal Church broke off from the Methodist Church, South, establishing an autonomous denomination, albeit one with close ties to white churches in many southern communities. Other southern denominations, the Presbyterians and Lutherans, for example, also separated along racial lines, while in most northern denominations, such as the Congregationalists, African-American members kept their membership in the church but organized into separate congregations.[20]

The African Methodist Episcopal Church (AME), founded in Philadelphia in 1794, had grown exponentially in the South, claiming 206,000 members by Reconstruction's end and over 750,000 by 1903. The number of black ministers had grown rapidly as well, with 265 in 1866 and almost 6,000 by the turn of the century in the AME alone. This remarkable growth cost money, and by 1903 the AME was raising $3.6 million annually for operating expenses. Between 1864 and 1903, the church raised an additional $300,000 for "Home and Foreign Missionary" work, which, combined with $770,000 from the General Fund, provided over $1 million to establish mission churches from Pittsburgh west to St. Louis and from Louisville south to New Orleans. In the wake of the Civil War, African Methodism spread to Texas, Kansas, the Rocky Mountains, and the Pacific coast, as well as throughout the former Confederate states of Florida, Georgia, South Carolina, Virginia, Alabama, and North Carolina. In addition, the AME church established 180 missions, gained 12,000 members in Africa, and worked in Canada, the West Indies, and South America as well. By 1903, the valuation of AME church property had topped $9 million. As the twentieth century began, seven-eighths of the entire black population of the United States, over four million people, worshipped in their own self-sustaining, self-governing church bodies.[21]

As African American churches sustained post-war life spiritually and materially, the building of schools endowed the succeeding generations of students with the practical and professional skills required by the economy of the New South. W. E. B. Du Bois's *Economic Co-operation among Negro Americans*, an extensive study of industry and education published in 1907, traced a remarkable age of miracles in education. "To the Negro slave, freedom meant schools first of all," the section on education began; "consequently schools immediately sprang up after emancipation." A list organized state by state followed, beginning with Georgia, where Du Bois reported, "In December 1865, the colored people of Savannah, within a few days after the entrance of Sherman's army, opened a number of schools, enrolling 500 pupils and contributing $1,000 for the support of teachers. Two of the largest of these were in Bryant's Slave Mart." State by state, the list of educational accomplishments went on. In Arkansas, freedmen established "the first free schools that ever were." In Florida, the all-black African Civilization Society and the Home Missionary Society of the African Methodist Episcopal Church worked to educate freedmen who built schoolhouses at their own expense, supported teachers, and cooperated with the Freedmen's Bureau in furnishing school lots and erecting buildings. Freedmen in Kentucky provided the main support for the thirty schools established there after the Civil War. In North Carolina, freedmen sustained teachers "until the last cent [they] could command was exhausted." At the end of 1868, the Freedmen's Bureau documented 1,198 day schools and 228 night schools across the South, collectively employing over 1,700 teachers, 713 of whom were African American. Over 80,000 students were enrolled in these schools, 469 of which were sustained wholly by freedmen themselves. Tuition paid by freed families totaled over $65,000, fully half of the cost of running the schools. And yet in 1869, not more than one-tenth of the children of the formerly enslaved attended school, largely because their parents did not earn enough to pay the tuition.[22]

Du Bois's own experience teaching elementary school in Alexandria, Tennessee, in 1886, the summer after his sophomore year at Fisk University, had opened his eyes to the enormous challenges involved in building, staffing, and funding schools for African American students across the South. He, too, often saw ambitious dreams hit up against the hard realities of persistent poverty and increasing debt. And yet he took solace in the fact that the "Negro carpet bag governments established the public schools" and argued that "although recent researche[r]s have shown in the South some germs of a public school system before the war, there can be no reasonable doubt but what common school instruction in the South, in the modern sense of the term, was founded by the Freedmen's Bureau and missionary societies, and that the state public school systems were formed mainly by Negro reconstruction." Du Bois quoted Albion Tourgée, the leading white lawyer working for black equality, who wrote that post-Emancipation African American education advocates had "instituted a public school system in a region where public schools had been unknown."[23]

In 1907, Du Bois reported that the efforts of African Americans to encourage education took three forms: creation of church schools, aid to private schools, and aid to public schools. The African Methodist Episcopal Church, the Colored Methodist Episcopal Church, the African Methodist Episcopal Zion Church, and the Negro Baptist Church established and ran over 280 educational institutions, from elementary schools to colleges. The list of private schools in operation in 1907 included over seventy-four universities, colleges, institutes, seminaries, normal schools, and grammar schools. In addition, Du Bois reported that African Americans in different communities across the region conducted several hundred other private and "unrecorded primary schools" each year.[24] Families in some communities worked regularly to supplement public school funds in order to lengthen the school term. African American public schools for the years 1870–1899 cost a total of seventy million dollars, of which black taxpayers paid twenty-five million in direct school taxes and forty-five million in indirect taxes and endowments. Du Bois's report concludes, "if Georgia be taken as a typical state in this respect, then . . . the Negro school systems of the former slave states have not cost the white taxpayers a cent, except possibly in a few city systems."[25]

Du Bois argued that, contrary to conventional wisdom and notwithstanding the enormously helpful contributions of white philanthropists, African American men and women paid dearly to educate their children, and it was their donations and volunteer labor that funded the lion's share of the dramatic expansion of schools in black communities. Often, only the confluence of funding from churches, tuition payments, taxes, and private donations provided enough money to keep struggling African American schools open.

After presenting images of churches and schools, the Exhibition of

American Negroes directly addressed the issue of housing, which had been a pressing concern for African Americans throughout the South since Emancipation Day. In 1869, General O. O. Howard, chief of the Freedmen's Bureau, reported that "in every state many thousands were found without employment, without homes, without means of subsistence, crowding into towns and about military posts, where they hoped to find protection and supplies. The sudden collapse of the rebellion, making emancipation an actual, universal fact, was like an earthquake. It shook and shattered the whole previously existing social system." Afraid to "stay on the same soil that they had tilled as slaves lest by some trick they might find themselves in bondage again," many freedmen and freedwomen migrated in search of work and a new home. "The wonder is not that so many, but that so few, have needed help," wrote General Howard, "that of the four millions of people thrown suddenly upon their own resources, only one in about two hundred has been an object of public charity." Howard emphasized the connection between land ownership and the manhood of those released from slavery when he wrote, "the one thing needful to the freedmen is land and a home. . . . Without that a high degree of civilization and moral culture is scarcely possible. So long as he is merely one of a herd working for hire, and living on another's domain, he must be dependent and destitute of manly individuality and self-reliance."[26]

Howard's gendered sentiments notwithstanding, in many areas where the federal government planned to allocate lands to the formerly enslaved, strong resistance from white neighbors prevented African Americans from taking possession of these lands. Where blacks did acquire land of their own, General Howard reported, they "commenced work with energy, building houses and planning." In 1869 in Orangeburg, South Carolina, he found that "hundreds of colored men have bought lands and are building and settling upon them." Outside the city limits, he found a settlement of a hundred families who had purchased small homesteads and were "joyously cultivating their own gardens and provision grounds" as well as finding day work in the city. The Freedman's Savings and Trust Company, created by the U.S. government to encourage savings, thrift, and economic stability, operated until 1874. In Texas, the Farmers' Improvement Society organized ten thousand members "to fight the credit or mortgage system, which is the Negro's second slavery" and "to buy and improve homes." The organization's pledge to its members read, "We believe in good homes and good people inside of them with plenty of good food raised at home or bought for cash." By 1898, African American building and loan associations were reported in Maryland, the District of Columbia, Virginia, Georgia, Florida, and Arkansas, and black-owned real estate firms opened in cities across the South.[27]

The photographs of housing in the Exhibition of American Negroes displayed a range of structures occupied by African Americans across the South, but as with the images of churches and schools, these pictures reflected the ideal rather than the reality of African American housing in 1900. Most of the homes featured in the exhibit were in middle-class urban neighborhoods in which a strong and growing group of business owners and professionals lived and worked. Turn-of-the-century census figures recorded a different picture, one in which 75 percent of black southerners lived in rural areas. In urban and rural areas combined, approximately 20 percent of African Americans owned their own homes, compared to almost 50 percent of white Americans. As African Americans sought to rent, buy, or build solid housing stock, numerous obstacles stood in their way. Low wages, restricted access to reasonable loans, unscrupulous landlords, high rents, lack of land available for purchase, hostile white neighbors, and increasingly segregated neighborhoods all took a toll. And yet during the months that the exhibit was on display in *l'Exposition Universelle*'s Palace of Social Economy, an alternative truth was visible: African Americans owned and occupied fine homes across the United States. This was true even in the South, where 90 percent of black Americans lived in 1900, three-quarters of those in rural areas, just as they had in 1880.[28] Throughout the exhibit, Du Bois's images emphasized a reality that he knew to be true for some and believed could eventually become true for a majority of African Americans in the twentieth century.

Despite the many factors that prohibited the expansion of housing for African Americans, black communities across the region included a skilled workforce of builders and carpenters ready to construct new homes, churches, and schools. Black expertise in the trades had developed in the crucible of slavery, and by the summer of 1865 the sound of post-war rebuilding rang out in the hot, humid air from Richmond, where observers reported that the noise of "hammer and saw lasts the livelong day," to New Orleans, where the promise of African American freedom was realized in the spirit of mutuality and self-help.[29] Black industrial schools thrived in the recovering southern economy of the 1870s and 1880s, and after the war, education and labor went hand in hand as the students themselves helped to build major structures on campuses from Virginia to Alabama, learning architecture and construction in the process. Black southerners knew how to build houses as well as bridges, roads, boats, and cotton gins, and in many areas black men maintained a near monopoly in the skilled trades. African American builders, carpenters, plasterers, and masons constructed a majority of the red brick textile mills and tobacco factories of the New South. This reliance on black expertise continued for a number of years before African American craftsmen began to lose out in competition with both newly trained white men and cheaply produced machine-made goods.[30]

The Morrill Act of 1862 had established land-grant institutions of higher education in Union states, and African American representatives elected to serve in southern state legislatures during Reconstruction were instrumental in persuading four former Confederate states to use funds from the Morrill Act to establish black land-grant schools. In 1871, Mississippi established Alcorn University, the first black land-grant institution in the United States. Virginia used half of the state's Morrill Act funds to establish Hampton Institute; South Carolina used all of its funding to establish Claflin University in 1872; Kentucky waited until 1897 to utilize funds from the act to establish the Kentucky State Industrial School. The Alabama legislature established Tuskegee Normal and Industrial Institute in 1881, which was not officially a land-grant college although the U.S. Congress did grant the school twenty-five thousand acres of land in 1899. In 1890, a second Morrill Act stipulated that states with racially segregated higher education systems must establish black land-grant institutions. This federal legislation achieved tangible results when sixteen public institutions in states across the South, from Delaware to Oklahoma, opened their doors to black students between 1890 and 1910.[31]

The Exhibition of American Negroes that Du Bois took to Paris showcased black professionals and the businesses run by black entrepreneurs and craftsmen across both the South and the North. It included photographs of dentists in training, doctors visiting patients, and funeral directors in front of the homes they owned and operated. Watchmakers, pharmacists, laundry owners, grocers, and shoe-store owners posed in front of their shops; tobacco inspectors at their posts; professional laundry operators by the huge mangles they owned, operated, and repaired. In the virtual community Du Bois and his colleagues created within the exhibit, the emphasis returned again and again to expertise and skill, ownership, and entrepreneurial savvy.

The Paris exhibit also underscored the importance of black newspapers, showing photographs of the composing and press rooms of the *Planet* in Richmond, Virginia, and the printing presses used to train students at Claflin University in Orangeburg, South Carolina. The life of the mind took center stage in photographs of university libraries, classrooms, and laboratories and in the classic image of a piano teacher and his student.[32]

W. E. B. Du Bois was a contemporary of photographers Jacob Riis and Lewis Hine, whose skillful use of images advanced their own agendas for immigration reform and the prohibition of child labor. Although there is no evidence that Du Bois used a camera himself, his innovative approach to public documentation at the *l'Exposition Universelle* in Paris demonstrated the power of visual culture on an international stage and gave him national and international recognition as a leader in the new field of sociology.[33] In the years that followed, a host of other African American educators followed Du Bois's lead and produced a vast number of photographic images of their schools, teachers, and students, many of which were reproduced as postcards. These educators, while disagreeing among themselves about the specific route to achieving what Booker T. Washington called the "Christian Citizenship in this Republic," all knew that the powerful combination of church, school, home, and work was the key to lifting millions of black southerners out of the poverty and lack of opportunity that had been slavery's legacy.[34] The body of photographs they produced disseminated images that reinforced their shared ideology of uplift, their belief in the promise of education, and their collective faith in the future.

Prior to the Paris exhibit, African American schools, including Fisk, Atlanta University, Tuskegee, and Hampton, had documented major school events and historic milestones with made-to-order double-image stereograph cards that created a three-dimensional image when viewed through a handheld stereoscope. As photographers opened studios in small towns across the South and the price of cameras and developing film decreased, photographs and photographic postcards gradually replaced stereographs, and hundreds of images of these rapidly expanding African American educational institutions were disseminated to donors, alumni, potential students, and the general public. Samuel Armstrong at Hampton Institute and Booker T. Washington at Tuskegee hired well-known photographers, black and white, to document the ongoing work of their schools, replicating and extending the work of visually representing African American success and achievement that Du Bois had set in motion in Paris. Mary McLeod Bethune, who in 1904 opened the Daytona Educational and Industrial Training School for Negro Girls (later the coeducational Bethune-Cookman Institute) in Daytona, Florida, and Nannie Helen Burroughs, who in 1911 founded the National Training School for Women and Girls in Washington, D.C., also made frequent use of photographs as they courted both black and white donors to support their institutions.[35]

The representations these educators chose uniformly emphasized hard work, order, and respectability. Each institution, from training school to university, put a premium on educating black men and women as Christian citizens who took pride in their work and responsibility for their actions. Comportment, dress, manners, dignity, and pride were the hallmarks of African American life, the symbols and the realities of the educational, social, and economic transformations that continued in the post-*Plessy* years.

Figure 2.13. Mary McLeod Bethune and her students at the Daytona Educational and Industrial Training School for Negro Girls, ca. 1905. Courtesy of the State Library and Archives of Florida.

Figure 2.14. New Library, Fisk University, Nashville, Tennessee, built 1910. Postcard owned by author.

While many of the tens of thousands of U.S. citizens traveling to *l'Exposition Universelle* in Paris viewed the Exhibition of American Negroes and even more Americans saw the exhibit at the Buffalo Pan American Exposition that drew some eight million visitors, it was the increasing dissemination of photographs and postcards of African American progress and prosperity through the mail and in newspapers and periodicals that familiarized northerners and southerners alike with the types of images Du Bois had selected for the exhibit. Like others influenced by Du Bois, African American writer Pauline Hopkins consciously used both visual and written images in her own work to counter negative racial stereotypes, arguing that images provided a special kind of literacy through telling a story in a way that was accessible to everyone, even those who could not read.[36]

The metaphysics of color that W. E. B. Du Bois explored in the Paris exhibit and that others continued after 1900 affirmed the presence of the black body in the United States and the black presence in American history while demonstrating the essence of life and energy in the rich and varied racial heritage of the American people. In 1900, on the cusp of a new century, Du Bois and his colleagues made a conscious choice to exhibit photographic representations of African Americans who had claimed freedom together with the symbols of black success and transformation—churches, schools, homes, and businesses. But as Du Bois and Thomas Calloway left Paris to return to the United States, the men, women, and children whose portraits they had transported across the Atlantic to *l'Exposition Universelle* were already becoming the targets of white resistance in a new wave of racial conflict that would substantially change the South and the nation. In 1898, a white mob had seized control of the municipal government in Wilmington, North Carolina, burned down the building that housed North Carolina's only black newspaper, and killed an unknown number of African American citizens. What few at the time knew was that Wilmington marked the advent of a new wave of racial conflict in which those African American citizens who had most successfully embraced the civil society of the post-slavery New South would be increasingly in danger of attack from white supremacists.[37]

"Days of Disillusion": A Counter-Narrative of Violence, Fear, and Death

The images displayed in the Exhibit of American Negroes in Paris put faces to the experience of African Americans in the United States and defied the color line established in the *Plessy* case. Following the Paris exhibit, however, Du Bois entered what he called the dark "days of disillusion" as destructive forces worked to unravel the social and economic foundations of the black community and the concept of American progress became intertwined with the ideology of racial segregation. In the wake of the Paris exhibit, a war of conflicting images ensued, searing dozens of incompatible representations into the minds of the American public, white and black alike. At one end of the spectrum were the visual representations of the prosperous and striving African American men, women, and children in the 1900 exhibit; at the other, horrifying photographs of lynchings in communities across the United States.

Between 1898 and 1923, fourteen episodes of massive racial violence occurred across the South, along with an untold number of more isolated incidents. No southern state was spared as African American citizens in towns and cities in the Carolinas, Louisiana, Texas, Tennessee, Florida, Georgia, Virginia, Arkansas, and Oklahoma faced terrifying violent assaults from white citizens. The brutality unleashed in Atlanta in 1906 foreshadowed the ensuing racial bloodshed in the North, beginning in 1908 in Abraham Lincoln's hometown of Springfield and spreading in 1917 to

East St. Louis, Illinois. Between 1917 and 1923, racial violence raged in Chicago; Omaha, Nebraska; Duluth, Minnesota; and Washington, D.C. Labor strife between white and black workers sparked deadly massacres in Charleston, South Carolina; Longview, Texas; Knoxville, Tennessee; and Elaine, Arkansas.

None of these events followed a single pattern, but several common elements influenced most if not all of the major incidents of racial violence between 1898 and 1923: sensationalist newspaper coverage that included visual images; reports of alleged rapes of white women by black men; ongoing competition for jobs between black and white workers; contentious political elections; and the self-defense of black citizens. Writing in the *Crisis* in 1919, W. E. B. Du Bois called the white American press a "riot-mill" that churned out copy in which "all the possible resources of 'make up' were brought to play." Newspapers, he claimed, routinely covered assault charges brought by white women in prominently displayed articles that provided "a multiplicity of details" and usually some "attempt at an exact description of the alleged assailants"; if the charges proved false, as they often did, notices that a case had been dropped or that the charges had been "a fabrication" were printed in tiny articles "tucked away" in the back pages. Frequently, by the time the initial headlines were in press, a mob had formed and was growing out of control.[38] Du Bois' charge describes the formulaic pattern of racial violence in this period, in which a specific sequence of events and circumstances resulted in a conflagration of racial hatred and brutality.

Historians have long emphasized the ways in which accusations, rumors, or even the discussion of interracial sex in any form, from marriage to consensual intercourse to rape, could become the catalyst for racial violence in both the South and North.[39] This proved true in case after case: in the Wilmington, Atlanta, and Tulsa riots discussed below; in Longview, Texas, in 1919, where a purported interracial love affair became the catalyst for a lynching, a cover-up, and a wave of destruction and murder unleashed by a mob of over a thousand; in Duluth, Minnesota, where, in the summer of 1920, thousands of white citizens took to the streets and lynched three young black men falsely accused of rape. In each of these communities, the mass violence followed reports of interracial rape that circulated throughout the community, both by word of mouth and through powerful white-controlled newspapers that used print culture to control the flow of information at the local, state, and regional levels.[40]

But in most cases, such rumors or accusations of interracial sex or rape were the spark that ignited the already smoldering fires of white resentment. In the face of increasing economic rights for freedmen and freedwomen, unresolved issues of work and labor, competition for jobs, and interracial organizing created a flammable brew, ready to ignite at a moment's notice. As Daniel Levering Lewis argues, while the immediate cause of the violence that erupted in Atlanta in 1906 was the "newspaper drumfire of alleged assaults upon white women by black men," the underlying cause could be found "in the politics of class conflict" and the use of African Americans as "a labor reserve against white workers."[41] The majority of the fourteen violent mob attacks that targeted African Americans in the South between 1898 and 1923 involved rumors of rape that masked the wage and labor issues that pitted white workers against black in an economy marked by recurring depressions, high unemployment, and increasing mechanization. In 1913, the Federal Mediation and Conciliation Service, which was established to receive arbitration cases, filed approximately thirteen thousand cases involving African Americans. Wage rates for black and white workers deviated sharply in this period as race-based conflicts swept the South, interracial competition for jobs and wages killed the possibility of interracial organizing, and white supremacists fought to reestablish political control.[42]

Visual evidence from three of these horrifying episodes—in Wilmington, North Carolina (1898); Atlanta, Georgia (1906); and Tulsa, Oklahoma (1921)—reveals the escalation of racial brutality in the first two decades of the twentieth century. Drawings and photographs played an essential role in these racial conflagrations, as the interplay of visual images and print media reinforced and disseminated the views of editors, writers, and commentators. Extant photographs document these violent "days of disillusion," leaving a visual record of trauma and memory. Images, visual and literary, tell a story of communities caught in the "riot mill" and provide stark evidence of economic conflict across the color line dividing "black" and "white."

In the late summer of 1898, various conditions made Wilmington ripe for conflict. The municipal government was in the hands of a coalition of black and white Republicans, while statewide, a whites-only Democratic party was determined to reestablish political control. An educated group of black professionals had made tremendous strides economically, socially, and politically in this majority-black community. Josephus Daniels, the editor of North Carolina's leading newspaper, the *Raleigh News & Observer*, made Wilmington an example of "Negro domination," against which he issued racist diatribes. In Wilmington, local white leaders of the Democratic Party heightened fears of "Negro rule" by circulating sensational stories and images that implied black men were raping white women throughout the state, and Daniels fueled these stories with editorials and cartoons. As the "riot-mill" churned out this material, a strong retort came from Wilmington when Alexander Manly, editor of the *Daily Record*, North Carolina's only black newspaper, refuted the charges, arguing that these were consensual relationships and that white men should be "more protective of their women against sexual advances from males of all races." Manly, known as the "fighting editor," was the "black" descendent of North Carolina's white former governor, Charles Manly. Seeking to expose the sexual indiscretions of white men, including those of his own relatives, Manly wrote that it "is no worse for a black man to be intimate with a white woman, than for a white man to be intimate with a colored woman." White supremacists pounced, accusing Manly of questioning the virtue of white women and committing "literary rape." Daniels printed three hundred thousand copies of Manly's editorial and sent them out across the state.[43]

At this point, into Wilmington strode "Pitchfork" Ben Tillman, U.S. senator and former governor from South Carolina, who, addressing a rally of Democrats on October 20, 1898, asked, "Why didn't you kill that damn nigger editor who wrote that?" A band of white men, calling themselves the Red Shirts, organized in response to Tillman's challenge. A few days later, Alfred Moore Waddell, a veteran of the Confederate Army and former U.S. congressman from North Carolina, gave a speech declaring that he would rid Wilmington of Manly and "Negro Rule," "even if we have to choke the Cape Fear River with carcasses." Early in the morning on November 10, Waddell led a white mob of former Confederate soldiers and businessmen to the offices of the *Daily Record* and burned the building to the ground. Manly had already fled the city, but the mob roamed the streets of Wilmington, firing hundreds of shots at African American citizens. The estimated death toll ranged from six to one hundred. That afternoon, Waddell and his supporters forced the resignation of the duly-elected Republican mayor and Wilmington's biracial city council, and a hastily convened new city council elected Waddell mayor. Put in office by a coup d'état, he would serve for the next six years.

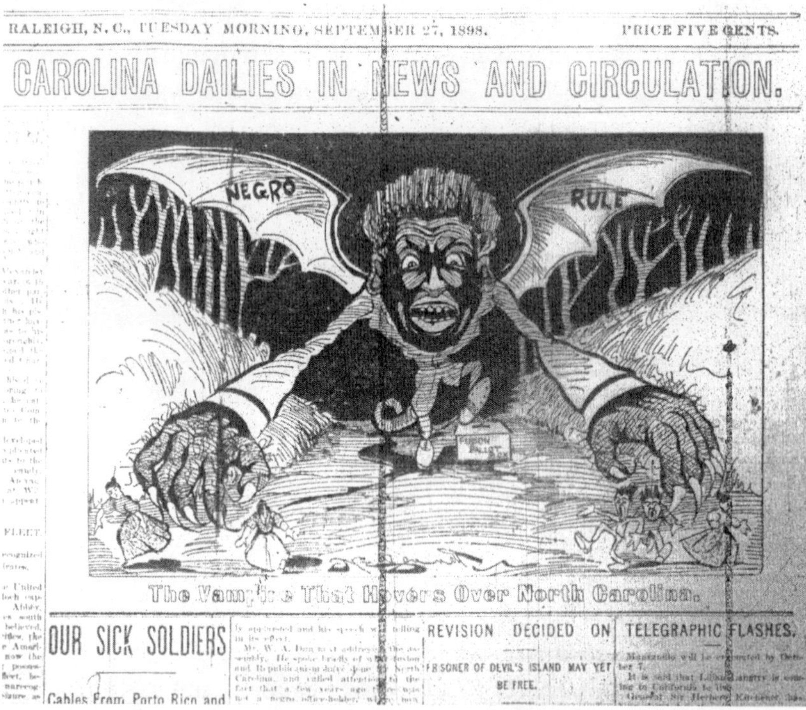
RALEIGH, N.C., TUESDAY MORNING, SEPTEMBER 27, 1898.
PRICE FIVE CENTS.
CAROLINA DAILIES IN NEWS AND CIRCULATION.
NEGRO
RULE
The Vampire That Hovers Over North Carolina.
OUR SICK SOLDIERS
Cables From Porto Rico and
REVISION DECIDED ON
PRISONER OF DEVIL'S ISLAND MAY YET BE FREE.
TELEGRAPHIC FLASHES.

Figure 2.15. "The Vampire that Hovers Over North Carolina." Cartoon. *Raleigh (N.C.) News & Observer,* 27 September 1898. Courtesy of the North Carolina Collection, University of North Carolina at Chapel Hill.

Two powerful visual images serve as bookends to the horrific events that took place in Wilmington. The first was a political cartoon titled "The Vampire that Hovers Over North Carolina" drawn by Norman Jennett, a young North Carolina artist hired by Daniels, which appeared in the *Raleigh News & Observer* on September 27, 1898.[44] The second, "Scene in the Race Disturbance," was by Hugh W. Ditzler, a young Illinois artist who had come to New York City in 1889. Commissioned by New York–based *Collier's Magazine*, it was chosen for the cover, but not necessarily intended as such, of the November 26, 1898 issue, published one week after the insurrection in Wilmington, along with an essay by Waddell. This work, which historian Joshua Brown calls "truly malevolent," erroneously interpreted the events in Wilmington for a national audience and propagated the lie that "gun-toting" African American citizens had provoked the riot.[45] These representations, drawn by young, supposedly "progressive" artists, framed the events in Wilmington and thereby shaped history through what anthropologist Richard R. Flores calls "those deeply experienced and highly entangled narratives of remembering that form for us the workings of historical discourse."[46] Jennett's cartoon, one of many he produced, imitates the popular racist caricatures, often printed on small trading cards, that denigrated African American economic success and circulated widely during Reconstruction and in the decades that followed. Here, a devilish figure with simian features, an enormous mouth, terrifying eyes, and claws steps forward on the "Fusion" ballot box, representing the coalition of Republicans and Populists, as he grabs helpless white citizens in his clutches. In the *Collier's* rendition of the Wilmington riot,

Figure 2.16. *Collier's Weekly* cover illustration for 26 November 1898, "Scene in the Race Disturbance at Wilmington, 1898"—N.66.7.119. Courtesy of the North Carolina Office of Archives and History, Raleigh, North Carolina.

Figure 2.17. "Love & Charity Hall Burning," 10 November 1898, H. Cronenberg, photographer, Wilmington, N.C. Courtesy of New Hanover County Public Library, Wilmington, North Carolina.

angry well-dressed African American men wield guns in the foreground while a black man pulls a white woman from her house and a huge, menacing, black mob surges forward.

In the full sweep of images of the Wilmington massacre, however, a single photograph has preserved a wholly different story. Made into a postcard, this photograph of the angry white throng posing for the camera both memorializes the massacre and provides powerful evidence of what actually happened. In front of the offices of the *Daily Record*, a fearless mob poses for the camera, smiles on their faces, guns in full view, with no fear of indictment for the crime they have committed.[47] In this case, the "lynched" subject was the black press—the voice of African Americans in the state of North Carolina—run by an editor who dared to talk back on the issue of rape.

Different images played a role in Atlanta in September 1906, when an angry, rioting crowd of ten thousand white citizens brutally murdered between twenty-five and forty African Americans and wounded more than a hundred. The mob destroyed black-owned businesses and stormed the streetcars, throwing black riders into the street. This time it was not visual but written images in the pages of Atlanta's white newspapers that lit the short fuse of growing white resentment over black economic and social mobility. At a time when younger white men in the city felt financially marginalized, rumors of black domestic workers organizing for higher wages and speaking back to their white employers only stoked the fire. Growing financial uneasiness played out against concerns about Atlanta's rapidly increasing population and rising crime rate. Many leading citizens blamed the saloons and bars frequented by black and white men in the heart of Atlanta for the city's declining morality. These establishments, notorious for their dark interiors filled with smoke and pictures of nude white women hanging over the long wooden bars where black and white customers stood drinking, were seen as evil dens replete with cocaine, alcohol, and lewd dancing to the "devil's music." Against this backdrop, white newspapers churned out one sensational article after another decrying the city's declining morality and then upped the ante by feeding on deep-seated white fears of interracial sex and the rape of white women by black men.[48]

Just before the riot began on a warm Saturday night in late September, metaphors and similes made pictures out of words as extra editions poured from the presses at the Atlanta *Journal* and *Evening News* on September 21, 1906: "NEGRO DIVES AND CLUBS ARE THE CAUSE OF FREQUENT ASSAULTS"; "NUDE PICTURES OF WHITE WOMEN FOUND"; "HALF CLAD NEGRO TRIES TO BREAK INTO HOUSE"; "Negro Attempts to Assault Mrs. Mary Chafin Near Sugar Creek Bridge"; ANGRY CITIZENS IN PURSUIT OF BLACK BRUTE." The *Evening News* issued five extras during the afternoon of September 22 with bold headlines covering the top half of the front page: "TWO ASSAULTS" read one, and within hours, another screamed "THIRD ASSAULT." Newsboys stood on every downtown street corner shouting the newspapers' headlines that a total of four white women had been assaulted in the city. Anxious citizens scrambled to get the latest news. Whites who read these headlines and heard the rumors that spread like wildfire across the city envisioned another wave of attacks on the heels of those already reported; African Americans grew increasingly uneasy about what might happen and began contemplating how to defend themselves and their families.[49]

By evening, the crowd of white citizens who had started gathering at Five Points, in the center of downtown, that afternoon had grown into a mob of several thousand and was becoming increasingly agitated. The tension broke shortly after eight o'clock when the mob lost control and fanned out across the central business district, smashing windows and demolishing black-owned businesses. White men forced their way onto streetcars and grabbed black passengers, unmercifully beating men and women. City officials waited at least four hours before shutting down the streetcars and calling in the militia. The crowd finally dispersed when a thunderstorm broke over the city, pelting everyone with heavy rain. The next day, while the state militia patrolled the streets, rumors that African Americans were gathering weapons sent armed white vigilantes into black neighborhoods. The day after that, police armed with rifles moved into Brownville, the neighborhood surrounding Clark College and Gammon Theological Seminary, described by journalist Ray Stannard Baker as "a self-respecting community of hard-working negroes, disturbing no one."[50] As the police entered the community, heavily armed blacks defended themselves and in the process shot one white officer. In response, three companies of militia descended on Brownville, seizing weapons and arresting over 250 black men.

The most graphic verbal image of the Atlanta riots of 1906 remains the description of three horribly mutilated, naked black bodies dumped in an alleyway at the intersection of Marietta and Forsyth Streets, "almost within the shadow of the monument of Henry W. Grady," the "New South" newspaper editor who had argued in 1886 that the New South had a record of "honor and equity" in dealing with race relations. Grady's newspaper, the *Atlanta Constitution,* reported that two black barbers at work in their shop had offered no resistance when the mob threw a brick in the face of one and fired shots at point blank, killing both men. The bodies were kicked and then dragged from the shop. Still unsatisfied, the mob tore off their clothing, with "many of the crowd taking these rags of shirts and clothing home as souvenirs or waving them above their heads to invite to further riot." Dragged across the street, the bodies were dumped in the alleyway. Soon the mob brought down another man, "felled with a single blow." Shot repeatedly after he was "far beyond any possibility of struggle or pain," the *Constitution* reported, "his body was thrown by the side of the two negro barbers and left there, the pile of three making a ghastly monument to the work of the night."[51]

When news of the Atlanta riot reached W. E. B. Du Bois in Lowndes County, Alabama, where he was working for the U.S. Census Bureau, he returned to his wife and daughter, who, together with other faculty families living on the Atlanta University campus, had taken refuge at home. Du Bois, boarding a segregated train to return to the city where, as the *Constitution* reported, "the sidewalks ran red with the blood of dead and

Figure 2.18. Scene at the intersection of Walton and Peachtree during the Atlanta riot of 1906. Photograph published in *Harper's Magazine* (vol. 50, p. 1458). Courtesy of the Kenan Research Center at the Atlanta History Center.

dying negroes," wrote a prayer poem, "A Litany to Atlanta," beseeching that a "Silent God, Sit no longer blind, Lord God, deaf to our prayer and dumb to our dumb suffering." Riding in the segregated Jim Crow car, the cotton fields of rural Alabama a blur at the window, and frantic for his family's safety in a city heavy with "the black and rolling smoke of sin, where all along bow bitter forms of endless dead," Du Bois pleaded:

> The God of our black fathers. . . . But whisper—speak—call, great God, for Thy silence is white terror to our hearts! Kyrie Eleison! [Lord have mercy!]. . . . Our hearts sink in silence and in night. . . . In night, O God of a godless land! Amen! In silence, O Silent God, Selah![52]

Where were the cameras during the Atlanta riot? The few extant photographs reflect none of Du Bois's anguish—no smoke, no blood, no dead bodies. It seems that Atlantans brought out their cameras only after the mayhem had subsided to capture posed images of occupation and control, not those of violence and decimation. One photograph, taken at the intersection of Walton and Peachtree Streets, shows militia members standing at attention next to a streetcar, white men in suits and hats standing nearby. There is no hint in this photograph of what had transpired hours earlier, no signs of destruction or death. No memory of the African American man thrown from the streetcar viaduct to his death below; no record of the dozens of other black men who died. Another photograph, this one of the Georgia State Militia, included an inset of a building in the African American neighborhood of Brownsville surrounded by a posse. Again, the focus is on armed white men, most wearing official uniforms, fulfilling their responsibilities to keep public order.

Determined to mend the damage to their city's image, white Atlantans experienced an astonishing collective amnesia following the riot. Across generations of white families, public memories of those September days almost completely disappeared. Official histories of the city omitted all references to the riot; teachers eschewed the subject. The opposite occurred in the black community, however, where men, women, and children had to deal with the lasting effects of lives lost, lasting injuries, destroyed businesses, and severe psychological trauma. As Ray Stannard Baker put it, "A riot is not over when the shooting stops!" An interracial committee of white and black elite Atlantans formed in the wake of the riot set the tone for the city's future by looking forward and studiously avoiding the subject of the past.[53]

In 1921, the Tulsa Riot followed a pattern eerily similar to that of Wilmington and Atlanta: rumors of rape ignited the already smoldering fires of economic resentment. Again the local newspaper played a major role in inciting violence. Intense opposition on the part of city fathers to interracial organizing by the Industrial Workers of the World (IWW) preceded the unprecedented conflagration that obliterated the prosperous African American community of Greenwood. Dozens of successful black-owned businesses, churches, schools, and homes were burned to the ground across a forty-four-block area.[54] As they had in Atlanta, blacks fought back in self-defense. In contrast to Atlanta, however, the camera's mechanical eye recorded what happened in Tulsa while the violence and burning was still underway, as well as in the aftermath of what historian Scott Ellsworth has called "Death in a Promised Land."[55] After the dead had been buried, a set of horrifying photographs made into postcards spread the story of Tulsa far and wide, providing a visual narrative of trauma, memory, and the destructive power of the white mob.

Handwritten captions on the fronts of these postcards recount what happened. Homes, schools, churches, and the black body itself—the hallmarks of African American life that Du Bois had heralded two decades earlier in the Exhibition of American Negroes in Paris—all lay charred and ruined in what had been a thriving African American community in the center of the United States. *Kyrie Eleison.* The destruction of African American lives, community, hard-won success, security, and spiritual well-being that shook Oklahoma and the nation on those fateful days in late spring 1921 left scars that never healed. The work of claiming freedom seemed to have no end.[56]

The photographs of Tulsa that were made into postcards and mailed around the country portrayed the heart-wrenching aftermath of the riot.[57] These intimidating images served both as evidence of the injustice that took place in Tulsa and as a powerful warning of what could happen to African Americans in any U.S. community. The images on each of these postcards carry enormous historical weight; the captions tell a specific narrative. In Fig. 2.19, the description "Little Africa on Fire, Tulsa Race Riot, June 1st, 1921" brings to mind Agassiz's message of separate creation and white superiority in the 1850 "Portrait of Renty," the African-born enslaved man whose photograph was used as scientific visual evidence of the superiority of the white race. The neat homes of Greenwood, the flourishing businesses of "Black Wall Street," the Dreamland Theatre, all burned beyond repair, are not referred to as part of Tulsa but as "Little Africa," an outpost of the continent that represents the real home of the "other" who lived in this part of town. The caption on the postcard in Fig. 2.20

Figure 2.19. Handwritten caption on front of postcard: "Little Africa on Fire. Tulsa Race Riot, June 1st, 1921." Courtesy of the Department of Special Collections, McFarlin Library, The University of Tulsa.

Figure 2.20. Handwritten caption on front of postcard: "Burning of church where ammunition was stored during Tulsa Race Riot." Picture of Mt. Zion Baptist Church taken near Cameron St. and Elgin Ave. The church was rumored to have been a storehouse for weapons and ammunition. Courtesy of the Department of Special Collections, McFarlin Library, The University of Tulsa.

rationalizes the act of burning a church by declaring that it was "where ammunition was stored." The elementary school and Masonic Hall shown in ruins in Fig. 2.21 symbolized both education and the free association of black men, powerful icons in Tulsa's upwardly mobile African American community. The caption in Fig. 2.22, "All that was left of his home," tells the viewer that this man, standing alone and forlorn, quite literally no longer lives here, not in this home or in this town. Finally, in Fig. 2.23, the callous heading "Charred Negro killed in Tulsa Riot" sends an unmistakable message to African Americans that a horrendous death awaits those who get in the way of white power; to white viewers, the image speaks consciously or unconsciously of the lethal dimensions of white power. This final postcard, so like lynching images from the same period, shows a body lying burned beyond recognition on the ground. From the ruins of Greenwood, this photograph, quickly converted to a postcard, carried the terror of Tulsa across the nation.[58]

Photographing sites of racial violence, whether the mass destruction of a black community or the tortured death of a lynching victim, became standard practice in the late nineteenth century and continued beyond

Figure 2.21. Handwritten caption on front of postcard: "Ruins of the Tulsa Race Riot, 6-1-21." The ruins of Dunbar Elementary School and the Masonic Hall (501 N. Greenwood) are in the background. Courtesy of the Department of Special Collections, McFarlin Library, The University of Tulsa.

Figure 2.22. Handwritten caption on front of postcard: "All that was left of his home after Tulsa Race Riot, 6-1-1921." Courtesy of the Department of Special Collections, McFarlin Library, The University of Tulsa.

Figure 2.23. Handwritten caption on front of postcard: "Charred Negro killed in Tulsa Riot 6-1-1921." Courtesy of the Department of Special Collections, McFarlin Library, The University of Tulsa.

the 1930s. The year after the Paris exhibition, ninety-nine documented lynchings took place in the United States, and photography became an integral part of the ritualized violence of these public events as picture postcards of lynchings were reproduced and shared. In sharp contrast to the portraits displayed in the Exhibition of American Negroes at *l'Exposition Universelle*, these horrifying images of torture and murder allowed white spectators to deny the similarities between themselves and the African American victims of extralegal violence. According to literary scholar Richard Brodhead, just as "whipping is *the* central image of slavery," so lynching is the "synecdochal image of the post-Reconstruction condition of the freedperson."[59] As Shawn Michelle Smith argued above, the widespread popularity of such representations reinforced the dichotomy of race and obliterated the "bridge of visual signs of similarity" between white viewer and black subject at work in the exhibition Du Bois compiled in 1900. In contrast to what Du Bois had accomplished, photographs of riots and lynchings further severed the connection between blacks and whites by denigrating the humanity of black victims, stripping them of citizenship and marking them as criminal.[60]

The war of images escalated dramatically with the release of D. W. Griffith's silent film *Birth of a Nation* in 1915. The film broke new cinematic ground even as it grossly distorted the history of slavery, the Civil War, and Reconstruction. "The harm it is doing the colored people cannot be estimated," wrote NAACP secretary Mary Childs Nerney from Chicago, who also had "no doubt that this was in the mind of the people who are producing it." President Woodrow Wilson showed the film in the East Room of the White House, declaring that it was "like writing history with lightening" and "all so terribly true." W. E. B. Du Bois advocated censoring the film and, failing that, urged that the most odious sections be deleted. In sharp contrast to the nuanced and multifaceted visual images Du Bois had assembled for the Exhibit of American Negroes, *Birth of a Nation* was "potent propaganda," in the words of Du Bois biographer Lewis. Du Bois argued in despair that the film left "the Negro represented either as an ignorant fool, a vicious rapist, a venal or unscrupulous politician or a faithful but doddering idiot."[61]

Destroying the "signs of similarity" between black and white southerners facilitated the institution of racial segregation in public facilities and within the workplace. Repeated episodes of extralegal violence in the form of riots and lynchings and the magnification of those events through visual records like the picture postcards accelerated the movement of African American men, women, and children out of the South. After a "holocaust of lynchings" killed at least six men and one woman in Brooks and Lowndes counties, Georgia, in May 1918, NAACP assistant secretary Walter F. White reported that "more than five hundred Negroes have left the immediate vicinity of Valdosta [in Lowndes County] alone and many more have expressed the determination that they too were going to leave as soon as they could dispose of their lands and gather their crops." Newspaper editor Alexander Manley was not the only African American to flee Wilmington. After the riot and takeover of the city government by the white mob, white Democrats in Wilmington promised jobs for white workers and waged a "banishment and intimidation" campaign against black skilled workers, entrepreneurs, attorneys, doctors, ministers, teachers, and postal workers. "Negroes Still Going North," read a New Bern headline in 1899, as the paper reported "the tide of negroes from Wilmington to new homes in the north, continues to flow." In 1898, black citizens had constituted 56 percent of Wilmington's population; after the riot, the city's demographics changed dramatically as 14 percent of its black residents left Wilmington permanently. From Atlanta, Ray Stannard Baker reported that "after the riot was over, many negro families, terrified and feeling themselves unprotected sold out . . . and left the country, some going to California, some to Northern cities." As in Wilmington, "the best and most enterprising" moved away. Labor, he argued, will be "scarcer and wages may be higher in Atlanta because of the riot," pointing out that the mob had targeted the middle class and that every one of those African Americans killed or wounded "was industrious, respectable and law-abiding." The words "RUNNING THE NEGRO OUT" scrawled across one picture postcard of fire destroying the thriving black community in Tulsa succinctly captured the motivation of the white mob.[62]

The year after the Atlanta riot, W. E. B. Du Bois addressed this issue when he wrote, "If my own city of Atlanta had offered it today the choice between 500 Negro college graduates—forceful, busy, ambitious men of property and self respect, and 500 black, cringing, vagrants and criminals, the popular vote in favor of the criminals would be simply overwhelming." He continued, "Why? Because they want Negro crime? No. . . . They fear Negro ambition and success more." "The South," Du Bois argued, "can conceive neither machinery nor place for the educated, self-reliant, self-assertive black man."[63]

The Metaphysics of Race

In 1900, when Du Bois was preparing the Exhibition of American Negroes, his determination to counter the nineteenth-century separate-species argument touted by his professors at Harvard had led him to play with the metaphysics of color and to mock the color line that the *Plessy* case had drawn through every southern community and every northern town. Two decades later, as he tried to comprehend the meaning of the Tulsa Riot, the metaphysics of race, not of color, weighed heavily on his mind. The system that determined the ways that race operated within American life functioned according to a fundamentally different calculus than the metaphysics of color Du Bois had so creatively explored in his exhibit. The metaphysics of color was rational; the metaphysics of race defied reason. Homer Plessy's case was argued according to the logic of color: a "white" man of African American ancestry could not be denied the right to buy a first-class ticket, and therefore any person of African

American origin had the right to ride in the first-class coach as long as the passenger could afford to purchase a first-class ticket. In sharp contrast, the U.S. Supreme Court decided the *Plessy v. Ferguson* case according to a metaphysics of race, whereby everyone of African American descent, no matter how remote that ancestry, was subject to segregation according to the new formulations of law and practice being enacted in communities across the United States. Riots and lynchings also operated according to a metaphysics of race that extended the evils of slavery and played on whites' fears of the black presence, which stemmed in large part from their own role in perpetuating a system first of enslavement and then of oppression and denied citizenship.

The visual culture of race affected black and white Americans in fundamentally different ways. For those on opposite sides of the color divide that Plessy and Du Bois had worked so hard to remove, the Janus-face of race showed a different past and a dissimilar future for African Americans and for those who identified themselves as white. As conditions for African Americans became increasingly perilous in the decades after *Plessy v. Ferguson*, photographic images of violence and lynching first competed with and then gradually displaced those of education, prosperity, and promise so carefully recorded by educators like Du Bois, Washington, and Burroughs. For a long time, images of violence seemed to carry the day. In the process, the narrative of black life in the South changed dramatically, from stories of claiming freedom to cries for justice like the one Du Bois recorded in the prayer poem he wrote after the Atlanta riot: "The way, O God, show us the way and point us the path. Whither? North is greed and South is blood; within the coward, and without the liar."[64]

The riot in Atlanta changed Du Bois in fundamental ways. After 1906, he kept a double-barreled shotgun in his home. He sharpened his opposition to Booker T. Washington's accommodationist strategies, and a short while later he left Atlanta and academia. He moved with his family to New York City, where he helped establish the National Association for the Advancement of Colored People (NAACP). As founding editor of the *Crisis* and director of publications and research, Du Bois became the sole African American to serve as an NAACP executive in its early years.[65] Touring the country for the NAACP in what he called his "annual pilgrimage to see The Problem first hand," Du Bois reported on racial inequities. In the spring of 1926, after stops in Ohio at Youngstown and Toledo, Du Bois headed west to Fort Wayne, Indiana, took a quick detour to Detroit, and then "flew nine hundred miles over land and river, by field and village, city and town, through poverty and wealth, smoke and sunshine, across the vale of the Mississippi, through . . . Missouri . . . to Oklahoma." As he rolled along on the Frisco line, Du Bois remembered, "I felt the thrill I always feel as I enter the land of slavery. It was like the nerves in a plunge in icy waters." Approaching the Oklahoma state line, Du Bois's train stopped at Monette, Missouri, where he changed trains and walked into the coach car. As "we rolled to the border," he wrote later, "the conductor glanced at me and went on. Then he came back." The conductor first begged Du Bois's pardon and then asked for his nationality. Later Du Bois reflected, "Wasn't it funny I could have been anything on God's earth but what I was and ridden in that coach into Oklahoma. I could have been Indian, Mexican, Philipino, Igorrote or lap dog. I could have been a murderer, rapist, thief or swindler." The one thing that "called for insult" was, Du Bois wrote, "my American citizenship for six generations." Knowing that he could have denied his identity, lied outright, or jabbered "Spanish, French or Hoglatin" and been undisturbed, Du Bois nevertheless answered honestly, "I am an American Negro," and was promptly escorted to the "Jim Crow" car.[66]

Thirty years after *Plessy v. Ferguson,* the long arm of the Supreme Court pulled Du Bois back into the small, dirty, smoke-filled "Negro section," where because of the legal authority vested in a white train conductor, he completed his journey into Tulsa. Five years had passed since the white mob burned the African American neighborhood of Greenwood to the ground. Having studied the photographs that poured out of Tulsa after the fires of 1921, Du Bois was overwhelmed by what he saw when he left the railroad station. Black Tulsa, he wrote later, "stands almost trim in new brick and wood. Scars are there yet, here and there, but the city is impudent and noisy. It believes in itself." As Du Bois toured the city in the hours before he was scheduled to speak to the Oklahoma Negro State Teachers Association, he saw rebuilt homes, schools, and churches, a "happy city" that had "new clothes" and was "young, gay and strong." Five years after "fire and blood and robbery leveled it to the ground, flat, raw, smoking," the city had "reeled to its feet blindly," wrote Du Bois, and "Black Tulsa rose triumphant from the dead." That evening, as he stood to address an overflowing crowd of eight hundred teachers and local citizens, Du Bois found himself briefly at a loss for words. "What should I say in this curious land?" he wondered as he looked out on the "fine, intelligent faces" before him. "I stand before Tulsa with uncovered head," he began. Writing in the *Crisis* after he had returned to New York, Du Bois admitted, "Tulsa helped me." Black Tulsa, he wrote, "did not cringe before riot and lynching. She killed the beasts and died and rose again."[67]

In November 1900, as Du Bois's Exhibit of American Negroes closed in Paris, members of the Phyllis Wheatley Club of Colored Women organized a protest rally at the Michigan Avenue Baptist Church in Buffalo, New York, to pressure the board of managers of the Pan-American Exposition to be held in Buffalo the following year to name a "colored commissioner" to represent the two thousand black citizens in the city. They also called on the board to invite Du Bois and Thomas J. Calloway to bring the Exhibit of American Negroes to Buffalo for the Exposition. A few months later, 850 miles due south in Charleston, plans were being made to display the Exhibit of American Negroes in the "Negro Building" at the South Carolina Inter-state and West Indian Exposition scheduled to open on December 1, 1901. The photographs Du Bois had assembled and shipped to Paris and back resonated with Americans who attended these exhibitions, although the war of images that raged during the early decades of the twentieth century was in evidence in both cities. In Buffalo, Du Bois's depictions of the range of African Americans' accomplishments in work, education, professional training, and business vied for attention with reproductions of slave cabins and native African tribesmen on parade in the midway. An exhibit titled The Old Plantation that stereotyped blacks as slaves and minstrels particularly aggravated the women of the Phyllis Wheatley Club, whose hard work was responsible for bringing the Exhibit of American Negroes to Buffalo. In Charleston, a similar controversy ensued over a statue commissioned by the Board of Directors slated for placement in front of the Negro Building that housed the Exhibit of American Negroes. This image, designed by Charles A. Lopez of New York, featured a young black woman balancing a large basket of cotton on her head. On one side of her, a muscular man, modeled after Booker T. Washington, held a plow in one hand and leaned against an anvil; on the other, a young male worker in a leather apron played the banjo. Black Charlestonians condemned the statue as an affront to "every hopeful, aspiring, self-respecting black person," and when they demanded that it be removed, the Exposition organizers complied.[68]

The body, as Foucault reminds us, "is the site for the inscription of justice," and in the post-Emancipation South the black body became the primary object that white southerners sought to control.[69] The black body in motion, the focus of the *Plessy* case that pivoted on travel by railroad, drew the attention of white southerners determined to reestablish racial supremacy and political, economic, and social control. Legal restrictions on the movement of racially defined bodies were at one end of a broad spectrum of social controls that ended with black bodies suspended from the end of a lynch rope, the most extreme form of extralegal violence perpetrated against African Americans in these years. Visual images reinforced this form of control—and with each passing year of the twentieth century, they increased in importance as tools for shaping public and private perceptions of history and race. The opposing forces of transformation and resistance fought hard for control of the message: uplift on one side, decline on the other. The shape of the future hung in the balance.

II

WOMEN AND DISSENT

3

· · · · · · · · ·

"I Got So Mad, I Just Had to Get Something off My Chest"

The Contested Terrain of Women's Organizations in the American South

In the last two decades of the nineteenth century, manufacturers and business leaders drew up blueprints for a New South that publicly embraced the doctrine of "separate but equal" by gradually extending segregation into every aspect of southern life. At the same time, they endorsed an industrial program that promised economic well-being but delivered low wages to workers who entered mills and factories. During this period, significant cohorts of black and white southern women promulgated their own views of how the New South should be developed and shaped. Southern churchwomen envisioned the South as God's kingdom on earth—a beloved community in which individuals lived, worked, and loved in harmony with one another.[1] Southern suffrage activists sought women's right to vote as citizens entitled to the full privilege of the franchise. Women workers in the region, rapidly increasing in numbers, spoke out for better working conditions and more equitable wages. This chapter examines the effects of racial and class divisions within groups formed by southern women to foster political and economic change, taking a close look at black and white Methodist women's associations, the campaign for women's suffrage in Atlanta, and two organizations that promoted the organization of southern women workers, the industrial clubs established by the Young Women's Christian Association (YWCA) and the Southern Summer School for Women Workers in Industry, a workers' education program for southern women.

As Reconstruction ended, women's organizations took root in every small town throughout the region. Church groups, literary societies, neighborhood organizations, and garden clubs became the warp and woof of southern small-town life and an increasingly visible aspect of the regional urban culture that developed in cities like Richmond, Charlotte, Atlanta, and New Orleans.[2] These organizations provided important collective outlets through which women could express their individual beliefs about gender, race, citizenship, and civic participation. Southern women across class and racial lines saw active participation in women's associational life as the most effective way to achieve the reforms that would realize their vision of what the New South could become. But although cross-class and interracial cooperation became the hallmark of some southern associations as women walked what historian Glenda Gilmore has called "the tightrope of interracial politics," racial and class-based tensions invariably marked the psychological landscape of these organizations. Tensions among black and white women otherwise engaged in cross-racial and cross-class cooperation frequently simmered below the surface. The contestation that characterized southern women's organizations through which black and working-class women found a voice is exemplified by Beulah Carter, a hosiery worker who claimed she finally spoke out in a group of middle-class women because "I got so mad, I just had to get something off my chest." Friction across class lines often developed as women in organizations as diverse as church groups, suffrage organizations, YWCA clubs, and the Southern Summer School constructed their public identities by speaking out, each in their own way, about the complicated economic and social issues confronting the New South.[3]

Within this context, white and black Methodist women focused on shaping a new society that accounted for the human costs of racial, industrial, and economic progress. They developed specific ways of working together based on mutual dependence and a transformative process that profoundly affected their agendas for broad-based social and economic reform. These strategies, honed within a common church tradition, did not transfer to the Atlanta campaign for women's suffrage, where demarcating rather than transcending racial and class divisions became an integral part of the political agenda. Divisions across class and racial lines also affected the work of southern women workers as they became increasingly active within the southern labor movement. Like women working within the church and the campaign for women's suffrage, women workers in

YWCA industrial clubs and the Southern Summer School expressed their own views about the development of the New South.

The women's organizations that were formed in the South exhibited the distinctive gender, class, and racial dynamics of a society forged in the aftermath of post-war Reconstruction. Historian Anne F. Scott, observing that southern "women were always reminding each other of the importance of being ladylike," quotes Nellie Nugent Somerville, a Mississippi suffrage leader, who in 1898 warned those working with her in the South that "an unpleasant aggressiveness will doubtless be expected of us" but nonetheless encouraged her co-workers to "let us endeavor to disappoint such expectations."[4] In the very process of speaking publically about their beliefs, these diverse groups of southern women deviated from traditional gendered behavior by making their views public, taking decisive action, and openly showing frustration and anger. As a consequence, in the years between 1880 and the 1930s, women dramatically changed the performance and significance of their associational lives. At the same time, several national organizations, both religious and secular, in the suffrage movement and in the labor movement, offered many southern women support they could not get inside the South itself. National groups working for racial reform, women's suffrage, and workers' rights also recognized that their success ultimately depended on their gaining the support of southern women.

Southern Churchwomen and the Process of Transformation

As economic and social changes reshaped the South in the wake of Reconstruction, white and black churchwomen became increasingly aware of the human costs of rapid industrial development and racial segregation. Empowered by their belief in women's civic and religious responsibilities, white women in the Methodist Episcopal (M.E.) Church, South, the southern Methodists who had broken with the national Methodist Church over the issue of slavery before the Civil War, became regionally and even nationally recognized as leaders in industrial and interracial reform and part of an amalgam of white religious and secular women's groups working for social change within the South. At the same time, black churchwomen, faced with building a free society within the post-Emancipation restrictions established by southern whites, saw the church as an institution through which they could successfully gather resources, create and sustain schools, deal with housing and social welfare concerns, and address political and economic issues crucial to the well-being of black southerners. Women in the Colored Methodist Episcopal (C.M.E.) Church joined the broad social reform movement organized by southern black women in the 1880s. Less politically active than their counterparts in the northern-based, more independent African Methodist Episcopal Church, C.M.E. women became cooperative partners with white church-women in the M.E. Church.[5]

An analysis of interactions between black and white Methodist women in the South between the 1880s and the 1930s reveals that while patterns of cooperation and animosity co-existed, white and black churchwomen also developed relationships that were based not on collaboration or enmity but on mutual dependence. This type of relationship occurred largely because women in the C.M.E. church, who were primarily grass-roots leaders based in small towns or rural areas, actively engaged in what I call a process of transformation through which they converted their concerns about the economic and social conditions faced by black southerners into a format that was acceptable to white women and that could be incorporated into the white agenda for social change. Because of this process, actively practiced by black women but invisible to whites, white churchwomen came to rely heavily on their counterparts within the black church for help in developing reform agendas and in carrying out interracial programs.

This process of transformation involved interactions between white and black southern churchwomen that allowed white women to preserve the power they derived from their race. For decades, white women did not acknowledge the help they received from black women, instead reporting (in both M.E. and C.M.E. records) that they were the ones "teaching" and "helping" the black women with whom they met. In fact, C.M.E. women expressly controlled their interactions with M.E. women so that they always appeared to be "learning" from and "being assisted" by whites. These ritualized interactions reinforced white dominance while simul-taneously allowing black women to maintain what Darlene Clark Hine has termed the dynamics of dissemblance, namely, "behavior and atti-tudes of Black women that created the appearance of openness and dis-closure but actually shielded the truth of their inner lives and selves from their oppressors."[6] Self-imposed dissemblance afforded black women a protective shield of invisibility, the safeguard they needed to survive in a white-dominated society. This shielding, combined with the process of transformation through which black women proactively converted the black agenda for economic and social change into a format that white women could understand and support, provided a way for African American reform goals to become part of the white agenda and, eventually, to be realized through programs that white women sponsored and black women implemented.

A close examination of the dual religious traditions of whites and blacks in the Methodist Episcopal Churches (South and Colored, respectively) reveals the interactions of southern women bound together in a common church tradition—racially separated but organizationally and theologically united. With the founding of the Colored Methodist Episcopal Church in Jackson, Tennessee, on December 12, 1870, southern white Methodists were forced to recognize black freedom and religious autonomy.[7] Wanting to retain some contact and control over black Methodists, white southern Methodists offered "assistance" to newly formed black congregations. For example, M.E. congregations were encouraged to donate land and to assist in building C.M.E. church houses. These forms of assistance perpetuated white control and extended black dependence on, and allegiance to, nearby white congregations.[8] The system cut two ways, however, and continued white control also meant that the Methodist Episcopal Church, South could not separate from its black counterpart. Whites had to openly acknowledge the existence of black Methodists who were part of the same religious tradition and were, in theory, "brother and sister Methodists." The shared rituals, liturgy, and administration of the Methodist Episcopal Church provided a common language and organizational structure that facilitated interracial contact and perpetuated white involvement in the black church and vice versa.[9]

The Methodist Episcopal Church, South and the Colored Methodist Episcopal Church also shared a tradition of male dominance. Women church members could not vote or serve as lay leaders or ministers. Women were expected to perform the invisible tasks that held a congregation together: running church schools, furnishing parsonages for ministers, cleaning the church, and preparing food for church suppers. Moreover, women formed a social service network within the churches, ministering to the sick and caring for grieving families, needy children, and the elderly. Both black and white Methodist women raised substantial amounts of money to build and maintain churches and parsonages. Both provided funds for ministers' pensions and cared for ministers' widows. This shared patriarchal tradition united black and white southern churchwomen more than any other common aspect of their lives.[10]

Within this context of male leadership and female service, Methodist women activists created organized sisterhoods that, while divided by race, affirmed them personally and professionally. These black and white southern churchwomen working in local communities had much in common, but there were also great differences between them. Their interaction, sustained for over half a century, took place in the context of the disenfranchisement of black citizens, sustained extra-legal racial violence, and increasing racial segregation. Resisting these forces, southern churchwomen established a record of cooperation across racial lines. They shared similar visions of southern progress, and over the years they associated with one another in mutually sustaining ways. As Dr. Mattie Coleman, the first president of the C.M.E. Woman's Connectional Council, emphasized when addressing the Council's first meeting in 1918, "There has always been a close relationship between the sisters of the M.E. Church, South and the sisters of the C.M.E. Church. . . . We have long since realized that each one is dependent on the other."[11]

The parallel histories of these churchwomen underscore the common experience faced by women who lived in a hierarchical society divided by gender. Both black and white women sought to expand the work they performed within their churches, to be recognized for their contributions, to make their invisible work visible. Both groups of women began by campaigning for voting rights within the church; both called for the ordination of women ministers. And both fought against men within the church, ministers and laymen alike, who opposed the women not for the work they did, but for their insistence on equal rights. White and black churchwomen crossed the thin line separating congregational service from what came to be defined as home mission work. They began by teaching Sunday school and caring for sick church members; they moved on to addressing regional public health issues, the biracial system of southern education, child welfare, racial inequity, and women's working conditions.

One major difference between the two groups involved the elaborate reform agendas and political programs developed and endorsed by M.E. women, who after the turn of the century developed a more active political program focused on industrial development and interracial cooperation. M.E. women developed bureaus and commissions, study groups, and committees to examine social issues and determine the official position of the M.E. Woman's Missionary Society (WMS) on such questions as child labor, protective legislation for hours and wages, collective bargaining, rural conditions, convict leasing, and racial segregation.[12] The development of such a bureaucracy held little appeal for C.M.E. missionary activists. C.M.E. leaders instead designed programs that could be easily adapted by the diverse groups of women, small and large, urban and rural, educated and uneducated, that made up the C.M.E.'s constituency. C.M.E. women saw their role as one of "Christianizing" their people. Christianization was a full-fledged program spoken in a one-word code. It meant not simply becoming Christian but becoming literate and economically secure. It meant being counted as a citizen, voting, and having access to public resources. Although these goals had political overtones, C.M.E. women protected themselves from reprisal by *not* taking official stands on public issues. To protect themselves and their families, they kept their political agendas hidden. They did not publish the proceedings of their meetings, as the M.E. women did, and their publications rarely included articles on controversial subjects. They did, however, openly applaud some of the public positions taken by the white M.E. women. When M.E. women spoke out against lynching, for example, or in favor of improving black schools, C.M.E. women supported the white reform platform.[13]

This indirect form of speaking out was especially important for southern black women who were not well-known and were working at the grass-roots level—women who were not protected by position, northern connections, or reputation. C.M.E. women did not hesitate to employ the protective strategy of showing their support for certain social or economic changes obliquely by endorsing a platform put together by white women. How could black women be attacked for supporting something that white churchwomen advocated? Moreover, by the time it was adopted, the platform formally endorsed by white Methodist women had been proactively shaped and re-shaped by black churchwomen who used the dynamic of dissemblance and the process of transformation to transmit their ideas to white Methodist reformers.

The white reform platform underwent numerous changes between 1906 and 1928, as M.E. women worked hard to realize their own vision of southern progress by embracing an increasingly public role in southern political life. They campaigned against the convict-lease system and endorsed bills in southern and federal legislatures on issues that affected southern women and children. They supported compulsory education and urged employers to stop using child labor. They also raised questions about the social costs of industrial development, ran boarding houses for women industrial workers, and helped fund welfare programs within southern mills.[14] But industrial reform proved to be a treacherous arena. Many white Methodist women were related to mill managers or to town merchants or professionals who had to maintain good relationships with industrialists. Consequently, while they could belong to a Missionary Society that theoretically endorsed collective bargaining, they regularly shied away from taking sides during local strikes or supporting specific unions.[15]

In this contentious climate, churchwomen increasingly turned their attention to interracial work, the third rail of M.E. missionary activism, and made relationships between black and white women their top priority. Connections between the two missionary societies, one white and one black, increased in both frequency and intensity after 1918, when the newly elected C.M.E. Missionary Society president, Dr. Mattie Coleman, requested to regularly attend M.E. Woman's Missionary Council meetings as a delegate. C.M.E. women were eager to meet with the M.E. sisterhood, and through the process of transformation, they were ready to provide the white women with both the information needed to set an agenda and the labor needed to implement interracial programs in communities throughout the South.[16]

With the guidance of C.M.E. women, white Methodist women gradually intensified their focus on southern African Americans, whom they referred to as "the dark faces of the alien race that looked daily into theirs."[17] Their endorsement of the Social Platform of the Federal Council of Churches in 1913 had an important impact on the M.E. Missionary Society's work with southern black women. That year, in her annual address to the membership, WMS President Belle Bennett reiterated the platform's first plank, a commitment to standing "for equal rights and complete justice for all men in all stations of life." At the same time, she endorsed the work of Deaconess Mary DeBardeleben in the black community in Augusta, Georgia, and issued a strong statement against "the barbarous crime of lynching," proposing, "we therefore, as an organized and representative body of southern women, should declare our disapproval and abhorrence of the savagery that provokes this crime, and by tongue and pen and, in those States where our women have the power of suffrage, by the ballot arouse and develop a public sentiment that will compel a rigid enforcement of the law against such violence until it is no longer known among us."[18] By 1918, M.E. Church, South women had adopted the argument that "the 9,000,000 negroes located in the South constitute the biggest opportunity for the Church to build up a citizenship which will make this country God's country."[19]

Clearly then, white Methodist women increasingly regarded their work with black southerners as the central focus of their domestic missionary program. But their approach to this work continued to be condescending and oppressively maternal toward African Americans. White women were surprised at "discoveries of negro efficiency" and considered southern blacks their "own peculiar charge." After Mattie Coleman became president of the C.M.E. Woman's Missionary Society and began attending the white M.E. Woman's Missionary Council meetings, however, the substance and tone of the reform agenda regarding the "negro" changed.[20] In the years that followed, both groups reported numerous gatherings between C.M.E. and M.E. women. These meetings routinely followed the prescribed "helping/learning" format, a posture that partially obscured the most essential aspects of the relationship between these women of different races: their mutual dependence and the process of transformation through which black churchwomen's ideas about economic justice became an essential part of the white agenda for social change.

For example, in the only history of women in the C.M.E. church, written in 1934, Sara McAfee tells the story of "Mother Sawyer," an elderly black woman who lived in Nashville, Tennessee, at the turn of the century. Mother Sawyer cared for children whose parents worked from dawn to dusk. Frequently she wept for her people, whom she saw suffering from unjust racial discrimination, inadequate schooling, and low wages and as vulnerable to unhappiness, hopelessness, and despondency. One evening after the last child had gone home, so the story goes, Mother Sawyer "lifted her soul in fervent prayer," asking for a way to help. Then, "as if in answer to her prayer, Mother Sawyer learned of the work that the Southern Methodist women were doing for the neglected white people of the city through their Wesley Houses," and "a hope was born in her heart for similar work for her own people." Certain she had received her answer, Sawyer made an appointment to see Mrs. R. W. MacDonell, the white general secretary of the M.E. Woman's Board of Home Missions. MacDonell sent her to see Miss Sara Estelle Haskin, who was in charge of community service. Haskin listened as Sawyer presented her case, describing crowded living conditions, children with no place to play except back alleys, babies left helpless while mothers worked, children with curable diseases but no treatments. Haskin's heart "was touched," and she promised to help. Shortly after this, Haskin reportedly "walked through the Negro section of Nashville in search of a place" to begin solving these problems. As she walked, she happened to notice "the flood of sunlight" in the basement of a local church. She asked the pastor if he would be willing to help sponsor a kindergarten in the basement of his church. He was willing and the school was opened, funded by the M.E. Woman's Missionary Society.[21]

Sawyer's story, told so eloquently in the C.M.E.'s history, does not appear in the M.E. Woman's Missionary Council records, which simply contain a reference to "the mission being developed in Nashville, Tennessee, by Miss Haskin, of the Methodist Training School."[22] Sawyer and hundreds of women like her in communities across the South were involved in this process of transformation, translating the massive economic and social needs of individuals and groups within the black community in a way that white women reformers could understand. They gave white churchwomen lists of specific social problems and suggestions for their solution (as Sawyer gave McDonnell and Haskin information about her community). White reformers then took this information and incorporated it into their own agenda. Black women, in a largely invisible way, controlled the process: they determined which needs were most pressing, they suggested solutions, and in most cases, they did the work of setting up and running the programs.

While white Methodist women looked to C.M.E. women to carry out their interracial missionary programs, C.M.E. women looked to white Methodist women for financial backing—funding they saw as their due, in lieu of the unpaid wages of slavery and the low wages they had received after freedom. Black women attended M.E.-sponsored leadership training schools and reported, "these schools have been much help to us, to the extent that we feel we are due." C.M.E. women also looked to M.E. women for support at critical times, such as when the C.M.E. men opposed their establishing a Woman's Council. At the invitation of the C.M.E. missionary society, they reported, M.E. member Mrs. Hume Steele "went with us to the seat of the Conference, aiding us in getting our bill passed" and "stood by our organization until it was perfected and the first officers initiated." Black women declared themselves willing to "join our sisters in the M.E. Church." They felt white women worked "side by side" with them, and as they expanded their role within the church, C.M.E. women believed they were "well assisted by the missionary women of the M.E. Church, South."[23]

Increased contact with organized C.M.E. women had a major effect on the work of the M.E. Woman's Missionary Council. In 1920, M.E. women formed a "Committee to Establish Policy for Negro Work," and the following year they began to organize interracial committees in communities throughout the South. Two years later they issued a new call to abolish mob violence and lynching. By 1923, 445 interracial committees had been organized; by 1927, the number had grown to 666, with most classified as "working in a spirit of cooperation, confidence, and mutual respect." During the twenties, M.E. women redefined what they meant by interracial cooperation, arguing for "face-to-face and hand-to-hand work with our Negro neighbors." Gradually white Methodist women shifted away from the patronizing language they had used for so long. They began to insist that charity was *not* interracial cooperation, and they recognized that "fear, the closed mind and heart, the credulity of the masses, sentimentalism, emotionalism, patronizing attitudes and low standards" impeded constructive interracial work.

As the 1930s came to a close, white M.E. women expressed their desire to integrate their reform program into the church at large, where it could transform a broader constituency. On this issue, they met stiff opposition from the male laity and leadership in their own denomination. Nevertheless, they continued to bear witness to the positive effects of acting on their own ideals. In this, they had the steadfast support of the C.M.E. women, whose beliefs in justice and opportunity they had adopted, through the process of transformation, as their own. White women had followed black women's lead in fighting for laity rights and in campaigning for the ordination of women ministers. When C.M.E. women "began to agitate the question of woman's rights" within their church in 1906, M.E. Church, South women took notice and three years later began their own fight for suffrage and equal rights within the church. C.M.E. women started working for the ordination of women in 1902. M.E. women followed suit, but waited until 1930 to press the issue.[24]

Both groups of Methodist Episcopal women participated to some degree in the campaign for women's suffrage that swept the South during the same decades that these churchwomen were working to advance their shared agenda for progressive reform. In some ways, the fight for women's suffrage in the southern states mirrored the campaign for voting and laity rights within the churches, but in this secular endeavor, black and white remained as separate as the fingers on the hand—they neither joined forces nor influenced each other's agendas. Unlike the interracial networks established by M.E. and C.M.E. women, which were the result of over forty years of cooperation, black and white women campaigning for suffrage had no history of shared traditions, no common administrative structure, and perhaps most importantly, no shared language to help them bridge the racial divide on this important issue. To Mattie Coleman's consternation, in the case of women's suffrage, black and white women each remained independent of the other in their struggle for full citizenship.

Southern Women and the Spectacle of Suffrage

Many southern African American women carried their fervor for equality and voting rights within the church into the fight for women's suffrage. Southern white women, on the other hand, were more sharply divided on the issue. In fact, the struggle for and against women's suffrage was the most contested issue in southern women's associational life. Historians Marjorie Spruill Wheeler and Elna Green have gone a long way toward reconstructing the narratives, defining the arguments, and exposing the strange bedfellows that defined white suffrage politics in the South.[25] As they have shown, the issue of women's suffrage detonated deep-seated feelings on all sides, especially in southern states that after Reconstruction had been reshaped first by the enfranchisement of black men and then again by their disenfranchisement. Proponents and opponents of women's suffrage—women and men, black and white—engaged in expressive public rituals and dramatic spectacles. Women's associations worked passionately on both sides of this issue. Emotions ran high as the tension between pro- and anti-suffrage advocates resonated across the entire South, from New Orleans to Washington, D.C. The spectacle of women's suffrage in the South turned on race and class. In sharp contrast to the mutual dependence of black and white churchwomen in the Methodist Episcopal Church, in the suffrage movement, there was no process of transformation that could shape an agenda that met the needs of women on both sides of the racial divide.

The struggle over women's suffrage in the South became publically visible when in 1895 the National American Woman Suffrage Association (NAWSA) chose Atlanta as the site of their first annual meeting to be held outside of Washington, D.C. NAWSA, acknowledging the South's importance in the fight for women's suffrage, set up headquarters at the newly opened Aragon Hotel on Peachtree Street and convened their meeting in the elaborate main hall at DeGive's Opera House. One hundred white delegates from twenty-eight states traveled to Atlanta in early February. Local visitors and guests filled the galleries, and dozens of reporters gathered, drawn into the spectacular convergence of white southern women and the politics of gender and race. Reports from the *Atlanta Constitution* followed the convention hour by hour, and one reporter, having "studied" the suffragists over the course of the week, noted with obvious sexism and condescension, "there are some gifted man-handlers in the body, and the way they take up a poor writhing male being, tear him to pieces, expose his impudent usurpation and twirl him about, stripped bare of every moral vestment is a caution."[26] When Rev. Anna H. Shaw preached the "Annual Sermon" on Sunday afternoon, the paper reported that an audience of two thousand crowded into the theatre and "there was not an empty chair in the house, every aisle was crowded and people anxious to hear the sermon . . . had invaded the stage."[27]

During NAWSA's convention in Atlanta, the issue of suffrage for black women played out in ways that foreshadowed the direction that the national suffrage movement would take over the next two decades. Susan B. Anthony herself, not wanting to alarm white southerners, had suggested that Frederick Douglass, an ally of woman suffrage, stay away from the Atlanta convention.[28] Other African-American men and women were overtly excluded from the meetings, except for a few, like Alabama minister Rev. R. M. Cheeks, and Adella Hunt Logan of Tuskegee, Alabama, who could pass as white and did. Anthony blamed the decision to exclude black participants on southern white women, who, she argued, would not accept a racially integrated convention. She nevertheless acted out her own deep ambivalence about racial justice by stealing over to Atlanta University's all-black campus during a break in the NAWSA proceedings. There she addressed an audience of ardent pro-suffrage African American women who believed that universal woman suffrage offered one of the best hopes for the re-enfranchisement of black men as well as suffrage for themselves.[29]

Other national leaders on both sides of what was euphemistically referred to as "the southern question" expressed their sentiments at the NAWSA convention in Atlanta. Henry B. Blackwell, the husband of Lucy Stone and an "ardent suffragist," openly endorsed extending the franchise only to those with an adequate education. In an interview with the *Atlanta Constitution* during the convention, Blackwell reportedly said, "the only solution to 'the southern question' is to enfranchise the educated women and disenfranchise the negroes who are uneducated—which would mean nearly all—and the illiterate whites."[30] The following day, Clara B. Colby, a white suffrage activist and journalist from Washington, D.C., and Rev. R. M. Cheeks, an African American pastor of the St. John's A.M.E. Church in Montgomery, Alabama, both of whom were attending sessions at the NAWSA convention, were guest speakers at Sunday services at the Big Bethel African Methodist Episcopal Church. There they addressed one thousand black congregants, assuring them that despite their exclusion from the convention, "the colored people had many friends" in the NAWSA.[31] The exclusion of black women from the NAWSA convention in Atlanta left no middle ground on which black and white pro-suffrage women could meet, exchange ideas, or strategize. In 1895, the only mutual tradition these women shared was that of segregation.

This tradition of exclusion was continued by the white organizers of the Atlanta Cotton States Exposition, which opened on September 18, 1895, and ran through the end of the year. African American women were not invited to place exhibits in the Woman's Building at the Exposition. Moreover, once the Exposition opened, they were denied access to that "lily-white" edifice.[32] Black women reacted to this exclusion with bold attacks on both white racism and the accommodationist rhetoric of Booker T. Washington, who had delivered his famous Atlanta Compromise Speech on the opening day of the Exposition. Washington made no reference to suffrage rights or disenfranchisement, but, speaking for the "Negro race," addressed the "Gentlemen of the Exposition," saying, "as we present to you our humble effort at an exhibition of our progress, you must not expect overmuch."[33]

The expectations of African American women for the Exposition, however, were anything but humble. They channeled enormous energy and hard work into organizing displays and exhibits from their local communities and institutions for the Negro Building and organized a Congress of Women to be held on December 27, just before the close of the

Exposition. African American women from eighteen states came together at Atlanta's Big Bethel African Methodist Episcopal Church, sitting in the same sanctuary where eleven months earlier Colby and Cheeks had addressed the black suffrage supporters excluded from the NAWSA convention. Members of the Big Bethel congregation had encouraged African Americans to boycott the segregated Atlanta Exposition, which they saw as a public space in which blacks were made "to feel inferior to other American citizens."[34] With the church members' support, the Congress of Women addressed the most contentious issues of the day. They passed a resolution calling for the separation of the sexes in railroad cars; they spoke out against the rape of black women by white men; they argued for the repeal of anti-miscegenation laws that denied legal marriages across racial lines; and they expressed their outrage at lynchings of black men, which were often based on no more than the rumor of an interaction with a white woman. Challenging African American women to take action in their local communities, they called for better schools and teachers for black children. They demanded legislation that would require landlords to improve their rental properties. They spoke out against racially segregated railroad cars and condemned the convict-lease system. They demanded that the press use "Mrs." or "Miss" when referring to black women and capitalize the word "Negro."

The resolutions, recommendations, and demands articulated by the Congress of Women that cold December day at the end of 1895 helped shape a national platform the following year, when African American women organized the National Association of Colored Women (NACW) in Washington, D.C. Atlanta had been, as one historian put it, the site of "a flourishing urban resistance campaign" for a number of years before the 1895 Exposition, and the energy that emanated from the black community there spread across the South as black citizens organized strikes, protested lynchings, and demanded better social services, including schools and police protection.[35] African American women across the region, from those active in C.M.E. churches in rural areas to suffrage activists like Lugenia Burns Hope of Atlanta and Adella Hunt Logan of Tuskegee to those who participated in the Congress of Women, saw the Exhibition as an important turning point, after which they began to look beyond the South for support on issues like women's suffrage.[36]

Following the events of 1895, Atlanta continued to be a site of contestation regarding the vote for both women and African Americans. The

Georgia Women's Suffrage Association (GWSA) held its first convention in the city in 1899, passing a resolution that if women could not vote, they should not have to pay taxes. Atlanta women activists sought to vote in municipal elections in 1902, but their petition was rejected. Endorsements for woman suffrage came from diverse quarters: the Prohibition Party of Georgia included a women's suffrage plank in its platform; the Georgia Federation of Labor endorsed women's suffrage in 1900 and encouraged local unions to sign on; even some members of the Ku Klux Klan supported women's suffrage.[37] Each of these groups saw increasing the number of white women voters as a political opportunity and an effective way to realize their own special interests, whether that involved controlling alcohol consumption, organizing labor, or maintaining white supremacy.

In 1908, two years after a rampage by mobs of white men had killed at least twenty-five black Atlantans and wounded many more, a majority of the white city fathers voted to disenfranchise black male voters.[38] The same impulse that disenfranchised black men in the aftermath of the Atlanta riot also fueled efforts to achieve woman suffrage in the state of Georgia. As they sought suffrage for themselves, white women closed ranks to the large cohort of "New Black Women" whose commitment to public service was evident throughout Atlanta's African American neighborhoods and in uplift programs focused on black mothers and their children. White woman suffrage activists continued to take their cue from Booker T. Washington's Atlanta Compromise Speech of 1895, in which he argued that the races should "be as separate as the fingers," although they ignored his rejoinder to also be "yet one as the hand in all things essential to mutual progress." The *Atlanta Constitution* established a woman suffrage department in 1913, and white women in Atlanta spearheaded support for a suffrage amendment in both the state and the region by founding the Georgia Woman Equal Suffrage League, the Georgia Men's League for Woman Suffrage, and eventually the Equal Suffrage Party of Georgia.[39]

Pro-suffrage women organized a large rally in Atlanta in March 1914, with Jane Addams as their speaker. The *Atlanta Constitution* reported that Addams and her "co-warriorettes for suffrage" came "loaded to the muzzle" to do battle, but "found none to fight." Atlantans filled the theatre beyond capacity, and after the speeches, "questions popped up all over the house like clay pigeons at a shooting tournament." The visiting suffragists "shot them down with guns of logic and statistics ere the voice that asked the question had ceased to echo."[40] On May Day the following year, Atlanta's pro-suffrage supporters staged a protest on the steps of the state capital, and in November they planned a major march through the streets of Atlanta to end the city's Harvest Festival celebration. The elaborate plans for the first suffrage parade ever to be held in Georgia called for multiple committees to handle such details as business issues, floats, tissue paper decorations, and automobiles. Little Victory, the "little yellow auto" sold by Anna Howard Shaw to pay "unjust" taxes in New York and donated to the pro-suffrage forces in Georgia, led the way for a brass band, students dressed in caps and gowns, and fifty decorated automobiles. In what the *Atlanta Constitution* called "a prophetic spectacle," a large sign reading "Georgia Catching Up" was attached to a pony cart filled with yellow chrysanthemums.[41]

During weeks of planning, Eleanore Raoul, the organizer of the Fulton and DeKalb Equal Suffrage Party, chairwoman of the parade committee, and driver of Little Victory, worked closely with the Atlanta police to secure special protection for suffragists during the parade. Raoul took every precaution, writing to Chief W. W. Mayo and receiving his assurances in writing that the necessary police protection would be furnished. The Harvest Festival commenced with a municipal parade that included a King and Queen, groups of pilgrims, members of the United Daughters of the Confederacy (U.D.C), the fire and police departments, and sanitary workers. The woman's suffrage procession was set to follow when the clock struck noon. But just as the first group of women moved out onto Peachtree Street to begin their march downtown, the police stopped holding back the traffic and "the suffragettes collided with street cars, automobiles, trucks, cabs, wagons, and other vehicles that had been turned into the street after being held in the side streets for an hour and a half."[42] Outraged by this deception and trickery, Miss Raoul severely criticized the police and demanded that the city authorities investigate the matter. "The girls and women on foot were in danger," she told the *Atlanta Constitution*; "this difficulty was inexcusable. It marred our process completely." Raoul immediately contacted NAWSA headquarters in New York City and assured local organizers that "further protest will be made against the failure of the police to give the marchers protection."[43]

The spectacle of suffrage that played out in Atlanta over the twenty-five years after the NAWSA convention exposed every gendered, classist, and racial dimension of southern women's clubs. Allegiances shifted over time. White women united across class lines on this issue, as groups as diverse as teachers and businesswomen in the Georgia Woman Equal Suffrage League and factory workers in the YWCA Industrial clubs came together to support woman suffrage. Ties between local women's groups and national suffrage organizations also remained strong throughout this period. African American women drew strength from the NACW and depended on their connections in Washington, D.C., and New York City to assist them in their fight for suffrage in states like Georgia and Alabama. White suffragists like Susan B. Anthony and Henry B. Blackwell depended on southern white women to support their argument that, as Blackwell put it during a visit to Atlanta in 1895, "in every state save one, there are more educated women than all the illiterate voters, white and black, native and foreign."[44]

The exclusion of most African American women and men from the 1895 NAWSA convention, the racial segregation of the Atlanta Exposition, and the barring of black women from the Woman's Building rendered moot the possibility of collaboration on an issue crucial to enacting the New South society envisioned by those black and white women committed to mitigating the human costs of industrialization and degradation of racial segregation. White women who desired "to gain the vote by an appeal to reason and fair play" lost sight of all that was at stake for African American women working toward the same goal. The aggressive exclusion of black women by white activists inspired a new boldness in the language and actions of those African American women who spoke out unequivocally for racial equality and justice. This boldness only increased in the years after World War I, when black activists increasingly sought opportunities to collaborate with white women.[45]

Historian Glenda Gilmore tells the story of Charlotte Hawkins Brown, an educator and activist who worked for over a decade to develop connections with white women before she was invited to speak at the white North Carolina Federation of Women's Clubs convention early in 1920. In her speech, Brown laid out three goals that echoed some of the same demands the Congress of Women had made in Atlanta twenty-five years earlier. She called for an end to lynching and racial violence. She advocated collaboration between black and white women to build a home for delinquent black girls. And she underscored the right of black women "to share equally the franchise which would soon be granted to the womanhood of the state."[46] By assertively calling for woman's suffrage across racial lines, Brown's speech broke new ground. She knew that winning the fight for suffrage in North Carolina would require nothing less than a political alliance between black and white women, and in what Gilmore has characterized as a "preemptive strike," Brown issued the call to women on both sides of the racial divide.[47]

Shortly after Brown spoke to the white federation, she traveled to Tuskegee, Alabama, for the biennial meeting of the National Association of Colored Women. There the importance of forging interracial alliances continued to be stressed. Lugenia Hope of Atlanta had drawn on her connections with white women in the Methodist Episcopal Church and invited Carrie Parks Johnson and Sara Estelle Haskin, the woman who had "helped" Mother Sawyer seven years earlier, to come to Tuskegee and work with the women there to establish secular women's organizations to improve race relations. In the meeting, Hope spoke directly to Johnson and Haskin and challenged them to "help us find a place in American life where we can be unashamed and unafraid."[48] Deeply moved, the two white Methodists invited the black women to send delegates to the white Women's Missionary Convention meeting that fall in Memphis. Carrie Johnson specifically invited Charlotte Hawkins Brown to address the Convention, and Brown accepted.[49]

A few months later, Charlotte Hawkins Brown, while traveling to the Memphis meeting where she was to give her address, was forced from the Pullman car by several white men who marched her back to a seat in the Jim Crow car. Filled with fear, humiliation, and anger, Brown passed a number of southern white women also traveling to the Memphis meeting, who sat in silence as Brown was forced to leave the car. As Gilmore points out, one of those women was Gabrielle De Rosset Waddell, the wife of Alfred Waddell, the man who had led the Wilmington Massacre in 1898. Two days after the incident on the train, Brown made her speech before the assembled white Methodist women. She told the story of being thrown out of the Pullman car, and then she urged the white women to "recognize the dignity of the African American woman" and join in the ongoing fight to stop the lynching of black men. Brown's speech concluded with a warning: "You are going to reach out for the same hand that I am reaching out for but I know that the dear Lord will not receive it if you are crushing me beneath your feet."[50] In the year that followed the Memphis meeting, Women's Committees of the Commission on Interracial Cooperation were established in many southern states. But even with this goal accomplished, white and black women remained miles apart on two key issues: the protection of African American voting rights and the condemnation of lynching. On both questions, the white women drew back, refusing the outreached hands of the black women who did not hesitate to raise their voices in opposition to lynching and to speak out in support of universal suffrage.

Southern Women Workers Speak Out

As the fight for woman suffrage concluded with the passage of the Nineteenth Amendment in August 1920, coalitions of middle- and working-class women hailing from both sides of the Mason-Dixon Line began to focus more intently on the treacherous arena of industrial reform that Methodist Episcopal women had avoided in their platform for southern progress since they began their work in 1886.[51] Two organizations had an enormous impact in this area, the industrial clubs of the Young Women's Christian Association and the Southern Summer School. Each focused initially on organizing white women workers, particularly in the rapidly expanding textile and garment industries, and gradually expanded their outreach across racial lines throughout the South. As groups headquartered outside of the region, these organizations offered southern women new ways of dealing with the persistent problems of low wages, opposition to collective bargaining, and the exclusion of women from many trade unions.

The Young Women's Christian Association (YWCA) began as a voluntary organization committed to serving the needs not only of young women, but also of the elderly, soldiers, prisoners, orphans, and hospital patients. The YWCA's work with women industrial workers began in Michigan in 1904 and rapidly expanded several years later, when six hundred local associations with a collective membership of almost two hundred thousand joined together under one national board. In 1907, the YWCA Industrial Department was established in New York City, and the philosophy of the organization's work with industrial women changed dramatically. As Florence Simms, the director of the YWCA Industrial Department, wrote, "We began to change from the type of work in which we were doing *for* girls, thinking *for* them[,] to that in which we began to feel the solidarity of the whole human family." As a result, Simms began to fight for self-governing YWCA industrial clubs in factories, laundries, stores, and mills.[52] As these industrial groups secured the freedom to prepare their own constitutions and design their own programs, greater numbers of working-class women began to address such issues as wages, health standards, working conditions, and protective legislation.

In 1915, there were 375 industrial clubs; by 1918, that number had risen to over 800. Increased participation by working-class women brought about a crucial shift within the YWCA from the idea of community service to an emphasis on changing the industrial system. At the YWCA's national convention in Cleveland in 1920, delegates representing thirty thousand women workers pressed for the adoption of a new set of industrial standards that included collective bargaining and equal pay for equal work. Fireworks ensued as a sharply divided group of two thousand women delegates debated the collective bargaining plank. Despite serious opposition from upper- and middle-class board members, the delegates from the Industrial Department stood their ground, eventually threatening to withdraw the industrial membership from the association. Their threat worked; National Board members yielded to the industrial membership and adopted the new set of standards. The Cleveland resolutions, along with a commitment to programs for industrial women that provided leadership training and the skills needed to push for industrial reforms, formed the core of the Industrial Department's program in the 1920s.[53]

But increasingly, the YWCA Industrial Department could not ignore the South, which in the words of National Women's Trade Union League organizer Elisabeth Christman, "looms up as a giant" in terms of industrial production in the textile and garment industries.[54] Shortly after the Cleveland convention, Florence Simms appointed Louise Leonard, an energetic white YWCA secretary whose work with women textile workers in the coal-mining region around Wilkes-Barre, Pennsylvania, had been noticed by the National Board staff, to head south to organize YWCA industrial departments throughout the region's burgeoning industrial cities and mill communities. As YWCA national industrial secretary for the South, from 1920 to 1926 Leonard traveled throughout the region supervising the work of YWCA secretaries in dozens of local associations.

At the time Leonard began her work in the South, the governing boards of the region's YWCAs were made up of middle- and upper-class women, the wives of industrialists and managers, who were financially secure and had enough free time to serve as volunteers. YWCA staff members and industrial women dubbed them "the ladies with the hats." As Leonard traveled from city to city to meet with YWCA board members and sell them on the idea of industrial work, she frequently complained that many were overcommitted women who took "too many trips abroad." Leonard reported that in Norfolk, Virginia, a community she described in 1923 as "overridden" with women's organizations whose efforts to provide social services were noticeably lacking, the head of the YWCA's board also served on nine other boards in the city.[55] In an effort to circumvent these city boards, Leonard established industrial committees made up of middle-class women without corporate ties, often a town's lone female lawyer, physician, or professor or the spouses of professors, ministers, or journalists. Over the years that Leonard worked in the South for the YWCA, she identified a network of progressive individuals in each community whom she characterized as "strong women." The allies Leonard depended on to fight for industrial programs on the local level included women like Mary C. Barker, an Atlanta school principal and active leader in the American Federation of Teachers; Mary O. Cowper, a Kansas native and suffrage activist who lived in Durham and served as a state officer in the League of Women Voters; and Alice Baldwin, the dean of women at Duke University. Because of their community status, these women often could obtain financial support for the YWCA from wealthier and more conservative local citizens; because of their personal belief in the need for industrial reform, they praised, sometimes *sotto voce*, the national YWCA's commitment to collective bargaining and trade unionism.[56]

By 1925, over fifteen southern cities had separate YWCA Industrial Departments. Southern working-class women responded so enthusiastically to the industrial program that in many communities membership in the industrial department exceeded that of the Business and Professional Women program, which served white-collar workers, and the Girl Reserves program.[57] In some communities, concern mounted among upper- and middle-class board members that the YWCA was becoming "dominated by workers." That may have been the case in terms of membership numbers, but spatial divisions within YWCAs across the region reflected the organization's strict segregation of women by race and class. African American women and girls had separate meeting facilities in towns across the South and could not access the elegant brick buildings with swimming pools, gyms, and dining rooms that the white women enjoyed. Within these structures, white industrial workers were often assigned meeting space in the basement, while white "ladies with the hats" lunched on the main floor. Such spatial segregation within the YWCA reflected and reinforced the rigidly defined class and racial parameters of the southern social order.[58]

Despite the class hierarchy within the organization during the 1920s, white women workers increasingly used YWCA facilities for weekly club suppers, parties with male friends, and study groups. In most southern towns, including Durham, Greensboro, Charlotte, Atlanta, Macon, and Birmingham, the YWCA ran a residence hall for working women. So while prominent community women controlled the YWCA's governing boards and met for lunch in the YWCA dining room, women workers spent more time in the buildings, booking rooms for meetings and reserving halls for speakers and dances and, in many cases, living on the premises. In autonomous YWCA industrial departments, women workers established priorities regarding social legislation and discussed their ideas about fair wages and hours. Gradually, the working-class arm of the YWCA grew stronger, in the South and nationally. By 1925, southern industrial departments had become some of the most vocal independent groups within the YWCA and also most likely to cooperate with African American branches of the organization. Cross-racial collaborations were most evident in the cities of Baltimore, Richmond, and Atlanta. In Baltimore, for example, ties between black and white women forged in the YWCA and the Colored Young Women's Christian Association (CYWCA) were sustained in other racially segregated but interracially cooperative organizations, including the white Women's Civic League and the African American Cooperative Women's Civic League.[59]

As industrial women assumed increasing responsibility within local YWCAs, their interests, not surprisingly, conflicted with those of the middle- and upper-class women who controlled the purse strings of the organization. The most dramatic clashes occurred over the issue of collective bargaining. When union organizing efforts were underway in a specific community, or when local workers went out on strike, Industrial Department members sought to offer assistance through *their* organization, the YWCA. Board members, despite the rhetoric about self-governing industrial clubs, usually sided with local manufacturers, defeating the Industrial Department's proposals that YWCA members provide strike relief, find housing for evicted strikers, or even walk a picket line. Thus, despite the National Industrial Department's support for labor and the Cleveland vote for collective bargaining, the grass-roots class struggle continued in YWCA industrial departments across the South.[60]

After serving for six years as national industrial secretary, Leonard saw the Industrial Department as both the most vital and the most vulnerable division within the YWCA. She recognized the YWCA's susceptibility to industrialists who could control available funding and consequently influence the scope of YWCA programs. In 1926, several local associations had refused to pay salaries large enough to attract a qualified industrial secretary, and other southern YWCAs threatened to disband their industrial departments altogether. Support from the National YWCA, particularly on the issue of collective bargaining, had waned. When southern associations divided on the issue that year, the national organization stayed out of the fray, letting local opinion prevail; the tide turned, and national-level support for the unionization of industrial workers weakened further. Without a counterforce to balance the local boards, the YWCA began to drop out of the picture as a force for progressive industrial reform. Leonard, reading the writing on the wall, decided to work with southern women outside of the YWCA Industrial Department to start a new organization, a school for southern women workers.

The Southern Summer School for Women Workers in Industry opened its doors in 1927 as a residential school for women industrial workers in the southern region. Modeled on the Bryn Mawr Summer School in Pennsylvania, the Southern Summer School placed a premium on creating an environment that would support and nurture southern industrial women intellectually, emotionally, and physically. The school's faculty envisioned a place where women workers—long used to being told what to do at home, in school, and in the workplace—could find their own voices and learn to speak their own minds. Many students invited to attend the school had already demonstrated their potential as grass-roots leaders by having found jobs, interacting with their bosses, joining industrial clubs or unions, and speaking out. Underscoring the entire Southern Summer School program was its founders' belief that real education involved convincing students that they could think for themselves, analyze complex information, and solve their own problems. The school was designed as an open place, a free space, where for six weeks every summer two to three dozen students and a cohort of educators, most of them women with newly minted Ph.D.'s, could meet together in a camp-like setting in the southern mountains. Classes in economics, labor history, and public speaking met each morning; hiking and swimming filled the afternoons; union organizers, political activists, leaders from women's organizations, and a vast array of other northern and southern guests spoke to the students in the evening. Throughout the summer, students experienced a milieu of cooperation and autonomy rather than authority and hierarchy.[61]

As the economy contracted in the early 1930s, most white Methodist women grew increasingly fearful of workers' autonomy as expressed in the nascent industrial unions and in groups like the Southern Summer School and the Workers' Alliance. In 1931, they declared that industrial issues posed "not only a live question but a dangerous one at present." By 1935, little remained of the substantial industrial reform program that southern churchwomen had developed in the 1910s and 1920s. White church-based activists had played an important role in bringing industrial concerns to the attention of secular reform organizations throughout the South, but after years of championing the needs of industrial workers, they only reluctantly endorsed the New Deal and grew increasingly wary of programs designed to address collective bargaining.

On the other hand, the Southern Summer School strongly backed trade unions throughout the region and provided strong support for workers' strikes and walkouts in communities from Virginia to New Orleans. By the early 1930s, the school had developed a close working relationship with Pioneer Youth of America, a Left-oriented independent children's organization that had a camp in North Carolina. The school also cooperated with labor activists across the left wing of the political spectrum even as it worked to maintain a neutral political stance based on the principles of academic freedom and free speech. Women students who attended the Southern Summer School frequently became active in the labor movement as organizers and leaders in local unions. Many became mainstays of the school's network of alumnae involved in a range of community organizations in towns and cities throughout the South.[62]

Among the southern industrial women who attended the school, political ideology usually took a back seat to local concerns and ideas of the common good shaped by experience. As Thelma Brown, "a silk mill girl," revealed aspects of her life and work to the other students and faculty, for instance, she also spoke openly about her husband's membership in the Ku Klux Klan. Another student talked about how the Klan protected women from domestic violence by threatening husbands who beat their wives. On the other side of the political spectrum, Bertha Hendricks, who attended the school in the 1930s, had been active in the Gastonia textile strike of 1929, and she and her husband had joined the Communist National Textile Workers Union (NTWU) in response to pressing issues of wages, jobs, safety, and respect. Interracial organizing in Gastonia had appealed to women like Bertha Hendricks and her co-worker Ella May Wiggins, who helped bring black workers from nearby Stumptown, a small community outside Gastonia, into the union. During the 1930s, the school began to organize interracial workers' education programs in Atlanta and Washington, D.C., to support workers in their efforts to moderate the harsh conditions of New South industrial life.[63]

"This is my show and I am the boss"

Increasingly, from the 1920s into the 1940s, white working-class and African American women shaped their identities as women and citizens through club membership. They contested the leadership of middle-class women and shaped clubs in ways that served their own needs and reflected their own cultural beliefs and values. Across class and racial lines, previously marginalized southern women found their own collective voices: "Shall we know our own minds?" wrote Sudie Grady, a student at the Southern Summer School in 1933, adding, "Shall we cooperate and be as one large family, or shall we continue living as far apart as if we were in separate worlds?"[64] In the 1920s and 1930s, hundreds of women in local communities across the South began to speak out and express their ideas about work, economic change, and social justice. We can recover their words in letters they exchanged with each other, with government officials, and with other individuals and groups with whom they shared concerns. A new boldness, much like that shown by African American women beginning in 1895, emerged during the 1920s, as women workers interacted in greater numbers with those holding positions of authority. Increasingly, women workers at the local level set their own agendas for change. They made demands in their churches and unions; they stood up to their employers; they spoke their minds as individuals, as women, as workers, and as citizens.

Examples of this new boldness abound. Ruth Culberson attended the Southern Summer School in 1931. Returning to her job in a Durham, North Carolina, tobacco factory, she worked with the YWCA Industrial

Club, the Workers' Alliance, and then in 1934 with Howard Bridgman on the New Deal FERA project in North Carolina. Culberson tried to start a workers' center in Durham during 1935, and by 1936 she had become the force behind the decade-old workers' education committee in Durham. She worked closely with Alice Baldwin, dean of women at Duke University, and grew skilled at simultaneously keeping former Summer School students involved and engaging middle-class supporters. When she approached a "Mrs. Hicks," a former YWCA supporter who told Culberson she had left the "field of social work entirely" and was no longer interested in workers' education, Culberson pressed the issue. "I 'out-talked' her!" Culberson wrote Louise McLaren, director of the school, in late 1936. "She is going to meet with us and help all she can—*ha ha*."[65]

Hosiery worker Beulah Carter went from her job at the Marvin Carr Silk Mill in Durham to the Southern Summer School in the North Carolina mountains. Later she attended the Bryn Mawr Summer School in Bryn Mawr, Pennsylvania, and after that she studied at Brookwood Labor College in Katonah, New York. In 1933, Carter returned to Durham, where she worked as an organizer for the Hosiery Workers' Union. She extracted a promise from a "group of middle class people" that they would make arrangements to bring the League for Industrial Democracy (LID) lecture series to the city. In a letter to A. J. Muste, the head of Brookwood Labor College, Carter described what happened when "as usual, they got cold footed and voted not to bring them here": "I got so mad I just had to get something off my chest. So I told them what I thought of the middle class, and how little they were contributing toward educating the public." Carter's outburst took everyone at the meeting by surprise, but, she wrote, "of course they hung their heads and were too polite to talk back."[66]

When her middle-class allies backed out at the last minute, Carter wrote to the LID and reported what had happened. When they replied that they were willing to come to Durham on the basis of her cooperation alone, Carter signed a contract to pay $400 ($6,000 in 2009 dollars) to the LID and issued a press release, presenting herself as a "committee of Durham citizens." When the newspaper wanted the name of the chairman, Carter felt she "was in a terrible mess." Thinking fast, she remembered an old Durham man, a retired mail carrier, well respected and with a college degree, who for years had voted the Socialist ticket. She told him that Norman Thomas would be one of the speakers, and that if he would agree to let her call him chairman, his picture would be in the newspaper. He agreed. She then went back to the middle-class group that had earlier contacted thirty-five people to guarantee the $400. Carter told them she had signed the contract and was depending on those guarantors to pay the amount they had promised. "This embarrassed the professors," Carter wrote later, "because they told these people that they would hardly have to put up any money—only if there was a deficit." Rather than embarrass themselves by imposing on their friends, the group decided to sell tickets. "I am sure we will raise the entire $400.00," Carter wrote confidently. To encourage hosiery workers to attend the lecture series, Carter decided to give them a "season ticket" for free. She also decided to admit all unemployed workers without charge. She told A. J. Muste that "some of the middle-class are raising their voices because I am letting the unemployed in free, but there is nothing they can do about it, because this is my show and I am the boss."[67]

"Out of the ordinary sphere"

The South underwent dramatic change as, over time, women across the lines of race and class began speaking out on economic and social issues. Important paradigm shifts took place: from the ritualized "helping/learning" performance of black and white Methodist women as they inched toward interracial cooperation to the increasingly inclusive policies in the YWCAs as black and working-class women gradually assumed leadership roles and gained power within the organization to the assertive discourse of women who, like Beulah Carter, trained at the Southern Summer School and returned to their local communities ready to speak their minds. On the other hand, in the same period, despite the work of diverse groups of women to shape, each in its own way, a new society in the South, racial segregation became increasingly entrenched in southern culture and economic life. Despite great difficulty and awkwardness, M.E. and C.M.E. women prioritized interracial work as an essential part of their New South agenda; in contrast, black and white women in the southern suffrage movement never attained the same level of interaction across racial barriers. In the spectacle that was suffrage in Atlanta, they did not even come close. Race remained a primary factor in the long and drawn-out debate over women's suffrage, and women themselves divided rather than united across racial barriers as they struggled separately to obtain full citizenship as women. Throughout the 1920s and 1930s, women's organizations for southern working women remained segregated. The YWCA Industrial Department and the Southern Summer School held a few carefully orchestrated mixed-race programs in the 1930s, but the organizations themselves did not become racially integrated in any meaningful way until the 1940s. Through these organizations, white women workers were encouraged to speak out in ways denied to the majority of black women until the civil rights movement of the 1960s.

In the multiplicity of women's groups of different shapes, sizes, and affiliations that flourished in the 1920s and 1930s, benefits accrued to all who belonged: female companionship, intellectual stimulation, opportunities for leadership, and a sense of being part of something larger than oneself. But the emotional culture of women's clubs varied dramatically from group to group.[68] In some southern cross-class clubs, working women sacrificed equality in order to sustain their membership. In others, working-class women fought to wrest the leadership from dominant middle-class members. Racial issues, overt or concealed, permeated every southern women's group, from church-based organizations to the YWCA to trade unions to political, cultural, and civic associations. Nevertheless, these organizations transformed the lives of those women who took an active role. As southern women entered the industrial workforce in greater numbers during the 1920s and 1930s, they gained a new collective identity based on common needs and shared aspirations.[69] Bound together by work and region as well as by family and community, they began to participate in a remarkably broad range of organizations: community associations, trade unions, church-based women's groups, women's auxiliaries, and workers' alliances. Southern women's organizations and societies flourished in these years across an astoundingly wide political spectrum, from women's groups within the Socialist and Communist parties, at one end, to women's auxiliaries of the Ku Klux Klan and the Knights of the White Camellia, at the other. The more intense the commitment of the group's membership, whatever the cause, the more active the organization tended to be. This held true at both ends of the political spectrum.[70]

Historian Anne F. Scott has argued that clubwomen in the late nineteenth and early twentieth centuries worked hard to present themselves as "models of harmony," no matter how much they argued internally.[71]

M.E. and C.M.E. women fit this model as they sustained the pretense of white women helping and black women learning, when in fact the reverse was more often the case. Among southern women who campaigned for suffrage, no one, white or black, could pretend that pro-suffrage forces were united across racial lines. YWCA industrial clubs presented themselves as internally harmonious, but class and racial tensions affected the organization as a whole, and contestation regularly carried the day. This was a time when women from multiple walks of southern life, some with shared traditions, others living in completely different worlds, asked questions, sought answers, and, as M.E. activist Bertha Newell put it, thought and acted together to reach ends that were "out of the ordinary sphere of their thought and action."[72] This activism happened in a range of different ways. Black church leaders like C.M.E. activist Mother Sawyer worked to bring about change by recognizing the mutual dependence of black and white women and trusting the process of transformation. As one of the many women wanting full citizenship and the right to vote, Adele Logan risked passing for white to attend the NAWSA meeting in Atlanta. Eleanor Raoul, a woman of social and racial privilege, stepped forward to organize a suffrage spectacle in downtown Atlanta only to be tricked by the city's policemen. Labor movement activist Beulah Carter learned to speak her mind and confronted and challenged middle-class allies who openly opposed her, as well as those who passively withdrew their support.

Southern women's organizational work had a huge impact on women workers for whom membership was often a matter of economic survival as well as an experience in community building and leadership. Generations of southern women, from Beulah Carter to Crystal Lee Sutton, whose story is told in the Hollywood film *Norma Rae*, got "mad as hell," as Sutton put it, about the low wages, poor working conditions, anti-unionism, and management strategies used to divide the southern workforce by race and gender. Sutton, who defied the J. P. Stevens Company to help start an interracial union in Roanoke Rapids, North Carolina, spent years doing low-paid shift work in a mill town where, she recalled in a interview in 1980, "All my life, textile workers were looked down on." A courageous woman with deep convictions and a desire to be heard, Sutton was fired for "insubordination" when she attempted to expose Stevens' racist anti-union tactics.[73]

Southern women, from Dr. Mattie Coleman, the C.M.E. church activist, to Crystal Lee Sutton, have a long history of finding first their voices and then the courage to stand and speak. From the late nineteenth century on, unwilling to accept the blueprint of the New South envisioned by manufacturers and business leaders, diverse groups of southern women put their own imprimatur on the New South by carefully deciding "which side they were on" and then working to shape southern society according to their own principles and priorities.

4

. . . .

Beyond Heroines and Girl Strikers

Gender and Organized Labor in the South

By standing up to the timid middle-class activists in Durham, North Carolina, in 1933 and becoming "the boss of her own show," Beulah Carter found herself negotiating new terrain between two powerful gender-based stereotypes that dominated the public discourse about women workers in the twentieth-century South: *heroines*, individual women who played exceptional roles within the labor movement, and what journalists of the time called *girl strikers*, women workers who protested collectively in public spaces across the region, from the streets of downtown Atlanta to the coalfields of West Virginia. These images of heroines and girl strikers resonated profoundly in southern culture and proved useful in attracting southern women into the labor movement. But even though they represent two important aspects of women's labor involvement, these stereotypes have also obscured the efforts of rank-and-file women workers to join and participate in unions on an equal footing with their male counterparts, thereby overshadowing the complex and nuanced roles that women like Beulah Carter played in the southern labor movement. This chapter both examines the important role these stereotypes played in the labor movement and looks beyond them to more adequately acknowledge the full range of southern women's involvement in organized labor. First it looks at the importance to the movement of three of the region's best-known labor heroines, Mother Jones, Ella Mae Wiggins, and Lucy Randolph Mason, and then of the often unnamed women leaders who led hundreds of workers out of factories, walked in the front ranks of strike parades, and filled conspicuous posts on picket lines. Lastly, it discusses important contributions of women to the labor movement in the South that have been largely overshadowed by the focus on those two more visible groups of women.

Heroines of the Southern Labor Movement

Despite the considerable differences between Mary Harris (Mother) Jones, Ella May Wiggins, and Lucy Randolph Mason as individuals and even as activists, examining their careers alongside one another can help us piece together the characteristics that made them effective heroines within the labor movement in the South and gain insight into both the power and the limitations inherent in that role. These women became legendary figures long remembered in story, song, and oral history. While living, they represented tens of thousands of southern workers in their fight for social and economic justice. After death, they continued to inspire generations of American workers and labor activists. Larger than life, they combined a motherly persona with an outpouring of love for humanity in general and workers in particular to send a powerful message of courage and militancy. Their stories have been told repeatedly, often as a way to inspire action and commitment in the midst of a labor struggle. As often happens in the telling of legends and myths, the facts of the actual lives these women lived have been modified or changed, exaggerated or deleted. In the process they became exemplary martyrs to the movement and heroes of their own lives.

Mary Harris Jones, the wife of iron molder George Jones, bore four children and raised them until their tragic deaths in a yellow fever epidemic in Memphis, Tennessee, in 1867. Her husband also died in the epidemic, and at the age of thirty she found herself a childless widow who, as historian Elliott Gorn has written, "carried to her grave these days of sorrow."[1] Soon after the epidemic ended, Mary Jones left Memphis for Chicago, where she supported herself as a seamstress and opened a dressmaking shop. Tragedy struck again four years later when on the night of October 8, 1871, flames whipped through the city destroying seventeen thousand buildings, leaving a hundred thousand people homeless and three hundred dead. Jones's shop was consumed in the fire's deadly wake, and she, like thousands of others, ran east to the lake for refuge. Jones's autobiography recounts how she thereafter joined the Knights of Labor, where she was welcomed as a woman, a worker, and the widow of George Jones, who had been a fervent unionist and member of the International

Iron Molders Union.[2] Clearly, at some point after the Chicago Fire, Jones went through a conversion that changed her life. Mary Jones, the widow who had watched four of her children die, effectively faded away. In her place, "Mother" Jones cast her lot with the labor movement, and from that point on she claimed to make her home "wherever there is a fight." Adopting American workers *en masse* as her children, she encouraged workers across the country to call her "Mother." She first entered the southern coalfields as an organizer in 1891, answering a request for help from miners out on strike from the Dietz mine in Norton, Virginia. Over the next three decades, Mother Jones traveled to mining areas in West Virginia so often that she came to consider the state her "stepdaughter of misery." She organized workers in different areas and diverse industries throughout the region. She saw the southern coal fields as "medieval" places where "cruel is the life of the miners with the weight of the world upon their backs . . . and their wives and little children in dire want."[3]

Ella May Wiggins was born in 1900 in the mountains of Cherokee County, North Carolina, near the town of Bryson City. Sent to work in a nearby spinning mill to help support the family, Ella May met and married a fellow mill worker named Johnny Wiggins. Together they left the mountains, migrating to the burgeoning industrial region of Gaston County, North Carolina, and settling in Bessemer City, where Ella May and Johnny took jobs in the American Mill in 1919. Over the next decade, Ella May worked as a spinner, bore seven children, and was deserted by her husband. At the age of twenty-nine, she worked the night shift in order to stay with her children during the day. Money and food were scarce, and two of the children died. When employees at the Loray Mill in Gastonia went out on strike in April 1929, workers at the American Mill staged a spontaneous walkout to show their support and joined the National Textile Workers Union (NTWU). Wiggins emerged as a strong leader of the strike, frequently leading the singing among workers attending mass meetings at Loray, recording the events of the strike in original lyrics that folklorist Margaret Larkin claimed at the time were "better than a hundred speeches." On September 14, 1929, on the way to a NTWU protest rally, the truck in which Ella May was riding was stopped by vigilantes who opened fire, killing Ella May and wounding two other strikers. Buried in an unmarked grave in Bessemer City's public cemetery, Wiggins, the "songstress of the mill workers," was declared a martyr by the NTWU, and her image as a heroine of the southern labor movement has endured ever since.[4]

Lucy Randolph Mason was born in 1882 in Alexandria, Virginia, into a family that traced its lineage to Virginia's early political leaders, including George Mason, author of the Virginia Bill of Rights. Mason's father was an Episcopal minister, her mother "a born social worker" who ran a half-way house for recently released convicts in their Richmond home, where they had moved in 1891. Despite his professional standing, Mr. Mason's church income was so limited that Lucy and her younger sister had to leave high school to work as stenographers to help support the family. Working as a secretary throughout her twenties, Mason also began teaching Sunday school classes to groups of industrial workers, predominantly young women between the ages of fourteen and twenty-five, and grew increasingly concerned about the effects of ten-hour workdays and meager wages on Richmond's women workers. In time, convinced that neither the church nor the efforts of well-meaning individuals could change these workers' conditions, she began to advocate protective legislation and found her strongest allies in the labor movement. Mason began working for the YWCA in 1914, as industrial secretary of the Richmond, Virginia, branch. In 1923, she assumed the post of general secretary in Richmond, a position she held for nine years. In 1932, she moved to Washington, D.C., to become a lobbyist for New Deal labor legislation as the general secretary of the National Consumers League (NCL). The League's failure to get protective legislation passed, especially in the South, made Mason reconsider her focus on protective legislation as a means of changing conditions for workers, and in the spring of 1937 she returned South as the southern director for textiles and clothing based in Atlanta. Mason reported to John L. Lewis, president of the United Mine Workers of America, and Sidney Hillman, the founder and president of the Amalgamated Clothing Workers of America (ACWA) and head of the Textile Workers Organizing Committee (TWOC). Soon it became clear that Mason, a forceful speaker adept at articulating policy and organizing workers, would become the public face of the CIO in the South. Mason joined picket lines and protected workers from vigilante violence. She also spoke directly to employers, ministers, newspaper editors, and members of the southern establishment about workers rights, collective bargaining, and the advantages of union membership.[5]

Despite the different paths by which Jones, Wiggins, and Mason became heroines of the labor movement, they were all described by reporters, workers, and labor leaders alike as "motherly" women. Being seen as mothers afforded them a degree of respect and a justification for their leadership that increased their effectiveness as labor organizers. With no children of their own, over their long careers Jones and Mason assumed roles through which they could channel motherly concern and love to workers and their families.

Mother Jones was seen by one friend as "almost like a biological mother to the miners," a mother who "goes through the shadow of death in order to endow her child with life." She also was the mother who gave birth to "the revolt which simmered within them."[6] This image helped Mother Jones work with great effectiveness in the matriarchal culture of mining communities, as she endorsed the miners' concept of ideal womanhood as "militance combined with motherhood," as Priscilla Long puts it, and argued "that a woman's work in the family gave her rights in the struggle."[7] For her part, Ella May Wiggins had joined the movement as a real mother, seeing in the union struggle a better way to provide for her children. As she put it in a speech delivered shortly before her death, "If we don't stand up for our rights . . . we are fighting ourselves and fighting our children." Framing her union activities as atonement for the tragic loss of two of her own children imbued her leadership with even greater emotional power and moral authority. Wiggins insisted that she "never could do anything for my children, not even to keep 'em alive. That's why I'm for the union, so's I can do better for them." With her murder, she became a labor movement heroine and a cause célèbre among southern liberals in large part because of the sympathy people felt for a mother slain simply for working for a better life for her family. Although Lucy Mason had no biological children, she had, in the words of an admiring journalist, "white hair and a warm, motherly smile," much like Mother Jones. Journalists portrayed her as a woman who, according to one, would "do almost anything to protect her 'boys,'—the union organizers who are leading the struggle to organize the South."[8]

For Jones, Wiggins, and Mason, being seen as a mother usually elicited a positive response from unionists and the general public. But this motherly guise also served all three as a shield against the oppressive dichotomy of being seen as either a good or a bad woman. Mother Jones, for example, had lived on her own ever since the deaths of her husband and children in 1867, and her traveling alone and staying overnight in private homes, hotels, and jails led some to question her personal life. Critics and enemies frequently attacked her moral character; Jones was regularly accused of having been a prostitute, of having run a house of prostitution, and of having been arrested at various times for "drunkenness and disorderly conduct." At one point, these allegations against Jones were read into the *Congressional Record*, and in southern West Virginia they were printed onto broadsides and tossed from a railroad car.[9] Jones's frequent use of rough, bawdy language reinforced her image as a coarse fighter, willing to lash out at coal operators, ministers, the press, and even the miners themselves. Yet she was simultaneously seen as a motherly figure, her impassioned actions the result of "a mother's heart torn by the sufferings of the poor." In the words spoken at her funeral, "Her faults were the excesses of her courage, her love of justice, the love in her mother's heart."[10] The purity of intention implicit in this motherly image undoubtedly reinforced the propensity of editors of both mainstream publications like the *Boston Herald* and as well as labor journals like the *Miner's Magazine* to refer to Mother Jones as "an American Joan of Arc," an "angel of light," and a revolutionary comparable to the French socialist Louise Michel, the "Red Virgin of Montmartre."[11]

Ella May Wiggins, too, had to deal with charges of immorality, especially as her life became more public during the Gastonia strike in 1929. Her husband, John Wiggins, had a reputation as "a ladies' man," and after he deserted his family around 1925, Ella May had started living with Charley Shope, a man she referred to during the strike as her cousin but who was, in fact, the father of her youngest daughter, then thirteen months old, and of the unborn child she was carrying when she was murdered.[12] The union tried to protect Ella May from adverse publicity, no doubt because such exposure would further damage the NUTW's reputation in North Carolina. In the articles following her death, Wiggins's role as mother was constantly emphasized, although probably because of her unmarried status, no mention was made of her being pregnant at the time she was shot. In mainstream newspapers, she was portrayed as a "mother of five, separated from her husband." According to the *Charlotte Observer*, "Mrs. Wiggins . . . had been going under her maiden name, Ella May Mays," under which she had joined the strike, become a union member, gone to New York to raise funds for the strikers, and been shot in an "anti-red demonstration." In this newspaper account, it was Ella May Mays, the independent, single (separated) woman, who had gone astray; Mrs. Wiggins, the mother of five, was never referred to as a union member or a murder victim. In the trial of the vigilantes accused of Wiggins's death, the defense attempted to sully her reputation by presenting evidence that her children had been born out of wedlock. Whether or not this influenced the case, her assassins were exonerated. All fourteen defendants were acquitted.[13]

Even Lucy Randolph Mason, whose life was a model of religious devotion and dedicated social service, was not exempt from whispered questions about her personal life. It was rumored that Mason had come into the CIO because she was in love with John L. Lewis, a story that had no factual basis but served as an explanation for the seemingly irrational decision of someone of her class to affiliate herself with the labor movement and promote the cause of unions and workers. Yet even Mason's partnership and rumored liaison with Lewis could be viewed in a positive light by her supporters: his status as the "father" of the CIO made her, by implication, the "mother" of the union, thereby casting her actions in terms of protecting southern workers, the "children" of this personal and professional alliance.[14]

These heroines were also frequently described as angels, evoking the common metaphor of mothers as the "angels of the house," or as women endowed with magical qualities who transcended normal moral categories. Like fairy godmothers, these women (in the words of Clarence Darrow's 1925 introduction to Mother Jones's autobiography) "always appeared in time of need," bringing "a ray of hope" before leaving for the next place to work their magic.[15] These allusions to seemingly supernatural powers both masked and overlooked the hard-headed determination and political savvy it took to design the successful strategies these women employed. They regularly circumvented the legal system by petitioning judges and shaming sheriffs. They subverted normal political channels, appealing directly to governors, senators, the President and First Lady. They used extraordinary means to communicate labor's message to the public by composing songs, contacting editors, ministers, writers, professors, and even by appealing directly to employers. They amended union protocol, bringing in new members whenever and however possible. When told she could not initiate a group of miners because she did not have a copy of the induction ritual, Mother Jones retorted, "The ritual, hell, I'll make one up!"[16]

Male union leaders often believed that women, especially older women, would be protected by southern chivalrousness and therefore could safely take risks that would bring certain attack upon men. As Mason herself quipped to journalist Lawrence Lader, "After all, who'd hurt a little, white-haired old woman?" But the reality of the southern labor movement was that no organizer was immune from attack. Jones, Wiggins, and Mason each faced real danger. In the traditional heroic sense, they willingly and bravely stood up to enemies larger than themselves. In her autobiography, Mother Jones tells the story of how in 1902 she went into Laurel Creek, West Virginia, after seven organizers had been shot, beaten, and chased from town at gunpoint. When one union man warned, "Mother, you mustn't go up there. They've got gunmen patrolling the roads," she replied, "That means the miners up there are prisoners and need me." Ella May Wiggins was one of just two women traveling with twenty-two unionists to a union meeting on September 14, 1929, when vigilantes blocked the road and fired point-blank into the back of the truck. Her daughter later claimed that her mother "knew she would get killed, but that she was not afraid." In 1941, the Amalgamated Clothing Workers asked Lucy Mason to go into Sparta, Georgia, a town that CIO labor leader Buck Borah de- scribed as "too hot to stay in" and "too dangerous for [CIO organizer] Ed Blair to return to." But being women clearly brought only limited protec- tion at best: Jones several times served time in jail, Wiggins was fatally shot, and Mason knew that as a representative of the CIO she risked fla- grant violations of her civil rights.[17]

Mother Jones, Ella May Wiggins, and "Miss Lucy" were successful in large part because they did not directly challenge gender norms in their interactions with their male colleagues. For example, as Elliott Gorn re- counts in his biography of Mother Jones, when a reporter at the *National Labor Tribune* called Jones a "New Woman" in 1897, he clarified that he did not mean the vain, bloomer-wearing kind who liked to make a "show of herself." Likewise, the *New York World* reported that "Mother Jones embodied a new style of female activism." Gorn contends that Jones put forward a "persona of militant working-class womanhood" that merged the archetypes of warrior and saint. As a woman who gave up everything for "her boys," Mother Jones was a martyr to labor's cause, an angel and a "hell-raiser" who reached out to union men with the power of love and what Gorn calls "charismatic motherhood." Men listened to her, did what she told them, and took courage from her strength. Her effect on women was equally powerful, but her message to miners' wives and sisters was less clear-cut. Mother Jones organized women to participate in strikes and protests, but spoke against women's suffrage. She emphasized the blessedness of home and family and the sacrosanct roles of wife and mother, but eschewed domesticity in the radical life she forged for herself. Mother Jones was known as a male-centered woman—she was drawn to powerful men, spent her time with male labor leaders, organized male workers, and had much less to do with women.[18] One could argue that the same applied to Ella May Wiggins, who was as strong and fearless as any man and a force to reckon with in the community of Gastonia strikers. Wiggins embodied the ideal of militant working-class womanhood. Lucy Randolph Mason also aligned herself with powerful male leaders in the CIO and proved most effective as a spokesperson for labor in the South when she confronted manufacturers, bankers, merchants, newspaper editors, and ministers in local communities across the region. Small and white-haired, older and from an aristocratic family, her credentials as a "lady" gave her access; her bravado belied her real power.[19]

If bravery is not a quality generally associated with women, these women's heroism also partook of a quality that men have traditionally admired in women, especially in their mothers: self-sacrifice. In their work to organize the South, these women gave to the movement without thinking of themselves, and each in her own way became a martyr for the cause. Ella May Wiggins was literally a martyr, giving her life for the union cause. Mother Jones dedicated herself to the labor movement, traveling across the country for over fifty years and frequently coming south to stand by the coal miners. When she died in 1930 at the age of one hundred, at her request she was buried alongside the martyrs of the Virden Massacre of 1898 in the Miner's Cemetery in Mt. Olive, Illinois. To Jones, "those brave boys" epitomized the determination and sacrifice of labor's struggle to which she also aspired. During her years with the CIO, Mason also devoted her life to a movement that took all of her time and energy. When journalist Lawrence Lader asked CIO leaders about Mason's retirement the year she turned sixty-five, they replied, "Retire? She'll never retire. As long as there's a fight going on down here, Miss Lucy will be right in the middle of it."[20] Jones, Wiggins, and Mason all devoted their lives to a cause they believed would change the world.

These labor heroines protected themselves from criticism, scorn, and physical danger by drawing on the evocative power of motherhood. In the process, they forged new roles as militant matriarchs who spoke out for working people, for justice, and for change. Viewed as women with magical powers that enabled them to do the impossible, their hard work, intelligence, and political know-how oftentimes remained invisible or certainly unheralded. They were lauded for subverting normal channels and using extraordinary means to accomplish labor's goals. These women did not challenge the status quo when it came to gender norms. They admired, worked closely with, and supported their male colleagues, as well as the other men in their lives. They saw themselves as womanly and strong, and each of them reached out to other women: to miners' wives, sisters, and daughters, in the case of Mother Jones; to other mothers who "slave for the bosses" while their "children scream and cry," as Ella May Wiggins wrote in her ballad "The Mill Mother's Lament"; and to female workers and activists in woman-centered organizations like the YWCA, the National Women's Trade Union League, the National Consumers League, and the Southern Summer School, in the case of Lucy Randolph Mason. Brave and powerful, these labor heroines left strong and complex legacies to succeeding generations in the southern labor movement.

Girl Strikers in the Southern Labor Movement

In contrast to the maternal heroines of the southern labor movement, girl strikers represented the daughters of the southern workforce—young women whose courageous, feisty, or "disorderly" behavior expressed the intense desire of such women to define their own lives as workers.[21] Strikes initiated by women workers and the role of women strikers in job actions that included both men and women punctuated southern labor history throughout the twentieth century and came to represent the collective defiance of the region's entire workforce.

The attention paid to women strikers during southern strikes was no mistake, as it was often encouraged by unions themselves. Throughout the century, unions organizing southern women workers repeatedly emphasized the presence of young women workers. In North Carolina in 1900, for instance, the American Federation of Labor (AFL) quietly organized local unions in textile mills across the state, and although women constituted only 20 percent of the membership of these locals, walkouts were often triggered by the grievance of a young woman worker. As one journalist observed in 1901, female workers, most ranging in age from ten to thirty, were placed in the limelight so frequently that managers in a number of communities perceived unions as "being made up largely of women and children."[22] The CIO used the same tactic of consciously emphasizing the participation of women in confrontational situations. For example, in 1938, the *CIO News* coverage of a raid on CIO headquarters featured a front-page headline reading "Girls Jailed By New Orleans Cops" above a photograph of six "girl workers at the CIO office" ranging in age from twenty to forty, even though most of the eighty-four CIO union officials and members arrested by the police were men.[23] A decade later, in 1948, when Bessie Hillman, *Advance* reporter and wife of ACWA head Sidney Hillman, visited an ACWA local in Atlanta, she described the "thrill" she experienced when she met the "beautiful girls" who had "forged a union during the heat of the 1941 struggle to organize Cluett's" (the Cluett Peabody plant). Meeting with workers who were opening a new union center, Hillman "witnessed the same enthusiasm, the same loyalty, devotion and love" that she herself had experienced "as a girl striker in Chicago in 1910."[24]

This focus on young women served the unions in several ways. For one, the conspicuous activity of women strikers in organizing parades or on a picket line was one way in which the labor movement could counteract the disproportionate focus on violence in the strike coverage of mainstream newspapers. Press releases and articles about girl strikers helped neutralize headlines about dynamitings and shootings that usually implicated union men. For another, girl strikers provided excellent publicity, as members of the public, both within and outside a local community, found it difficult to ignore the plight of young women who reminded them of their own daughters. The younger the workers involved, the greater the sympathy that could be elicited from the community at large. Mill managers already had significant difficulty defending the practice of child labor, and paying "girls" pennies an hour for a fifty- to sixty-hour workweek conjured up the practice of hiring children to work in the mills. At Elizabethton, for instance, although the women strikers ranged in age from fourteen to thirty-five, they were described in both the labor press and in daily newspapers throughout the South as "very young girls." According to one labor reporter, "An outstanding feature of this most unusual rebellion is that it was led by children, the little girls in the inspection rooms. They were not only the first to come out but among the most determined. Numbers of them addressed the mass meetings of strikers which were held every day, pleading, in their piping, childish voices, for the 'grown folks' not to weaken." In the *American Federationist*, photographs of the Elizabethton "strike leaders" featured four young women; none of the male strike leaders were mentioned. In a mixture of paternalism and male voyeurism, author Sherwood Anderson, covering the southern strikes in 1929 and 1930 for the *Nation*, wrote of seeing "Girls everywhere": "And many of these mountain girls are lovely little creatures. They have, at least when excited, straight hard little bodies, delicately featured faces. I sat beside a child that couldn't have been over thirteen—no matter what her 'mill age'—and as I looked at her I thought how proud I would be to have been her father."[25]

The perceived vulnerability of girl strikers could cut both ways, however. While journalists and union officials sought to provide protection for these workers, employers and community leaders attempted to reassert their control over mill daughters fighting for autonomy and decent wages. During a sit-down strike in Tupelo, Mississippi, in 1937, the union and the management of the plant competed for the allegiance of the town's young female workforce by appealing not to the workers but to their parents. The local newspaper would not print the union's announcements, but sold the management space for numerous advertisements addressed to "The Farmers of This Territory, If your daughters or any of your relatives work in the garment factories," whom they advised to "stick by the homefolks. . . . Advise your daughters and relatives to stick to their jobs and beware of outsiders' counsel." In intentionally suggestive language, southern fathers were urged to protect their daughters by "keeping the virgin Southland free at the present from a communistic organization."[26]

Thus although the image and pre-adolescent implication of the term *girl striker* strengthened their identification as "daughters" (albeit errant) of the community, thereby conferring some degree of protection during their periods of open defiance, it may also have perpetuated managerial paternalism in the face of persistent labor militancy throughout the South. Such was suggested in a ballad written by Odel Corley in Gastonia in 1929: "Manville Jenckes was the millionaire's name, He bought the law with his money and fame. . . . Told Violet Jones if she'd go back to work, He'd buy her a new Ford and pay her well for her work."[27] Likewise, in the 1937 Tupelo sit-down strike involving 400 workers, management encouraged women workers to expel the union's organizers. A group of 150 women cooperated, "escorting" two women organizers from the International

Ladies Garment Workers Union (ILGWU) out of town. To show their appreciation, management treated 375 women workers to a seventy-five-cents-a-plate celebration dinner at the local hotel; "Girl Workers Given Dinner," read the headline in the *Memphis Press-Scimiter*.[28]

Despite the pervasiveness and usefulness of the image of the girl striker, it ultimately distorted the day-to-day reality of southern working-class community life. Strikes, whether they lasted two hours or two years, were sporadic events, although in southern communities in the years before World War II they occurred often enough to become ritualized affairs. Parades, picket lines, relief stations, speeches, rallies, and meetings lent most strikes a sideshow atmosphere, and the presence of journalists, visitors, and observers from outside the community made it impossible for anyone in the community to ignore the strike. The presence of extra police or military personnel further transformed the routine of local community life, heightening underlying tensions between competing groups of citizens and often unleashing previously dormant hostilities. Celebration, excitement, fear, confusion, and violence occurred simultaneously, bringing intense feelings to the surface and leaving individuals exhilarated and drained at the same time.

In these atypical situations, women workers readily assumed the role of girl strikers, but it was a role that did not reflect their actual involvement in the labor movement. Being viewed as a girl striker did not confer equal status with men within the union. After a strike ended, girl strikers often returned to being simply "girls" in the eyes of male union leaders who were unwilling to consider women as co-equals within the organization. Thus it could be argued that the girl striker image actually made it more difficult for women to be taken seriously within the labor movement and to realize their full potential as union members.

Claiming Unions as Their Own

By the same token, the stereotypes of heroine and girl striker have impeded a more comprehensive analysis of women's roles in the history of organized labor in the South. These circumscribed views of women's participation do not make clear their involvement in the day-to-day maintenance work of the union, their contributions as auxiliary members, their struggles for leadership roles within their locals, and their alliances with middle-class women. Furthermore, these stereotypes, based on the contributions of white women, leave out the important role played by black women in southern labor organizing. Thus we must look beyond these stereotypes to fully understand how labor women attempted to incorporate their own political agenda into southern unions.

Perhaps the images of the heroine and the girl striker have been so prevalent because they represent women's commitment to an agenda shared by the largely male leadership of the labor movement. Thus the focus upon them, among unionists and historians alike, has distracted attention from the ways in which the roles and interests of women workers have been different from, and sometimes in direct conflict with, those of their male co-unionists.[29]

Chief among these differences is that southern labor women, from the late nineteenth century through the twentieth, often proposed that the labor movement address a broader range of issues that would go beyond wages and working conditions to also speak to social and familial concerns. For example, women unionists argued that "working conditions" included not only wage and hour issues, but hours off for meals, maternity time for bearing and nursing children, and housing policies (especially in the years before 1940 when many workers lived in company-owned houses). These issues brought women into conflict with union leadership, and women members frequently described themselves as being "in the minority on policies." This was particularly true in the late 1930s, when male labor leaders accused women unionists of moving too quickly on certain issues, including racial integration. For example, women members of the Textile Workers' Union local in Roanoke, Virginia, proposed to the membership at one meeting that the union should put into practice the official ideology of "equality and justice for all workers" by opening the union to black workers in the factory. Because of the large percentage of women members in the union, the issue passed, but the women, having taken union leaders completely by surprise, were harshly criticized for "not working through proper channels."[30] Despite opposition from the male union hierarchy, a significant minority of white southern women continued to advocate a union agenda that transcended wage issues, addressed the needs of all union members, and included black workers.

As workplaces and unions did become increasingly integrated, black women also came to play important roles within the southern labor movement. Bringing with them generations of organizing experience in the church and the civil rights movement, black women proved exceptionally adept as leaders within the labor movement, contacting unions, getting cards signed, fighting legal obstacles, and participating in contract negotiations. In the South after 1965, cooperation between black and white women workers in textile, garment, and tobacco factories became the most critical factor in winning union elections. As the number of black women workers in southern mills continued to increase in the late 1960s and early 1970s, a majority of black women workers within a plant could usually convince younger white women to join them in supporting the union, and with this interracial coalition, election victories became more frequent.[31]

Extending our view of women in the southern labor movement beyond the activities of heroines and girl strikers also allows us to see more clearly the importance of women-based networks in supporting women workers, and through them the labor movement more generally. At the local level, in the 1910s through the 1930s, such networks might include branches or committees of the YWCA Industrial Department, the National Women's Trade Union League, or the Southern Summer School for Women Workers in Industry; in the 1970s and 1980s, these would include chapters of the Coalition of Labor Union Women (CLUW). Through these local organizations, southern women, white and black, participated in regional meetings of the YWCA, the Southern Summer School, the National Women's Trade Union League, CLUW, and the Southern School for Union Women established in the 1970s. At times, unions themselves responded to initiatives by their female membership to form subgroups within a local union and then participate in regional meetings with women unionists from across the South.

As southern women workers built local and regional networks, they sometimes looked to cross-class, in addition to interracial, women's organizations for support. In the 1920s and 1930s, the YWCA, the National Women's Trade Union League, the Southern Summer School, and even the League of Women Voters fostered the work of women unionists by offering strike support, workers' education, and a commitment to industrial organizing. In the 1960s, middle- and working-class southern women joined forces again as they worked for women's equality through organizations like the National Organization for Women. Throughout the twentieth century, these alliances often created tensions within the labor movement as male unionists feared that women workers' affiliations with middle-class allies would weaken their allegiance to the class-based labor movement.[32]

In the 1920s and 1930s, as the National Women's Trade Union League, the YWCA, and the Southern Summer School for Women Workers in Industry reached out to southern women workers in an effort to bring them into the labor movement, each group faced opposition from organized labor itself. AFL leaders feared that the NWTUL's organizing work would lead to a separate union structure for women that would undermine AFL supremacy. As students trained at the Southern Summer School formed local networks of women workers in dozens of communities across the region, AFL leaders accused them of "dual unionism," that is, of establishing an autonomous workers' organization that might compete with official trade unions. In Mobile, Alabama, in 1935, a group of five women garment workers who found themselves branded as "radicals and agitators" by the union leadership appealed to the regional labor boards in both Atlanta and New Orleans, claiming that their situation was "just another case of the industrialist trying to crush the workers and in so doing, being protected by an old conservative international." In 1942, Molly Dowd, a longtime labor activist in Alabama, wrote to Margaret Drier Robins of the NWTUL that she was pleased that her work with the State Labor Department under the progressive Governor Bibb Graves "gave me a chance to be of some help to the workers in our state, especially the women who are always so neglected," adding that "the men in the Labor movement are paying a little more attention down here than they once did because it's a matter of self-defense, but sad to say the only part they let women play is the paying of dues. They are not interested in developing any sort of leadership among their women."[33]

The participation and leadership patterns of southern women within the labor movement have differed significantly from those of their male colleagues across time and place, from the organization of black washerwomen in Alabama in the 1880s to the walkouts of young white textile workers in the southern strikes of 1929 to the CIO activists who worked across racial lines to organize the unorganized in plants and factories throughout the South. Both black and white southern women have been most active in union work when they were not heavily involved in childrearing, meaning that women activists within a union usually were clustered into two groups: one of eighteen to twenty-five year olds, another of thirty-five to fifty-five year olds. Active male unionists did not follow this pattern but rather entered the union when they entered the workforce and rose within the ranks throughout their career until they reached their late forties. Because of this bimodal age distribution, middle-aged women often found themselves competing for leadership posts with men who were a decade younger but had more experience as union activists, having held minor offices since they were in their early twenties. This lack of seniority within the union, resulting from the discontinuity that so frequently marked women's working lives, hampered women who sought leadership positions within the labor movement.[34]

In the union roles they did fill, women in many locals took responsibility for the "invisible" work of the union. The important but behind-the-scenes work these women accomplished included helping other workers on the shop floor, providing food for union-sponsored activities, working to provide food and housing relief during a strike, fundraising for the union in the local community, tending union children so young parents could attend union functions, as well as numerous clerical tasks. Women undertaking this type of work for the union frequently held offices like recording secretary or shop steward, but on a sporadic basis. Usually their work went unrecognized and often unappreciated by the union hierarchy.

Another largely unexamined venue through which many southern women participated in the labor movement is the women's auxiliaries of craft unions, as well as those in coal and steel unions. Women's auxiliaries have had a long history in the South. Throughout the twentieth century, union leaders in the skilled trades, such as the Machinists' Union founded in the South in the 1890s, encouraged their members' wives to organize local auxiliaries to support the membership, and dozens of these groups thrived in communities throughout the region.[35] Southern women's auxiliaries also existed in the building trades as well as in the railroad unions and the coal industry. In tightly knit industrial communities, women's auxiliaries merely formalized existing networks of women whose husbands or fathers worked for a particular company, while in larger communities, auxiliaries brought together women who had little in common except their husbands' union. Auxiliaries grew in the postwar period, but as more women entered the workforce in the fifties and sixties, the number of active auxiliary members declined. In the seventies, as women moved into nontraditional jobs, especially in coal mining, women who would have joined the auxiliary joined the union instead, although as layoffs forced women out of mining in the 1980s, former women miners once again joined auxiliaries.

Although auxiliaries often provided women an avenue for participation in the labor movement, their influence was clearly limited. Women did not become full-fledged union members by joining a union auxiliary but rather served as the "wives" of the movement, a role based solely on providing support. As such, these women often played crucial roles as ambassadors for the union within the community, as relief workers during strikes, as mothers rearing their children in the traditions of unionism. Yet the work these women performed for the union, within their households, and within the labor force was viewed within the context of a properly functioning union family with a male unionist as the head. Union auxiliaries were recognized as effective organizations in expanding the influence of the union, but the female auxiliary member was not recognized as having autonomy, as being an equal within the movement or within the southern wage economy.[36]

In fact, organized labor's view of women's participation in auxiliaries quite accurately reflected the attitude of many union leaders toward women workers themselves, regardless of these workers' depth of involvement in or commitment to the union. Even in the face of overwhelming evidence to the contrary, unions continued to look at women workers as "temporary" members of the workforce or as workers who would not, for one reason or another, become a permanent part of the labor movement. The persistence of the occupational segregation of women in low-wage jobs in the textile, garment, food, and service industries reinforced the idea that women workers were different from men, and these "women's" industries—in contrast to higher-paying "male" industries such as steel, auto, and rubber and the building trades—had consistently low levels of unionization. Despite the consistent gains in female union membership as manufacturing jobs generally held by men were eliminated, the predominately negative view of women in organized labor changed little over the course of the century.[37]

Because of negative experiences in unions, women workers often viewed unions as male-dominated organizations in which they had little control, gained only sporadic access to top-level leaders, and had to wage constant battles on the grass-roots level to express their ideas and have them heard. All unions were not the same, of course, but examples abound of women unionists running headlong into conflict with union

leaders. Unions organizing in the South consistently paid women organizers lower salaries, often left them to work in complete isolation, and
ignored their requests for assistance. In addition, union administrators
often took the work of women organizers for granted. In a 1938 report,
ACWA president Hillman admitted that "this is a man's world . . . even
in an organization that represents so many women" and apologized for
having "failed to mention the women" in his discussion of the leadership of the southern organizing campaign. Many women argued that their
unions didn't "accept the idea of girls being active," and a lot of union
women would have sympathized with Virginia unionist Jennie Spencer,
who described the first year of her life in the union as "a period in which
my spirits had been broken, all except a single thread."[38]

In its failure to recognize, accommodate, and legitimate women's various roles in the movement, organized labor failed to live up to its own
ideology of universal equality and justice. For many women, this was a
particularly bitter pill to swallow, for it was this very ideology that had
drawn them into union participation as members, activists, strikers, auxiliary members, and supporters. As an ideology that had universal application, unionism was not gender-based. From the beginning of the twentieth century, the language of equality and justice permeated the rhetoric
of unions as they campaigned for new members. Labor slogans crafted
by generations of unionists encapsulate this sentiment: "All for One and
One for All," "Labor Omnia Vincit," "Workers Unite!" "In Unity There
is Strength," "Solidarity Forever." This language was particularly appealing to women, and at times unions explicitly articulated their ideology of
unity and fair treatment as a way to recruit women workers into the labor
movement.[39]

The inclusive, democratic ideology of the labor movement also offered
southern women an alternative to prevailing norms regarding female behavior, which no doubt accounts for some of the enthusiasm with which
they responded to the movement. Women who joined unions signed on
as individuals, in their own names. As unionists, they acted independently
of their fathers or husbands and of the company. For women raised in a
culture that taught them to be subservient to God and man, this independent status had the appeal of underwriting their autonomy; it also had
the threatening potential to reorder gender relationships in the workplace
and the home.

This is precisely what happened throughout the South as female membership in unions increased during periods of rapid economic change: in 1900, in the early and late 1920s, during the 1940s, and when the economy surged in the late 1950s and 1960s. For southern working-class men, union membership meant assuming an adversarial stance vis-à-vis an employer, a risky undertaking in a culture based on adherence to a rigid social and economic hierarchy. The risks multiplied for southern women who joined unions to improve their conditions as workers and became part of an organization that was independent of both the private and public spheres in which they normally lived and worked. Over many decades, while women workers, black and white, sought to claim unions as their own, to establish themselves as participants and leaders, the relationship between women workers and organized labor has also been one plagued by discontent and unhappiness, feelings never reflected in the static images of the heroine and the girl striker.

"A Bond of Silk"

Given the actual diversity of southern women's involvement in the labor movement, what explains the persistence of the predominant images of them as heroines and girl strikers? One explanation is undoubtedly that these models of women's behavior and roles reflected the limitations placed on women by the labor movement. Young women could be "strikers," acting alone or as part of a group, as long as they could also be viewed as daughters, young and impetuous, disconnected from the responsibilities and roles of adult society. If they were older, or dead, they could become heroines, motherly or grandmotherly figures who loomed larger than life.

These stereotypes also resonated so powerfully in southern unions because they reflected southern cultural views of women. Nowhere are these views more clearly expressed than in southern country music, where mothers are idolized and daughters are adored. But southern men were rarely acculturated to treat women as equals, and many had tremendous difficulty doing so. In those same country ballads, the wife, the partner, the co-equal was more frequently the source of trouble and woe.[40] Within the labor movement, this cultural standard also held: women could be mother-like heroines or daughter-like activists, but when women unionists (often emboldened by the democratic rhetoric of the union itself) demanded or expected equality within the union, they tended to be seen as troublemakers and faced an uphill struggle at best.

In the 1980s, many of the advances made by the labor movement during the previous two decades were eroded by a deep recession in the South's basic industries—textiles, tobacco, furniture, and steel. In 1989, the strike against the Pittston Corporation once again drew national attention to the intransigence of employers and the determination of southern workers to fight for their benefits and rights. Following in a long tradition, women again played a crucial role in the Pittston struggle. The "ladies auxiliary" of the local United Mine Workers of America (UMWA) re-named themselves "The Daughters of Mother Jones." In keeping with a strong heritage of female militancy and union loyalty, they fed three thousand strikers and their families as well as thousands of union supporters who visited

Figure 4.1. This angel of the labor movement embodied the protective characteristics of labor's female heroines. The engraving appeared on the cover of the *American Federationist* in 1900 and 1901. Courtesy of the George Meany Memorial Archives.

Figure 4.2. Untitled Farm Security Administration photograph by Jack Delano [?] of women textile workers on CIO picket line in Greensboro, Georgia, May 1941. Reproduced from the Library of Congress, Washington, D.C.

the strike area, walked the picket lines for over eight months, served time in jail, traveled north to raise money, and chronicled the strike in song. They participated in the union struggle exactly as southern women had done since the nineteenth century. Their decision to declare themselves the daughters of Mother Jones confirmed their understanding of southern labor history. They appreciated the power that images of mothers and daughters held for the labor movement, and in uniting these two images, they forged a new and more powerful role for themselves, which the UMWA acknowledged by assigning an organizer to this group of women activists.[41]

Symbolic representations of idealized figures were frequently used in labor movement publications as Americans entered the twentieth century. The Mariana figure on the cover of a 1900 edition of the *American Federationist*, for example, incorporates aspects of both labor heroines and girl strikers. She is huge and strong looking, she is young and beautiful. She holds olive branches in both hands, from which flow streamers printed with the motto "A Bond of Silk, Stronger Than Brass or Steel." She figuratively protects the two male workers, trade tools in their hands, who sit at her feet. She is inspirational—and imaginary.[42] Four decades later a

Figure 4.3. Photograph by Jack Delano. Farm Security Administration. Title: "Union meeting of textile workers in Greensboro, Greene County, Georgia." 1941. Reproduced from the Library of Congress, Washington, D.C.

photograph of women workers on strike in Greenboro, Georgia, in May 1941 captures the energy and feisty defiance of a group of primarily young women standing on the picket line outside the mill, signs held high in protest. They are angry, proud, speaking out, and going public to change their lives in the workplace. A third photograph, less dramatic than the other two, reflects the middle ground of women's lives in the southern labor movement. Taken at a regular meeting of the textile union six months after the end of the Greensboro strike, it shows five CIO women, one with her children in tow, listening attentively. Unlike Mother Jones, who made her home wherever the fight was, and in sharp contrast to the picket line on which some of these women had stood months earlier, they sit together, serious and calm, at the meeting in the town where they live and work. Neither heroines nor girl strikers, but conscious of that history, these women have taken their place in the union and see their future and that of their children in the labor movement.

III

LABOR RIGHTS TO CIVIL RIGHTS

5

· · · · · · · · ·

Labor Looks South

Theory and Practice in Southern Textile Organizing

Women textile workers in southern mills envisioned gender equality as the most promising way to resolve the problems of occupational segregation and discriminatory wage differentials within the industry. Their use of collective action to realize that vision at times put them at cross-purposes with the efforts of organized labor to unionize southern workers. From the late nineteenth century on, the basic theory of the labor movement had remained the same: organizing southern workers would protect northern wage scales and prevent runaway shops. Indeed, fears of a non-unionized workforce in the American South ran deep among northern workers.[1] Whenever faced with job flight to the South, leaders realized that the survival of the U.S. labor movement would depend on the successful organization of unions among southern workers. This chapter examines the theory and practice of organizing in southern textile mills by focusing on the efforts of different unions and labor organizations active in the South. Yet strategies and tactics are not the same, as becomes clear when we compare the theoretical framework used in organizing southern textile workers with the actual tactics used in specific strike situations and organizing efforts.

Goals and Challenges

Since the 1880s, organizing campaigns mounted by virtually every branch of the American labor movement have swept through the South. The Knights of Labor was the first group to recognize the strategic importance of organizing in the South. Then, in the 1900s, the American Federation of Labor (AFL) looked to "The Awakening of the South," promising to enter the region "like a solid wedge against the injustice and wrong of child labor and overlong hours."[2] Theories about organizing textile unions put forward by both the Knights of Labor and the AFL addressed major issues in southern society: the role of the South in the national economy, the intransigence of both southern employers and northern industrialists based in the South, and the economic relationship between black and white workers. The strategies and tactics used by specific unions raised important questions about labor's commitment to organizing rank-and-file workers, the role of women in the textile industry and in the labor movement itself, the involvement of the political Left in union organizing, and the impact of liberal support.[3] From the 1880s through the 1910s, organized labor worked to increase union membership among southern workers and in so doing to eliminate North/South wage differentials and stop industrial migration into the South. Cheap southern labor posed the greatest single threat to the American labor movement, and the fear of losing jobs to the South permeated the workforce of every major industry in the United States. In the textile industry, this fear became a reality in the early 1920s as an increasing number of northern manufacturers began moving their textile operations to the South, setting in motion a relocation process that took almost four decades to complete.

American textile unions have always faced the difficulties inherent in organizing a labor-intensive industry with the nation's lowest wage rate and a workforce composed mostly of women (and in the earliest decades, children). In addition, in the 1920s, the industry was composed of several autonomous sub-industries, including plants that produced cotton, silk, wool, hosiery, synthetic yarns, and garments, and even as late as 1935, the number of individual employers exceeded six thousand. To make matters worse, unions faced attacks not only from employers but from other textile unions as well. Constant conflicts among the unions attempting to organize textile workers exacerbated an already difficult situation by diverting the labor movement's limited resources from the task at hand.[4]

Even in the Northeast, textile organizing had never been easy, despite the region's long union tradition, urban industrial settings that facilitated the mobilization of support for strikers, a labor movement with political influence, and substantial liberal support. Although the South's seemingly unending labor supply and poverty-level wages would seem to make the region ripe for unionization, the paternalism of southern employers and the migration to the South of anti-union northern industrialists created a social and economic environment hostile to union organization. From the beginning, the labor movement fought an uphill battle in organizing textile workers in the South, where manufacturers effectively maintained control of local law enforcement officials and the state National Guard. The rural nature of the industry, with numerous isolated mills dispersed over huge areas, further hampered organization. In addition, the labor movement in the South lacked political influence and liberal support, and pro-labor groups never matched the overall strength of the region's conservative forces.[5]

Yet it was the division of the industry into northern and southern spheres that proved the most difficult obstacle for the labor movement to overcome. As northern textile manufacturers sought to control their southern competitors, northern textile workers fought to maintain their wage rates in the face of being undercut by southern labor. Through the labor movement, workers in the Northeast tried to equalize northern and southern wages, hoping that by raising southern rates they could stop the migration of the industry to the South. But the persistence of a North/South wage differential ensured the continuation of runaway shops and a steady decline in the percentage of organized textile workers.[6]

Throughout the 1920s, unionists from the Northeast, especially those in the cotton textiles, garment, and hosiery industries, sought to organize southern workers in order to stabilize their industries and save their unions. The independent CIO also launched intensive drives to organize southern workers between the late 1930s and the early 1950s. Beginning in the 1960s, black women played an increasingly important role in organizing workers in the garment, tobacco, and textile industries. In the 1970s and 1980s, as the number of manufacturing jobs in the region declined and women workers took new jobs in the service and clerical sectors, other national unions, including District 1199 and the Service Employees International Union (SEIU), saw the South once again as ripe for labor organization.[7]

Labor Looks South

In the nineteenth century, the most successful labor organization in the South was the Knights of Labor. The Knights' national policy of including women and black workers in its membership was particularly important in the South. In 1889, there were already over fifty women's local assemblies in the region, which comprised 30 percent of the Knights' women's assemblies in the United States. A fifth of those women's assemblies in the South had been organized by black women. By 1890, however, membership in the Knights began to wane nationally, and labor organization among southern workers fell to its nadir. After local orders of the Knights had dissolved and the cotton textile industry in the South had grown sufficiently large to challenge New England's supremacy in the production of coarse cotton goods, the AFL-affiliated National Union of Textile Workers (NUTW) began to organize in southern mills. A craft union, the NUTW organized only skilled male operatives, and by 1900 it had claimed as members only five thousand of the ninety thousand textile workers in the South. Not until a generation later would southern women textile workers organize on a large scale.[8]

In the 1920s, the pleas of spontaneously militant workers and the potential for vast gains in membership enticed unions into the South. The South's growing importance within the national industrial economy also commanded the attention of the labor movement. As Edith Kowski, a Brookwood Labor College student and labor organizer, put it after spending the summer of 1928 in the South, it was necessary to "worry about the south . . . if for no other reason than to save our own union hides from an onslaught of company unionism and open shop drives."[9]

Late in the decade, a considerable amount of labor activity in the South centered on the Full-Fashioned Hosiery Workers, a Philadelphia knitters' union whose members were determined to organize southern workers in order to protect their own jobs and wage levels throughout the East. Alfred Hoffman, an organizer for the Hosiery Workers, established the Piedmont Organizing Council in 1927 and invited the AFL to assist with general organizing work in the South. Although southern delegates at the AFL's convention in New Orleans in 1928 mapped out a plan for organizing the South, the Federation actually put few organizers in the region and offered local organizing drives little monetary support. AFL backing of southern textile strikes in 1929–30 was minimal, and women strikers received more support from middle-class reform groups within the region than from the AFL.[10]

Technological Change and Labor Dissent: 1929–1931

The wave of southern textile strikes in 1929–1931 was the direct result of fundamental technological changes that first became evident in the early 1920s, when many mills purchased and installed new equipment designed to increase production. In northern mills, these changes in work speed and load had coincided with the installation of new equipment following World War I. Northern workers had reacted to an increasing workload and decreasing wages by striking, and the UTW-AFL had responded by sending organizers into strike situations, working out compromises with management, and trying to grow newly established unions under extreme circumstances. In practice, the efforts of the national unions were often discredited, as was the case in the Amoskeag strike of 1922, where workers never identified with the union leaders, who came from outside the region; in the end, these workers felt betrayed by a union that offered hungry strikers little more than "flour and beans."[11]

Many of the southern mills with more modern plants had also purchased new equipment around the same time, increasing southern production but, at least initially, leaving wage rates and individual workloads unaltered. But in the mid-1920s, overproduction and severe price competition forced southern manufacturers to maximize the efficiency of the new equipment they had purchased earlier in the decade. Southern management increased the hours in the workweek, escalated the workload, accelerated the machinery, and cut wages. This stretch-out/speed-up combination sparked protests by southern workers who, like their northern counterparts a few years earlier, simultaneously felt the strain of working harder for even less pay.[12]

Southern textile workers reacted to the stretch-out of 1929 by walking out of mills across the South. Some 3,200 workers in Elizabethton, Tennessee, struck at the local Bemberg and Glanzstoff mills in March. The workers at the Loray Mill in Gastonia struck in April, and on July 11, 650 textile workers in Marion, North Carolina, walked out to protest the firing of fifteen union members and working conditions that outsiders described as "unbelievable" and "atrocious." The strike in Marion stretched on into the fall of 1929. Early in 1930, H. R. Fitzgerald, owner of the enormous Dan River and Riverside Cotton mills in Danville, Virginia, forced through a 10 percent wage cut. For eight months, the workers in Danville, led by an independent local of loom-fixers that had formed in

1919, refrained from striking, until that September when 2,500 workers were discharged for union activity. These strikes—Elizabethton, Gastonia, Marion, and Danville—have become legendary episodes in southern labor history and the most celebrated of the strikes that took place in the South in 1929.[13]

Competing for Southern Textile Workers during the Great Depression

In the late 1920s and early 1930s, four labor organizations competed for dominance over the agenda for organizing southern textile workers: the United Textile Workers (UTW), the most important but then still weak AFL-affiliated textile union whose membership comprised less than 3 percent of the workers in the industry (in 1929, thirty thousand); the Conference for Progressive Labor Action (CPLA), directed by A. J. Muste and committed to industrial unionism and organizing the unorganized; the National Textile Workers Union (NTWU), founded in 1928 by the Communist Party; and the National Women's Trade Union League (NWTUL), officially allied with the AFL but with a special commitment to organizing women workers. Three of these organizations—the UTW, the CPLA, and the NWTUL—shared the belief that to protect the interests of northern workers, southern textile workers had to be organized. The fourth, the communist-dominated NTWU, espoused a different rationale for their work in the South, arguing that southern mill workers needed to be developed as an integral part of the class-conscious proletariat.[14]

The UTW looked south in the mid-1920s, desperate to save the union from the declining membership and shrinking treasury left in the wake of the disastrous New England strikes of 1921 and 1922. As a UTW resolution before the AFL Convention in 1929 argued, "Southern workers, if not organized and assimilated with the American Labor Movement, will become a more dangerous menace to the progress of the Organized Workers than can be found in any other economic obstacle now confronting them."[15]

In agreement with the UTW, A. J. Muste of the CPLA believed that with the South "unorganized it will become more and more impossible to hold what little we have in the North." Muste viewed a "non-union, trustified, industrial South" as a threat to the future of the American labor movement, writing, "if this enemy is not conquered . . . while he is young and has not yet reached his full strength, it is useless to expect that anything can be done with him later." An organizer sent to the South from Brookwood Labor College in 1928 reiterated the theoretical position that the UTW-AFL and the CPLA both espoused, arguing that it was necessary to get "down to the business of helping the next fellow (the southern worker) even if for no other reason than to save our own union hides from an onslaught of company unionism and open shop drives. The sooner the South is organized, the sooner the time will come when we will not need to carry on six and nine month strikes to get tolerable conditions in the North."[16]

The NWTUL also believed that organizing in the South was essential to saving the labor movement for northern workers. The NWTUL launched a southern organizing campaign in 1926, explaining that the growing number of women workers in the expanding southern textile industry needed the support of an organization committed to bringing unskilled women workers into the labor movement. The NWTUL saw in the southern strikes of 1929 "the possibility of holding up the standards of living for millions of northern workers menaced by long hours and starvation wages paid to the workers in the southern mills."[17]

The theoretical framework regarding organizing in the South shared by the UTW, the CPLA, and the NWTUL was on the whole accurate. The South's cheap labor force was, as an article in *Business Week* reported in 1929, "the lure dangled before the noses of harassed New England mill owners," and textile unions in the Northeast were in fact eventually crippled by the lack of organization in the South.[18] But although labor's theory proved correct, its approach paralleled the manufacturers' colonial approach to southern industrialization, which dealt with southern textile workers solely in terms of what would benefit those in the North. As a consequence, organizing efforts in the South began and remained extrinsic to southern working-class society, and hence many of the strategies and tactics used by organized labor in the South were inappropriate for the task at hand.

The strategy that the AFL had devised for dealing with the South relied heavily on the cooperation of southern craft unions and the marketing potential of the Federation's reputation for respectability. The AFL hoped that its conservatism and formula of union-management cooperation would prove an "'open sesame,' swinging wide the gates of southern industry to organized labor," as the economist Jean Carol Trepp observed in 1933. Plans to include textiles in a southern campaign had been delayed throughout the 1920s, and only after the walkouts of 1929 did the AFL promise to launch an official campaign in the South and assist the UTW by providing them with organizers and financial support.[19]

To obtain financial backing from the AFL, the UTW agreed to carry the AFL banner of union-management cooperation into the South. To convince the South of the advantages of collective bargaining, AFL president William Green assured the UTW of the AFL's peaceful mission: "We come with the hand of friendship extended to you. There is no sword in our scabbard. There is no weapon in our hand. We come not with the mailed fist but with the open hand to the employers of the South, appealing to them to give us the opportunity, to try us out and see whether we can help this industrial situation in the South."[20]

But AFL support proved totally inadequate to the task. The UTW basically followed "the strategy of the empty treasury," constantly claiming that there was no money for strike relief and refusing to officially sanction strikes by workers in newly organized UTW unions. By 1930, the AFL had virtually abandoned its southern campaign. Francis Gorman, vice-president of the UTW, reported at his union's convention in 1930 that organizational work in the South had been seriously retarded because the UTW had been able to provide only three organizers to cover a territory comprising 1,440 mills and 300,000 workers.[21]

Leaders of the CPLA, a coalition of unionists and intellectuals that advocated industrial unionism, worker control of industry, and labor militancy, adopted the same general theory regarding the necessity of organizing in the South. The CPLA, however, had predicted that the AFL's strategies of cooperation and limited financial backing would never succeed in bringing southern workers into the labor movement. Instead, A. J. Muste—the CPLA's founder, head of Brookwood Labor College, and arch-foe of the AFL's William Green—argued in 1928 that the "southern situation must be tackled soon and on an adequate scale." The CPLA severely criticized AFL efforts in the South for failing to commit sufficient numbers of organizers and financial resources to the task. The CPLA advocated a more militant campaign and stressed the importance of supporting the many spontaneous strikes by workers angrily walking off the job across the region. Muste's group also pointed out that craft union organizing was inappropriate for the southern textile industry and urged the inclusion of unskilled and semiskilled workers in organizing drives.

Muste's small group of progressive labor activists became heavily involved in the Marion strike of 1929 when Tom Tippett and Bill Ross stepped into the leadership vacuum left by the UTW, which would not supply an organizer to coordinate the strike. When the UTW refused to provide strike relief in Marion, the CPLA established an Emergency Strike Relief Committee with Norman Thomas, leader of the Socialist Party, as its chairman.[22] On October 2, 1929, six strikers were killed by deputies at the gate of the East Marion mill, an act of retaliation and resistance so severe that workers throughout the South took heed. Muste, a minister as well as a labor activist, traveled south to officiate at the funeral of the Marion strikers. He spoke to the hundreds of workers gathered before him, sharing in their grief and offering whatever comfort and solace he could. Later, in a statement on "The Marion Murder" issued by the CPLA, Muste addressed the AFL leadership in an attempt to spur the Federation into action. He wrote, "The deaths of these comrades is a challenge to the AF of L. Southern textile workers have in recent months been knocking at its doors clamoring to be organized. . . . But the AFL must have the will, the intelligence, and the courage to seize the opportunity. It must meet the challenge that has been thrown down to it here." Muste effectively articulated and publicized a critique of AFL strategies for organizing in the South, calling for "an immediate, large-scale campaign" to organize southern textile workers and challenging the AFL to raise a million-dollar fund "in memory of the martyrs of Marion" for future organizing and strike relief.[23]

The CPLA itself approached the Marion situation pragmatically, providing leaders and organizing strike relief. But despite their arguments that the AFL was not committing adequate resources to the southern campaign, CPLA efforts also remained minimal. Although Muste theorized about the critical importance of the South, he spent little time in the field and offered only long-distance advice to Brookwood graduates who went south to organize while providing virtually no day-to-day leadership. As Tom Tippett remarked sardonically in a report to Muste on the Marion situation, "Reading [about] it at Brookwood will be 'interesting.' Down here it is tragic." After the period between 1929 and 1931, the CPLA's influence in the South waned, although their belief in the strategic importance of organizing unskilled workers and their endorsement of militant tactics paved the way for the CIO's entry in the next decade.[24]

The NWTUL, the last of the three major organizations to launch a campaign to organize southern textile workers in the late 1920s, previously had developed the successful strategy of supporting spontaneous strikes by women workers as a way to build permanent union shops in the major cities of the Northeast and Midwest. Between 1903 and the mid-1920s, the League expanded its influence and activities, establishing branches in two-dozen cities. Never a chartered union of the AFL and suspect because of its cross-class membership and female constituency, the League continually struggled for legitimacy within the labor movement. Firmly committed to the principles and politics of the AFL, the NWTUL sought to demonstrate its sincerity and potential value by channeling aid to striking AFL union members in cities with NWTUL branches. A decade after its founding, the League had managed to win some recognition from the AFL for its organizing efforts, but its strict allegiance to the AFL's craft unionism and organizing tactics, which targeted skilled workers, actually hampered the League's work.[25]

Once the League turned its attention to the South, the membership pledged to train a "corps of organizers" to undertake what the organizer Elisabeth Christman described as the "southern task which . . . looms up as a giant." The League openly criticized the AFL's refusal to organize unskilled workers, large numbers of whom were women. Matilda Lindsay, an organizer for the League, played a crucial role in the Elizabethton and Danville strikes, both of which involved large numbers of women workers. Mary Anderson, director of the Women's Bureau, argued that "if it had not been for Tillie Lindsay the strike in Elizabethton would not have amounted to anything" and cited Lindsay's ability to keep the women together as more "evidence that it takes real women to organize women."[26]

Thus, despite its close contact with the AFL, the League did develop certain strategies that worked well in the South. Lindsay's contact with women strikers proved effective; the NWTUL coordinated local strike relief efforts in both Elizabethton and Danville and gathered support from unions and middle-class sympathizers across the nation. In 1929, the League inaugurated a nation-wide campaign to help "Organize the South." To raise money for organization and relief work among southern textile workers, members sold small lapel pins, which were cast in the shape of a shield with a tiny spinning wheel in the upper half and intended to remind the wearer "of Gandhi's stupendous effort to free the wage slaves of India."[27]

Unlike the NWTUL, the CPLA, and the UTW, the Communist-affiliated National Textile Workers Union was not invested in preserving the labor movement as it existed in the late 1920s and thus was not interested in organizing southern textile workers for that purpose. Nonetheless, the strategies and tactics the NTWU developed in the South in 1929 had important long-range implications for organizing within the region. These included recruiting black and white workers into integrated unions, organizing unskilled industrial workers, bringing women into unions on an equal basis with men, openly avowing worker control of industry, and endorsing Leftist political positions. With regard to racial equality and worker control, the NTWU openly supported strategies that the CPLA only covertly endorsed, and while these positions hampered the NTWU's campaign in 1929, the importance of the union's racial policy in the long term cannot be underestimated. The NTWU drew attention to a central issue in southern labor organizing—namely, the biracial nature of the southern workforce—and helped set the stage for later organizing campaigns that overcame intense opposition from segregationists to unite black and white southern workers. Here, however, we remain focused on the central, but sometimes overlooked, role that North-South tensions played in the labor movement during this period of rapid southern industrial expansion.[28]

New Organizers, New Tactics

In the strikes of 1929–1931, southern textile workers reacted to the stretch-out in the same way their northern counterparts had a few years earlier. But despite efforts to bring workers in the South's largest industry into the labor movement and thereby salvage the unions and jobs of northern textile workers, none of the groups organizing in the South in 1929 had the strategic vision and resources necessary to wage an effective campaign. From the 1930s through the early 1960s, the persistence of the North/South wage differential, the continued flight of northern manufacturers to the South, and the growth of indigenous southern industry only reinforced labor's belief that the South held the key to the survival of the American labor movement.

During this period, campaigns to organize textile workers in the South continued to be designed to protect northern wage scales and curb

employer migration to the region. Although this underlying strategy remained the same, the lack of significant union gains following these early
strikes led the movement to change its tactics. The AFL's commitment to
union-management cooperation, without militancy, strikes, or unreason-
able demands that would make industrialists or the public apprehensive,
had had little effect. Moreover, hampered by a shortage of funds and organizers, the AFL had made little headway in organizing workers in the
anti-union South. Francis Gorman, vice-president of the UTW, reported
at the UTW convention in 1930 that the union had been able to fund only
three southern organizers to cover a region that included nearly 1,500
mills and more than a quarter of a million workers. The future, critics like
the economist Jean Trepp warned, would require "a policy of militancy
rather than respectability." There was no easy road to organization. As
Trepp argued, less should be heard about cooperation and more about
"strike funds and workers' rights . . . all [of which] are needed to hew a
path into the forest of opposition."[29]

The generation of southern women workers who had joined the NW-
TUL, attended sessions at the Southern Summer School, or become active in a local YWCA Industrial Club were trained in the principles of
industry-wide union organization and committed to bringing southern
workers in large unorganized industries such as furniture, tobacco, and
cotton textiles into the ranks of organized labor. To these women, the
AFL, with its emphasis on craft organization, could not provide the leadership so desperately needed in the South, and they became a natural base
for the CIO drives of the 1930s and 1940s.

After 1931, the UTW underwent several transformations. As a direct
result of the difficult campaigns of 1929–1931, the UTW changed its organizing policy to focus on rank-and-file workers, regardless of occupation,
rather than on bringing the most highly skilled employees into the union.
The union also began to recognize the militancy of southern workers,
which was confirmed in September 1934 when 170,000 men and women,
two-thirds of the textile workers in the region, walked off the job to protest abusive new efficiency measures instituted by their employers. This
powerful strike united textile workers across regional lines as workers
from the North joined those in the South, seeing themselves for the first
time as allies, not rivals. Three weeks into the strike, President Roosevelt's
assurances that the abuses in the nation's textile mills would be addressed

led the UTW to call off the walkout, a decision many workers came to regret when they faced a virulent blacklist and could not return to work.

Realizing how difficult it was going to be to organize the increasing number of southern workers, the UTW in 1936 joined the Committee for Industrial Organization (CIO), and that June the UTW Executive Council met to prepare a new plan for organizing unorganized textile workers. The Council's plan emphasized the need "to stimulate a new trade union consciousness and militancy in the South" and underscored "the fact that organization of the East and the North without simultaneous organization in the South merely means speeding the migration of all industry from the North to the South." As part of the UTW's new strategy, organizers sent into the South would receive intensive training in southern industrial development, southern labor history, and analyses of the anti-union tactics of southern manufacturers.[30]

In March 1937, the UTW and the CIO formed the Textile Workers Organizing Committee (TWOC), announcing that "the protection of the textile worker depends up[on] the unionization of the south." The TWOC outlined new strategies for tackling the still untamed southern giant. The CIO worked to provide adequate finances and to use southern organizers whenever possible. The TWOC worked to avoid strikes and to run a broadly based publicity campaign to educate both workers and community members about the value of unions. Echoing the AFL strategy of 1930, TWOC leaders encouraged organizers in the southern field to emphasize to unions and industrialists alike the union's role in stabilizing the industry and promoting industrial efficiency.[31] Women organizers, especially native southerners, were now hired to work in the South. The CIO increasingly looked to organizations like the Southern Summer School to provide women leaders, and ten students from the School became organizers in the TWOC campaign. Among those who had been initially exposed to the concept of industrial organization in the YWCA, gone on to work with the Southern Summer School, and then been hired by the CIO were middle-class women like Lucy Randolph Mason, the CIO's southern public relations representative; Mary Lawrence, hired from the Highlander Folk School staff to work with TWUA; and Pat Knight, who led education programs for the Textile Workers Union of America. Other southern women workers who followed the same path included Hilda Cobb (Amalgamated Clothing Workers of America), who organized a campaign in Richmond, Virginia, in 1936; Polly Robkin (TWOC), who was sent to a small community in south Georgia to organize workers there; and Jennie Spencer (TWOC), who worked as an organizer at the American Viscose plant in Roanoke, Virginia.[32]

Part of the TWOC's new plan for the South included accelerating demands for National Labor Relations Board (NLRB) elections and contract negotiations. A key component of the TWOC's southern strategy involved the NLRB's recommendation of a minimum wage of forty cents per hour to stabilize the industry. TWOC leaders saw the minimum wage as a viable way of ending to "the ruthless competitive process" at work in textiles. At last, they believed, the movement of textile employment from North to South could be stopped. "The migration to the South," a TWOC report argued in 1938, "has meant not only low wages in the South, but also low wages in the North." After finding that the rate of return by southern mills exceeded that of their northern counterparts by 5–6 percent, the TWOC Research Division argued that the southern branch of the industry could easily absorb higher wage rates and establish wage levels on par with those in the North.[33]

More carefully planned than any previous textile campaign, the TWOC's drive in 1937 brought approximately 25 percent of workers under contract. By October 1938, the TWOC had spent $1.5 million on its southern campaign. When the TWOC was reformed as the Textile Workers Union of America (TWUA-CIO) in the spring of 1939, about 20 percent (or 70,000) of the South's 350,000 cotton mill workers carried union cards, and that year about ten thousand southern workers were under TWUA contracts. By the end of the campaign, the North/South wage differential had been narrowed by three percentage points, raising southern wages from 80 to 83 percent of those in the North. The economic threat posed by southern workers had not been eliminated, but the success of the strategies and tactics used in the 1937 campaign inspired organized labor to continue their efforts to raise the economic level of southern workers and, in the process, to protect the wage rates of those already in the union fold.[34]

The CIO and Operation Dixie

The theoretical assumption that organizing southern textile workers would protect the benefits of those in the North persisted beyond the

Depression and World War II, culminating in Operation Dixie, the CIO's campaign to organize the South that began in 1946 and continued until 1953. The CIO sponsored a southern drive because, as one leader emphasized, "the competition of unorganized southern plants with CIO-organized northern industries could in time of depression threaten the whole CIO national position." In addition to the immediate economic goal of raising southern wage levels and eliminating the threat of the open shop, the CIO campaign had two objectives: socially, to organize the region's significant number of black and female workers and, politically, to eventually unseat the conservative southern Democrats in Congress, who were powerful opponents of labor in general and the CIO in particular.[35]

The CIO launched Operation Dixie with the goal of signing up one million workers in twelve southern states. As George Baldanzi reiterated in 1946, "Low incomes in the South are a threat to the prosperity of the entire country. . . . [As] long as wages remain low in any one section, . . . there is the threat of sweat-shop competition with other sections. We, in the textile industry, in our fight to raise the wages of textile workers everywhere, have had to fight constantly against the low wages paid southern textile workers." The CIO dedicated two hundred organizers and one million dollars to the effort during the first year of the campaign, and optimism ran high. The effort focused on the textile industry, which the CIO believed was the key to organizing the South. At that time, 75 percent of the nation's organized textile workers worked in the North, but almost three-fourths of the nation's workers in the textile industry were employed in the South, where just 15 to 20 percent were organized.[36]

Textile wage rates increased in the South in the postwar period, and southern workers began to catch up with their northern peers. The TWUA-CIO claimed credit for this new prosperity, announcing that "the growth of unionism in the South during recent years" was the most important factor in raising the per capita income of the South. But by 1947, successfully negotiated wage increases in northern mills once again increased the North/South differential, and the TWUA was forced to counter southern employers' justifications for their textile workers' lower earnings and to demand new wage negotiations.[37]

In this period, women workers made up over 50 percent of the industry's workforce in most southern states, and the Operation Dixie campaign focused specifically on union benefits for women workers. A pamphlet prepared by TWUA in 1946 promised "that women get whatever men get" in a union drive and concluded "THAT'S WHY ALMOST HALF OF TWUA'S 400,000 MEMBERS ARE WOMEN." Efforts to attract southern women to the CIO were quite successful. Of the four hundred thousand new union members recruited between 1946 and 1948, at least half were women. But the CIO campaign was arduous. Bitter conflicts between the AFL and the CIO in the South impeded organizing efforts. Employers, aided by local law enforcement officials and the National Guard, often met the drive with armed violence and blacklisting. Furthermore, the work of local organizers, especially women, was often slowed by union administrators who hired women on a temporary basis for one-half to two-thirds of the salary paid to men doing the same work.

In practice, the financial demands that the southern campaign made on northern unionists proved to be Operation Dixie's greatest obstacle. Nevertheless, the CIO felt that organizing southern workers was an inviolate imperative, and in 1948 the convention voted in a three cents per capita increase in dues per month, two cents of which went to support the organization of southern workers. At that time, however, the TWUA-CIO was plagued by a series of internal disputes that, while they had little to do with southern workers, severely hampered the completion of the southern drive. In 1952, the CIO claimed 120,000 textile workers in the South, 90,000 of whom were under contract, but the percentage of organized textile workers in the region had actually declined, from 20 percent in 1945 to 15 percent in 1952.[38]

The End of an Era

Organizing in the South, as elsewhere in the nation, grew increasingly difficult in the 1950s and 1960s, although organized labor's determination to unionize workers in the South never waned. State, federal, and municipal anti-labor legislation, combined with unsuccessful strikes and declining membership, forced unions to abandon massive region-wide campaigns like Operation Dixie and concentrate on more localized efforts to organize workers in specific plants. White southern women, still the overwhelming majority of the female industrial workforce in the South, played important roles in these drives. In the strike in Henderson, North Carolina, in 1958 and in the later campaign against J. P. Stevens in Roanoke Rapids, North Carolina, women campaigned actively for the union, picketed, arranged strike relief, and traveled north to raise money.[39]

TWUA organizers considered the Henderson strike, which lasted from 1958 through 1961 and was the largest strike in the TWUA's twenty-four-year history, crucial to the union's efforts to maintain and extend its southern base. The 1,038 workers at the Harriet-Henderson mills walked out in November 1958 to protest management's insistence that the union amend its arbitration clause to permit the company to veto demands. The Henderson strikers proved to be courageous and strong, and their unified determination closed the plant for three months. In February 1959, the company hired strikebreakers and re-opened the mills. A wave of violence ensued, union leaders were convicted of conspiring to damage company property, and the two-and-a-half-year strike, which cost union members $1.5 million, ended in defeat.[40]

TWUA's rationale for supporting the Henderson strike was the same rationale labor had used regarding organizing the South since the 1920s. In its efforts to raise money for the North Carolina strike among locals in the Northeast, TWUA emphasized that "the struggle the Harriet-Henderson workers are undergoing is our fight too." In 1959, Sol Stetin, the TWUA's regional director for New Jersey, Pennsylvania, and Delaware, argued that the "union-busting campaign" in Henderson was "aimed at the destruction of the very life of our union in the north." Eighteen months into the strike, the president of the New Jersey State CIO Council concurred:

> For us in the North, there is special significance in this strike—indeed in any strike in that area of the country. The Middle Atlantic States are continuing to lose jobs to the South. Not only in the textile industry, but in the electrical, chemical, apparel industries, as well as many others, employers, attracted by low wages and tax "breaks," have shut down plants leaving their workers to fend for themselves. The employer offensive against unions in the south is a prelude to an acceleration of the industrial migration already under way. For if they are able to defeat the union at Henderson, another barrier to the runaway shop will have been removed. It is therefore, in our own interests to continue support for the Henderson workers.[41]

The Henderson defeat heralded the end of an era in southern textile organizing. From the 1920s until 1960, unions based in the North had believed that to save the labor movement they had to organize the South—indeed, that organizing the South was tantamount to organizing textiles. After Henderson, this theory no longer carried the same weight. The bulk of the industry had come south, the small portion of the industry left in the Northeast had reached a new production equilibrium, and the North/ South wage differential became less significant with the diversification of southern industry in the 1950s and 1960s.

After 1960, however, southern workers faced the threat of runaway shops just as generations of northern workers had before them. In 1965, fewer than 8 percent of workers in southern textiles belonged to a union. But that year, with the implementation of the Civil Rights Act passed in 1964, the industry experienced a significant transformation as black southerners were actively recruited for production jobs for the first time. The leadership in southern union organizing efforts came increasingly from black women. Brought up in opposition to white authority and trained in the civil rights movement, in many southern mills black women were the workers most responsive to seeking cooperative solutions to work situations. Previously excluded from production jobs, by the late 1980s black women had moved into over 50 percent of the operative positions in some southern plants. Many black women entered textiles after having worked in domestic service; unlike their fathers and brothers, they came into the mill without previous industrial experience, and often without having worked outside the region. Yet they brought with them a firm commitment to improving their lives by working together, the way their mothers had worked within the church.[42]

The difficult process of uniting black and white southern women within the union was repeated across the region. After 1965, the relationship between black and white women workers in garment factories across the South became a critical factor in whether union elections were won or lost. As the number of black women in southern mills began to increase in the late 1960s and early 1970s, the number of successful union elections also increased. Black women took the lead in contacting unions, getting cards signed, fighting management's legal obstacles, and participating in contract negotiations. A majority of black women workers within a plant could usually convince younger white women to join them in supporting the union, and with this interracial coalition, an election could be won.[43]

Both management and the unions were fully cognizant of the correlation between a high percentage of black workers in a plant and the viability of the union there. After black women were hired at the Oneita Knitting Mills in Andrews, South Carolina, in 1964, the configuration of the workforce changed, and so did the union's chance for success. In 1971,

75 percent of the workers were black and 85 percent were women, and the union easily won an election for bargaining rights. As their actions opened a new chapter in the history of black workers in the textile industry, these women became part of the story of black workers in southern mills that stretches back to the photographs W. E. B. Du Bois had assembled for the Exhibition of American Negroes in which African American mill owners and machine operators proudly posed for the camera.[44]

In the South, a region where anti-union resistance has often succeeded, the story of labor activism, of strikes and walkouts, protests and boycotts, has always been a powerful counter-narrative that speaks to the militancy and power of southern workers. There is a long history of workers across the South taking action in the workplace, in individual confrontations on the shop floor, or in collective actions that involved every worker in a factory or mill. As more women entered industrial work in the early decades of the twentieth century, they advanced gender equality as a way to resolve problems of occupational segregation and discriminatory wage rates; as African American workers gained access to the region's increasing number of industrial jobs, especially after World War II, they also fought to be treated with respect and to receive fair compensation for their work. Organized labor did not always share these concerns, in large part because northern-based unions sought to organize southern workers primarily to protect northern wage scales and prevent the spread of runaway shops. They knew that the survival of the U.S. labor movement depended on establishing strong unions in the American South. To this end, unions, from the Knights of Labor to the CIO to the SEIU, looked south to bring new workers to trade unionism. Support from liberal allies and the political Left affected the trajectory of labor organizing in the region as organizers worked to balance union goals and local concerns. Theory and practice often diverged in the southern field when strategies and tactics forged on the ground in communities across the region had to shift and change in response to the intransigence of southern manufacturers and the necessity of organizing hundreds of thousands of workers, skilled and unskilled, who were new to industrial life. The increasing participation of women, in the workforce and the labor movement, also changed the calculus of labor organizing and brought new organizers and new issues to the top of labor's agenda. Over the decades from Reconstruction to the end of the twentieth century, cheap southern labor threatened the future of the American labor movement. Textile unions, like those in every major U.S. industry, reacted to the fear of losing jobs to a nonunionized southern workforce with intense efforts to bring southern workers into the union fold. In the process, they were forced to work on every front to protect the jobs and wage rates of American workers, North and South, without regard to gender, race, or region.

6
· · · · · · · · ·
"Living in Two Worlds"
Civil Rights and Southern Textiles

The movement of black workers into textile mills across the South transformed the industry and the relationships between black and white workers in ways that paralleled the efforts of black activists like W. E. B. Du Bois to shape the national reform agenda. Black men worked to improve conditions in the mills just as they and their families had worked to build schools and churches in communities across the region. Black and white southerners lived, worked, and worshipped in separate spheres before, during, and after the southern textile workforce became integrated. Nevertheless, significant transformations did take place. As John Foster, an African-American textile employee from Alabama who came up through the ranks over the four decades between 1940 and 1980, put it, "I consider myself as living in two worlds, the one I remember and the one that I'm involved in now."[1]

Despite the overt exclusion of black workers from most southern textile manufacturing jobs between 1880 and 1965, the ongoing threat of extralegal violence, and the oppression of black men and women in the segregated South, a closer look shows that black workers had continued to make slow but steady gains in industrial employment, especially during World War II and in the years leading up to 1965. Hard-won positions within the region's industrial workforce made possible the growing solidarity and collective political action of black textile workers in local southern communities. Their involvement in early civil rights activism and in grassroots work for social, political, and economic change laid the groundwork for the increasingly powerful roles they would play in efforts to organize the textile industry after 1970.

Between 1940 and 1980, workers in the southern textile industry experienced rapidly changing patterns of employment, and the slow but steady movement of black employees into mills across the South gradually transformed the workplace and relationships between black and white workers. Before 1940, African Americans made up less than one-tenth of the southern textile workforce, and of those, 80 percent toiled as "mill laborers" in non-production jobs. By 1978, the composition of the workforce had changed significantly: one in five textile workers was African American, and black workers held one-fourth of all operative positions. In the 1980s and 1990s, African American workers represented the largest group of recently recruited workers within the industry, and in many southern mills they constituted the majority of the workforce.[2]

Traditional discriminatory patterns of employment in the South eroded rapidly during World War II. Black workers who previously had been relegated to jobs in agriculture or domestic service found new positions opening up as thousands of white male recruits left southern mills to join the military and white women moved from textiles to work in better-paying munitions factories. As the wartime labor shortage grew more severe, manufacturers turned to African American workers, men and women, to fill the region's growing need for industrial labor. After the war, many black workers lost those positions to returning white veterans. But by the early 1950s, the growth and diversification of southern industry resulted in a renewed need for African American workers, many of whom found jobs as steelworkers, rubber workers, or autoworkers. These changes, combined with the impetus of federal civil rights legislation in the 1960s and pressure from locally organized civil rights groups, resulted in the acceptance of black workers in a broader range of job classifications within the textile industry that for so long had been perceived as reserved for white workers.

Prior to these changes, black workers throughout the South had faced severely restricted employment options. Manufacturers ostensibly reserved jobs within textiles, the South's most rapidly growing industry, for white workers. This hiring principle, a cornerstone of the segregated New South, became a regional imprimatur, a way of southern life encoded in law by the *Plessy* decision. A closer look, however, reveals a different story. First, the statistics that indicate that only a small percentage of blacks worked in the South's most important industry do not include the thousands of African American workers who were hired as "mill laborers," a title that masked the true nature of work that ranged from the least to the most skilled of any performed in the mills. Second, black workers composed a reserve labor pool that management could and did tap whenever necessary. Third, although black workers were only occasionally used as strikebreakers, their mere proximity to southern mill communities functioned as a threat to white job security and served to keep the demands of white operators to a minimum. Southern mill owners continually considered hiring greater numbers of black workers and did so whenever a shortage of white labor appeared imminent. For example, during both World War I and World War II, the percentage of black workers in the mills increased. Not until the 1960s, however, did the shortage of white workers grow severe enough that black workers were hired in dramatically significant numbers. After 1965, black men and women were finally actively recruited for production jobs in textiles.

The History of Black Participation in Southern Textiles

The long history of black participation in the southern textile industry reaches back before the Civil War, when slave labor was used in the home to spin and weave cloth. According to historian Eugene Genovese, slave women on southern plantations often returned from a day of hard fieldwork to "spin, weave, and sew well into the night." In the Southeast, the transition from home to factory production was made by bondswomen and bondsmen who were either owned by industrial entrepreneurs or hired out by their owners to work in the small antebellum mills that dotted the streams and rivers of the Piedmont. Prior to 1860, no one questioned the ability of black workers to handle industrial work. To the contrary, industrialists praised the virtues of black labor over white, and slave labor over free.[3]

After the Civil War, southern workers faced a reorganization of the region's occupational structure and a redefinition of the occupational status of the black worker. In plantation areas, the transition from slavery to share tenancy resulted in black workers' attaining virtually the same economic rank as non-landowner whites. In cities and small industrial towns, however, changes in the occupational alignment of black and white workers resulted in the loss of skilled and semiskilled positions for blacks. In urban mill communities and industrial villages, this meant that black workers who had been textile operatives before 1865 began to be replaced by white workers. The number of mills in the South increased by two and a half times between 1880 and 1900, and as new mills were built, jobs as spinners and weavers went to white workers, predominantly women and children who left small farms to work in textiles. In this way, the workforce of mill operators, which had been largely black before the Civil War, became predominantly white by the turn of the century.[4]

By 1900, the proportion of black workers in textiles had declined to less than 2 percent of the total labor force. In response to the white backlash following Reconstruction, industrialists in effect granted white southerners limited protection from direct competition with black workers for positions as operatives. Within the mills, moreover, more rigid racial divisions were established, reflecting twentieth-century patterns of racial segregation throughout the South. As part of the growing segregation of the years following *Plessy v. Ferguson* (1896), an ideology developed regarding blacks and industrial work in general that simultaneously reflected and reinforced the occupational segregation of black workers that had already taken place in textiles. As Herbert Lahne wrote in 1944, "There appeared to be no limit to the supposed justifications of the exclusion of the Negro from the work of operatives—Negroes were said to be temperamentally, morally, physically, etc., etc., unfit to be anything but laborers. All these reasons were, of course, beside the point."[5]

By 1915, most southern industries had instituted segregated labor systems. In South Carolina, an extreme example of such segregation was evident in the textile industry when a new occupational code that virtually excluded black workers from operative positions was written into law. Passed by the state's General Assembly in 1915 and not rescinded until 1960, this legislation called for separate weave and spinning rooms for black and white employees and effectively banned black workers from the primary work areas of the mills. The act read in part, "Be it enacted by the General Assembly of the State of South Carolina, that it shall be unlawful for any person, firm or corporation engaged in the business of cotton textile manufacturing in this State to allow or permit operatives, help and labor of different races to labor and work together within the same room." The act's second clause, however, excluded it from being applied to "firemen as subordinates in boiler rooms, truckmen, or to floor scrubbers and those persons employed in keeping in proper condition lavatories and toilets, and carpenters, mechanics and others engaged in the repair or erection of buildings."[6] The evidence suggests that mill owners violated this law whenever convenient or necessary, although its second clause left considerable leeway for hiring black employees in a variety of positions. Textile entrepreneurs across the South clearly wanted the flexibility to hire whomever they pleased, but as concessions to white southerners, they gave white employees priority, hired black workers only as needed, segregated the workforce within the mill, and used the title "mill laborer" as the job category for most black employees, no matter which tasks they actually performed.

Mill Laborers and Industrial Observers

It was as "mill laborers" that black workers in southern textile mills carried out tasks that ranged from cleaning floors to installing electrical wiring, repairing looms, and constructing mill buildings and mill housing. In the years after they were segregated out of operative positions, thousands of black workers continued to perform essential functions within mills. The work of black men and women included, for instance, the most arduous tasks of lifting and loading bales of raw cotton and rolls of finished goods, as well as assignments in the opening and carding rooms, the sections of the mill with the highest concentrations of cotton dust. In addition to performing the most disagreeable jobs, black workers made the lowest wages in the textile industry, a result both of being restricted to the lower-paying textile jobs and of wage discrimination on the basis of race. Gender provided a third discriminatory factor, for white men made more than white women and black men earned more than black women. Race was the predominant wage determinant, however, for black men were paid less than white women. For example, in Georgia in 1938, black men made 65 percent of the wages paid to white men; black women earned only 56 percent of the wages paid to white women; and black men were paid 78 percent of the wages paid to white women.[7]

Clearly, black workers received lower wages than their white counterparts no matter what type of work they performed. Over time, however, these significant wage differentials have obscured the fact that the 80 percent of black workers categorized as mill laborers actually held a wide range of jobs within the mills. As early as 1900, an Atlanta cotton manufacturer testified before the United States Industrial Commission that he never attempted to work black and white labor together "except when the white help goes out to get a can of snuff the colored sweepers run the loom."[8] A 1922 study of 2,750 women (840 of whom were black) in ten textile firms found that black women worked in all of the twelve occupations in which white women were employed, although the black women also worked at cleaning and feeding, two jobs not performed by the white women.[9] The list of jobs held by my sample of 115 black employees who had worked in textiles in LaGrange, Georgia, for at least twenty-five consecutive years (within 1925–1969) comprised thirty-eight job classifications, including master plumber, skilled carpenter, card stripper, card tender, picker tender, mechanic, machine fixer, and landscaper, in addition to the work performed by a woman who stenciled flower designs and a man who retired as a loom fixer in 1969.[10] A 1951 survey of seventy textile mills in Virginia, North Carolina, and South Carolina reported that black workers were employed as painters, plumbers, carpenters, and electricians as well as truck drivers, sweepers, and janitors. In the late 1960s, Richard Rowan reported in his study of black workers in southern textiles that although the job description nomenclature for black textile workers had not changed since the early 1900s, "close scrutiny of the jobs in the laborer category would probably result in some of them being reclassified as semiskilled. . . ."[11]

In other words, black workers held positions in southern textile mills that required greater skill than southern industrial lore has recorded. Moreover, mechanics, teamsters, painters, carpenters, and sweepers had considerable mobility within the mill. Unlike white operatives who could not leave their spindles or looms, black workers had the freedom to move from one section of the mill to another. As roving workers, black employees observed industrial work and learned about the overall operation of the mill. Black workers laboring as mechanics and loom cleaners became familiar with industrial machinery; as carpenters, electricians, and painters, they worked as craftsmen within an industrial setting. Black workers employed in textiles prior to 1965 became what I call "industrial observers," knowledgeable about the organization of the industry and the hierarchy of the workforce and accustomed to the pace and environmental conditions of industrial work. Hired in significant numbers in many mills, these workers formed a substantial cohort of minority textile employees, forerunners of the thousands of black workers who moved into operative positions after 1965.

The work histories of two of the Georgia textile workers I interviewed illustrate the role of the industrial observer in more concrete terms.[12] Both

Julian West and Minnie Brown grew up in West Point, Georgia, where their fathers worked in the mill. When West turned eighteen in 1932, he entered the mill as a full-time worker. Brown took a mill job in 1942, when she was twenty-eight years old, after having worked for over a decade as a domestic worker. When West and Brown retired after 1975, their work lives had spanned four decades of change for black workers in the industry. Their careful descriptions of their work delineate the parameters of their industrial experience and demonstrate the subtle distinctions that must be made when correlating job descriptions with job classifications.

Julian West's family moved to West Point in 1920 when he was six years old, after his father got a job as a sweeper in the mill. As teenagers, Julian and his two brothers went down to the mill with their father to help out in the cloth room for a few hours a day, and by the time West was eighteen, he had a full-time job at the mill cleaning and "chucking cloth." He left the mill in 1943, went to Michigan for several months, and upon his return asked for a job in the carding department. Hired immediately, West stayed in the carding department until he retired in 1978, and it was in the card room that he became an industrial observer. Familiar with the mill since he was a child and already knowledgeable about the cloth room where he had worked with his father and two brothers, West entered the card room as a sweeper in 1943. Promoted to lap racker in 1948, West became a card tender in 1965. But as he explained, he had known how to tend cards long before he got promoted to a card tender's position:

> Well, you see, when I was a lap racker I'd put up a bolt of cotton on this card machine. Well, maybe now the end of that card has stopped. I mean the cotton has broke out and the card has stopped or either kept running and run over. Well, I would go over there. Now the card tender, he'd possibly be way down the line somewhere, and he got a card up here that's overrunning. Well, I would stop and pick that cotton up and put it back in there and start it back to running, although that wasn't my job. But I'd do it, see, and that's the way it'd run.

For seasoned industrial observers like West, the transition to a production job did not involve additional training. By allowing West to "learn cards" and help the white card tender, management had ensured his training, and when the time came that West was needed as a card tender, he was well prepared:

They wouldn't bother you, you see was alright if the racker would help the card tender keep his job up. I had to be around the machine anyway because I had to service the machine. What I meant by that is that I had to keep enough cotton up here for the card tender to run. I couldn't let the cotton go out of the machine. And at the same time, when I got through supplying the machine, putting enough cotton on the machine, then, see, I had to sweep around it and keep the floor clean and all that kind of thing. So every chance I got to get up an end, as we call it, and start that machine back running, well then it was a help to that card tender, and finally, a long time before they gave me a job running them, I'd learned how to do it. One day the boss came out there and he asked me, "Julian, you reckon you could run a set of those cards?" I told him, "Yes, sir." And the next morning he gave me a job on them.

Unlike Julian West, who changed positions three or four times during his work life in the mill, Minnie Brown worked for thirty-four years in the same job. Hired in 1942 as a "cleaner," she retired in 1976 in the same position. As a child, Brown remembered "going to the mill carrying my daddy's dinner," and when, years later, one of the few jobs available to black women opened up, she was eager to earn the money paid in the mill, wages much higher than those she could make as a domestic worker. Brown's job as a cleaner took her "all through the mill from one end to the other." But Brown did not just clean. Through her "white friends" in the weave shed and spinning room, she learned how to weave, decided against spinning ("I'd seen how it was done all right, but I didn't fool with it"), and settled on work filling batteries:

> I'd be caught up with my job, you know, and I'd go down there and they'd let me fill batteries. Just every night I'd go on back down there to the weave shed. I'd get down there and they'd say, "Start up there." And I'd throw that spool in and whip it around there and like that. And I began to like it. They had so many to do. I didn't charge nothing 'cause I was just learning. They'd say, "When you get ready, just come on down here" and I'd say, "All right."

The testimony of workers like West and Brown confirms the existence of an informal work structure within the mills that differed from the formal job and wage classifications used by management. While they were classified as holding "non-production" jobs, both West and Brown performed tasks that directly affected production. Moreover, although they worked within "segregated" mills, West and Brown labored side by side with the white workers who trained them. White employees expressed appreciation for the help they received and, according to West, would reciprocate with cash payment or favors. Thus, everyone benefitted in some way from the operation of this informal system. White production workers received much-needed assistance, black workers got industrial training and some extra pay, and management gained from increased production without additional wage costs. In the long run, the industry benefited most from the existence of a well-trained reserve workforce of black men and women eager to move permanently into higher-paying jobs as production workers.

Farm to Factory Migration among Black Textile Workers

The historical and political significance of this group of industrial observers is two-fold. First, although the black textile workers hired in non-operative positions in the decades between 1900 and 1940 had, like their white counterparts, come from agricultural backgrounds to take jobs within the mills, the general movement of black workers into industrial work in textiles was in fact a three-step process that spanned three generations of employees: the initial migration of black workers from farms to southern urban and industrial communities where they worked non-production mill jobs like sweeper and cleaner; the movement of their children into higher-level jobs such as picker tender and lap racker; and finally, in the mid-1960s, the large-scale movement of the next generation of black southerners into operative positions. Second, within the context of local southern communities, these individuals formed a small but important group of workers whose ability to earn regular cash wages augmented their standing within the black community and their power within the white community. For example, among my sample of 115 long-term black workers in the LaGrange mills, at least 40 percent owned their homes and many had credit at local furniture and clothing stores. It was the norm for the children of these workers to finish high school, and many sons and daughters of this black community graduated from college. Active in church work, a majority of the workers in my sample served as officers, deacons, or lay preachers within local black congregations.

The experience of LaGrange's black textile workers was not unique. In West Point, Georgia, the "relatively progressive community" in which Julian West grew up and then raised his own children, the prevailing philosophy of life was "if you work hard, you can make it." Black families coming into town from nearby farms sought to buy a plot of land, build a house, and send their children to school. Parents worked hard to keep their children out of the mills. Mattie Ivey, whose grandfather had been a slave and whose father worked on the railroad, worked the 6 p.m. to 2 a.m. shift as a cleaner in an Alabama mill and held two additional domestic cleaning jobs to put her four children through college. She stated emphatically when interviewed in 1982 that she and her husband, a mill elevator operator, "survived and succeeded through hard labor." They labored in the mill for over thirty years, "did not drink, smoke or party," and used what little money they had so their sons and daughters could "follow what they learned." African American children who grew up in southern black communities adjacent to textile mills were taught to work hard and maintain their allegiance to church and school.[13]

Firmly grounded in well-established black communities, the backgrounds of many southern black workers who entered the mills in the 1960s and 1970s were substantially different from those of the white operatives who had migrated from farm to factory between 1900 and 1940. Numerous black workers who became textile operatives after 1965 did not come from the agricultural sector. Rather, their families were already a part of a southern urban/industrial workforce, and they were second- or third-generation city dwellers and often second-generation mill workers. But unlike white southern textile workers, black workers had experienced little mobility within the mills and had made their homes in racially segregated areas, shut off from equal access to full political, economic, or social participation within in the larger community of textile workers. The combination of these two factors—being familiar with industrial work and skills and being denied equal participation—made southern black textile workers more predisposed to collective action and union organizing than the white workers who had preceded them into the mills.

For example, when Jim Thomas's grandson became a textile operative in the mid-1960s, his knowledge of industrial work was based in part on his grandfather's experience in the card, picker, and opener rooms of the Unity Spinning plant in LaGrange from 1929 to 1954. His familiarity with factory-town living came from his father, who held a position in the Elm

City weave room in the 1950s, and from his own childhood spent in La-Grange. Father and son had witnessed and supported efforts by AFL and CIO unions to organize the mills near LaGrange. For Julian West, who grew up in the black community in West Point, Georgia, and whose father had retired from the mill, a job in textiles meant continuing his father's fight for civil rights within the workplace. Inside the mill, working for equality meant fighting for the union, and West's allegiance was second nature. In the plant West worked for the union, and at home he fought to send his children to college rather than into the mill.[14]

Both Jim Thomas's grandson and Julian West worked in tandem with previous generations of black textile workers. The sons of men who believed that "if you were going to survive in this society, you had to be able to hold a job" struggled to provide their children with the employment opportunities they had been denied. Taught by their fathers to "go ahead but be careful," black workers in the period between 1940 and 1980 used their positions within the community and the plant to fight for the right to fill jobs they could already perform, to have access to better jobs, and to earn wages equal to those of white employees.

Rural Industrialization

A somewhat different version of the multi-step migration pattern by black workers who became textile operatives took place in eastern North Carolina and in low-country South Carolina, where mills were built and still operate in small rural communities. In these areas, the children of black sharecroppers quit farming and entered the mills in a way that initially appeared to duplicate the farm-to-factory migration of white workers in the years between 1900 and 1940. But the lives of black workers entering the mills in the 1960s and 1970s were influenced as much or more by their experience of the land as by the fact that their parents were sharecroppers. For example, when James Boone, a black North Carolinian in his early twenties, took a job as a doffer in 1971, he had already worked for several months in textiles elsewhere and as a store clerk in Washington, D.C. Boone had grown up in the country outside Roanoke Rapids, but he had come into town to attend high school and, unlike the white children of tenant farmers who had migrated to textile communities in the 1920s, was familiar with the local J. P. Stevens plants. His father had worked for many years in a paper mill and was a proud member of the International

Woodworkers Union of America. When union organizers came to the textile plant where Boone was working in 1974, he was "raring to go," saying, "blacks and some whites, too, are gonna make some changes here."[15]

In more rural areas, many workers continued to live with family members who farmed, depending on the land when work was irregular in the mills and vice versa. One advantage of this dual farm/factory work life for families was that as black workers organized in the mills, they had resources and options rarely available to earlier generations of white workers who lived in company-owned housing. For example, in a study of mill workers in a rural North Carolina community, Dale Newman reported that two black workers involved in collective action to improve working conditions in the plant expressed "sensitivity to the possibility their actions might result in losing their jobs but as they were both landowners, they and their wives were willing to take the chance."[16]

Changing Patterns of Employment

Black workers' presence in the textile industry changed dramatically between the 1940s and the 1980s. Between 1940 and 1978, the number of black textile employees increased six-fold, from 24,764 in 1940 to 152,458 in 1978. The greatest increase in black employment occurred between 1966 and 1968, when the proportion of black workers in the textile mills in North Carolina, South Carolina, and Georgia rose from 10 to 15 percent. In South Carolina and Georgia, the southern textile-producing states with the largest black populations, the percentage of black workers within the industry traditionally had been higher than the regional average. In 1920, for example, black workers constituted 10 percent of South Carolina's textile workforce at a time that the industry average was 2.6 percent. The representation of black workers was consistently highest in Georgia, where between 1966 and 1968, the percentage of black employees increased from 14 to 18 percent, with black men constituting 22.5 percent of all male textile employees in the state in 1968. The gains black workers made in the textile industry in the 1960s were consolidated in the 1970s. By 1978, in Georgia black workers held 28 percent of all available jobs within the industry there, and 58 percent of all black employees worked as operatives. That year, in Georgia and the Carolinas combined, black workers held 26 percent of all textile positions and 31 percent of all operative jobs in these states.[17]

The pivotal point at which textile employment in the South opened up to black workers came in the mid-1960s, a period that black workers refer to as "the change" and that Richard Rowan describes as "a virtual revolution in employment in the southern textile plants." The groundwork for this transformation, however, had been laid in the 1940s and 1950s. In the 1940s, with the growth of wartime industries and the subsequent diversification of local manufacturing in the South, textile firms began losing white employees. One Macon, Georgia, textile manufacturer lamented these changes, particularly in terms of the shifting racial demographics of the workforce. In an interview in the early 1980s, he looked back to the period after World War II, remarking that from that point on, "things started getting kind of rough. A lot of other industries came to this area, and your skilled people, such as loom fixers, were the first ones they would hire away from you." His reference to "getting kind of rough" was a euphemism for the changing racial demographics of the workforce, as white employees left textiles for better jobs in other industries and black workers were hired to fill this gap. In my sample of 115 long-term African American textile workers in LaGrange, fifty-five, or 48 percent, began work in the mills between 1940 and 1944, during and after the mobilization of World War II. Nevertheless, few black southerners who entered the mill during this period were classified as operatives. Instead, manufacturers moved black textile workers who were already employed in the mill into new positions as "picker tenders," "opener tenders," or "lap rackers." After the war, when white workers returned from military service, the black workers were demoted back to "mill laborers."[18]

In addition to the diversification of southern manufacturing, the post–World War II period brought significant changes to the black communities in southern towns and cities. Black veterans returning from the military saw their hometowns and local industries in a different light after traveling to other places in the United States and overseas. As described by John Foster, an African American man employed in textiles from 1949 to his interview in 1982, "It wasn't a whole lot better after we came back from the military, but we had been exposed to things a little different, and not so much of trying to change the system as to get the opportunity to participate a little bit more from the standpoint of things like voting, and registering to vote. They gave veterans the opportunity to do those things. A lot of us were determined to fight the system to see if we could do it." Fighting the system in the late 1940s meant battling for equal political participation. Gaining the right to vote was the first step, as Foster explained:

> We felt that as long as we didn't try to participate in the political side of this society, there was not a whole lot we could do. The guys who came back from World War II, we started opening up these little voter leagues you hear them talking about. We felt that if we could get involved in voter registration, then we could get others involved. The only thing you had to do was to get enough black people together to make a politician realize that they could make a difference.[19]

Gradually, with constant pressure from black veterans and others, rigid segregation within southern political, economic, and social systems began to give way. Within the textile industry, changes also came slowly at first. By 1954, John Foster, still actively working to register his people to vote, played baseball for the mill on an integrated team. After 1958, turnover among white male textile workers increased rapidly as they found higher-paying jobs in other industries. At the same time, southern white women, the workers on whom the textile industry had grown dependent for many jobs, were also leaving the mills, particularly for jobs in the clerical sector. Meanwhile, local black leaders in southern textile communities were biding their time. Floyd Harris, a black man who had risen to a management position in the industry, recalled, "I was active in the social revolution that went on from the fifties through the sixties and early seventies, so I was aware of what the black leaders were talking about. We wrote the laws and they passed the Civil Rights bill, and I knew that if the federal government made it a law, it'd have to be followed. Our management here is smart, and they knew it, too. Besides, that was the only way we could survive."

By 1964, when the Civil Rights Act passed, black workers and management both began to make cautious moves to change the system. Black workers already employed in textiles, many of them World War II veterans, wanted to "integrate things ourselves so there wouldn't be trouble." As Floyd Harris remembered, "Management would screen workers real carefully at central employment. You had to know somebody to get on. They would put a black here and a black there and this sort of thing." Thus, when "the change" took place, it was both carefully planned and swiftly implemented, as Harris described:

We didn't have such a difficult time inasmuch as the president of the company, when the bill was passed, had employment meetings, group meetings, and everyone was told in no uncertain terms that discrimination would not be practiced in this plant. Anybody caught doing this, of course, would be separated. Segregation was eliminated, and everybody had the right to the job they were capable of doing. Management, top management, made it clear that there wasn't going to be any trouble, so the transition wasn't bad because it came from the top.[20]

The relative willingness with which southern textile employers, a group generally intransigent in the face of federal mandates, responded to the regulations of the Equal Employment Opportunity Commission (EEOC) and the Office of Federal Contract Compliance reflected the industry's need for new workers and its growing reliance on black labor. Although a number of supervisors had to be replaced, by 1969 the initial transition had ended and management in most southern textile communities looked to hire black workers, in some areas quite literally to keep the mills running. In 1970, with unemployment low throughout the Southeast, Floyd Harris was promoted to a position recruiting black workers for the industry. Having a difficult time getting people to apply for the available jobs, Harris finally set up recruiting stations in country stores within a fifty-mile radius of the mills to try to attract local black men and women to work in the industry.

Double-Consciousness

In 1903, W. E. B. Du Bois described the experience of black Americans as one of "double-consciousness," the sense of seeing one's self through the eyes of others in a world in which they were both "American" and "Negro." This meant, in Du Bois's words, that "two souls, two thoughts, two unreconciled strivings" permeated the consciousness of every African American as the country in which they lived moved ever so slowly toward recognizing universal civil rights. This sense of "two-ness" increased for black men and women living in southern textile communities as they witnessed innumerable changes, both obvious and subtle, in the years following the transitions of the 1960s.[21] An exploration of the evolving relationships between black and white southern workers within the mills and within the larger community reveals that integration initiated within the workplace also began the process of transforming textile-dominated towns and cities with long traditions of racial segregation. Most agree that once the mills integrated, the effects spilled over into the larger community. As Julian West remembered, "The better it got down there at the mill, the better it got out here in the black community." Just about everybody other than merchants worked in the cotton mills, he noted, and "where it began to get better was on the job. Integration in the mills forced many white employees to recognize and come to terms with the abilities of black workers." As John Foster put it, "Any close contact between individuals in any specific area made it possible for people to do a better job of evaluating abilities. The people in the mills had an opportunity to compare white skills against black skills, and they found out that blacks did have skills, did have intelligence."

Foster and others agreed that one of the main things that black workers had to overcome was "the idea that Negroes were not intelligent enough to work with modern technology." Foster felt that "in each of the areas where Negroes had a chance to come together and work side by side with whites, they were able to more and more disprove some of those theories. Eventually it just got to the point where they accepted the fact that there were blacks who could do this work and blacks who could not, just like in any other ethnic group."[22]

Racial integration within the mills made white workers more aware of the skills and abilities of black workers than they had been when the range of jobs performed by many black workers remained hidden under the generic classification of "laborer." But despite white workers' reconciling black workers' evident abilities with their own longstanding presumptions about African American incompetence, few employees, black or white, forgot the past completely. For example, Floyd Harris, a mill porter until 1965, had delivered the mail to a plant where the receptionist, a white woman who sat in the front office, always called him "boy." Harris, then a man in his mid-thirties, had repeatedly tried to get the woman to address him by his first name. In 1970, Harris, newly elected as one of the two black members of the local city council, became assistant personnel manager in the mill where this receptionist still worked. No words were exchanged as the two adjusted to a new hierarchy that placed Harris in a supervisory role, but as Harris recalled, "I hadn't forgotten, and I'm certain she hadn't either."[23]

Nevertheless, as Julian West emphasized, once black workers could not be denied jobs in the production areas of the mills, "the atmosphere changed": "They changed and I changed. We got closer together in every way." The opening of production jobs to black workers in southern mills affected the ways in which black and white employees interacted in the workplace, and the higher wages earned by black workers new to operative positions brought material improvements to homes and businesses within the black community. Integration of the schools in most southern towns and cities followed closely behind integration of the workplace. But as Floyd Harris admitted, despite integration in the workplace and the schools, the mill community he lived in "remains segregated, like it was." John Foster agreed that "segregation is still a part of this society . . . you still have the same basic feeling being a minority, and you know that in everything you do, you will succeed or fail through how you respond to the majority."[24]

By the 1980s, the tangible differences between the totally segregated society of the past and the partially integrated communities of the South included that black children no longer had to leave the region to become successful, that a decent education in an integrated public school was attainable for both black and white students, and that black workers were not denied industrial jobs on the basis of their race. John Foster agreed that "there is a marked difference now, and people who couldn't get away from here fast enough are coming back comfortably."

Foster grew up in Alabama in the 1930s, served in a segregated unit in World War II, headed the mill-run recreation program for black workers while fighting for civil rights on the grass-roots level in the 1950s and 1960s, and by 1980 had become an employment manager for a major southern textile company. Reflecting on the changes he had experienced, Foster described his past and his present situation as two different worlds: "Now the younger black doesn't have the hesitancies that I have in a lot of situations because of the changes in the local area and in the southern region since he's been growing up. I find myself cautioning him about my experiences and about his relationship to the white majority."[25]

Black workers like Foster and Harris, among the few African Americans promoted to white-collar jobs in textiles, described themselves in these conversations as blacks first and textile managers second. Their allegiance was to their people, and in their capacity as employee counselors and grievance arbitrators, they argued that they could play the role of the union in their company's unorganized plants. But when interviewed in the early 1980s, these men were uncertain of what would happen next. Concerned that black workers had not moved into management jobs as rapidly as they had into operative positions, they noted that the affirmative action program that had "helped us get into these areas" was already under fire at both the federal and local levels.[26]

Textile Unions

Beginning in the days of the CIO, textile workers in the South came to symbolize both the hope of equality and the promise of justice under the law. In the 1950s and 1960s, black men like Julian West found themselves fighting for the union in battles that went on continuously, year after year. In West's plant in southwest Georgia, votes for and against the union consistently divided along racial lines:

> I was for it. If we could have got it in there, everybody felt like they would have bettered themselves. Where we didn't have a union and didn't succeed in getting it, well then, we just had to put up with what we did have. White voted it down. It meant equal rights. The white voted it down to keep me down. If the white had voted the way the black voted, then the union would have gotten in, would have taken over control. Then that would have made me get just as much as they get. They just didn't want it; it was a matter of keeping it segregated.[27]

West viewed the refusal of white workers to vote for a union as a political act executed to maintain the status quo both within the plant and within the community.

Just as the textile industry came to rely on black workers to run the mills, so too the unions organizing in southern textiles depended on them to organize workers, win elections, and fight decertifications. The effects of black participation on efforts to organize in textiles were evident in union elections across the South. For example, the favorable vote for the union at the Roanoke Rapids Stevens' plants in 1974 was ascribed to the fact that 70 percent of the voters were black. Although neither the

Amalgamated Clothing and Textile Workers Union (ACTWU) nor the International Ladies Garment Workers Union (ILGWU) recorded the race of their members in the South, unofficial tallies indicated a black majority. Union organizers like Bruce Raynor of the ACTWU began to argue that the unionization of textiles depended on black workers looking for the "promise of the civil rights movement." During the 1970s and 1980s, African American leaders coming to the fore in textile unions had grown up in southern urban/industrial areas, had learned their organizing skills in the civil rights movement, and had lived outside the region in New York, Chicago, or Detroit before returning south. These activists, together with local union leaders from both urban and rural backgrounds, formed a strong new core of southern unionists ready to organize the textile industry.[28]

This new cohort of southern textile union leaders faced many of the same problems that had always plagued those trying to unionize southern workers. Most importantly, the long-held anti-union stance of southern industrialists remained unshaken. Local southern Chambers of Commerce tried to entice northern industry south with promises of low taxes, inexpensive energy sources, and cheap, nonunion labor that duplicated almost word for word those issued in the 1920s. The companies that came south and those long entrenched in the region were literally invested in the belief and hope that workers of the South would remain unorganized. Among the most successful at fighting unions were the large textile chains, J. P. Stevens, Burlington Industries, and Cone Mills. In the 1970s and 1980s, these companies expanded their operations, especially following the elimination of the 1968 ban on mergers within the textile industry. For workers, this meant that union drives became more difficult as an increasing percentage of employees worked for major firms that could easily close plants or shift production schedules to fight organizing efforts within a local community.[29]

Although there were many similarities between the difficulties faced by union organizers in the southern textile industry in the 1980s and those that frustrated union drives among primarily white workers in the period before World War II, there were also many differences. Most significantly, by the 1980s, the paternalistic vise within which southern mill owners kept their workers had been loosened. The mill villages had been sold or torn down, and the majority of workers lived miles away from the mill in which they worked. Few, if any, young black workers had experienced life in a company town, and their willingness to respond collectively to their work situation underscored the different heritage they brought into the mill. Many black workers in southern textiles came from backgrounds, both urban and rural, in which racially cohesive institutions—churches, agricultural and educational improvement associations—had provided the means for collective action to solve common problems black communities faced. They brought values and attitudes shaped by generations of working together with them into the mill.[30]

After black workers entered the mills in unprecedented numbers in the mid-1960s, their initial response to unionization was so overwhelmingly positive that the unions tended to take that firm commitment for granted. As one organizer explained, "Back in the late 1960s, whenever you went into one plant the first thing you looked to was how many blacks are there working in here. And if there were forty blacks you could count on forty votes."[31] But after a decade, things began to change. Managers worked hard to break the racial solidarity of black employees by promoting black leaders and hiring some workers to spy against others. Southern black workers continued to respond collectively, but decades spent within the mill with individual production demands, pressure on individuals from foremen and supervisors, and rigid time schedules that curtailed communication among workers made it difficult to sustain the cooperative values with which most black employees entered the industry. For example, in a Macon, Georgia, organizing drive in 1979–1980, black workers voted solidly for the union, and they remained united until management withheld wage increases for two years and some of the black workers finally broke rank and participated in a successful decertification election. A year later, one of the black women leaders of the union campaign emphasized the necessity of continued efforts "to make our people understand" the ramifications of the tactics used by management.[32]

In many southern mills, the workers most responsive to solving work situations cooperatively were black women. Long excluded from production jobs, by the late 1980s black women held more than half of the operative positions in plants in the Carolinas, Georgia, and Alabama. Many black women entered textiles after having worked in domestic service; unlike their fathers and brothers, they came into the mill without previous industrial experience, and usually without having worked outside the region. For them, the transition from domestic work to factory work was most analogous to the farm-to-factory transition experienced by workers who entered the mills between 1900 and 1940. As a Roanoke Rapids woman who went to work for Stevens in 1971 recounted, "To tell you the truth, when I first went in there, I thought I had stepped into hell. I thought I knew what hard work was, but until I went in there, I didn't."[33]

Black women who began work in southern textile mills after 1965 often came from southern rural/industrial areas, where families both retained their ties to the land and worked in the mill. This rural pattern of industrialization, so common in the South, involved a complicated set of interactions between those family members who farmed and those who worked in the mill. In these families, black women were most often the steady textile employees: those who went to work in the mill at eighteen and stayed (with the exception of maternity leaves) throughout their childbearing years and beyond. Their fathers, brothers, or husbands were often seasonal textile workers who farmed, did pulpwood work, and labored in the mill in the winter when bad weather prohibited outdoor work. Women could get regular work in the mills more easily than men, as there were still more jobs designated as "female jobs" than "male jobs" and a steady demand for the "nimble fingers" of women workers.[34]

As we saw in chapter 5, although many southern black women came to textiles from nonindustrial backgrounds, they brought to the mills a clear understanding of how to work together for the common good that they had learned within the church. The two women who became leaders of the organizing drive in Macon, Georgia, "prayed for those yeses to come" as the National Labor Relations Board official counted the ballots at the Bibb Company's Bellevue Plant in the spring of 1980. Another woman, who worked as an inspector in the mill for three years before the election, equated working for the union with "working for God by working for humanity."[35]

Changing Roles and New Challenges

Even though southern black textile workers had already formed a significant part of the workforce in most southern mills by World War II, in the four succeeding decades they went from being marginal mill laborers to becoming the region's most prominent group of industrial employees. But despite the substantial changes they brought to the textile industry, they also inherited many of the traditional problems of this labor-intensive, low-wage industry that offered predominantly semiskilled or unskilled jobs. Throughout the 1970s, 1980s, and 1990s, textile workers remained among the nation's lowest-paid industrial workers. In the fall of 1980, the average wage for cotton textile workers in the South was $5.21 per hour while nationally the average manufacturing wage was over $8.00 per hour. Black operatives, like generations of white operatives before them, were also exposed to the crippling effects of byssinosis, a respiratory disease associated with exposure to cotton dust. Moreover, beginning in the early 1970s, many southern mills, faced with labor shortages and government pressure to reduce the levels of cotton dust within the plants, began to invest in new equipment and automated machinery that simultaneously increased production and reduced the size of the workforce. As a result, the number of U.S. textile workers, which in the 1950s had exceeded one million, had declined to 779,620 workers by 1966 and to 754,296 workers by 1978. The industry never regained the employment levels it had before the recession of 1974–1975. By 1980, over 12 percent of southern textile jobs had been permanently lost.[36] Unionized textile workers across the South were pressed for concessions on a model patterned after General Motors and Ford, but made one-fourth the wage of automobile work- ers. Textile employers from North Carolina to Alabama reduced workers' hours; in South Carolina, twelve mills closed in the last six months of 1981, putting 18,000 of the state's 133,000 textile workers out of work.[37]

Although black textile employees, the most recently hired group of workers in the industry, bore the brunt of this downturn, their solidarity and experience in grass-roots organizing had laid the groundwork for worker responses to the new waves of plant closings, unemployment, wage cuts, and union decertifications that affected the industry in the years after 1980. The struggle to raise regional wages to the national aver- age, to participate in industry decisions about automation and health and safety, and, most importantly, to gain union representation demanded all the strength, courage, and interracial cooperation of the men and women, white and black, operating the looms of the South. Although black and white southerners by and large continued to live, work, and worship in separate spheres, as black workers moved from being marginalized in the workplace to being more accepted by white workers and as interracial groups of southerners developed a greater awareness of their common needs, their experiences paralleled those of the black and white church- women who had gradually developed relationships based on mutuality and respect. The story of union organizer Crystal Lee Sutton celebrated in the film *Norma Rae* demonstrates the power of interracial unionism and the impact of the civil rights movement and the women's movement on the still burgeoning textile industry of the 1970s. As we shall see, future campaigns to organize the South would continue to emphasize the importance of the region's workers to the American labor movement, but the increasing competition of overseas textile mills and American-owned maquiladoras in towns along the Mexican border, combined with powerful anti-union forces and the increasing migration of Latino workers from Mexico and Central America into the region, challenged labor in ways that mirrored the situation unions had faced when looking south at the beginning of the twentieth century. In short, the changes set in motion as southern black workers moved into production jobs in the textile industry marked only the beginning of a series of demographic and technological transformations that would eventually reshape American industry and the economy and culture of the American South.

IV

FROM THE NEW SOUTH TO THE GLOBAL SOUTH

7

. . . .

Transformation and Resistance
in the Nueva New South

There's a place where I've been told
Every street is paved with gold
And it's just across the borderline
And when it's time to take your turn
Here's one lesson that you must learn
You could lose more than you'll ever hope to find.

"Across the Borderline," Ry Cooder, James Dickson,
and John Hiatt

The hard-hitting lyrics of "Across the Borderline," as sung by Ry Cooder in 1995, just as the North American Free Trade Agreement (NAFTA) took hold and immigration into the United States from Mexico and Central and South America soared, warn of the price of coming north and the dreams that can die in this "broken promised land." Evoking both hope and danger, the song's lyrics capture the high risk and elusive promise of traversing the Rio Grande to seek a better life in the United States. Cooder's music, steeped in history, invokes a sense of Pan-Americanism and a new "New South" that stretches from California to Cuba, from Texas to Virginia. This "New South" is a place that transcends borders, a place where no matter what, "hope remains when pride is gone." In the tradition of the dust bowl ballads of the Great Depression sung by Woody Guthrie, the haunting lyrics of "Across the Borderline" allude to the long history of the Latino South, the multi-generational issues inherent in immigration and transnational identities, and the high cost paid for the opportunity to work.

Globalization and Southern Transformation

Long seen as the region of the country most impervious to change, the American South has over the last fifty years nonetheless undergone a transformation as globalization—that shorthand term for the increased interconnectedness and mobility of capital, technology, labor, and goods and services throughout the world—has taken hold. A transnational history of the South opens, as one scholar put it, "a world of comparative possibility" by arguing that historical processes that evolve in different locations are constructed in the "spaces between" as people and ideas move from one place or region to another.[1] Since 1980, globalization has affected the U.S. South in three important ways. First, southern manufacturers slowly began to outsource their operations, initially across the border to Mexico and then overseas, particularly to industrializing countries in Asia. Second, immigrant workers were recruited to fill U.S. jobs in significant numbers, especially following the implementation of NAFTA in January 1994 and the Central America Free Trade Agreement (CAFTA) in 2005.[2] Although thousands of Latinos, the majority of them Mexican, had long worked as migrant agricultural workers throughout the region, new workers filled community-based jobs in the expanding poultry and pork processing industries, construction, service work, and landscaping. Finally, the U.S. South became a magnet for foreign investment as companies from outside the United States, producing everything from automobiles to microprocessors, tires to timber, staked their corporate claims.

A century earlier, in 1886, Atlanta newspaper editor Henry Grady had christened the region the "New South." Grady saw this New South as a "perfect democracy" imbued with "the consciousness of growing power and prosperity," a region built on "a diversified industry that meets the complex need of this complex age."[3] In a region scarcely one generation beyond slavery and in the midst of instituting a system of legally sanctioned racial segregation and African American disenfranchisement, Grady was astoundingly wrong about the democracy part. But he was on the money when it came to acknowledging the ascendant power and growing prosperity of the South. Grady, in his boosterism, accurately predicted the emergence of the post–World War II political influence of the South and the economic dominance of the Sunbelt in the later decades of the twentieth century.

As the fastest growing region of the United States between 1980 and 2010, the South has experienced dramatic cultural changes that run the gamut from the founding of multilingual newspapers, churches, and television stations to schools whose students speak two dozen languages. A new regional workforce, diverse advocacy groups and civic organizations, and immigrant worker centers, markets, restaurants, art galleries, theater troupes, and musical groups have transformed the region. The South is being made anew, from the hundreds of new businesses along Atlanta's Buford Highway, the central artery of immigrant settlement in the city's northeastern suburbs, to the rapidly growing Latino population in Carrboro, North Carolina, where language barriers and documentation issues shape the lives of new immigrants who in 2009 made up 12 percent of the population, to Yancey County, North Carolina, where Latino and Appalachian families compete head to head in the struggle to make ends meet.[4]

The impact of immigration on the South can be heard, seen, and measured in new languages and dialects, varied religious rituals, changing race relations, and tremendous economic growth. The southern population no longer conforms to the black/white paradigm held in place for so long by the twentieth-century color line described by W. E. B. Du Bois. Responses to this wave of new immigration have been mixed: immigrants have been welcomed and embraced; immigrants have been snubbed and rejected. Opposition to immigration runs deep among many in the South, black and white, while at the same time southerners, like others throughout the country, depend heavily on the strong labor force and economic growth that new immigrants have brought to the United States. The long-term effects of post-1965 migration into the region remain to be seen, but globalization and the increasing integration of trade, technology, capital, and labor markets clearly have had a profound impact on the region. The incorporation of millions of new immigrant southerners has transformed the labor force, recalibrated ethnic identification, and disrupted the biracial status quo established after Emancipation.

The demographics that had defined the South since the late nineteenth century first began to change in the 1960s, imperceptibly at first and then in ways that elicited remarks like those of Elton Corbitt of Pearson, Georgia, a white southerner born in 1930 who told an interviewer in 2006 that he saw immigration as "threatening everything that matters."[5] By that point, 1.6 million new immigrants, the vast majority from Mexico and Central America, had settled in Arkansas, Alabama, North Carolina, South Carolina, Tennessee, and Georgia. Across the region, Hispanic, Asian, and African newcomers have since transformed the biracial black-white demographics of southern society into a multi-ethnic population, with Latinos constituting the largest single group of new immigrants. Between 1990 and 2005, the number of Latino residents in Georgia and

North Carolina, the southern states with the highest rates of in-migration, increased by 480 and 600 percent, respectively, accounting for over half of the population growth in each state. In some local communities across the region, the number of Hispanic residents has surged even more dramatically. Gwinett County, Georgia, outside of Atlanta, for example, has the fastest growing immigrant population in the United States: between 1990 and 2007, its Hispanic population jumped by an incredible 657 percent, to constitute over 17 percent of the population.[6]

More significantly, since 2003 the rising number of U.S.-born children of Latino immigrants has outpaced immigration as the Hispanic population's primary source of growth.[7] This demographic transformation of the U.S. South has implications that go to the heart of the nation's understanding of democracy. As Leon Fink has written, "When it comes to the prospect for American democracy at the dawn of a new century, the welfare of new immigrant labor forces will likely tell us as much about our own dreams as about theirs."[8] In ways that mirror the connection between industrial rights and civil rights in the South in the 1930s, 1940s, and 1950s, the transformation and resistance engendered in the region by Latino immigration has reverberated throughout the United States. Traditional boundaries of race, class, and ethnic identity have blurred, opening what Saskia Sassen calls a series of "emergent possibilities" for the interplay between nationality and citizenship at a time in which the borders defining North, South, and West are being redrawn. Furthermore, the demographic transformation of the South and consequent dilution of the traditionally white southern political power structure may ultimately signal the demise of the Nixonian southern strategy built on white resistance to minorities.[9]

Ethnic Southerners

Henry Grady would have taken in stride the fact that in the twenty-first century, Atlanta has the fastest growing immigrant population in the United States and is a harbinger for a more racially diverse and pluralistic South. A sprawling metropolis covering twenty counties, Atlanta boasted a population of well over five million in 2009. Of these five million Atlantans, almost seven hundred thousand were new immigrants, two-thirds from Mexico and the remaining third from a dizzying array of nations, including India, Brazil, Guatemala, China, Cuba, Ethiopia, Haiti, Korea,

Iran, and Vietnam.[10] Current immigration to the United States follows longstanding patterns of chain migration, push/pull factors, and assimilation. Often, neighbors and relatives from specific overseas communities migrate in succession to a particular city or neighborhood in the United States. As in previous waves of immigration, difficult economic or political forces push emigrants out of their countries of origin, while the promises of jobs and freedom pull them to new destinations. The pressure to assimilate, a constant in U.S. immigration history, remains strong as individuals and families adjust to a new language, culture, and way of living. Unlike earlier generations of immigrants who entered the United States through Ellis Island, post-1965 immigrants have used the gateway cities of Atlanta; Austin, Texas; Charlotte, North Carolina; and Washington, D.C. as portals to a new life. A new and complicated cultural and ethnic landscape has emerged in southern communities in which residents can remember no previous in-migration. Each of these ports of entry has strong connections to global commercial networks and diverse economies that, at least until late 2008, have been hailed by manufacturers and government officials as engines of job creation.[11]

As noted, the South's growing diversity is eclipsing the black-white divide that has defined both Atlanta and the surrounding region for over a century. Beyond the statistics, the changing cultural landscape can also be observed in the comments of local residents like Christy Magbee, who lives eighty miles south of Atlanta in West Point, Georgia, a place she says is "starting to feel like a melting pot." Magbee was pleased when the Korean car manufacturer KIA announced that the company was going to open a plant in West Point. Looking at the old Pizza Hut, now a Korean Bar-B-Que, and the local KFC, now a Korean restaurant called Young's Garden, she commented, "You got the culture coming in. . . . You don't have to travel to Atlanta anymore. It's starting to come here."[12]

The rapid growth of the Hispanic population in the South has outpaced that of all other demographic groups. Between 2000 and 2008, in the twenty counties that make up greater Atlanta, the Hispanic population grew by 89.2 percent, from 274,853 to 520,158, increasing from 6 percent to 10 percent of the total population. During the same period, the black population of Atlanta grew by 36.4 percent, increasing from 29 percent to 31 percent of the total population. In contrast, the Asian population, while experiencing some growth, increased only from 3 percent to 4 percent of the total population. These gains of 3–4 percentage points, combined

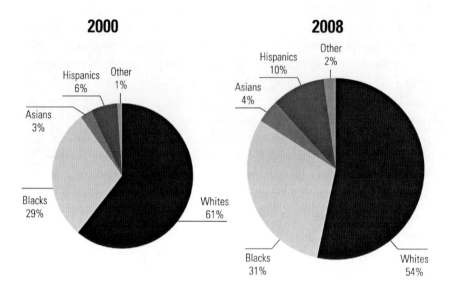

Figure 7.1. Pie charts of changes in ethnicity in Atlanta Metropolitan Area (Atlanta-Sandy Springs-Marietta), 2000 to 2008, from summary profile compiled by the Harvard School of Public Health from U.S. Census Bureau data.

Changes in Ethnicity in Atlanta Metropolitan Area, 2000 to 2008

	Total		Whites		Blacks		Asians	
	2000	2008	2000	2008	2000	2008	2000	2008
Population	4,281,896	5,376,285	2,594,165	2,880,146	1,223,940	1,669,518	142,090	224,506
Share of Population			61%	54%	29%	31%	3%	4%
% Increase	26%		11%		36%		58%	

	Hispanics		Other	
	2000	2008	2000	2008
Population	274,859	520,158	46,842	81,957
Share of Population	6%	10%	1%	2%
% Increase	89%		75%	

Figure 7.2. Table of changes in ethnicity in Atlanta tabulated from summary profile compiled by the Harvard School of Public Health from U.S. Census Bureau data.

with the smaller increases in the numbers of Asian and other Atlantans, reduced the percentage of whites in the total population from 61 percent to 54 percent. Thus, as the population in the twenty-county Atlanta area increased 25 percent between 2000 and 2008, the 11 percent growth in the white population was surpassed by a growth rate of 48 percent in the combined minority populations. White Atlantans are well on the way to becoming one of four minority groups in the city's increasingly diverse and multi-ethnic population.[13]

Although wages in the United States remain higher than those in Mexico and Central and South America, often by a factor of ten, 20 percent of Latino immigrants in the U.S. South live below the poverty level. As the U.S. economy began its downward spiral in 2007, documented and undocumented Latino immigrants endured the brunt of being "last hired, first fired" and a sharp increase in immigration enforcement. Layoffs, unemployment, and grim forecasts for the job market have slowed immigration by one-third. Estimates indicate that the undocumented immigrant population in the United States declined 13.7 percent between the summer of 2007 and the spring of 2009, when an estimated 10.8 million undocumented immigrants remained in the country. In 2006–2007, the growth in the Southern Latino population came from childbirth, not immigration, a reversal of the trend in the 1990s. As of 2006, one in four children under the age of five in the United States was Latino.[14]

The cultural complexities of the contemporary South go a long way toward dispelling images of moonlight and magnolias in a region many believe is still in the thrall of a *Gone with the Wind* mystique. Henry Grady's New South, built on textiles, sharecropping, and steel, is long gone, and even the late-twentieth-century vision of a modern, prosperous South, with Atlanta as its world-class capital, is fading in the face of the compelling global realities of immigration and investment in the region. At the same time that the South became the gateway of immigration to the United States, the new Ellis Island, foreign companies invested heavily in the region, drawn by state resources that include generous tax incentives, relatively cheap energy sources, inexpensive land, state-sponsored training facilities, the absence of trade unions, and a low-wage, hard-working, reliable workforce. Most recently, automobile companies from Germany, Japan, and Korea have flocked to the South, staking out territory for new factories and assembly plants along what has come to be called the Southern Auto Corridor, a broad swath that cuts through the region along I-85, following the tracks of the old Crescent line railroad and the string of once flourishing textile towns where for most of the twentieth century the mills ran late into the night. In 2009, foreign car manufacturers became the corporations infusing new life into former textile towns like Spartanburg, South Carolina, and West Point, Georgia.[15]

Southern state governments have actively courted this industry with multi-million-dollar packages, and local leaders across the region have responded with enthusiasm. BMW recently built a plant in Greenville, South Carolina, and KIA opened its billion-dollar state-of-the-art plant in West Point, Georgia, in February 2010. Toyota operates out of Georgetown, Kentucky; Hyundai has set up shop in Montgomery, Alabama; Nissan builds cars in Smyrna, Tennessee, and Canton, Mississippi; and Volkswagen will open a billion-dollar "green" plant in Chattanooga, Tennessee, in 2011. An auto plant is "the holy grail of economic development," Chattanooga Mayor Ron Littlefield remarked when VW signed the deal. "The car gods are smiling on Chattanooga," quipped Richard Casavant, dean of the College of Business at the University of Tennessee at Chattanooga.[16] And auto companies are but one of many industries looking south for bargains. Parts manufacturers, steel and semiconductor producers, and cleantech developers of solar cells and panels, emission regulators, and electric cars are all jumping on the southern bandwagon, attracted by the elixir of low wages, union-free workers, and state governments ready to make deals.

Across the South, states are sponsoring industrial development with a sharp eye toward job creation. But while jobs are a high priority, there are few guarantees about how many jobs will materialize from such development. There is also the question of who is going to be hired. Workers whose jobs have been lost to deindustrialization? Women? Men? Blacks? Whites? Latinos? When announcing the KIA deal in West Point, Georgia, Governor Perdue referred to wanting all of those jobs to go to "Georgians," but in an era of tremendous population growth, the majority of it from new immigration, who is a "Georgian?" Competition for jobs is fierce. Aging former textile workers are attending community colleges to retool their skills for the new economy, but at the same time, a generation of new workers stands ready to move into the workforce. Many younger workers are the sons and daughters of recent immigrants trained at the same regional community colleges and technical schools. The West Point

KIA plant received over 40,000 applications for 2,500 jobs before closing the on-line application Web site.[17]

At the same time, companies from tire manufacturers to poultry processors have recruited large numbers of immigrants to the region to work in factories, processing plants, construction, and service jobs. This influx of new workers and their families has escalated the need for adequate housing, multilingual schools, and an expanded infrastructure for water, sewage, and transportation. It has also put additional stress on an already precarious health care system and focused new attention on a bevy of workplace issues, including wage rates, health and safety regulations, industrial accidents, insurance, unions, and labor recruiting. The diversified economy of the U.S. South revved its engine throughout the 1990s, scarcely missed a beat during the post–9/11 economic recession, and kept going strong until late 2008, when the economy came to the brink of collapse. At that point, unemployment rose sharply across the South, and the effects of what is being referred to as the Great Recession can be seen in record numbers of home and business foreclosures in Georgia, Florida, the Carolinas, Alabama, and Virginia.[18]

The Latino South

While the South has become more diverse across the board and immigrants from around the world continue to flow into the region, it is the Latino population that has had the most dramatic effect on the region. The South's largest group of new immigrants, Latinos have been in the United States the longest and are most at home in the region. Mexican immigrants, who constitute by far the largest group of Latinos, have become especially well established in the South, its proximity to Mexico making it easier to travel back home than from, say, Chicago or New York. Established Latino communities throughout the region help new immigrants, who rely on networks of family and friends to help them find housing, jobs, and schools. Latino immigrants have to struggle to obtain one of the sixty-six thousand H-2B work visas awarded annually (and valid for less than a year) if coming to the United States to accept a temporary or seasonal non-agricultural job. Twenty-first-century Latino immigrants have no clear path to U.S. citizenship, unlike European immigrants entering the United States between 1870 and 1920, who could follow an established legal route to become naturalized citizens. Similarly, earlier generations of Latino immigrants, those who entered the country prior to 1965, could cross the southern U.S. border unimpeded. In addition, many pre-1986 immigrants were legalized by the Immigration Reform and Control Act of 1986, which granted amnesty to those who had entered the United States before January 1, 1982 and lived continuously in the country.[19]

For many who crossed the border during the boom economy of the 1990s, their work visas, if they ever had them, expired long ago. Becoming a U.S. citizen remains an elusive, often unattainable goal for such immigrants. Instead, men and women in the rapidly expanding Latino South continue to live on the borderline, an uneasy place where nightmares of deportation haunt hard-won dreams of supporting a family. The Latino South, a site of rapid demographic change, is a result of unprecedented labor migration during the boom economy of 1990–2005, when hundreds of thousands of young, predominantly male immigrants found work in states from Virginia to Texas. Men came first, to find jobs and make money, often as much in a day as they could make in a week in Mexico or Central America. Most sent remittances of cash to their families back home. Many eventually brought their family members to the States. Once across the border, additional children born in the United States easily obtained the citizenship rights that eluded their parents.[20]

The Latino Presence in Southern History

There is also a longstanding Hispanic/Latino history deeply embedded in the meta-narrative of the southern past. "We didn't cross the border, the border crossed us," was the rallying cry of Latino immigrants in the United States in the 1960s, and the slogan encapsulates a hidden chapter in American history rarely taught in U.S. schools. Latino immigrants have a history that is more closely interwoven with that of the United States than many Americans are aware. Texas, the only state in the region with an international border, was settled by Indians, Spanish, and Mexicans before the Anglos arrived. The influx of slaveholding southerners into Texas at the invitation of the Mexican government ultimately led to the secession of Texas from Mexico, in large part over the issue of slavery. The annexation of Texas to the United States in 1845 triggered the Mexican-American War the following year. Mexican Texans, or Tejanos, who remained on the Texas side of the border were increasingly relegated to second-class citizenship. Border wars between the United States and Mexico exploded in the years between 1846 and 1915 and have erupted sporadically ever since. Florida and Texas are among the traditional Hispanic areas in the South, states that had significant Hispanic populations long before 1965, and Alabama and Louisiana could be added to that list. The Spanish flag flew over New Orleans until 1803 and over Mobile until 1813, and sizeable Hispanic populations once thrived in both cities.[21]

Mexican-American author John Phillip Santos recounts in his family memoir that "we were required to study Texas history, but it was history from the viewpoint of the later Anglo settlers from the United States and Europe, beginning with the battle at the Alamo for Texas independence, and later, statehood." No lessons in the San Antonio schools in the 1960s focused on the Indians, or on the Spanish and the Mexicans "who had first built the city by the river." Over the years, Santos cobbled together a "secret history" from the legends and stories he grew up hearing from *las ancianas* of an extended family that had always straddled the Rio Grande. Santos's quest to discover the past proved arduous, for while he wanted to "bind Texas and Mexico together like a raft strong enough to float out onto the ocean of time, with our past trailing in the wake behind us like a comet tail of memories," many of the family members he spoke with had "made selective forgetting a sacramental obligation." He writes that sometimes it seemed "as if Mexicans are to forgetting what the Jews are to remembering." Leave the pain of the past in the past, his relatives urged him. "All that you were, and all that you could not be" should be let go of, if for no other reason than "there is pain enough in the present to go around."[22]

In similar ways, African American southerners have longstanding and painful historical connections to the Caribbean basin that stretch back to the seventeenth century, when generations of Anglo traders sailed throughout the region as dealers in global slavery. Enslaved men and women came from across the Caribbean into ports along the Georgia, Florida, Alabama, and Louisiana coasts. In New Orleans, as we saw in chapter 1, the city's diverse population included persons of African, French, and Spanish descent. Many families had come to Louisiana from the Caribbean islands, especially Cuba, Haiti, and Santo Domingo.

During the Civil War, Latino soldiers joined both the Union and Confederate armies. After the war, an undetermined number of ex-Confederates fled to Mexico and South America. In recent decades, business interests have pulled primarily white southerners into Mexico and Central and South America. Prosperous southerners have established second homes in Mexico; San Miguel de Allende in the state of Guanajuato, the Lake Chapala area in the state of Jalisco, and San Carlos in the state of Sonora are particularly popular U.S. enclaves. American snowbirds regularly travel by RV to Guaymas, a port city on Mexico's western coast, where they live for the winter. Each year, hundreds of retirees cross the border, going south to join a thriving U.S. ex-pat population estimated at between two hundred thousand to one million.[23] In sharp contrast to the Latino immigrants coming north, American citizens drawn south by business, retirement, or pleasure pass easily through customs in the twenty-one countries that make up "Latin America," although since 2009 their passage requires a passport rather than just a driver's license.

Latinos heading north, documented or not, have never been reciprocally received. In the 1910s and 1920s, the combination of a strong U.S. economy and the Mexican Revolution prompted hundreds of thousands of Mexicans to seek opportunities in the United States. As unemployment rose during the Great Depression, the Mexican Repatriation Program deported half a million workers of Mexican descent, including many U.S. citizens. The process began all over again when a decade later the Bracero Program, the official Mexican Farm Labor Program designed to alleviate labor shortages during World War II, drew hundreds of thousands of Mexican workers into the United States. The majority worked in agriculture, others on the railroad. Initiated in 1942, the program officially ended in 1947, but ongoing labor shortages prompted extensions of various kinds until 1967. In all, some 4.5 million Mexican workers came north as part of this program, many of them moving back and forth across the border according to the needs of U.S. employers. During the winter or when the economy slowed, workers returned home. Some left voluntarily, others when threatened with deportation through programs like "Operation Wetback," which the Justice Department initiated in 1954.[24]

When the U.S. economy began to expand again in the late 1950s, the cycle of crossing the border for higher wages began once more. In the half-century since then, U.S. perceptions about Mexico and nations further south have been affected by everything from border violence to trucking wars to the outbreak of swine flu. Popular ideas about Mexico and Central and South America run the gamut in the United States, from derogatory stereotypes to romanticized images. There is little middle ground in terms of recognizing Mexico's large and prosperous middle class, for example, or the intellectual depth and cultural richness of the nations of Central and South America. And while many Americans associate Latin America with weapons and drugs, few acknowledge the role the United States plays in that traffic or the negative view many of those south of the border have of the United States. The astounding number of guns flowing across the border from the United States to Mexico has prompted U.S. authorities to dub the weapons trade the "iron river." Meanwhile, the U.S. government estimates that its citizens pay billions of dollars each year to Mexican drug cartels in exchange for drugs sold north of the border.[25]

The Borderline as Contested Space

In the 1990s, the borderline Ry Cooder portrays became one of the most contested spaces in the world. Lives hang in the balance on that strip of land two thousand miles long, a place that is no place. The American dream is palpable there, but can slip away in an instant. Death is commonplace along this border, where between 1998 and 2004, 1,954 people died, the majority from exposure. In May 2009, the Department of Homeland Security announced that the construction of a planned "virtual fence" on the U.S.-Mexico border would continue. At an estimated cost of $7 billion, the elaborate system of cameras and surveillance equipment mounted on towers along the two-thousand-mile divide between the United States and Mexico will give twenty-five thousand Border Patrol agents the capability to control even remote desert areas. The goal is to stop 75 percent of those trying to enter the United States illegally, a number that in 2008 topped seven hundred thousand, 92 percent of whom came from Mexico.[26] Of the twenty-three million Americans of Mexican descent who live in the United States, one-third (about seven million) remain undocumented. One million workers without papers are deported each year, even as six hundred thousand new immigrants cross the border into the United States.[27]

From those impressive figures, however, a more complicated picture emerges. Although more prosperous than they would be in their home communities, many Latino immigrants remain isolated and alone. Alvaro, a construction worker from Veracruz, has worked in central Kentucky since 1999. He has steady employment and has bought a house, but, as he told an interviewer, he continues to feel alone: "In my house, I feel as if I were in a cage. You can put a bird in a cage, and even though the cage is made of gold, it's still a cage."[28] Kinship ties and linguistic connections within immigrant neighborhoods across the South mitigate the isolation many new immigrants feel as they stretch the bonds of family and reestablish ties from their birthplace in new communities. Social service agencies and religious organizations provide assistance with health care, language skills, and legal advice. Latino children have access to public schools and are able to take advantage of school meal programs for breakfast and lunch. With the immigration of more Latino women to the U.S. South in the early 2000s, a new gender balance and family stability has grounded the Latino community. Families provide strength and permanence, but also bring crushing responsibilities. Complex issues of continuity and change, of transnational identity and U.S. citizenship challenge family members across the generations. Many Latino men, women, and children continue to live on "the border"—on the edge of poverty; on the verge of arrest and deportment; in the lower margin of the middle class; in jobs that expand and contract with the economy; in a society that can be simultaneously welcoming and foreboding. Connections among recent immigrants within Latino communities in the South are strong, but the idea of regional and national belonging remains tenuous. For these new southerners, the South they would like to call home remains a contested space.

Crossing the border transforms individual lives, for better or worse, temporarily or forever. At the same time, the immigration of hundreds of thousands of Latino men, women, and children has changed the nature of the border itself. A new system of privately owned buses carries riders from towns and cities across the U.S. South to the Mexican border and then onto Mexico City and points further south. Adame Buses, Ltd. offers service from Atlanta, Nashville, Houston, and Durham, North Carolina. Stops along the route in North Carolina include Charlotte, Burlington, Greensboro, Raleigh, and Goldsboro. A one-way ticket from Durham can be purchased at stores in Carrboro or Siler City for about $300. No ID is required going south; visas are checked on the return trip. Faster and more direct than traveling by Greyhound, the trip takes between forty and sixty hours, depending on the exact destination. The buses from Durham are full from November to February, less crowded in the summer months when there is more work. But by the time they reach Atlanta, every seat is taken, no matter the time of year. A constant flow of people, luggage, and dreams moves back and forth across the border.[29]

Money, too, travels across the southern border. Latino workers in Memphis, Tennessee, for example, save one out of every three dollars they make and send two-thirds of those savings back across the border. In 2009, remittances to family members in Latin America sent from Memphis alone totaled over $125.6 million. Latinos throughout the United States sent a total of $50 billion in remittances to Latin America in 2005, $62 billion in 2006.[30] This flow of money sustains families left behind and fuels the dreams of immigrants planning to return home. The earning and purchasing power of new immigrants who settle in the U.S. South is highly prized on both sides of the border. In Georgia, in the less than two decades between 1990 and 2008, Latino buying power increased from $1.3 billion to $15 billion, a tenfold increase that is three times the national average. In Memphis, Latino workers earned over $570.8 million, of which $97.9 million was paid in taxes and $125.6 million was sent in remittances to family members in Latin America.[31] Money moves more freely than people across the contested borderline.

The New Minority

Siler City, North Carolina, where the Latino population grew from less than 1 percent to 40 percent of the total population in the decade between 1990 and 2000, has been described as a place where "outsiders came first in a trickle, then in a flood." These newcomers spoke a "foreign tongue" and brought "foreign ways," as Andres Viglucci, a reporter for the *Miami Herald*, put it. Once a small southern town and more recently a bedroom community south of Raleigh-Durham, Siler City is a place where "the oldtimers . . . have yet to recover from the shock." "The new name for Siler City," quipped Joe Langley, a clerk selling farm equipment in town, "is 'Little Mexico.'" The racial balance in Siler had not changed between Reconstruction and 1990, but at the beginning of the twenty-first century, longtime residents, black and white, find themselves "caught somewhere between welcome and animosity."[32] The *New York Times* reported in 2006 that Latino workers in Georgia have lower unemployment rates than black workers, that employers favor Latino over black employees, and that Latinos have an easier time operating small shops and stores than

African Americans. Many Latinos say that African Americans avoid hard work; African Americans argue that Latinos are "rate-busters" willing to work harder for lower wages because they are immigrants.[33]

As new immigrants, Latinos have benefitted in numerous ways from the political groundwork established by generations of African Americans who worked in the civil rights movement. The Voting Rights Act protects the ballot box; Title VI ensures nondiscrimination in federally assisted programs; access to public schools makes it possible to educate one's children; public libraries open their doors to all; public health programs immunize children and provide health care for low-income women and children. But as Latino Americans overtook African Americans as the nation's largest minority in 2007, what Latino columnist Ruben Navarette Jr. called the "black-brown thing" became shorthand for "the uneasy relationship between the nation's largest minority and the group that formerly held the title." In Dallas, Texas, in 2001, an African American candidate for city council was taped warning black business leaders, "You better wake up and look at your next-door neighbor, because now, your next-door neighbor is Hispanic. And they're moving in. And they're taking over. And they're pushing us out." After Hurricane Katrina, New Orleans Mayor Ray Nagin complained that his once black-majority city was being "overrun by Mexican workers." As Navarette sees it, aggravation cuts both ways: "African-Americans are frustrated because they think they're losing jobs to illegal immigrants. Latinos are frustrated that African-Americans—of all people—can't detect the racism that poisons this debate." Arguing that this is not a zero-sum game where only one group can be recognized at a time, Navarette concedes that "Latinos make the mistake of not paying respect to the unique place that African-Americans occupy in this country and its history." By the same token, he sees African Americans mistakenly "assuming that Latinos want to take their slice of pie, when Latinos just want a slice of their own."[34]

Southern Latinos, like southern blacks before them, have become scapegoats for pent-up anger over everything from the decline of U.S. power in the world to the stagnation of U.S. wages and the rising cost of health care. New to the region, immigrant workers who had little or nothing to do with the precipitous decline of southern manufacturing found themselves caught in the crossfire of job losses, declining wages, and diminishing community resources, making them easy targets for blame. The balance between welcome and animosity frequently tipped toward the latter, as when Mexican or Central American immigrants recruited for work in a local poultry processing plant in North Carolina or a catfish factory in Mississippi took the heat for whatever was happening in the community, whether that involved plant closings, union negotiations, or racial tensions at the local high school.

"We're becoming a Third World country," pharmacist Reid Ringer, a lifetime resident of Saluda, South Carolina, told a visitor as they passed by a dozen trailer parks where chickens and goats wander freely and garbage goes uncollected. "It wasn't like this 15 years ago," Ringer lamented as he recounted the problems with illegal immigration: "the slum lords, the declining education standards, the burden on emergency rooms, the increased crime rates."[35] Ringer's acrimony, however, ignores the South's dependence on Latino workers and turns a blind eye to conditions that black southerners endured for generations. And while many African Americans in the South admit to feeling uncomfortable that Latinos have "stepped into a place that we still haven't arrived at," the oppression faced by Latinos in the South is of concern to black southerners, who on the one hand envy rapid Latino success, but on the other deeply understand the politics of hate and the issue of color discrimination. The African American civil rights movement is clearly a model for Latinos as they fight for full citizenship rights. When Ilana Dubester of the community organization Hispanic Liaison heard the national call for Latinos to take to the streets in response to congressional inaction on April 10, 2006, she organized the largest march and rally in North Carolina. Thousands of Latinos (estimates ranged from 1,500 to 7,000) and other supporters of immigration reform walked peacefully through the streets of Siler City, North Carolina, chanting "¡Sí, se puede!" Dubester counted on the support of African American leaders that day, and they came through, speaking at the rally and marching side by side with Latinos and white North Carolinians in favor of immigration reform.[36]

Juan Crow and the Politics of Resistance

Anti-immigrant sentiment has increased in direct proportion to the number of immigrants entering the U.S. South. As *New York Times* reporter Rachel L. Swarns wrote about Pearson, Georgia (population 1,805) in 2006, "For generations, people here have savored the predictable cadences of small-town living. They knew their neighbors and their neighbors' neighbors, the sweet sound of Sunday church mornings and the rumble of tractors tilling the rich soil." And then, Swarns continues, "Mexican immigrants started streaming in," drawn by jobs in agriculture and manufacturing: "the newcomers landed in a town with one traffic light, no tortillas in the supermarket and residents who stared openly at foreigners in a county that saw its last wave of immigrants in the 1850s." In 1990, Latinos made up 3 percent of the population in Pearson, with the balance almost equally divided between blacks and whites; by 2009, the Latino population had grown to 28 percent of Pearson's total population, and the town found itself in what Swarns calls "a cauldron of demographic change." That cauldron of change is also a boiling pot of ethnic tensions. Longtime residents like Elton Corbitt, the Pearson resident who said that immigration threatened "everything that matters," are afraid that white southerners may soon become "outnumbered or irrelevant." His ancestors had helped settle the county in the 1800s, and now he fears that his children and grandchild are "going to become second-class citizens."[37] Corbitt's sense of loss is palpable, and Pearson's rapidly changing ethnic identity has left many whites feeling dislocated and angry. As newcomers to Pearson and similar communities throughout the South, Latinos struggle to establish themselves in communities that are at best ambivalent about their presence.

As is the case with black/white racism, the South hardly has a monopoly on anti-immigrant sentiment. Nevertheless, Latinos throughout the South find themselves living "under siege," in the words of a recent report from the Southern Poverty Law Center that documents abuses that include wage theft, discrimination, hostility, racial profiling, sexual violence, and harassment by racist extremist groups.[38] Throughout the region, weak labor laws and the absence of unions have left workers, new and old, unprotected and without the leadership a strong labor movement might provide. State and local governments in many parts of the South have exacerbated the situation by passing ordinances that deny services to undocumented immigrants and enforcing immigration laws in ways that promote systematic racial profiling and make Latino witnesses and victims of crime unwilling to cooperate with police. Moreover, tens of thousands of Latino immigrants who have entered the U.S. South over the last twenty years find themselves snared in a tangled web of laws and regulations that restrict their access to legal residency or citizenship.

Anyone who enters the United States, with or without documentation, is classified by the U.S. Citizenship and Immigration Services as an "immigrant" and an "alien" under the Immigration and Nationality Act (INA). However, without the presentation and official inspection of documentation at the border, an individual's status becomes that of "not a permanent resident alien." Lawful permanent residents receive immigrant visas or permanent resident status and are granted the privilege of residing permanently in the United States. Non-permanent resident aliens, commonly referred to as "illegal aliens" or "illegals," live in constant fear of arrest, imprisonment, and deportation. A disproportionate percentage of the undocumented immigrants in the United States live and work in five southern states (Texas, Florida, Georgia, North Carolina, and Virginia). This number topped four million in 2009, despite the recession and tightened enforcement at the border. Constantly on the lookout for the police or government immigration officials and vulnerable to unscrupulous employers and criminals who prey on immigrants, undocumented workers are the Latinos most at risk. But as one immigrant advocate in North Carolina reported, "The assumption is that every Latino possibly is undocumented, so [discrimination] has spread over into the legal population."[39]

The Southern Poverty Law Center (SPLC) found in 2008–09 that "even legal residents and U.S. citizens of Latino descent say that racial profiling, bigotry and myriad other forms of discrimination and injustice are staples of their daily lives." In April 2009, the SPLC argued that the systematic discrimination of Latinos in the U.S. South "constitutes a civil rights crisis that must be addressed." Forty-one percent of the workers surveyed by the center in 2008–09 reported having experienced wage theft. In New Orleans, four out of five immigrant workers involved in the rebuilding effort after Hurricane Katrina reported not being fairly paid for work they had completed. In 2007, at the Durrett Cheese Sales Company in Manchester, Tennessee, Latino workers repeatedly found their paychecks shorted and delayed. Finally, on October 22, 2007, a dozen workers decided to take action and refused to leave the break room until the company paid them. Their supervisor fired them on the spot, but they still refused to leave. Then company officials called the Manchester sheriff. A factory worker named Teresa reported being happy that the sheriff had been called, thinking "they would help us get the checks we were owed." But instead the deputies arrested and jailed the Durrett workers, charging them with trespassing. The company suggested the workers were undocumented immigrants, and agents from Immigration and Customs Enforcement (ICE) were called. A SPLC attorney finally got them released and a year later filed a federal lawsuit charging the company and the sheriff's department with "subjecting the workers to illegal retaliation and discrimination." This same company issued paychecks backed with insufficient funds to *Mixteco* indigenous workers hired in the Manchester area, workers whom company supervisors frequently referred to as "stupid Indians" and "donkeys."[40]

Latinos hired to work in the agricultural fields of the U.S. South face extremely difficult work situations, consistent violations of wage and hour laws, and a byzantine system of subcontractors and middlemen that makes it virtually impossible for them to defend their rights. One worker put it succinctly: "If you say something, they fire you." Latino farm workers in the South follow in a long tradition of exploited labor. As a grower in North Carolina told the SPLC, "The North won the war on paper, but we actually won because we kept our slaves. First we had sharecroppers, then tenant farmers and now we have Mexicans."[41] Senator Bernie Sanders of Vermont visited workers in the tomato fields surrounding Immokalee, Florida, in January 2008, prior to a Senate hearing on immigrant farm workers. "What is going on in Immokalee and other regions of Florida is deplorable," he reported, "and at its core repugnant to the values that our country is built upon." Concerned about the millions of U.S. workers who "are being forced into a race to the bottom," Sanders described the workers in Immokalee as "living on the lowest rung of the ladder in that race to the bottom." Exempt in most southern states from wage and hour regulations, immigrant farm employees across the region have worklives that grimly reflect those of antebellum slaves who toiled from "dark to dark." Modernity has brought the added threat of fields sprayed with pesticides and the constant exposure to chemical toxins. In Immokalee, Florida, in 2008, migrant tomato workers reported earning "40–45 cents for each 32-pound bucket of tomatoes they picked—or about $25 per ton." Farm workers are considered "guest workers," a category of employee rarely covered by workers' compensation provisions.[42]

The conditions faced by migrant agricultural labor in the U.S. South have been an issue for over half a century. In 1958, Eleanor Roosevelt wrote in one of her "My Day" columns, "It is curious to find that where men's pocketbooks are involved, they do things which they probably would be ashamed of if they were out in the open." For example, she asked, "would Senator Harry F. Byrd, the biggest apple grower in Virginia, point with pride to the conditions under which his migrant apple pickers live in a camp run by the Frederick County Fruitgrowers Association?" Roosevelt described the conditions for the readers of her column, which was syndicated in ninety U.S. newspapers and had a readership of over four million: "A room 25 feet square in which 40 Bahamians sleep in double-deck bunks less than a foot apart" and a "community bath, which is not very carefully cleaned. Garbage is left in the hot sun."[43] Two years later, Edward R. Murrow broadcast *Harvest of Shame*, a hard-hitting documentary aired right after Thanksgiving that included a report of the conditions of migrant workers at Sen. Byrd's Virginia farm during the recent apple harvest. Murrow's opening words, voiced over footage of African American farm workers being recruited in Florida, reflected his outrage: "This scene is not taking place in the Congo. It has nothing to do with Johannesburg or Cape Town. . . . This is Florida. These are citizens of the United States, 1960. . . . This is the way the humans who harvest the food for the best-fed people in the world get hired. One farmer looked at this and said, 'We used to own our slaves; now we just rent them.'" The migrant apple pickers Harry F. Byrd hired at his farm in the 1950s at least had mandatory health and accident insurance under their contract with the Fruitgrowers Association. AFL-CIO officials looked after their interests, making sure no violations of international labor agreements took place. The tragic irony is that in 2000, even though 70 percent of migrant and seasonal farmers in the United States are permanent residents, 85 percent do not have access to health or accident insurance, and few come under the purview of the AFL-CIO.[44]

The working conditions of farm workers in the twenty-first century, while in some respects even worse than those of fifty years ago, represent only part of the story of how the politics of ambivalence, neglect, and hate have manifested for Latino workers in the South. Six months after she took office, in July 2009, Secretary of Labor Hilda Solis related being "particularly concerned about our Hispanic workforce, as Latinos often work low-wage jobs and are more susceptible to injuries in the workplace than other workers."[45] The National Council of La Raza reported that "in 2006 alone, 990 Hispanics were killed on the job; that year, Latinos had a fatal occupational injury rate that was 20 percent higher than that of white workers and 26 percent higher than that of black workers. Racial profiling by police, long a severe problem for African Americans, affects Latinos as well."[46] Since 2006, with the establishment of the 287(g) Program, local police and sheriffs' deputies have been authorized to enforce federal immigration laws once they establish an agreement with federal agencies. Establishing checkpoints in Latino neighborhoods, local police act on behalf of the Immigration and Customs Enforcement agency and set deportation orders in motion. Two-thirds of the 287(g) Programs in the United States are located in the South.[47]

Targeted by local police, Latinos have been subject to a rising number of hate crimes. As the SPLC reported in 2007, "vicious public denunciations of undocumented brown-skinned immigrants are increasingly common among supposedly mainstream anti-immigration activists, radio hosts and politicians." This virulent rhetoric urges violence against Latinos, regardless of their immigration status, by depicting them as "invaders," "criminal aliens," and "cockroaches" that must be exterminated. Hate crimes create terror, while street crimes plague unarmed Latino workers who often carry large amounts of cash. Known as "walking ATM's" because they rarely use banks, undocumented immigrants are easy targets for robberies and muggings.[48] In 2007, a white supremacist group based in Birmingham, Alabama, prepared to attack Mexican immigrants with semi-automatic weapons and 2,400 rounds of ammunition. In Atlanta in May 2008, Rich Pellegrino, director of the Cobb Immigrant Alliance, received a death threat. White citizen's councils, so prevalent across the South during the civil rights movement, have formed again, this time with Latinos as their targets. In 2009, the Ku Klux Klan, which claims it opposes any illegal behavior and is not a hate group, nonetheless places "adopting laws requiring immediate deportation of all illegal aliens" at the top of the list of things they support.[49]

The threat of deportation remains a powerful tool, and the immigration process itself works effectively to control behavior and keep Latinos from living openly. Anti-immigrant forces frequently ask, "Why don't they come legally? Why don't they wait in line?" But as Jeffrey S. Passel, a demographer at the Pew Hispanic Center, explains, "For most Mexicans, there is no line to get in." In 2005, the United States allotted five thousand permanent visas worldwide, just *two* of which went to Mexicans. Recruited by U.S. businesses such as the poultry processing titans Tyson and Gold Kist, Mexican workers responded to billboard promises like those

Gold Kist put up in Tijuana, Mexico, offering "much work" (e.g.,"Mucho Trabajo en Russellville, Alabama") and providing the telephone number of a local labor recruiter. Once stateside, there are no guarantees; there are no streets paved with gold, no line for citizenship.[50] The concerns that Eleanor Roosevelt had in the mid-twentieth century have only magnified in the twenty-first. The public housing initiatives she supported during the New Deal for those living below the poverty line are no longer on the table. The threat of deportation keeps the lid on complaints about housing, robberies, slurs, or threats of violence. Fearing any interaction with the police or the justice system, Latino women often remain silent about widespread sexual harassment in the workplace and incidents of domestic violence at home. Silence does not mean inaction, however, and Latino Americans living and working in the South have a long history of resisting the loss of their dreams in the "broken promised land" north of the Rio Grande.

The Latino Response

Resistance cuts both ways, and while there has been intense opposition to the Latino presence in the region, there has also been a long history of Latino resistance to the oppression they have met across the border. Traditionally this resistance has come from workers and speaks to what Sassen refers to as "the possibilities for a politics of membership that is simultaneously localized and transnational." Labor historian Leon Fink's pathbreaking study, *The Maya of Morganton: Work and Community in the Nueva New South*, turned on a question that emerged from a strike at Case Farms led by workers from Guatemala, the overwhelming majority of whom were indigenous people of Mayan descent from the mountains of Central America. The workers at Case Farms, a poultry processing plant on the outskirts of Morganton, North Carolina, united in their determination to win union representation and better conditions in the workplace. Their steadfast militancy in the face of seemingly overwhelming odds required their turning a blind eye to the realities they faced in North Carolina, a state "with not a single organized chicken-processing factory." "Who were these people," Fink asked; "where did they come from and why did they act the way they did?" Wondering if they were "crazy and disoriented" or if they knew "something about social struggles of which others were ignorant," Fink found that the Maya of Morganton drew their strength from a strong reservoir of family and community ties that stretched from the Highlands of Guatemala to the streets of Morganton, a town of fewer than twenty thousand people in the foothills of the Appalachian Mountains. Most importantly, Fink found that the life narratives of the Mayan workers at Case Farms had been defined by the Guatemalan civil war and experiences of terror and escape. These workers had a long history of relying on group ties in a hostile environment, a combination that, Fink discovered, created "an opening for worker mobilization."[51]

This historical ethnography has changed the way scholars look at immigration and the history of labor organization. Fink's emphasis on the intersection of globalization and community, both powerful forces that transcend borders, places contemporary responses to capitalism in the mainstream of American labor history. American Studies scholar Sheila Croucher articulates a similar theory, focusing on the fluidity and multiplicity of belonging that she argues is "as old as history," while emphasizing that "the contexts in which belonging is negotiated" continuously change. Globalization, she contends, reshapes the contours of belonging even as it necessitates expanding the boundaries of identities in ways that both reinforce existing connections and relationships and create new ones.[52]

A profound historical example of the ways in which Latino Americans have responded to oppression by drawing on ties to a cultural birthplace, kin and linguistic connections, and the strength of community comes from a series of strikes by pecan shellers in San Antonio, Texas in the 1930s. As in the Case Farms strike of the 1990s, the workforce in the four hundred pecan shelling sheds in West San Antonio was overwhelmingly Latino. In this case, Mexican workers hand-shelled pecans for two to three dollars per week, in one of the lowest-wage industries in the United States. Short strikes in 1934 and 1936 had gained union recognition by the International Pecan Shellers Union No. 172, a chapter of the United Cannery, Agricultural, Packing, and Allied Workers of America, part of the newly formed Congress of Industrial Organizations (CIO). In 1938, when Julius Seligmann, the head of the Southern Pecan Company, the largest of the San Antonio firms, announced a wage cut, workers again walked out in protest. Emma Tenayuca Brooks, a fearless Tejana leader who had cut her political teeth in the radical Workers Alliance during the early years of the Great Depression, led the strike. Pecan shellers in most of the firms in the city joined the walkout, more than eight thousand workers in all.

Virulent opposition from local authorities resulted in between seven hundred and one thousand arrests, underscoring the deep-seated animosity toward Mexican workers and fear of transnational Mexican–Mexican American political power harbored by Anglo city leaders of San Antonio. After six weeks and many acts of violence by police, both sides agreed to arbitration. But the issue of Tejano justice and Mexican civil rights remained on the table long after the strike ended. Emma Tenayuca, who fit both the heroine and girl striker profiles, fearlessly fought city authorities like police chief Owen Kilday, who, defending his use of force, declared, "It is my duty to interfere with revolution." Known as La Pasionaria (the Passionate One), Tenayuca grew up in a politically active Tejano family that was acutely conscious of its Mexican and Indian ancestry.[53]

Following the pecan shellers' strike in 1938, Tenayuca's reputation as a "fiery orator" led to her run for the U.S. Congress from San Antonio on the Communist Party ticket. As historian Zaragosa Vargas argues, she was a political leader who "put practice into theory," especially when she wrote about the right of Mexicans to self-determination and nationhood as a conquered population "sharing a common history, culture and language." Tenayuca's work was emblematic of the widespread labor activism of Latinos in the 1930s. The pecan shellers' movement eventually led to a substantial change in San Antonio's city government and to the founding of the Texas Civil Liberties Union. In the midst of the strike, as picketers surrounded the shelling sheds in West San Antonio, one activist claimed that political leaders in the city feared Mexican Americans would "become aware of their own power." The actions of the pecan shellers and their strike leader Emma Tenayuca, however, proved they already had. Grounded in a local community secured by language and kinship, the Tejanos of San Antonio had a deep connection with their own history and an understanding of the past that bound "Texas and Mexico together," as John Phillip Santos put it three generations later.[54]

The pecan sheller strikes of the 1930s and the Case Farms strike in 1996 are not isolated incidents. The story of workers drawing on a shared history of culture, language, and experience to organize and fight for dignity and full citizenship rights has been a common one, from the Knights of Labor to the AFL-CIO. Over the years, Latino workers have been adept at building on and then transforming traditional forms of successful organizing. Latino farm workers joined the Southern Tenant Farmers' Union (STFU) in Arkansas in the 1930s and the Farm Labor Organizing

Committee (AFL-CIO) in North Carolina in the 1990s. Labor activist and intellectual Sara Estela Ramírez organized workers in Laredo, Texas, for the AFL-affiliated Federal Labor Union No. 11953 in the early twentieth century and then worked along the border to unionize Mexican railroad workers. Puerto Rican women, important rank-and-file members of the International Ladies Garment Workers' Union, organized workers beginning in the 1920s in a diaspora that stretched from Puerto Rico to Florida to New York City. Male and female Cuban and Puerto Rican cigar workers in Florida joined working-class organizations like the Federación Libre de Trabajadores. Through unions like the ILGWU and the United Farm Workers, Latina women and Latino men across the South participated in a national movement that drew in rank-and-file members, spouses, and labor leaders.[55]

As the pecan shelling companies left Emma Tenayuca's old neighborhood in West San Antonio in the 1930s to avoid paying higher wages, garment manufacturers moved in. Latina women still made up over 90 percent of the workforce when in the 1990s Levi Strauss began to close its plants, leaving thousands of longtime workers unemployed. In the wake of the layoffs, the women organized Fuerza Unida/Strength United under the motto "Unidos sin Fronteras/United without Borders" to fight for benefits and retraining programs. The Case Farm workers who organized in 1996 continued the long history of Latino labor activism a decade later when workers at Smithfield Foods' Tar Heel plant, the largest pork processing facility in the world, walked out in a wildcat strike. The workforce there, which was three-quarters African American and one-quarter Latino, had been trying to organize since 1994. After a long, complicated struggle, workers finally gained the right to hold an election in North Carolina, where only 3.3 percent of workers belong to a union—the lowest representation in the United States. On December 11, 2008, just a month after the election of Barack Obama, Smithfield workers saw themselves "on the verge of making history" as 52 percent of the plant's five thousand workers voted to unionize.[56]

Making history had also been on the minds of the Latino immigrants and their allies who in April and May of 2006 marched in more than a hundred cities across the United States in support of immigration reform. Communities across Alabama, Mississippi, North Carolina, South Carolina, and Georgia witnessed demonstrations that rivaled those of the 1960s civil rights movement. In Siler City, when some in town argued that the march "came across as an intimidating show of force," organizer Ilana Dubester responded, "Tough sh—." Determined to do what she could to work with others to fix this "broken Promised Land," Dubester spoke from the heart: "It's OK [with you] if we're invisible, it's OK if we're silent, it's OK if we hide in our houses, it's OK if we break our backs and twist our hands cutting your fricking chicken." But, she continued, "for us to stand in front of your town hall demanding better services, demanding a better life and a better future, that's too much." People think, "you brown people stepped out of your place." Emphasizing their place and belonging in the community, the Latino marchers in Siler City carried banners reading, "I love Siler City" and "I pay taxes." In Atlanta, as many as fifty thousand supporters gathered at the suburban Plaza Fiesta shopping mall on Buford Highway. Most wore white tee shirts and carried signs reading, "We Have a Dream, Too," connecting their struggle to the one led by Atlanta's revered civil rights leader, Martin Luther King Jr.[57]

Points of Connection

These points of connection between the Latino immigrant quest for civil rights and the history of the black civil rights movement lead us back to Sassen's concept of emergent possibilities and a construction of citizenship that is simultaneously local and transnational. The Latino community's strength and unity in 2006 demonstrated the power of "unauthorized yet recognized subjects," a power that, Sassen suggests, drove the civil rights movement and the earlier struggle for women's suffrage. The momentum that drew thousands of Latinos and their supporters into the streets across the South, however, slowed in the wake of the economic downturn that became evident in 2007 and reached a crisis point in October 2008. Marches and rallies led by immigrants calling for reform gave way to rising concerns about unemployment. As the recession took hold, Latino immigrants found themselves especially vulnerable to layoffs and discriminatory hiring practices. Remittances declined, and reverberations of the economic downturn echoed south, from Mexico to Nicaragua. In April 2009, remittances to Mexico alone were 18 percent lower than in the same month a year earlier.[58]

The fiscal bubble in the South burst quickly and dramatically. The economic fallout in Carrboro, North Carolina (population sixteen thousand) tells the story. Once a textile mill town and now a suburb of the university community of Chapel Hill, Carrboro, like so many southern towns, saw its Latino population increase by 936 percent in fifteen years. By 2000, Latino residents, three-fourths of whom came from Mexico, made up 12.3 percent of the local population. Since the 1990s, Latino workers in Carrboro had been lining up every morning at dawn outside the BP station on Jones Ferry Road to wait for day work. Then the recession hit—hard.[59] One morning in late August 2009, over seventy-five men waited at the Jones Ferry Road BP as the sun came up. By noon, after hours of watching for contractors who never came, the line dispersed. It had been this way for months. The lucky ones who did find work clocked only a few hours in the course of a week. "I've been here eleven years and I've never been without work," one Latino man told Suzy Firestone, the Hispanic Services Coordinator at the Inter-Faith Council (IFC) for Social Services, as unemployment reached record levels in the spring months of 2009. The IFC was founded in 1963 as a volunteer group committed to addressing poverty-related issues in Chapel Hill and Carrboro. The group, which started a Hispanic Outreach Program in 1995, relies heavily on a volunteer staff. Their outreach to the community's growing Latino population has increased dramatically, especially since the fall of 2008, when the economy began to falter. By the summer of 2009, they were serving almost double the number of clients they had two years earlier. IFC works on a "first come, first served" basis, and by the time the staff arrived each morning, there were two long lines—one for English speakers, the other for those who only spoke Spanish. Clients waited to obtain groceries, clothing, or money for rent and utilities. Black and white southerners sat in the folding metal chairs that line the small waiting room; Latino clients usually stood in the hallway. In a perverse role reversal, black workers could be heard referring to Latino workers as "dogs" and "goddamned Mexicans." Joblessness and poverty have wreaked havoc on nerves already frayed by the anxiety of unpaid bills, the fear of eviction, and the agony of going day after day without work. Tempers flared and snapped; fights occasionally broke out. The police were called more than once as the long summer wore on. Latino clients waiting to be seen at the IFC were ready scapegoats, easy to blame for everything from declining wages to unemployment to crowded school and social services stretched thin by depressed city and state revenues.[60]

Borders divide, but they can also be points of connection. Writing in 2005, scholar David A. Davis observed that although the Mason-Dixon

Line has long served as the South's traditional border, its "northernmost reference point—a place to be south of," the South's other borders, to the west and south, "have always been and continue to be uncertain." Indeed, Davis continues, "on a transnational level the South's borders may be more ambiguous now than ever before."[61] The region has new internal borderlines as well, such as the Buford Highway, that six-lane-wide ribbon of immigrant-generated commerce on Atlanta's periphery. The old lines between North and South—the Mason-Dixon Line and the Ohio River—mean nothing to the 1.5 million new immigrants creating the Nuevo New South. That watery line that once divided free laborers from those enslaved has no currency among the sixty thousand Latino immigrants who have settled in the tri-state region shared by Kentucky, Indiana, and Ohio. Throughout the South, one hears complaints that Latinos are somehow outside the region's history, that *they* are not interested in or part of southern tradition. Latinos rarely describe themselves as "southerners," although as researchers at the Pew Foundation point out, this is probably because of the hostility with which many Latinos have been greeted by people who do.[62]

Before an audience while running for the presidency, Barack Obama referred to W. E. B. Du Bois's declaration that "the problem of the twentieth century is the problem of the color line." But now, Obama added, "the problem of the twenty-first century is the problem of the other." In the United States and around the world, he argued, people have difficulty accommodating people "who are not like us." Joseph Stewart, chair of the political science department at Clemson University, in Clemson, South Carolina, would agree. The response to immigration in the South is an "outsider-versus-insider reaction," he argues, adding "it's more of a visceral than an economic issue."[63] Scholar Julia Kristeva argues that the antidote to racism and xenophobia in a nation of immigrants is to realize that we are always, as the title of her book suggests, *Strangers to Ourselves*. "The foreigner is within us," she writes, and recognizing that can keep us from projecting our own alien nature, our "improper" unconscious self, onto the "other." In the context of the U.S. South in the twenty-first century, this requires coming to terms with the new and multiple meanings of regional identity. There are positive developments that affirm the growth of civil society in the South. But the answer to the question Leon Fink posed recently—is the glass half empty or half full when it comes to immigrant rights?—is still pending. Multiple non-governmental agencies, like the Inter-Faith Council in Carrboro, have stepped forward to meet the needs of new immigrants. In Clarkston, Georgia, a small town on Atlanta's eastern edge, the Fugees, a soccer team of boys from newly immigrated families, transcended local opposition and their own fears to create strong alliances on and off the field. A Latino team in Siler City has done the same. New histories that document the long-standing Latino/a presence in the South are being written. Heavily attended annual festivals in cities across the Nuevo New South display and affirm Hispanic/Latino culture. Hard-working immigrants and their families across the region pay taxes, save money, and participate in community life as parents, churchgoers, and taxpayers. At the same time, as noted earlier, the Ku Klux Klan supports immediate deportation for undocumented immigrants, 287(g) laws have empowered local authorities to stand in for the Immigration and Nationalization Service, and in the wake of what is being referred to as the Great Recession, Latino immigrants face increased discrimination and resistance.[64]

A system that denies citizenship to Latino immigrants who, like so many U.S. immigrants before them, have a right to the American dream runs a huge risk of reinforcing these structural inequalities. There is much to lose, and while, as Ry Cooder sings, "hope remains when pride has gone," the South and the nation need to get immigration right. The South, more than any other region in the country, knows the damage that can be done by a caste system like the one that plagued African Americans for centuries, in which gaps in wealth, health, and education become self-perpetuating. Immigration is a political red herring, its discourse characterized by distortion, rumor, and bald-faced lies. As the debate over reforming health care heated up in the summer of 2009, virulent outbursts conflating health care reform with an anti-immigrant agenda could be heard from New Hampshire to South Carolina to Arizona. At a town hall meeting in Portsmouth, New Hampshire, a white protester yelled through a megaphone, "We don't need illegals. . . . Send 'em back with a bullet in the head." When President Obama outlined his health care reform plan before a joint session of Congress on September 9, 2009, Republican Representative Joe Wilson of South Carolina interrupted the president's statement that "the reforms I'm proposing would not apply to those who are here illegally" by yelling "You lie!" across the chamber, eliciting a round of boos from Democrats and embarrassing some Republicans as well.[65] Wilson's outburst replicated town meeting outbursts and widespread outrage that health care reform intended to insure over forty million uninsured Americans might also include millions of undocumented immigrants when, in fact, the vast majority (80 percent) of the uninsured are U.S. citizens. This anger directed at immigrants and supporters of immigration reform is especially palpable in the South, where the rate of in-migration has increased so dramatically over the past two decades.

No one can change the past, but it is possible to shape the future. The long history of the Latino South tells us that immigration is both a moment in time and a permanent transition that affects the lives of subsequent generations. "We are a nation of immigrants," the United States Citizenship and Immigration Service declares on its website. "But," the director warns, "we are also a nation of laws."[66] Those laws remain unworkable for the hundreds of thousands of men, women, and children, many recruited by U.S. companies, who enter the United States from Mexico and Central and South America without required documentation. For those who enter on a visa or work permit that they cannot renew, the situation is much the same. Population growth through immigration helped fuel the southern economic boom of the 1990s, as did the combination of anti-unionism and the use of state resources to attract investors. The triumph of anti-unionism opened the region to global investment in a world that sees this newest New South as a model for capitalist development in the twenty-first century. But the New South of the 1880s and the Nuevo New South of the 1990s both fostered economic growth and development and set in motion a race to the bottom that eroded the standard of living of one group of workers by bringing new and cheaper workers on line. The mantra of New South industrial development—state incentives for business, no unions, and low wages—has been exported to the "Global South," that vast expanse of nations stretching from Mexico to Nicaragua, from India to Central Asia, China to Vietnam. As the quest for cheap labor continues, the haunting refrain from "Across the Borderline" hangs in the air. In seeking to find that place where "every street is paved with gold," everyone risks "losing more than they could ever hope to find."

8

. . . .

Back to the Future

Mapping Workers across the Global South

I heard the rhythmic clickity-clack whoosh, clickity-clack whoosh of the old looms before I saw them. By the time I crossed the dusty courtyard, where ripe apricots hung from trees in the noontime sun, and walked into the weave room, the noise was deafening. Once my eyes had adjusted to the dim light inside, I could not believe what I saw. There in Margilan, the silk capital of Uzbekistan, was a room full of cast-iron looms from the Carolinas. As incredible as it seemed, after flying halfway around the world to Central Asia, I had entered a weave room straight out of the 1920s. The story of how looms from the Carolinas ended up in Uzbekistan is not a straightforward tale of southern deindustrialization and Asian labor markets. Who makes what where, when, and why depends on a chase around the globe for cheap labor that involves overlapping waves of industrialization and deindustrialization. Some of these waves hit like tsunamis; others barely make a ripple.

Viewing the lives of women workers in Margilan in 2006 evoked a sense of time travel. I could have been stepping into the Odell spinning mill in Bynum, North Carolina, in 1900; the Erwin Cotton Mill in Durham in 1919; or the Baldwin Mill in Marion in 1929. The looms in the Margilan weave room had been manufactured in the United States and were the same machines that, by 1920, were being used all across the American South. But how had they gotten to Margilan? Why in 2006, in a country as old and full of contradictions as Uzbekistan, was there a weave room exactly like the ones in the Carolinas almost a century earlier?

Workers across the Global South share a history of work and protest, collective action, and individual survival with earlier generations of women in the American New South. The world economy is moving at full speed back to a future that has the potential to dramatically shift current levels of employment, exploitation, racial and ethnic divisions, poverty, and gendered divisions of labor. Workers' experiences mapped across the globe assure us that no one wins when companies "race to the bottom." The life histories recounted by generations of women who have migrated from field to factory demonstrate that local, national, and international efforts of workers to organize themselves offer the best opportunities for creating a world in which human rights are respected and social and economic justice becomes a reality.[1]

Historical Perspectives on the Global Workplace

Founded two thousand years ago, Margilan is one of the oldest cities in Central Asia. In the ninth century, the town was famous for its silk fabrics, which traders carried to Egypt, Greece, Baghdad, Khorasan, and Kashgar across the routes that made up the Great Silk Road. Margilan sits in the Ferghana Valley, known as the breadbasket of Central Asia and the most fertile agricultural area in the entire region. During the Soviet era, almost all of Ferghana was given over to cotton production, and the soil has suffered the ravages of that lucrative cash crop, the "white gold" that American southerners know so well. Since Uzbekistan declared independence from the Soviet Union in 1991, cotton production has declined, although the crop remains one of Uzbekistan's major exports. Throughout the summer, in the fields of white gold outside Margilan, groups of workers move up and down the rows chopping weeds with wooden-handled hoes. In the fall, students across Uzbekistan leave school for two months of mandatory work picking cotton, a strange echo of the forced labor used in the nineteenth-century U.S. South.[2]

Nineteenth-century Margilan was one of many Uzbek textile towns, such as Bukhara, Namangan, Samarkand, Shakhrisabz, Kitab, Karshi, Khojent, Urgut, and Khiva, that became famous for cotton, silk, linen, and wool production. By the 1890s, manufactured cloth had replaced handwoven goods, repeating what had happened in the Appalachian South when factory-produced goods replaced the homespun weaving of traditional designs throughout the region. In the Margilan factory I visited in 2006, the gender politics of occupational segregation mirrored those of the early twentieth century in the U.S. South: men supervised; women tended the looms. Three women workers taking their break in the courtyard outside the weave room smiled and greeted me. They were playing with the child of one of the workers, a little girl who in the Carolinas would have been called a lap baby. The vast majority of the workers were young women; a few were fifteen or sixteen years old, but most were in their late teens or early twenties. There were several mother-daughter pairs in the mill, and a number of the women working together were sisters. In striking contrast to the fenced, locked, and closely guarded southern mills in the early twentieth century, visitors to Margilan in 2006 could wander unaccompanied throughout the mill and even take photographs. But despite the relatively slow work pace, the hypnotic clattering of the old looms, the sisterly camaraderie of the women, the courtyard breaks, and the presence of a baby, workers were closely monitored and their purses searched as they queued up to leave the factory at the end of their shift.

Uzbekistan's history provides few answers to the question of how these American looms ended up there. Conquered by the Mongols in the eighth century and by Russia in the nineteenth, Uzbekistan became part of the Soviet Union in 1924 and reluctantly declared independence in 1991. Since then, Islom Karimov, the former First Secretary of the Communist Party, has twice been voted into office as president in elections considered neither free nor fair. Despite his Russian name, he has fostered anti-Russian nationalism, and 80 percent of ethnic Russians (some two million people) have fled the country. The Peace Corps left in 2005, the same year Karimov evicted the United States from the Karshi-Khanabad air base.[3] Although the Karimov administration restricts the movement of tourists within Uzbekistan, does not allow journalists to enter the country, and discourages Uzbek citizens from traveling abroad, its doors are wide open to international investors. In April 2008, the fourth Central Asian International Textile Machinery Exhibition—CAITME 2008—was held in the UzExpoCentre in Tashkent. In all, 130 companies from seventeen countries participated, among them Austria, Belgium, Great Britain, Germany, India, Italy, Russia, the United States, Turkey, Switzerland, France, the Czech Republic, South Korea, and Japan. The People's Republic of China and Taiwan participated in the CAITME conference for the first time in 2008. The meeting focused on textile machine building and the renovation, retooling, and modernization of the industry in Uzbekistan.

In sharp contrast to the international scope of the CAITME conference, the Southern Textile Association (STA) held its annual meeting that year at the Hilton Hotel in Myrtle Beach, South Carolina, with 150

Figure 8.1. Woman weaving on a Draper loom, Margilan Silk Mill, Margilan, Uzbekistan, 2006. Photograph by author, 2006.

participants from throughout the Carolinas in attendance.[4] As they have each June since 1908, STA members networked and exchanged information about the industry. The meeting's theme was "Looking at the Past/ Thinking about the Future." Members raved to Lillian Link, STA secretary-treasurer, about the booklet the STA staff had prepared on "The Past 100 Years." Many told her how much better the mood was in 2008 than at the annual gathering two years earlier. That was a "weird" affair, Link reported, when textile executives who had always attended "just did not show up" and it seemed that those members who did attend "were just going through the motions." When asked why the mood and attendance had improved, Link pointed to the lobbying efforts of the National Council of Textile Organizations (NCTO) in Washington, D.C. Those, she argued, "have made a big difference. . . . At least now we believe there will continue to be a textile industry in the United States."[5]

The future size and scope of the American textile industry remains to be seen, but those who attended the first Southern Textile Association meeting a hundred years earlier had been optimistic enough to found the new organization even though southern firms controlled just a small portion of the U.S. textile industry at the time. The national economy that year was still reeling from the Panic of 1907 in which financial markets tumbled, the stock market crashed, and banks closed. Even in 1908, southern textile manufacturers faced fierce national and international competition, feared labor unrest, and relied heavily on the China market for their profits.[6]

Spreading from one continent to the next since the eighteenth century, alternating waves of deindustrialization and reindustrialization point to contrasting narratives of progress and development. In all of this history, women have consistently played important roles in the production of textiles and garments, the traditional forerunner of industrial expansion in most national and state venues. Examples abound: in Britain and Europe in the eighteenth century; New England in the nineteenth century; the American South, Japan, Russia, and the Soviet Union in the late nineteenth and early twentieth century; and throughout the vast region that in the early twenty-first century we are calling the Global South.

Industrial Waves, 1780–2008

Comparing and contrasting historical statistics across two centuries is an imprecise process at best. Nevertheless, it is possible to broadly trace the major waves of industrialization and deindustrialization in the United Kingdom and Europe, the United States, and the Far East. As shown in Figure 8.2, an examination of the ratio of employment in manufacturing to that in agriculture from 1800 to 2000 shows the compression of the length of time encompassed by the rise and decline of manufacturing employment for each successive wave. Industrial production in the United Kingdom, employment in manufacturing, and sustained profits continued to increase for close to 150 years before declining. In the United States, after a difficult start because of British competition and the disruption of the Civil War, steady growth in industry lasted for over one hundred years. In Figure 8.3, we see that manufacturing employment rates in the Global South nations of South Korea, Brazil, and China follows a pattern of development much like that in the American South, with large portions of the working population in these countries remaining in the agricultural sector. These new industrializing economies have developed rapidly for a couple of reasons. Unlike in the United Kingdom in the late eighteenth and early nineteenth centuries, when industrial machines were in their infancy, the technology required for expansion is already in place and the equipment being installed in start-up factories has substantially higher production capabilities.

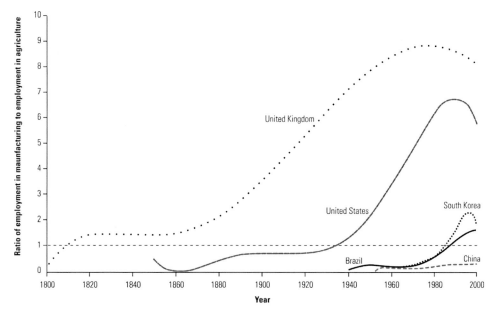

Figure 8.2. Ratio of employment in manufacturing to employment in agriculture, 1800–2000. Copyright: Peter Evans and Sarah Staveteig, University of California, Berkeley. Used with permission.

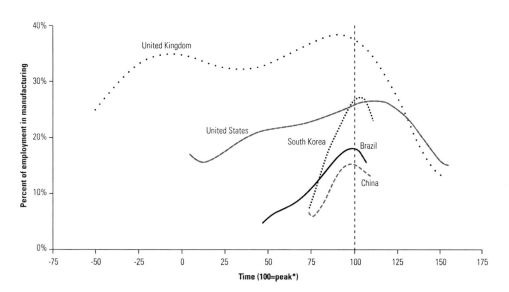

Figure 8.3. Percentage of employment in manufacturing at peak. Copyright: Peter Evans and Sarah Staveteig, University of California, Berkeley. Used with permission.

Rapidly industrializing regions, whether the New South in 1900, Ciudad Juarez in 1995, or China's Pearl River Delta in Guangdong Province in 2005, have taken full advantage of what has seemed an endless supply of migrant agricultural workers eager to fill industrial jobs. Such regions have also capitalized on increased automation and, in the twenty-first century, on computerized operations to reduce manufacturing employment levels and increase output. In twenty-first-century China, for example, 130 million migrant workers supply the labor for manufacturing, construction, and services. A 2006 survey conducted by the Chinese central government on the conditions these workers face documented that "only 12.5 percent have signed a labor contract and only 48 percent are paid regularly."[7] The vast majority work seven days a week and are "seldom paid the legal overtime wage." Ten million migrants cycle annually through the Pearl River Delta, now commonly referred to as the "factory of the world." One-third of China's total exports come from this coastal region, which enjoys easy access to Hong Kong. Ten percent of all Pearl River Delta exports end up on Wal-Mart's shelves. Growth in this sector of China's burgeoning economy has been so rapid (10–20 percent per year) that in May 2008 there were reports of a labor shortage of two million workers, despite the large numbers of new migrant workers arriving from the countryside. As a result, wages have begun to rise, and companies are leaving the region in droves (a thousand in December 2007 and January 2008 alone). "Turning a profit is becoming increasingly rare," reported a specialist who helps German companies enter the Chinese market. The U.S. Chamber of Commerce in Shanghai reports that one in five companies is considering pulling out of China in search of the next low-wage country. Vietnam, Bangladesh, and India top the list of contenders as many argue that China's position as "the ultimate low-cost production location is fast becoming history."[8]

The New South as Model for the Global South

New South industrialization became the model for subsequent development as investment extended beyond the borders of the United States and pushed further south into Mexico and Central America and west into Japan, Korea, and the Philippines, setting the stage for the twenty-first-century expansion across the larger Global South. Little of what we are witnessing in the Global South is new, but the scale and scope of contemporary industrial development around the world is unprecedented. U.S. industrialists began looking south for cheaper labor markets in the late 1870s, and investors, northern and southern, continued to pour money into the resource-rich New South for over a hundred years. Unlike previous models of industrialization in the United Kingdom and New England, in which regulatory laws, worker guilds, and unionization gradually mitigated the power of manufacturers, New South industrialization sustained and fostered persistent patterns of corporate control, low wages, and an anti-union climate reinforced by state and local governments. As in the New South, each new wave of industrial expansion in the Global South makes it increasingly difficult for workers to exert control over their own lives, to influence what happens on the factory floor, and to protect their political and economic interests. Corporate power, on the other hand, in the form of twenty-first-century multinational corporations, has continued to increase exponentially.

As industrialization gradually spread across the American South, the experiences of workers in the arc of states stretching from Maryland to Texas varied according to several factors, including whether factories were located in rural or urban settings; the experiences of first-, second-, and third-generation industrial workers; whether industrialization was occurring in unionized or nonunionized areas; and before 1965, hiring patterns that gave preferential treatment to white southerners. Between 1870 and 1970, companies operating in the region continued to thrive, first by pulling in new employees—initially, large numbers of women and men from agricultural areas in the southern mountains and the Piedmont region and, after 1965, large numbers of African-American workers—and second by continuing to expand the economy of the New South through the construction of new factories and mills in previously undeveloped areas. In 1900, industry moved into southwest Georgia and Alabama along the Chattahoochee River; in the 1970s and 1980s, U.S. industrialists moved into northern Mexico, opening "maquiladoras," factories that import materials and equipment for assembly or manufacturing and then re-export the assembled product, usually back to the originating country; and in the 1990s, these same companies invested in operations throughout the Global South.

Throughout this process, manufacturers have constantly sought fresh sources of low-wage workers. "Cheap and contented labor," as Sinclair Lewis put it in 1929, often meant young women who could be spared from family farms or sharecropping to work in a newly opened factory nearby or to migrate into urban areas in search of wage work. But it also meant increasing numbers of male workers who left agricultural jobs and began to dominate the cotton textile labor force as early as 1900, when 56 percent of this labor force was male. By 1920, this figure had risen to 63 percent.[9] To fully understand the New South industrial experience, we must mark, as historians have for earlier expansions in New England and the United Kingdom, the historical moments when changes in the composition of the labor force produced major social and economic shifts. This includes examining how gender, ethnicity, and race affected these changes, as, for example, when immigrant workers entered the New England labor market in the 1850s or formal racial barriers in southern industries were finally broken down in the 1960s.

At first glance, it might seem that industrialization in the New South was a repeat performance of what had happened in Britain and the northeastern United States, but the New South paradigm differed in important ways. Unlike the workforces in Britain and New England—where workers' collective action became institutionalized in the form of guilds, cooperatives, and trade unions that engaged in formal negotiations with employers and exerted considerable political power—the southern workforce relied more heavily on informal influence, both on the factory floor and through the political system. As the southern workforce matured, union and nonunion workers alike exerted considerable political influence and developed effective ways of indirectly controlling changes in the status quo. Spontaneous walkouts and strikes that were often bitterly fought and involved hundreds or thousands of workers exerted a kind of veto power over wage cuts or increases in workloads. This was especially important in nonunion mills and factories.

Southern workers who grew up in the mills and worked there as adults developed firm ideas about equity and fair dealing. They also relied on and benefited from efforts to reform the industry by northern trade unions, religious organizations, private organizations like the National Consumers' League and the YWCA, progressive political activists including American socialists and communists, and the small number of government inspectors/officials charged with enforcing labor laws. The actions of southern workers to change what they saw as violations of the moral economy of labor relations, combined with regional and national attention focused on southern industry at certain historical moments, helped mitigate labor abuses in the region, although not to the extent that formal unionization had made possible in New England and the United Kingdom.[10]

Throughout the Global South, however, a sense of rights, individual and collective, has been slow to develop as industrialization has spread. Nevertheless, as in the New South a century ago, the work of international labor organizations and non-governmental organizations (NGOs) such as Oxfam, Human Rights Watch, China Labor Watch, the National Labor Committee, the Clean Clothes Campaign, Anti-Slavery International, and Free the Children have supported dissent and played the role that in an earlier era was played by organizations like the YWCA Industrial Department, the National Women's Trade Union League, the National Child Labor Committee, the Chinese Working Women Network, and the International Labour Organization. By monitoring wages, working conditions, and human rights violations, these groups are focusing attention on the human costs of international capitalist development and working to shape and re-shape the global economy that has emerged since the 1980s.

Women Workers in the New Global South

As New South industrialization became the model for global development in the late twentieth century, the life patterns adopted by women working in factory jobs across the Global South have followed a template set by women workers of the American South. Competition for wage jobs in the New South was fierce, and newly opened southern factories had little trouble filling their spinning and weave rooms with young women workers who migrated from rural areas into mills and factories. Manufacturers touted the dexterity and "nimble fingers" of female employees, who nevertheless were classified as unskilled labor. Small female hands were considered ideal for the tasks of textile work, perfect for tying broken threads as well as plying needles in the garment trade throughout the region. Considered cheap but diligent labor, women were seen by employers as more content than their male counterparts, more easily "cowed" and less likely to participate in walkouts or strikes.[11] Over the past two decades, this pattern has been repeated on a massive scale throughout the Global South. In 2008, the "nimble fingers" of women workers were in high demand around the world, from Managua, Nicaragua, to Margi-lan, Uzbekistan, to the Pearl River Delta in southern China. Indeed, the majority of the workers in export-oriented manufacturing units in the Special Economic Zones of China are young women between the ages of sixteen and twenty-five, who are preferred because, according to one report, they have "small delicate hands that can do fine work, are willing to spend long hours at a stretch on repetitive tasks, and are obedient and easy to control."[12] Seen by their employers as key to the economic miracle of globalization, women workers themselves speak of "falling through the floor [of] the world's factory," sinking below the minimum standard for socially acceptable work as defined by the International Labour Organiza-tion (ILO).[13]

The experiences of women in the New South in the late nineteenth and the twentieth centuries provide compelling historical precedents for Global South workers in the twenty-first century. Despite enormous ob-stacles—child labor, low wages, occupational segregation by gender and race, virulent anti-unionism, absentee owners, isolated mill communities, and complicit state and local governments—southern women workers re-sponded to the economic and social changes confronting them by turning to specific forms of gendered resistance. Collective organization, strikes, workers' education, and cross-class cooperation were the hallmarks of women's activism for social and economic justice in the U.S. South. The success of these efforts depended on women workers' ability to find places in which they could see themselves as part of a collective, find their voices, and openly "speak their minds." Venues where this could happen var-ied from the factory floor to company housing, from YWCA industrial clubs to union halls. For textile workers from the Baldwin Mill in Marion, North Carolina, who went on strike in 1929, the Southern Summer School for Women Workers in Industry provided such a space. Students and fac-ulty from the school joined together to support the Marion strikers as they walked the picket line. When the strike ended, women from Marion became part of the school's effort to build networks of women organizers and activists across the region.

Like those in Mexico and China in the twenty-first century, women in the southern United States were often the first members of their fami-lies to move from farm to factory and take an industrial job. The major-ity of these women began mill work between the ages of fourteen and twenty-four, though many were even younger. As late as the 1970s, some southern women still at their looms had first entered southern factories as children of ten or twelve. From the beginning, economic and political factors particular to the New South economy made engaging in collective organizing more difficult for southern women workers than for their counterparts in the industrial Northeast. Barriers to collective action and trade union organization in the U.S. South included the persistence of child labor until World War I, a surplus of workers in the region, rural-based industries far from urban labor centers, a manufacturing base largely controlled from outside the region, a repressive political system firmly allied with manufacturers, and a high concentration of women workers in agriculture and domestic service. These same factors were shaping the global economy in 2008 and still cast a shadow on the work lives of women around the world.

The percentage of women working in manufacturing in the southern United States remained low throughout the twentieth century, just as it has in the Global South. As mechanization increases with each new industrial wave, it becomes possible to achieve higher production levels with even fewer workers. In 1910, 83 percent of the female workforce in the South remained in agriculture and domestic service, compared with 33 percent in the North. By 1940, 46 percent of women wage earners in the South (compared to 24 percent in the North) still worked in agriculture or service jobs, which historically have received little attention from organized labor.

As late as 1950, less than 18 percent of southern women workers worked in manufacturing, the segment of the economy most likely to be unionized, compared with almost twice as many, 34 percent, of their peers in the North.[14] Southern women in other sectors, and especially in agriculture, constituted a large pool of workers waiting to "move up" to manufacturing work. This labor surplus reduced the job security of industrial workers and increased the leverage manufacturers had over them. Mexico faces a similar situation in the early twenty-first century, with only 24 percent of its workforce occupying industrial jobs as of 2003. In China, despite its rapid industrialization in recent years, in 2006, 43 percent of the population continued to work in agriculture, while only 25 percent were employed in industry. In a report published by the Bureau of Labor Statistics, Judith Bannister estimates that there are as many as two hundred million "surplus" workers currently unemployed in China's agricultural sector. She predicts that five hundred million peasants will have migrated to Chinese cities in search of factory work by 2016.[15] As in the U.S. South, although on a scale several orders of magnitude larger, these workers form a surplus labor force that waits in reserve for industrial jobs.

Child labor also severely hampered the organization of women workers in the U.S. South. The low standard of living among southern families and the lack of legislative restrictions on manufacturers in the region perpetuated the use of child labor long after it had disappeared in New England. Between 1880 and 1900, the number of children working in the mills and factories of the industrialized southern Piedmont region quadrupled. The proportion of adult women workers declined from 47 to 33 percent, while that of children under sixteen increased to 26 percent.[16] This shift had an adverse impact on organizing in the region. "Unionism is a signal failure in textile work, as cotton mills employ too many children," the secretary of a textile union reported in 1911. In Texas, she noted, "About one-third or more of the hands are children, most of them too small to take into a union."[17]

Because of the detrimental impact of child labor on adult jobs, wages, and organizing efforts, the Knights of Labor, the American Federation of Labor (AFL), local textile affiliates, and state federations concentrated on eliminating children from southern factories. In 1901, child labor bills were introduced in the region's four leading textile states, the Carolinas, Georgia, and Alabama, where they met stiff opposition. Underage workers continued to labor in large numbers throughout the South until World War I. In 1946, southerners made up 25 percent of the nation's population but received only 8 percent of the national income, a circumstance that continued to encourage early entrance into the workforce. Because wage rates were low for all workers, southern families often depended on the wages of two or more family members, including underage children.[18] Similar circumstances now shape the lives of families on the industrializing edge of the Global South. In 2004, the ILO estimated that worldwide, 218 million children between five and seventeen years of age worked as agricultural laborers, domestic workers, and service employees.[19]

As discussed in chapter 6, the biracial and segregated nature of the southern workforce proved a formidable challenge to the labor movement in the South. Rural workers, white and black, male and female, constituted an enormous reserve labor force that management used to threaten industrial workers throughout the region. Racial segregation in the southern workforce exacerbated the tensions that already existed between white and black workers. Even though black workers were only occasionally used as strikebreakers, the lower wages they received threatened white job security and kept the demands of white operatives to a minimum.[20]

Following a similar pattern, the workforce across the Global South is separated into regional, national, and ethnic categories that are hierarchically ranked and constantly pitted against one another. Workers in Mexico, Central America, and the Caribbean have lost jobs to lower-wage workers in southern China. Chinese workers already have seen their jobs outsourced to Vietnam. And garment workers in Vietnam, where inflation reached 27 percent in July 2008, have participated in wildcat strikes, sought trade union representation, and lobbied for a minimum wage, leading manufacturers to move quickly to relocate factories to India and Bangladesh, where they can pay lower wages and find workers who will acquiesce to seventy to eighty hours of required overtime per month. In every nation from Mexico to Brazil, from China to Vietnam, the workforce, already divided by ethnicity and gender, has been further fragmented by the migration of indigenous populations to cities for work, religious differences, and preferential hiring practices. In the Xinjiang region of China, for instance, newly opened mills give Han Chinese migrants preferential treatment in the hiring process, while denying equal access to jobs to the traditional Uighur population, which is primarily Muslim.[21] Mexican workers compete against both workers in the United States and workers further south as maquiladoras open across Central America. And with increasing frequency, Chinese workers vie for jobs with lower-paid workers in Vietnam and Cambodia.

Still other characteristics of the industrial economy in the American South made collective action and unionization difficult to achieve. The manufacturing sector was geographically dispersed across a thousand-mile stretch of Piedmont from the Appalachian Mountains to the eastern coastal plain. Long distances between factories and mills made it difficult for workers to communicate and arduous for organizers to cover their assigned territories. Many southern factories located in remote agricultural areas far from urban centers of skilled workers provided the only wage work available for miles around, so that while many workers competed for the few available jobs, few factories had to compete for workers. When southern industrial workers organized, they generally did so in isolation. The assistance of nearby farmers who supplied food during southern strikes could not take the place of sympathetic unionists in an urban environment who would honor a picket line or strike in support of fellow workers. Identical problems currently persist across the Global South, a region that stretches for almost ten thousand miles, literally around the world, from one continent to the next. In individual countries, including Mexico, Brazil, and China, isolated manufacturing corridors are hundreds of miles apart, divided by expansive agricultural areas, and often closed off to outsiders, much like New South company towns.

To encourage the development of industrial communities throughout the South, southern state and local governments provided multifaceted assistance to manufacturers, including low-cost utility services, roads, and tax breaks. In return, manufacturers built company towns that provided workers with double-edged benefits: rental housing that was close to the mill or factory but tightly regulated, and a tightly knit community that kept outsiders at bay but limited personal independence. Desirable amenities came at a cost. Edith Kowski, a New York City garment worker and Amalgamated Clothing Workers of America (ACWA) member, visited one of these towns in 1928. The mill in West Durham, North Carolina, employed 1,100 workers and provided housing, a community center complete with gym, bowling alleys, library, movies, night high school classes, and clubs for everyone from babies to grandmothers. According to Kowski, the workers' lives were "so absolutely entrenched in the village life that there is no leaving it and Mr. Erwin, the owner, reigns as 'God Almighty.'"[22] Many decades later, in 2004, a reporter visiting the Guangdong Chigo factory in Nanhai, China, described August 3 as a "red-letter day" for dozens of workers who stood in line for "a rare treat in this dusty industrial town: free run of the shady, company-owned orchard, filled with ripe pomegranates." Chan Ya-xi, a twenty-one-year-old worker, flashed her company ID at the guards and rushed past the gate. "This is a very nice benefit," she told Mei Fong of the *Wall Street Journal*. Between 1999 and 2004, Chigo's owner, Li Xinghao, the "Mr. Erwin" of Nanhai, built "a swimming pool, new housing and a reading room for his workers" and countered high turnover rates with higher salaries and bonuses for workers who stayed more than three years.[23] Today, Chinese workers migrate to join companies that provide benefits, just as manufacturers, in both the New South and the Global South, built factories in areas offering tax exemptions, low utility rates, cheap land, low-wage workers, and often state-supported technical education programs. Both the New South and the Global South have been touted as havens from organized labor, and state and local governments throughout both regions have strived to maintain both the image and the reality of union-free states. Company benefits, from pomegranates to swimming pools, have proved to be powerful antidotes to unionization around the world.

From the beginning of the twentieth century, southern states provided manufacturers with military assistance in strikes. Local government authorities there routinely routed union organizers from their communities, often at gunpoint. After 1947, many southern states passed "right-to-work" laws that prohibited "closed union shops," workplaces where union membership was a condition of employment. Fearing the competition of union labor, manufacturers in nonunion strongholds within the region have since used their political influence to prevent unionized firms from moving into the area. In today's Global South, thousands of worker protests against low wages, withheld pay, and abusive working conditions have been treated as illegal demonstrations. As a consequence, workers from Mexico to China, from Uzbekistan to Vietnam, have been arrested, detained, and sentenced to prison terms for protesting working conditions and organizing collectively.

Despite American human rights protests in opposition to such heavy-handed government intervention against worker's rights, these actions merely repeat the script of labor relations in the New South, a dramatic narrative in which workers regularly faced shootings, abductions, and arrests. For example, in Georgia in 1934, Governor Eugene Talmadge earned mill owners' unwavering gratitude when he declared martial law and held picketers in concentration camps behind barbed wire.[24] And last though not at all least, the use of convict labor had a profound and lasting influence on the New South model of labor relations and the shape of southern workers' lives. Karin Shapiro's examination of how workers in Tennessee coal mining communities stood against the oppression of convict laborers, for instance, demonstrates "that in the postbellum South, as in so many other historical contexts, the actions of men and women could unleash a very different future from the one they expected or for which they hoped," thereby revealing not only "the often cruel legacies of that region's embittered past" but also "a profound sense of new possibilities in the American South."[25]

Parallel Lives across the Globe

Thus, the life stories of women in the American South during the first half of the twentieth century and in the Global South during the early twenty-first century are strikingly parallel. In each of these "Souths," women migrated to factories from rural areas and were often the first members of their families to work in a factory and, not infrequently, the first to earn cash wages. All of the women involved, across time and place, have worked for wages so low that they could not support themselves or their children above the poverty level; in both cases, these wages were the highest of any available job except prostitution. As Jane L. Collins observes in *Threads*, her book on the global apparel industry,

> When we hear about the movement of jobs to Mexico or China, we tend to think of new industries with new male workers. In some cases this is a true picture, but as Jefferson Cowie has noted, the fact that women are often the first to be hired into assembly work and are often the most disposable workers in the chain or production "places them at the heart of the story of both industrialization and deindustrialization." Not only do women make up the majority of workers in the world's new export assembly zones, but ideologies of gender and ethnicity are crucial to the political strategies through which employers recruit and administer a low-cost, efficient, and orderly labor force.[26]

In the U.S. South, white women entering racially segregated factories came from families whose economic situation was in decline, and a similar situation marks today's Global South, where decreasing standards of living and downward mobility in agriculture across generations delineate the lives of workers in the maquiladoras and in mills and factories throughout Central and South America, Central Asia, China, and Vietnam. In many of these areas, as in the U.S. South, young women come of age in communities where religion reinforces traditional ideas about male authority and female submission. In the U.S. South, many of these young women came from families whose harsh childrearing practices socialized both girls and boys to accept emotional and physical violation. In the Global

South, *machismo* and domestic abuse have similarly restricted the lives of both women and men. In all of these locations, incidents of exploitation within the family increased exponentially during periods of economic crisis. The women weavers of Margilan live in a region where an estimated 40 percent of the female population suffer from domestic abuse.[27]

The colonial nature of industrialization in the U.S. South, where a high percentage of manufacturers were based outside of the region, parallels the current system of outsourcing used by U.S. firms in the Global South. Mills and factories in the American South operated with a 1:4 wage differential compared with northern factories. In the Global South, that differential is even greater, with some workers earning less than 10 percent of the wages earned by their counterparts in other parts of the world. In both areas, women were lured into factories by the promise of jobs and cash wages and by hopes for a better life and an increased measure of personal autonomy.

In the U.S. South, industrialists practiced a relentless and severe form of paternalism that appears almost benevolent when compared with twenty-first-century management styles in a global market economy that emphasizes supply chains and human resources over manufacturers' responsibilities. In the early twentieth century, most factory owners had names and faces; twenty-first-century corporate structures encourage industrial anonymity. A 1938 feature story in *Fortune* touted "The Industrial South" not as the nation's "No. 1 economic problem" but as the nation's "No. 1 economic opportunity" for industrialists. With abundant natural and human resources, the South was ripe for development, the article advised American investors. In mining, timber, textiles, cotton spinning, hosiery production, cigars, and canneries, the New South, from the Chesapeake to the Gulf of Mexico, had vast potential, *Fortune* readers were told; low labor and energy costs, low taxes, and low levels of unionization all meant high returns on every dollar of investment. A colorful map oriented readers to the region's diversity and promise.[28]

Seventy years later, the Global South, and more specifically the Pearl River Delta area located on the China/Hong Kong border, was widely hailed in the business press as the "superior investment environment" of 2008. The "Invest Huadu" website, for instance, reads like a page right out of the 1938 issue of *Fortune*, detailing the region's industrial potential, transportation network, population, climate ("neither sweltering in summer, nor cold in winter"), natural resources, low tax rates, and government support for industrial investment. Beautiful pictures show the range of features that Huadu offers: a convenient location, an economic growth rate of 20 percent, "green mountains, clear water, blue sky," and even "the vice center of the North" (e.g., gambling and prostitution), the latter being the only feature that was not openly touted in the New South. Hallmarks of such appeals include outstanding opportunities for foreign trade and economic cooperation; superior housing; and the industrial production of everything from cars to textiles, jewelry, leather products, and parts of all kinds. In Mexico, signs advertising land available for maquiladoras also tout the availability of energy, transportation lines, and urban services.

Gendered Resistance in the New South

Industrial advertising campaigns like those run in *Fortune* in 1938 or on the Huadu website in 2008 are written in coded language that obscures gender, hides race and ethnicity, and renders workers invisible. Deconstructing these ads, reading them inside out, we find the parallel landscapes of the New and Global Souths: low wages, virulent anti-unionism, significant labor unrest, and massive state support for industry. Women workers, essential to the economy of the New South and the "backbone industries" in Huadu and similar regions across the Global South, do not appear on these maps at all. But in both of these places, workers have mobilized extensively to resist oppression and shape the worlds in which they live, despite pervasive obstacles. Gendered resistance, actions through which women (or men) speak out individually or collectively to change the conditions of their lives, played a role in shaping the New South and will have a profound impact on life in Huadu as well.

Women in the New South engaged in ongoing labor struggles for many decades and made substantial gains in wages and in working and living conditions. The activism of southern women workers grew out of the strategies they used to control their work lives in the mills. The high turnover rates at factories and mills throughout the New South represent the most common action individuals used to deal with bad working conditions, abusive bosses, and low wages. Interviews conducted with southern women workers in the 1920s indicate that the turnover rate (e.g., the rate at which women terminated employment) ran as high as 198 percent annually, twice as high as the rate for women workers in the North. Throughout southern mills, what researchers at the Women's Bureau called "the shifting element" made up 56 percent of the workforce, and only 25 percent of southern workers stayed in the same mill for twelve months or longer.[29]

Over time, spontaneous local collective actions that established the limits of behavior that women were willing to accept from management expanded into formal labor protests or formed the germ of union organizing efforts. Gradually a strong cohort of activist women workers, union organizers, scholars, and writers, along with representatives from women's organizations, workers' education alliances, and political organizations, focused their attention on the South and argued that the future of the U.S. labor movement depended on the successful organization of the thousands of young women filing into mills and factories across the region. These activists sought to address the human costs of southern industrialization and mitigate the effects of rapid development that emphasized investment returns over wages and working conditions.

Unions organizing in the U.S. South initially denied the importance of women workers, but as early as 1900, women came to play key leadership roles in strikes and lockouts in three-dozen North Carolina cotton mills. The walkouts of the pre–World War I era, the wave of strikes in southern textiles from 1927 through 1934, labor battles in the post–World War II period, and later union struggles in the Civil Rights decades of the 1960s and 1970s all involved thousands of women workers. Women played multiple roles in these fights, at times leading hundreds of male and female workers out of factories, walking in the front ranks of strike parades, or filling conspicuous posts on picket lines. Without question, the actions of women workers were crucial to labor's struggles in the South throughout the twentieth century.[30] Specific efforts to attract southern women to the unions were quite successful, although each campaign involved bitter intra-union conflicts, anti-union police and National Guard forces, and employers' retaliation with blacklists and armed violence.[31]

As we have seen, working women in the New South were particularly adept at garnering the support of cross-class women's organizations that offered educational resources and information about strategy and tactics. Groups like the National Consumers League (NCL) provided information about how to organize boycotts and label campaigns; the League of Women Voters (LWV) supplied information about legislation and government procedures; the YWCA organized dozens of "industrial clubs" in communities across the South in which women factory workers met on a regular basis to discuss working conditions and wages, factory rules, and educational opportunities. These clubs thrived, especially in communities where union organizing was difficult, if not impossible. Although feminist cooperation across class lines in the South was never a substitute for unity among men and women in factories and unions, such alliances became resources that women workers could tap as they sought more education and expertise. For the women who participated, these women-centered organizations offered vital social spaces in which they could articulate opinions, stake out positions, argue, compromise, and grow.

During every effort to organize workers in the New South, women organizers worked closely with activist workers across the region. Heroic leaders like the "Hellraising" Mother Jones, the martyred Ella Mae Wiggins, and the grandmotherly Lucy Randolph Mason drew attention to women's issues in the workplace, the home, and the community. But it was on the shop floor and in working-class neighborhoods that women forged the connections they needed to commit themselves to collective action. Gendered resistance had a powerful multiplier effect in workplaces and communities where women transformed their autonomy as workers into acts of confrontation and made conscious use of their gender identity in resisting oppressive conditions. Southern women workers, like their predecessors in the North, gradually changed the terms of their employment by speaking their minds, whether quietly to each other or loudly in walkouts or strikes.

Southern industrial women increased their effectiveness as labor activists on the local level by connecting with workers' education programs established in the region after World War I. National programs such as the National Women's Trade Union League (NWTUL), Brookwood Labor College, and the Bryn Mawr Summer School sponsored major southern organizing initiatives in response to the region's increased industrialization. As discussed in chapter 3, the Southern Summer School for Women Workers in Industry was established in 1927 as a residential program to train grass-roots leaders in union organizing, labor history, economics, and public speaking. Students shared their individual life stories and came to see themselves as part of a long history of labor activism and struggle. In 1932, the Highlander Folk School established a workers' education program in Tennessee that served both men and women. Both the Southern Summer School and Highlander ran educational programs in numerous local communities and provided direct assistance to striking southern workers.[32]

In the 1950s and 1960s, a later wave of deindustrialization shut down factories in northern communities from Woonsocket to Yonkers, relocating industries in towns further south. Union organizers renewed their campaign to bring southern workers into labor's camp, both as a way to stabilize wages in the North and to protect the interests of the growing number of southerners in the textile, steel, furniture, and food processing industries. As industries continued to move south, southern workers maintained what had become a long tradition of struggling against low wages, undesirable working conditions, and the lack of autonomy. In the 1950s, women workers played critical roles in the textile strike in Henderson, North Carolina, which lasted from 1958–1960, and in the early 1960s when workers at the Oneita Knitting Mills in Andrews, South Carolina, walked out after their contract expired and the company refused to negotiate a new one. The seven-month strike at Oneita was finally won after a successful boycott. In 1963, the campaign to unionize the J. P. Stevens Textile Company got underway. One of the most ambitious campaigns ever waged in the anti-union South, this arduous effort lasted for seventeen years, included a sexually savvy "Don't Sleep with Stevens" boycott of Stevens' bed sheets, and ended successfully in 1980 with the organization of 3,500 textile workers in twelve southern mills. [33]

Women workers played key roles in each of these strikes, and in the Stevens campaign, African American workers new to southern mills were able to demonstrate their widespread solidarity with the union for the first time. The Oscar-winning film *Norma Rae*, based on the heroic actions of Stevens worker Crystal Lee Sutton, resonated with workers throughout the United States as they witnessed a dramatic standoff between industry and the union and the actions of a woman who knew without question which side she was on. The Stevens campaign brought American labor a major victory that raised the hopes of workers throughout the country, and for a brief moment, it looked as if a century of runaway industrialization in the New South could be staunched and the American labor movement could carry on much as it had since the 1930s. As it turned out, however, once the anti-union Reagan administration gained the White House, the "southernization" of American industry continued unabated. The federal government abandoned the labor movement, steady deindustrialization eroded the weakened manufacturing base in states from

Maine to Michigan, and manufacturers continued their ongoing quest for cheap labor and new sources of "nimble-fingered" women laborers to work the looms and ply needles in the increasingly global textile and garment trades.

Actions by U.S. industrialists in the New South throughout the twentieth century foreshadowed later expansion into the Global South. In fact, by 1980 such expansion was well underway.[34] Wal-Mart, the most successful corporation operating in the global economy of the twenty-first century, grew organically out of the American South in the 1970s and 1980s, integrating every facet of the New South industrial model: low wages and benefits, opposition to trade unions, high turnover rates of 50–75 percent, and the use of child and convict labor. Wal-Mart has added its own twist to the system by buying from non-U.S. subcontractors, Global South–based private manufacturers who hire the workers and take responsibility for the day-to-day production of goods for western markets. Reports issued in 2008 on the use of child labor by subcontracting firms with direct ties to U.S. corporations implicate Wal-Mart, Disney, Dell, and Hasbro.[35] In June 2008, the U.S.-China Economic and Security Review Commission held hearings on the state of China's prison labor system (*laogai*), examined how products made in Chinese prisons enter the United States, and analyzed the effects of the "Memoranda of Understanding between the U.S. and China Regarding Prison Labor" issued in 1992.[36] Wal-Mart, a capitalist phenomenon that historian Nelson Liechtenstein calls "a kind of combination manufacturing and retail global corporation" that now serves as the template for corporations around the world, is the epitome of New South industrial development.[37]

Holding the Line in the Global South

Today in communities across the Global South, new leaders—among them, "Hellraising" Martha Ojeda, the supporters of the martyrs of Ciudad Juarez such as Mireille Rocatti and Lourdes Portillo, and Alma Mejia and Yesenia Bonilla of Honduras—are once again putting themselves on the line for economic justice, working through independent organizations or in trade union federations such as the Frente Auténtico del Trabajo (FAT).[38] In China, Pun Ngai and Chan Wai Ling head the Chinese

Working Women Network (CWWN), a Hong Kong–based NGO committed to community-based labor organizing in the Special Economic Zone of Shenzhen.

Like workers' education activists in the New South, the CWWN operates outside the traditional trade union model to establish a platform from which to begin organizing. Its programming focuses on educating workers about labor rights, protecting themselves against sexual discrimination, and legal and health issues. Pun Ngai advocates cultural projects that encourage migrant workers to collectively fight for, in her words, "their labor and feminist rights." CWWN publishes a Chinese magazine titled *Voices of Dagongmei* (women workers) and is compiling a collection of oral stories of migrant women workers "to engender common and collective working experience and class consciousness." The Women Health Express, a mobile van equipped with diagnostic equipment, provides outreach to women suffering from occupational diseases in three industrial towns in the Pearl River Delta, an area where workers collectively break or lose forty thousand fingers a year and self-organized strikes involving over a thousand workers happen at least once a day. Pun Ngai argues that workers empower themselves when they act collectively to transcend differences in "localities, ethnic origins, gender, age, work positions and the like."[39]

Separated by time and place, these groups of "southern" women workers share the legacy of the human costs of industrialization and globalization. Both groups migrated to factories to earn cash wages, commonly in order to support families left behind in rural areas. Low wages, long hours, and the rising cost of living have made it difficult, if not impossible, to get ahead. Often illegally hired as young girls, workers have faced a plethora of wage violations: not being paid on time or at all, no overtime rates, broken time clocks, and pressure to take work home. Safety violations abound: fire hazards, the absence of safety guards, exposed belts and pulleys. Women industrial workers have risked their health through exposure to poor ventilation, heavy dust, toxic materials, poor lighting, and inadequate rest rooms. As in the New South, terminating their employment is the most frequently used form of protest for women workers throughout the Global South. Turnover rates among women workers in Mexico, Central America, China, and Vietnam remain high, exceeding 50 percent per year in many Chinese factories. Like the women workers charged with "disorderly conduct" in the strikes that spread throughout the New South in 1929, when Ding Xiulan and Liu Meifeng led protests of several hundred workers at the Zhongheng Textile Company, demanding back pay for layoffs in 2004, Chinese authorities arrested them on charges of "disturbing social order."[40]

Among the twenty-first-century groups fighting for workers' rights in the Global South are two organizations that evolved from the Southern Summer School and the Highlander Folk School of the 1920s and 1930s: the Southern School for Union Women and the Highlander Research and Education Center. In addition, STITCH's Women Organizing for Social Justice in Central America, US/LEAP's Labor Education in the Americas Project, the United Electrical Workers Union's FAT Labor Workshop and Studies Center, and the AFL-CIO's Solidarity Centers in Guatemala and El Salvador are working to end discrimination against women on the job and to help women workers become strong union leaders. Each of these groups affirms the experiences of individual women workers and the power of the collective and runs leadership training and research and education programs with a transnational focus in communities throughout the Americas.[41]

In 2009, transnational feminist organizations include the Coalition for Justice in the Maquiladoras, Women on the Border, the Coalition of Labor Union Women (CLUW), the Colectiva Feminista Binacional and La Mujer Obrera, the Association for Women's Rights in Development (AWID), and the Comité Fronterizo de Obreros (CFO) Committee of Women Workers, as well as long-established groups such as the YWCA and the League of Women Voters, both of which have global initiatives that target women and build leadership skills through education and exchange programs.[42] Oxfam International works with thirteen organizations on three continents to fight poverty and injustice and regularly documents working conditions around the world, exposing the practices of individual companies by documenting abuses on a case-by-case basis.

In China, evidence suggests that labor unrest increased between 2002 and 2009. Some reports indicate that the number of workers involved in strike actions doubled in the first half of the 1990s, others that thirty thousand workers' protests of "significant size" occurred in 2000 alone, averaging more than eighty per day. As China has become known as the "workshop of the world," or as some say, "the sweatshop of the world," workers facing ten- to twelve-hour days, rigid production quotas, and abysmally low hourly wages or piece rates have begun to use tactics pioneered in the 1930s by industrial unions in the United States. For example, in late 2001, two thousand workers occupied the Shuangfeng Textile Factory, protesting pay cuts and missing pension funds. Workers refused to leave the factory and went back to work only after the company promised to return lost savings and pensions worth US$14 million.[43]

In 2002, workers at the Nanxuan Wool Textile Factory in southern China's Pearl River Delta region participated in a three-day riot. By 2004, such strikes and protests had increased dramatically as China sold off more than 190,000 state companies to private investors: 6,800 workers went out for seven weeks at China Resources, a Hong Kong-listed retailer in northern China; in Shaanxi province, another 7,000 workers, the majority of them women, struck at the Tianwang Textile Factory. According to China Labor Watch, a U.S. labor-rights group, "about 1,000 police appeared at the factory gates with water cannons four days into the strike" and "were met by thousands of workers who surrounded them, forcing them to back down."[44]

In January 2008, amid labor shortages in south China and high inflation rates, labor activists reported rising labor unrest throughout the country. By June 2008, the *China Labour Bulletin* reported that a "continuous wave of industrial action" had forced the government to reassess workers' needs in light of a 1982 constitutional amendment that made the word "strike" (*bagong*) taboo. Although China has trade unions—tightly organized and boasting the world's largest membership rosters—they are widely considered "an embarrassing joke," and Chinese workers do not have the constitutional right to strike. But like their counterparts in the New South in the 1920s and 1930s, they are walking out anyway—and the cumulative effect of thousands upon thousands of shutdowns, slowdowns, and sit-downs is becoming difficult to ignore.[45] Factories in Vietnam, one of the fastest growing economies in the Global South, have also been hit by waves of strikes since 2005.

Protests against low wages and harsh conditions have increased in number and intensity as growth has slowed and inflation soared. On PBS's *Bill Moyer's Journal* on August 22, 2008, Moyers interviewed Philip Pan, author of *Out of Mao's Shadow: The Struggle for the Soul of a New China* (2008). The heart of the interview was a discussion of women factory workers that complicated the spectacular picture of a "new" China portrayed on NBC television during the 2008 Olympics:

BILL MOYERS: I was watching the beach volleyball the other night. And suddenly, I got up and looked at the T-shirt I was wearing. And it had a "Made in China" label. Help us understand what life is like for the women who made that T-shirt.

PHILIP PAN: Most of the women in these factories, they're from the countryside, poor villages. Many of them are young, often underage, who have been pulled out of school because their parents can't afford to pay the taxes just based on their farm income. They have to send their children to the cities to make extra income, in order to just pay taxes. Their opportunities are limited. In these factories, their rights are limited as well. They cannot form unions. They have very few venues to complain about working conditions. And because the labor force is so large, they have little leverage as well, in terms of wages. At the same time, though, these factories are paying them much more than they could have ever made in the countryside. And so, they're willing to take these jobs, and often times, they improve their lives through these jobs, if they can survive the conditions.

BILL MOYERS: In other accounts, I read of women crammed into dark and damp dormitories, working seven days a week with three days a year off. Their workshops filled with smoke, their eyes burning and watery, the skin on their hands peeling and painful. I read of 50,000 fingers slashed off in China every year, of more than a million workers contacting fatal diseases, of workers trying to organize, as you say, and being beaten and hauled to jail. And the picture that emerges to me is of a communist police state enforcing the most extreme model of capitalism.

PHILIP PAN: There are officials in this party who still cling to the old communist values, I would guess, of egalitarianism, of labor rights. You know, after all, this party did promise a worker's paradise. And so, there are parts of the party that are concerned about this issue. And other parts of the party are also concerned, just simply because they're worried that if conditions get too bad, they would have a revolution on their hands. But generally, yes. You know, they call themselves Communist, but they've adopted a form of capitalism, capitalism without democratic checks on it, essentially. And so, you have market forces in the extreme, as you say, with very few options for workers to fight back.

Along with the debut of communist capitalism on the world stage has come what some critics have called "an era of silence and forgetting" in which the historical excesses of both communism and capitalism have been ignored.[46] In many parts of the Global South, losses outweigh gains for women workers caught up in a form of economic development that has replaced New South paternalism, and in some places Communist paternalism, with a production process based on a subcontracting model in which workers have no contracts, no voice, no grievance system, and little knowledge about the firms for which they work. At the plants that Jane Collins studied in Mexico (Burlmex and Confitek), workers are "not laboring in a nascent industry in a nation that is taking its first steps toward economic development" but rather "working for multinational corporations in a globally organized production process that, in the case of Liz Claiborne, encompasses thirty-two countries." As U.S. activists in the United States had done through groups like the WTUL in the 1910s and the National Consumers League in the 1920s, Collins calls for "new international communities of accountability, focused on particular firms and their brands." These strategies, used effectively in the first half of the twentieth century, have the potential, Collins argues, to counteract corporate investment strategies that determine the fate of workers throughout the Global South, from Mexico to China to Uzbekistan, where women workers in Margilan spend hot summer afternoons and cold winter mornings weaving on Carolina looms.

Margilan Weavers and Carolina Looms

Looms removed from New England mills made their way south in the decades after 1880. In the 1940s and 1950s, looms from the Carolinas made their way to Texas and then even further south.

The looms I saw in Margilan in 2006 were, in fact, U.S.-made looms manufactured by the Draper Company in Hopedale, Massachusetts. The first Draper loom appeared in 1895; the ones in Margilan are Model K and Model XK looms, which went into production in 1918 and in the 1930s, respectively.[47] How did these looms get to Uzbekistan? No one in Margilan was sure, but one likely scenario is that they were shipped south from Massachusetts in the 1920s and early 1930s and then overseas as southern mill owners who could afford to do so replaced their outdated looms with new equipment in factories throughout the region. Many of the older

Figure 8.4. "Elliott White Springs pictured with old mill machinery at Lancaster Cotton Mill." Reproduced from *The Springs Story: The First One Hundred Years*. Courtesy of the William Elliott White Homestead Archives, Fort Mill, S.C.

looms, most of them Draper models, were sold abroad. Elliott Springs, for example, inherited six South Carolina cotton mills, a lot of outdated equipment, and a passel of creditors from his father in 1931. Faced with how to dispose of these outmoded looms, Springs sold as many as he could (see Figure 8.4).[48]

During the 1930s, U.S. machinery dealers shipped both new and secondhand looms all over the world, often directly from a factory that was upgrading or closing. Around this time, the Soviet Union (USSR) purchased a large amount of industrial equipment from the United States, including many obsolete looms from the Carolinas, as it expanded its manufacturing sector in textiles, automobiles, farm equipment, locomotives, military equipment, and steel. From there, the looms were either sent directly to Uzbekistan, whose textile industry began its slow rise after Stalin came to power in 1927, or found their way there sometime before or after being used in Russia. A major textile factory was built in Margilan in 1930 because of its close proximity to the cotton fields of the Ferghana Valley. After the German invasion of Russia in 1941, more than 280 manufacturing enterprises, including numerous textile factories and their looms, were moved to Uzbekistan. The Uzbek Republic became one of the USSR's leading wartime arsenals, and these evacuated enterprises produced everything from planes to grenades to parachutes.[49]

Another possible scenario is that after being replaced with newer models at some point between the late 1920s and 1940, these Draper looms languished in a mill warehouse in the American South until the early 1970s, when they were shipped to Uzbekistan to outfit the Yoderlik Mill in Margilan, which the British Council in Uzbekistan helped establish. A few southern U.S. mills used their Draper looms well into the 1960s and even beyond; some were still intact in the Santee Mill in Bamberg, South Carolina, until the mill shut down for good in 1986. As the New South gradually deindustrialized, mill owners unloaded as much equipment as possible, either for much-needed cash or for installation in new factories elsewhere. Norris Dearmon, who worked for Cannon Mills in Kannapolis, North Carolina, for forty-three years, remembers when the giant plant employed eighteen thousand people. After changing owners and more than a decade of laying off workers, the mill closed in July 2003, and according to Dearmon, "all the equipment's been stripped out and sent to China, India, Mexico, wherever. They really cleaned it out."[50] In early 2008, the Lancaster, South Carolina, company that Elliott Springs saved from bankruptcy in 1931 merged with a Brazilian firm to become Springs Global. Donnie Ingram, who was laid off after more than thirty years of work in what had been the largest fabricating and finishing facility under one roof in the world, told a reporter that "the machines inside are being moved to Brazil." The business of recycling mill equipment has gone on for well over a century.

In recent years, the massive deindustrialization of the former Soviet Union has sent countless trucks loaded with dismantled factory equipment and industrial infrastructure roaring across Central Asia on their way to China. As the world's new industrial power, China has become a magnet for valuable metal from around the world, most of it now in the form of scrap. As the old New South divested itself of both its industrial equipment and its place as the textile center of the world, those red brick mills that once stretched "like pearls on a necklace" from Richmond to

Birmingham began to be rehabbed into trendy apartments, lofts, and offices that were then purchased by folks whose mortgages are held by Chinese lenders, another example of the retrofitting of the obsolete. These changes remind us that what is obsolete in one venue is cutting edge in another. They bring us back to a future that underscores the complicated and intertwining stories of industrialization, deindustrialization, material culture, gender, and work. "Who makes what, where, when, and why" has been and continues to be a complicated question that mirrors the intricacies of local and global economic, political, and cultural systems of production and consumption.

Uzbekistan's textile industry is a case in point, for in 2003, a new factory opened several miles down the road from Margilan's Yodorlik Mill. An Uzbekistan-Turkey joint venture, this mill has modern facilities, new equipment, and a growing and mostly female workforce that produces 5,200 tons of 100 percent cotton carded yarn for the expanding textile manufacturing markets of Central Asia, Turkey, Iran, and China. Representatives from each of these markets traveled to Tashkent in April 2008 to attend the CAITME Conference, where they planned the reindustrialization of Uzbekistan. Three years earlier, in the same city, the Tashkent Women's Resource Center (TWRC), an NGO committed to improving women's economic and political status, had closed under pressure from the Uzbek government. Women activists throughout Uzbekistan continue to monitor the conditions of women workers in this rapidly changing country in *sotto voce* collaboration with regional and international women's organizations.[51]

The New South

The New South template of industrial development, that venerable dream of progress and profit, has both a history and a future: from England to New England, from New England to the U.S. South, from the U.S. South to Mexico, and then on to Central and South America and around the globe. Africa alone remains untapped by massive industrial expansion, and Chinese companies are already actively investing there and hiring the next generation of "nimble fingers." The metaphoric point at which "the developed North" meets "the undeveloped South" is constantly shifting. But the significance of women's activism does not change. Workers' efforts to organize themselves and negotiate collectively for fair wages and safe working conditions offer the most promising path to realizing basic human rights and social and economic justice, locally, nationally, and internationally. In 1948 when Eleanor Roosevelt asserted, "Where, after all, do universal human rights begin? In small places, close to home—so close and so small that they cannot be seen on any maps of the world," she affirmed the power of the individual within the collective milieu of the community and workplace. These are the places, she argued, that people seek "equal justice, equal opportunity, equal dignity without discrimination," concluding that "unless these rights have meaning there, they have little meaning anywhere. Without concerted citizen action to uphold them close to home, we shall look in vain for progress in the larger world."[52]

In the Global South today, cross-border cooperation involves negotiating different boundaries and new forms of organization. Today's activists need access to the contested and suppressed labor history of "other Souths," for while each generation creates its own future, the collective historical consciousness of workers, activists, and trade unionists can move the struggle forward toward economic justice. Each new wave of industrial development brings with it optimism and despair. As Tina Rosenberg acknowledged about globalization in the *New York Times* in 2002, "Since the mid-1970's, Japan, Korea, Taiwan, China and their neighbors have lifted 300 million people out of poverty, chiefly through trade." But the protestors are also right, she argues, for "no nation has ever developed over the long term under the rules being imposed today on third-world countries by the institutions controlling globalization."[53]

In the ongoing story of capital migration, as historian Jefferson Cowie contends, "new locales were always sites of tremendous optimism for women and men eager to work for a living." The "dour tale of plant shutdowns" and the "hopeful story of plant openings" are, he points out, opposite sides of the same coin.[54] By the same token, narratives of having a steady job and making money—or as Janet Patterson, the first black hemmer in the sheet department at Cannon Mills, put it, of making "good money, even to the point I used to make *enough* money"—are balanced by concerns about exploitation and oppressive conditions.[55] At the first Southern Summer School in 1927, Elbe Robertson, a textile worker from Virginia, posed the question, "Should we spend our lives making others richer, while our own wants are deferred?" Eighty years later, Alma Mejia, a worker in Honduras, told STITCH interviewers that "the transnational companies have always wanted to exploit and pay women less." In 2006,

Ms. Zhang, a factory worker in China's Pearl River Delta, spoke of the need for women to act on their own behalf. Given the conditions, she warns, "the first step is difficult enough," but "what women workers need the most is to know something about the law . . . [so they] can protect their rights, . . . make progress and improve their condition." As Lynda Leech, a member of the United Electrical, Radio and Machine Workers of America, wrote recently about UE's "Hands Across the Border" program aimed at organizing women workers internationally, "Let history repeat itself, as oppression is overcome."[56]

Coda

Southern Workers on the World Stage

Looking south across the Ohio River from Cincinnati, architect Daniel Libeskind's post-modern high rise on the Kentucky side stands as a material reminder of the South's prosperity and promise in the years when the crumbling infrastructure of the Rust Belt gave way to the economic and demographic transformations taking place in the Sunbelt. The oil crisis of 1973, the triumph of southern anti-unionism during the Reagan years, the deindustrialization of the Northeast and Midwest, and the beginning of a new wave of globalization shifted the center of U.S. economic activity and population growth to the region of the nation that had long been considered the most traditional and backward.

Almost overnight, in the 1990s the South became the focus of national attention as cities across the region, led by Atlanta, doubled in size. In those years, new construction hit record levels, industrial output remained steady, and the population boomed, largely as the result of in-migration from northern cities like Detroit and Cleveland as well as new immigration from Mexico, Guatemala, and points even further south. The industries that built the New South—textiles, tobacco, and steel—gradually left the region, but new businesses emerged—from poultry processing to auto manufacturing to financial services, information technology, and tourism. The region's economy became more diversified, both economically and demographically, than at any other time in its history.

The essays in *Looking South* reflect on major transitions in southern history by examining two paradigm shifts in the region's workforce, the first occurring at the end of the nineteenth century in the wake of Emancipation, the second at the end of the twentieth century with the economic changes brought about by deindustrialization and globalization.

As we have seen, the tangible material, political, and cultural successes of the first generations of freedmen and freedwomen included creating communities from scratch in the perilous period after the Civil War, constructing churches and schools, developing independent businesses, and actively participating in local, national, and international organizations and associations. These remarkable achievements, often accomplished with meager funds and a reliance on a unique combination of mutuality, innovation, and savvy, were met with damningly virulent negativism and hostility by white southerners who could not bear to see the upward mobility and material success of a population they had once enslaved. The quest for universal citizenship moved southern African Americans from enslavement to independence, but slavery and segregation continued to cast deep shadows. Hopes for full citizenship for all southerners gave way to divisions marked by race, ethnicity, class, and gender. Today's generation of southern workers, in contrast, live in a South where the black/white color line established by *Plessy v. Ferguson* in 1896 has given way to new divisions in a population rapidly becoming not simply African American and Anglo but Latino and Asian as well and in a world in which their history is being reenacted in the new Global South.

The argument that runs throughout *Looking South* is that the labor systems that were adopted as the South industrialized in the late nineteenth century became the model for U.S. industrial expansion in the twentieth century and the paradigm for industrial development exported abroad beginning in the 1950s. In the early years of the twenty-first century, the model of industrial expansion and production that was created in the era of the New South and fully developed in the second half of the twentieth century became the template for global capitalist development. The Global South is heir to the New South, with the powerful triptych of antiunionism, low wages, and state-supported industry firmly in place.

The dream of universal citizenship in a free and civil society that Lillian Smith's *Killers of the Dream* depicted being destroyed by hatred, greed, and reactionary traditions emanated from a history marked by slavery and oppression. This was the dream sought by African American men and women after Emancipation, pursued by black and white southern women who wanted the vote in their congregations and in their communities, and by southern workers across the generations, regardless of race, ethnicity, or gender. At different points in its history, the South has been a place of promise and hope. This was true after Emancipation and during

Reconstruction; it proved true again in the 1920s, when a huge sign over Birmingham welcomed visitors to "The Magic City" and across the South an economic boom supported by textiles and steel promised prosperity and plenty, if not for all, at least for some. The civil rights movement of the 1950s and 1960s set in motion the hope of new freedoms and opportunities to millions of men, women, and children across the South, the nation, and the world. In the Sunbelt years, the South again proffered images of prosperity and expansion that drew people in from far and wide.

Yet each of these periods has, in its own way, fallen short of its vision, or worse. The dream of freedom and universal citizenship promised by Emancipation and Reconstruction died in the extralegal violence unleashed across the region that killed thousands of African Americans and destroyed black communities in Wilmington, North Carolina; Atlanta, Georgia; Tulsa, Oklahoma; and Rosewood, Florida, just four of many places where white rioters wreaked deadly havoc. The majority of African American men had been disenfranchised by the turn of the twentieth century, and black men, women, and children faced a destructive system of legal segregation that relegated them to second-class citizenship and made it increasingly difficult for them to make a living, let alone realize the lives that freedom had promised. White workers seeking new opportunities as they moved from field to factory in the early years of the twentieth century found little magic in the cities and textile towns of the South, where they worked long hours for paychecks that barely paid for food and rent. On many occasions, southern individualism gave way to collective action as workers sought to join unions to change the system and gain the respect and dignity they deserved. The dream of interracial solidarity, realized most completely by workers in unions with black and white members, remained a powerful vision. As George Pozzetta wrote two decades ago, the hope and optimism exuded by the very idea of the Sunbelt caused "a very diverse set of people to move to the urban South," including "impoverished Haitian boat lifters, retirees from ethnic communities in the North, Cuban exiles, undocumented Mexican migrants, Vietnamese refugees, and unemployed third- and fourth-generation ethnic Americans from nearly every part of the nation." Still seen as the gateway to a land of new opportunity for immigrants coming to the United States, especially those from Mexico and Central and South America, the South continues to diversify, proving Pozzetta's point that "the very term *South* itself implies a regional homogeneity that in fact does not exist."[1]

For a region the rest of the nation often views as static and traditional, the South remains a place of transformation and resistance. Change has been one of the few constants in a region where people have long been shaped by forces larger than themselves: slavery, war, freedom, segregation, industrialization, migration, immigration, and deindustrialization, to name only a few. The transformation brought by African American freedom and citizenship after Emancipation and again during the Civil Rights Movement and the white resistance to fundamental changes in the economic and social system together form the primary narrative of southern history. Now, at the beginning of the twenty-first century, at a time when southerners are more diverse than ever, there once again is an opportunity to write a new script, to transform the region, to overcome resistance and reaction, and finally to realize what has eluded previous generations—the dream of universal citizenship that can truly make the South a land of promise and hope.

Notes

Introduction

1. Lewis, *W. E. B. Du Bois: Biography of a Race*, 68–70.
2. Du Bois, *Autobiography*, 112.
3. Elisabeth Christman, "Letter to Members of the Executive Board," 29 June 1927, Reel 4, NWTUL Papers.

Chapter 1. Labor, Race, and Homer Plessy's Freedom Claim

1. "The Strike. Governor Foster Takes Steps to Increase the Militia," *New Orleans Times Picayune*, 10 November 1892, 1.
2. *Harrisburg Daily Telegraph*, 18 January 1863. The "vine and fig tree" reference comes from Micah 4:4–5. Booker T. Washington, *Up From Slavery*, 19. Anna Woods Interview with Mary D. Hudgins, Slave Narratives from the Federal Writers' Project, 1936–1938, Arkansas Narratives, Volume II, Part 7, 227, Library of Congress. Woods prefaced her story with her memory of the day and time when the Union soldiers arrived: "Seems to me like it was on a Monday morning when they come in. Yes, it was a Monday."
3. Winik, *April 1865*, 354.
4. Eric Foner, *Reconstruction*; Cimbala and Miller, eds., *The Freedmen's Bureau and Reconstruction*, ix; Berlin, Fields, Miller, Reidy, and Rowland, eds., *Free at Last*, 167–180.
5. The Thirteenth Amendment (1865) guaranteeing the permanent abolition of slavery; the Fourteenth Amendment (1868) securing the rights of those formerly enslaved, providing a broad definition of citizenship, and providing equal protection under the law to all people; and the Fifteenth Amendment (1870) prohibiting each government in the United States from denying a citizen the right to vote based on that citizen's "race, color or previous condition of servitude."
6. Barry Goldberg, "Slavery, Race and the Languages of Class," in Gates, ed., *Cultural and Literary Critiques of the Concepts of "Race,"* 104.
7. Medley, *We as Freemen*, 17, 27; Arnesen, *New Orleans Daily Picayune, New Orleans Times*, 17 June 1873; "Strikes and Conflict," in *Encyclopedia of U.S. Labor and Working-Class History*, 525. See T. Harry Williams, "The Louisiana Unification Movement in the United States," *Journal of Southern History*. Letwin focuses on interracial unionism among coal miners in the same period in *The Challenges of Interracial Unionism*.

8. C. Vann Woodward, "The Case of the Louisiana Traveler," in Garraty, ed., *Quarrels That Have Shaped the Constitution*, 157–74.

9. Similar restrictions in the form of written and unwritten racial codes also began to be instituted in towns and cities of the Northeast, Midwest, and West.

10. Medley, *We as Freemen*, 79–80. "Local Intelligence," "Classification of Cars," *New Orleans Crescent*, 7 May 1867; "The Car Question," *New Orleans Times*, 7 May 1867.

11. "Grand Unification," *New Orleans Times*, 15 July 1873, 4. The unification platform is also reprinted in Olsen, *The Thin Disguise*, 36–39.

12. Medley, *We as Freemen*, 86.

13. New Orleans city directories from 1886–1924 list his occupations as shoemaker, laborer, clerk, and insurance agent; see "Homer Adolph Plessy," Conrad, ed., *Dictionary of Louisiana Biography*, vol. 2, 655.

14. Daniel Rosenberg, *New Orleans Dockworkers*, 5–6. Only African Americans, free blacks included, were given the death penalty when convicted of arson or of raping a white woman.

15. Olsen, *The Thin Disguise*, 69; *Crusader*, June 1892, reproduced in Medley, *We as Freemen*, 146.

16. "Jim Crow is Dead," *The Crusader*, 28 May 1892.

17. See Rebecca Scott, "Public Rights, Social Equality, and the Conceptual Roots of the Plessy Challenge," *Michigan Law Review*.

18. Medley, *We as Freemen*, 37–52; Dresser, *African Americans on Martha's Vineyard*, 45–57.

19. Medley, *We as Freemen*, 45; "The Workingmen's National Union League," *New York Times*, 21 December 1863, 1.

20. As Woodward recounts in "The Case of the Louisiana Traveler," the first "Jim Crow" law that was applied to railroads was adopted by Florida in 1887. Mississippi followed suit in 1888, Texas in 1889, Louisiana in 1890, Alabama, Arkansas, Georgia, and Tennessee in 1891, and Kentucky in 1892. The Carolinas and Virginia passed similar legislation between 1897 and 1900 (Garraty, ed., *Quarrels That Have Shaped the Constitution*, 157–74).

21. Gordon-Reed, *Race on Trial*, 66. The Comité plan included Walker, with his experience in criminal law, handling preliminary matters in Louisiana, and senior counsel Ohio-born Union Army veteran Albion W. Tourgée taking the case to the United States Supreme Court.

22. *New Orleans States*, 13 October 1892.

23. Quotations from the *New Orleans Times-Democrat* cited in Philip S. Foner, *History of the Labor Movement in the United States*, 201; Olsen, 14; Medley, *We as Freemen*, 163.

24. *Minutes of the Loyal National League of Louisiana, 4 July 1863: Abstract of the Proceedings* (New Orleans: H. P. Lathrop, 1863), 6.

25. "A General Strike. The Amalgamated Council Finally Decides Upon the Step and Orders the Arm of Labor to Become Inert at Noon," *New Orleans Times Picayune*, 5 November 1892, 1.

26. "A General Strike," *New Orleans Times Picayune*, 5 November 1892, 4.

27. "The Blow Struck," *New Orleans Times Picayune*, 6 November 1892, 2.

28. News of the strike appeared in the following articles around the country: "The New Orleans Strike, City Gas Works Shut Down—Talk of Closing the Water Works," *Baltimore Sun*, 9 November 1892, 2; "New Orleans in Darkness," *Knoxville Journal*, 9 November 1892, 2; "The New Orleans Strike," *Dallas Morning News*, 9 November 1892, 2; "Without Change, The Strike Situations in New Orleans," *Duluth News-Tribune*, 9 November 1892, 4; "The Big Strike in New Orleans," *Springfield (Ill.) Republican*, 9 November 1892, 3; "The New Orleans Strike," *Idaho Statesman*, 9 November 1892, 5; "To Prevent Riot, The Governor of Louisiana Advised to Take Charge of the City of New Orleans," *Aberdeen [S. Dak.] Daily News*, 9 November 1892, 1.

29. "The Condition of Business," *New Orleans Times Picayune*, 9 November 1892, 4.

30. "The Strike Situation," *New Orleans Times Picayune*, 7 November 1892, 4.

31. "Let It Not Go By Default," *New Orleans Times Picayune*, 7 November 1892, 4.

32. "The Strike. A Day of Peace in Respect to the Election. The Freight Handlers Join in the General Strike." *New Orleans Times Picayune*, 9 November 1892, 1.

33. "The Strike So Far," *New Orleans Times Picayune*, 9 July 1892, 4.

34. "The Strike. Governor Foster Takes Steps to Increase the Militia," *New Orleans Times Picayune*, 10 November 1892, 1.

35. "Is It Treason? Pennsylvania's Chief Justice Charges the Grand Jury in the Homestead Affair," *New Orleans Times Picayune*, 11 October 1892, 11.

36. "The Strike So Far," *New Orleans Times Picayune*, 9 November 1892, 4.

37. "New Orleans; Governor Responded," *Trenton Evening Times*, 9 November 1892, 4.

38. "The Strike. Governor Foster Takes Steps to Increase the Militia," *New Orleans Times Picayune*, 10 November 1892, 1.

39. "Blood Flows. Pinkerton Men Attempt to Secure Possession of the Carnegie Works. The Strikers Resist," *New Orleans Times Picayune*, 7 July 1892, 1.

40. "A Flag of Truce Repeatedly Shot Down by the Maddened Laborers," *New Orleans Times Picayune*, 7 July 1892, 2.

41. "Settled. The General Strike Called Off This Morning," *New Orleans Times Picayune*, 11 November 1892, 1.

42. "The Strike. Still Smoothing the Rough Edges of the Recent Struggle," *New Orleans Times Picayune*, 19 November 1892, 6.

43. "Settled. The General Strike Called Off This Morning," *New Orleans Times Picayune*, 11 November 1892, 1.

44. Ibid., 1.

45. Quoted in Rosenberg, *New Orleans Dockworkers*, 36; see Nicholson, *Labor's Story in the United States*, 123.

46. Medley, *We as Freemen*, 46–47; "Chief Hennessy Avenged: Eleven of His Italian Assassins Lynched by a Mob," *New York Times*, 14 March 1891, 1.

47. Eric Foner, *Reconstruction*, 581–82. The "separate but equal" doctrine that resulted from the Plessy ruling remained in effect until 1954, when it was overturned by the Supreme Court decision in *Brown v. Board of Education*. It was rendered completely illegal by the federal Civil Rights Act of 1964. Although the Plessy case turned on racial

segregation in the transportation system, it nevertheless formed the legal basis for establishing and maintaining segregated school systems throughout the United States for the subsequent fifty-eight years. The case also had serious implications for occupational segregation in the workplace.

48. In April 1896, arguments for *Plessy v. Ferguson* began. There, Tourgée argued that the state of Louisiana had violated the Thirteenth Amendment, which granted freedom to slaves, and the Fourteenth Amendment, which stated, "no state shall make or enforce any law which shall abridge the privileges or immunities of citizens of the United States; nor shall any state deprive any person of life, liberty, and property, without due process of law." On 18 May 1896, the U.S. Supreme Court also ruled in favor of the State of Louisiana, with a majority of the court arguing that while the object of the Fourteenth Amendment was to "enforce the absolute equality of the two races before the law . . . in the nature of things it could not have been intended to abolish distinctions based on color." Quotations above from Albion W. Tourgée to Louis A. Martinet, 31 October 1893, reprinted in Olsen, *The Thin Disguise*, 78.

49. See Klarman, *Brown v. Board of Education and the Civil Rights Movement* regarding the impact of Court rulings and whether they matter. His argument that the "efficacy of Court decisions depends on certain social and political conditions" holds in the *Plessy* case, as the circumstances of the local strike in New Orleans and the "labor wars" in the North (Homestead in 1892 and Pullman in 1894) combined with the re-establishment of white political power in the South to influence Ferguson and the seven judges who supported him in 1896. Importantly, too, in 1896, the "nation," as it were, with the exception of the African American press and the AME Church, did not speak out against making racial segregation the law of the land. Tourgée argued that if one of the judges "hears from the country," he might change his mind and advised the Comité "to bend every possible energy . . . to reach and awaken public sentiment." In Olsen, *The Thin Disguise*, 79.

50. *Plessy v. Ferguson*, 163 U.S. 537 (1896) (Harlan, J. dissenting), in Olsen, *The Thin Disguise*, 113–21.

51. Like Plessy, Robert Harlan, the son of a white man and an enslaved woman who was three-fourths white, was himself the descendant of one great-grandparent of African heritage. See James Gordon, "Did the First Justice Harlan Have a Black Brother?" in Delgado and Stefancic, eds., *Critical White Studies*, 444–57; *Brown v. Board of Education*, 347 U.S. 483 (1954) in Martin, *Brown v. Board of Education*, 168–74.

52. *New Orleans Times Picayune*, 3 March 1925, 1.

53. Quoted in Blassingame, *Black New Orleans, 1860–1880*, 176.

54. Lewis, *W. E. B. DuBois: Biography of a Race*, 68; *Harrisburg Daily Telegraph*, 18 January 1863; Blight, *Race and Reunion*, 98–139.

Chapter 2. Transformation and Resistance

1. Shawn Michelle Smith, *Photography on the Color Line*, 1; Du Bois, *The Souls of Black Folk*, vii.

2. Du Bois, "The American Negro at Paris," *American Monthly Review of Reviews*,

576. On the Pan American Exposition in Buffalo, see Williams, *Strangers in the Land of Paradise*, 1–5, 183–84.

3. For a detailed catalogue of these stereotypical postcards, as well as a discussion of black stereotypes, see Mashburn, *Black Americana*, 19–21.

4. Du Bois, "The American Negro at Paris," 576.

5. Ibid.

6. Morrison, *Playing in the Dark*.

7. Blassingame, *Black New Orleans, 1860–1880*, 201.

8. Matthew Jacobson addresses the conflation of ethnic identity across the United States in the nineteenth and early twentieth centuries; see Jacobson, *Whiteness of a Different Color*, 68–119.

9. See Christopher Robert Reed, *All the World is Here!* 19–61. Du Bois was in Germany in 1893, the year of the World's Columbian Exposition in Chicago. Had he been in the United States, he would no doubt have become involved in some aspect of the protest against the restrictions on African American access to and participation in the Exposition. In Paris in 1900, the United States Commission made plans to include a "Negro exhibit" and asked Thomas J. Calloway of Tuskegee Institute to spearhead the project. Du Bois used the opportunity to outline an alternative future that rejected racial apartheid and "held out the possibility of decolonialization both at home and abroad." See Fischer and Docherty, eds., *Paris 1900*, 141–42.

10. Williamson, *The Crucible of Race*, 119–20; Wallis, "Black Bodies, White Science."

11. Lewis, *W. E. B. Du Bois: Biography of a Race*, 275.

12. Waligora-Davis, "W. E. B. Du Bois and the Fourth Dimension," 67.

13. duCille, *The Coupling Convention*, 8.

14. Shawn Michelle Smith, "'Looking at One's Self through the Eyes of Others,'" 591–92.

15. Homer Plessy, New Orleans, La. in the 1880, 1900, and 1920 United States Federal Census [database on-line]; Ancestry.com and the Church of Jesus Christ of Latter-day Saints, Provo, Utah.

16. Du Bois, *The Souls of Black Folks*, vii.

17. African American Photographs Assembled for the Paris Exposition of 1900. The Library of Congress holds approximately 220 mounted photographs that reportedly were displayed in the exhibition (LOTs 11293–11308), as well as material Du Bois compiled: four photograph albums showing "Types" and "Negro Life" (LOT 11930), and three albums entitled "The Black Code of Georgia, U.S.A.," offering transcriptions of Georgia state laws relating to blacks, 1732–1899 (LOT 11932). The materials cataloged online include all of the photos in LOT 11930 and materials in the other groups for which copy negatives exist.

18. Du Bois, "The American Negro at Paris," 575–77.

19. Du Bois, "The Negroes of Farmville, Virginia," in Lewis, ed., *W. E. B. Du Bois*, 232.

20. On Methodism in this period, see Bennett, *Religion and the Rise of Jim Crow in New Orleans*, chapters 1–4. For an overview, see Montgomery, *Under Their Own Vine and Fig Tree*, 142–90.

21. Du Bois, ed., *Economic Co-Operation among Negro Americans*, 54–58.

22. Ibid., 77; Jacqueline Jones, *Saving Savannah*, 53–55.

23. Du Bois, *Economic Co-Operation*, 79.

24. Ibid., 88. See James D. Anderson, *The Education of Blacks in the South, 1860–1935*, 4–32.

25. Ibid., 91.

26. Du Bois, *Economic Co-Operation*, 43.

27. Ibid., 173.

28. Lieberson, *A Piece of the Pie*, 9. Detailed information on internal and interregional black migration can be found in Trotter, *The Great Migration in Historical Perspective*.

29. Eric Foner, *Reconstruction*, 96, 101.

30. A post-war generation of New South whites, emerging elites whose wealth would not depend on agriculture, gradually turned their attention to the task of training white builders and engineers. To this end, beginning in the early 1870s several state-funded technical schools were established to offer exclusive training to white males in civil and electrical engineering, chemistry, physics, and industrial textiles. These institutions—the Virginia Agricultural and Mechanical College in Blacksburg (1872), the Agricultural and Mechanical College of Alabama (1872), and the Georgia School of Technology (1885)—excluded black men and all women without regard to aptitude, skill, or experience. Harbingers of the rigidly segregated workforce and educational system of the twentieth century New South, these land-grant schools funded by the federal government fore-shadowed the transformation of the agrarian South into an industrial economy. See Cross, *Justin Smith Morrill*; Sharpe, "All Land Grants Were Not Created Equal."

31. Jackson and Nunn, *Historically Black Colleges and Universities*, 11–14, 75–90.

32. African American Photographs Assembled for the Paris Exposition of 1900.

33. Smith, *Photography on the Color Line*, 1–7.

34. Washington and Du Bois, *The Negro in the South*, 41.

35. See Bieze, *Booker T. Washington and the Art of Self-Representation*. Images from the Nannie Helen Burroughs Papers. The Prints and Photographs Division of the Library of Congress contains 550 items dating from 1910 to 1958 that document the students and activities of the school for African American girls that Burroughs founded in Washington, D.C. in 1909.

36. Wallinger, *Pauline E. Hopkins*, 155.

37. Morrison, *Playing in the Dark*; Jimoh, "Playing in the Dark."

38. Du Bois, "The Riot-Mill," 306.

39. See Giddings, *A Sword Among Lions*; Hall, *Revolt Against Chivalry*; and MacLean, *Behind the Mask of Chivalry*.

40. Fedo, *The Lynchings in Duluth*, 52–123.

41. Lewis, *W. E. B. Du Bois: Biography of a Race*, 334.

42. Cassedy, "African Americans and the American Labor Movement."

43. Hirsch, *Riot and Remembrance*, 55.

44. Norman Jennet, "The Vampire that Hovers Over North Carolina" (cartoon), *Raleigh News & Observer*, 27 September 1898. Copy of cartoon available from *The North Carolina Election of 1898*, North Carolina Collection, University of North Carolina at Chapel Hill. [http://www.lib.unc.edu/ncc/1898/sources/cartoons/0927.html.]

45. "Hugh Ditzler Obituary," *New York Times*, 5 October 1949. "Scene in the Race

Disturbance" (cover illustration), *Collier's Weekly*, 26 November 1898. Brown, "Presidential Ears."

46. Flores, *Remembering the Alamo*, xvi.

47. Joshua Brown, "Presidential Ears."

48. See Godshalk, *Veiled Visions*, 28–31, and Hunter, *To 'Joy My Freedom*, 98–124.

49. John and Lugenia Hope, at Atlanta Baptist College, just southwest of Five Points, sensed the danger that evening. After the fire alarm sounded, John Hope left home to investigate the scene and found that it confirmed his worst fears. Godshalk, *Veiled Visions*, 90, and Hunter, *To 'Joy My Freedom*, 136–145.

50. Baker, *The Atlanta Riot*, 9.

51. The *Constitution* offered the fairest assessment of the riot of any newspaper in the city, reporting at one point that "white policemen stood by and watched as the racial brutality of Atlanta's citizenry mocked the New South's promise of hope and prosperity and eclipsed the city's reputation as the most progressive urban center in the region."

52. Du Bois, "A Litany of Atlanta," *Independent*, 11 October 1906, 856–58; reprinted in Du Bois, *Darkwater*, 19.

53. Recent works on the Atlanta Riot include Bauerlein, *Negrophobia*; Dorsey, *To Build Our Lives Together*; Godshalk, *Veiled Visions*; Mixon, *The Atlanta Riot*. Baker quote from Baker, *Following the Color Line*, 10.

54. Madigan, *The Burning*, 125–159; see also Brophy and Kennedy, *Reconstructing the Dreamland*, chapter 5.

55. Ellsworth, *Death in a Promised Land*.

56. The coda to the horror in Tulsa came two years later when a white mob destroyed the black community of Rosewood, Florida, less than fifty miles southwest of Gainesville, burning black-owned homes and businesses to the ground and killing an unknown number of the town's two hundred residents. The town itself ceased to exist. See D'Orso, *Like Judgment Day*, 26–55. See also Rucker and Upton, eds., *Encyclopedia of America Race Riots*, 572–77, for Rosewood and multiple entries listed by community for race riots in this period.

57. At a time when Comstock laws prohibited the mailing of information about birth control and contraception on grounds of obscenity, lynching images passed easily through the Post Office. See Boyer, *Purity in Print*. Recognized as controversial and incendiary, lynching photographs were included in an amendment to the U.S. postal laws in 1908 that forbade mailing "matter of a character tending to incite arson, murder or assassination." The law did not stop the practice, but it did result in many postcards being mailed inside envelopes. See Wood, *Lynching and Spectacle*, 109.

58. Photographs of the riot from Tulsa Race Riot of 1921 Archive, Collection 1989–004–5.

59. As quoted in Wallinger, 155. Wallinger points to Richard Brodhead's argument that the "embodiedness of whipping" and "the perfect asymmetry of power expressed in the whipping scenario" represented slavery in all its cruelty and imbalance of power.

60. The number of lynchings in the United States was significantly higher in the last years of the nineteenth century than in the first three decades of the twentieth. But increased press coverage, by white and black newspapers, and the picture postcards sent

through the U.S. mail broadened the effect of each of these sadistic ritualized murders. Postcards provided an especially important visual record of public events in the years before 1920 when most newspapers did not yet have the technology to print high-quality images. As Amy Wood argues, the "morbid popularity" of lynching postcards increased substantially after the Post Office initiated rural free delivery in 1898, expanding home mail service to millions of rural residents. Wood, *Lynching and Spectacle*, 107.

61. Lewis, *W. E. B. Du Bois: Biography of a Race*, 506–07.

62. Walter F. White, "The Work of a Mob," *Crisis*, May 1918, 221–23; "Negroes Still Going North," *New Bern (N.C.) Semi-Weekly Messenger*, 30 June 1899; Umfleet, *1898 Wilmington Race Riot Report*, 158–185; Baker, *The Atlanta Riot*, 10; Brophy and Kennedy, *Reconstructing the Dreamland*, 66.

63. Washington and Du Bois, *The Negro in the South*, 180.

64. Du Bois, "A Litany," 856–58, reprinted in Du Bois, *Darkwater*, 19.

65. See Sullivan, *Lift Every Voice*.

66. Du Bois, "Pilgrimage," *Crisis* 31 (April 1926), 267–70, reprinted in Du Bois, *The Crisis Writings*, 437–439. Quotations on 438–39.

67. In the audience with his parents that evening in Tulsa was eleven-year-old John Hope Franklin. "I recall quite vividly," Franklin wrote later, "his coming on to the stage, dressed in white tie and tails with a ribbon draped across his chest, on which was pinned some large medallion. . . . I had never seen anyone dressed in such finery." Franklin, "W. E. B. Du Bois," 410.

68. Williams, *Strangers in the Land of Paradise*, 183–84; Smyth, "Blacks and the South Carolina Interstate and West Indian Exposition," 217.

69. Docherty, *Postmodernism*, 22.

Chapter 3. "I Got So Mad, I Just Had to Get Something off My Chest"

1. Anne F. Scott first discussed the work of the women of the Methodist Episcopal Church, South in *The Southern Lady*. She re-emphasized the importance of this group as leading advocates of social change in the South in "Women, Religion and Social Change in the South, 1830–1930," in Hill, ed., *Religion and the Solid South*. Since the publication of these seminal works, scholars have continued to explore the reform agendas put forward by southern Methodist women. For a general history, see McDowell, *The Social Gospel in the South*, and Tatum, *A Crown of Service*. For an examination of Methodist women and racial reform, see Hall, *Revolt Against Chivalry*, especially 59–106. For an analysis of the industrial reform program endorsed by Methodist women, see Frederickson, "Shaping a New Society: Methodist Women and Industrial Reform, 1880–1940," in Thomas and Keller, eds., *Women in New Worlds*, 345–61. Anastatia Sims carefully examines the work of white Methodist women in North Carolina in "Sisterhoods of Service: Women's Clubs and Methodist Women's Missionary Societies in North Carolina, 1890–1930," in Thomas and Keller, eds., *Women in New Worlds*, 196–210, and in her book on women's organizations and politics, *The Power of Femininity in the New South*, 15–21, 190–91. The history of women in the C.M.E. church has received little attention from scholars. See McAfee, *History of the Woman's Missionary Society in the Colored Methodist Episcopal Church*.

2. Scott, *Southern Lady*, especially chapter 9; Scott, *Natural Allies*, 89–138; Blair, *The Clubwoman as Feminist*, 109-129; Gere, *Intimate Practices*, 54–92; Levine, *Degrees of Equality*, 8–43 and 60–116.

3. On the process of interracial cooperation and conflict, see Frederickson, "'Each One is Dependent on the Other,'" in Hewitt and Lebsock, eds., *Visible Women*; Gilmore, *Gender and Jim Crow*, especially chapters 2, 6, and 7; Robertson, *Christian Sisterhood, Race Relations, and the YWCA, 1906–46*, especially chapter 7; and Elsa Barkley Brown, "Polyrhythms and Improvisation." Cross-class interaction is examined in Payne, "The Lady Was a Sharecropper"; Mary Frederickson, "Citizens for Democracy: The Industrial Programs of the YWCA," in Kornbluh and Frederickson, eds., *Sisterhood and Solidarity*, 77–106; and Browder, "A 'Christian Solution of the Labor Situation.'" Kate Dossett's excellent *Bridging Race Divides* examines the literary, political, and social networks that black women established across the United States in the last decades of the nineteenth century and into the twentieth. Chapter 2 offers a compelling analysis of Black Nationalism and interracialism in the YWCA. Two studies of Durham, North Carolina probe the complex divisions of class, race, and gender at work in a southern community. Janiewski focuses on the barriers to collaboration in in *Sisterhood Denied*, while Brown analyzes the gendered dynamics of racial politics and the tension between mutuality and dissonance within the black community in *Upbuilding Black Durham*.

4. Scott, *Southern Lady*, 180.

5. These organizations spanned a broad political spectrum. At the center were Protestant religious reformers, led by the Methodists, along with the American Association of University Women, the League of Women Voters, the YWCA, and the National Women's Trade Union League; they were flanked on the right by the Women's Christian Temperance Union and the General Federation of Women's Clubs, and on the left by the Southern Summer School, union women, and women active in groups supported by the socialists and communists. See Levine, *Degrees of Equality*, on the activism and demographics of women in the American Association of University Women; on the involvement of the National Women's Trade Union League, see Payne, *Reform, Labor, and Feminism*. For a study of interactions between the groups along this spectrum, see Roydhouse, "The 'Universal Sisterhood of Women.'" Black women's organizations included the National Association of Colored Women's Clubs, the National Council of Negro Women, and the International Council of Women of the Darker Races. Southern black women joined southern affiliates of national organizations such as the YWCA and the Women's Christian Temperance Union, as well as neighborhood and community women's clubs such as the Tuskegee Woman's Club in Alabama, the Woman's Industrial Club of Louisville, Kentucky, and the Neighborhood Union in Atlanta. See Giddings, *When and Where I Enter*, 95–117; on the southern black women's reform network, see Rouse, *Lugenia Burns Hope*, 1–10. On the reform work of southern women in the black Baptist church, see Higginbotham, *Righteous Discontent*. Women's interracial work in the decades before 1940 laid the groundwork for the activism of southern women in the civil rights era; see Murray, ed., *Throwing Off the Cloak of Privilege*.

6. Hine, "Some Preliminary Thoughts on Rape, the Threat of Rape, and the Culture of Dissemblance," 915.

7. African Methodist Episcopal Church, *A.M.E. Year Book, 1918*, 4; McAfee, *History of the Woman's Missionary Society*, 32. On the formation of the C.M.E. church, see Lincoln and Mamiya, *The Black Church in the African American Experience*, 60–65; "Work With Negro Members," in Bucke, ed., *The History of American Methodism*, 279–87; Manning Marable, "Religion and Black Protest Thought in African American History," in Wilmore, ed., *African American Religious Studies*, 330–31; Hine, *When Truth Is Told*, 18; Gilkes, "'Together and in Harness,'" 678–682; and Boles, *Black Southerners, 1619–1869*, 201–02. For the white response, see Bailey, *Southern White Protestantism in the Twentieth Century*, 4–7, and Caldwell, *Deep South*, 194–98.

8. J. A. Martin, "Background of Missionary Activities," in McAfee, *History of the Woman's Missionary Society*, 33–35. From 1870 to 1890, between 50 and 60 percent of the rural church house lots of the early C.M.E. Church were given with conditional clauses stipulating that the property would revert to the original donor when the land or building was no longer used for religious services by the C.M.E.

9. Ibid., 35.

10. See McDowell, *Social Gospel*, chapter 1; McAfee, *History of the Woman's Missionary Society*, 41–64. In *When Truth Is Told*, 17–27, Hine writes of the "most 'invisible' constituency within the black church—the women."

11. McAfee, *History of the Woman's Missionary Society*, 145.

12. Methodist Episcopal Church, South, *Report of the 21st Annual Meeting, Woman's Missionary Council*, 126. In 1930, the Methodist Episcopal Church, South, Woman's Missionary Council's Bureau of Social Service established three separate commissions: the first dealt with Interracial Cooperation, the second with Industrial Relations, and the third with Rural Development. Each commission had a chairman who directed research and made recommendations. At the same time, the bureau organized standing committees on International Relations and World Peace, Christian Citizenship and Law Observance, and Cooperation with Welfare Agencies.

13. McAfee, *History of the Woman's Missionary Society*, 142–46, 149–56; *Handbook for Adult Missionary Societies*; and the *Messenger* (Jackson, Tenn.: Woman's Connectional Council of the Colored Methodist Episcopal Church).

14. Frederickson, "Shaping," in Thomas and Keller, eds., *Women in New Worlds*, 355–57; McDowell, *Social Gospel in the South*, 36–59.

15. Methodist Episcopal Church, South, *22nd Report of the Woman's Missionary Council* (1932), 142; Methodist Episcopal Church, South, *Report of the 24th Annual Meeting, Woman's Missionary Council*, 11.

16. Methodist Episcopal Church, South, *Report of the 28th Annual Meeting, Woman's Missionary Council*, 145; McAfee, *History of the Woman's Missionary Society*, 148.

17. Methodist Episcopal Church, South, *15th Annual Report, Woman's Parsonage and Home Mission Society*, 51–52.

18. "President's Message to the Woman's Missionary Council," in Methodist Episcopal Church, South, *Report of the 3rd Annual Meeting, Woman's Missionary Council*, 293–99.

19. Methodist Episcopal Church, South, *Report of the 5th Annual Meeting, Woman's Missionary Council*, 101; Methodist Episcopal Church, South, *Report of the 6th Annual*

Meeting, Woman's Missionary Council, 131–32; Methodist Episcopal Church, South, *Report of the 9th Annual Meeting, Woman's Missionary Council*, 80.

20. Methodist Episcopal Church, South, *Report of the 6th Annual Meeting, Woman's Missionary Council*, 131; McAfee, *History of the Woman's Missionary Society*, 148.

21. McAfee, *History of the Woman's Missionary Society*, 177–80.

22. Methodist Episcopal Church, South, *Report of the 3rd Annual Meeting, Woman's Missionary Council*, 298.

23. Quotations, in order, from McAfee, *History of the Woman's Missionary Society*, 159, 129, 174, 197.

24. McAfee, 121; on M.E. laity rights, see McDowell, *Social Gospel in the South*, 130–40, and Virginia Shadron, "The Laity Rights Movement, 1906–1918: Woman's Suffrage in the Methodist Episcopal Church, South," in Thomas and Keller, eds., *Women in New Worlds*, 261–75.

25. Wheeler, *New Women of the New South*; Green, *Southern Women and the Woman Suffrage Question*. For a general overview of black women's suffrage, see Terborg-Penn, *African American Women in the Struggle for the Vote, 1850–1920*.

26. Robert Adamson, "Topics of the Week," *Atlanta Constitution*, 3 February 1895, 5.

27. "A Woman to Women," *Atlanta Constitution*, 4 February 1895, 5.

28. Wheeler, *New Women of the New South*, 116.

29. Eltzroth, "Woman Suffrage."

30. "Let the Women Vote," *Atlanta Constitution*, 4 February 1895.

31. "Sermon to Colored People," *Atlanta Constitution*, 5 February 1895, 5. Cheeks added that the A.M.E. church "knew no race or color, but made all races welcome to her community." On Colby, see "Clara Colby," Wishart, ed., *Encyclopedia of the Great Plains*, 327. Information about Rev. Cheeks in Washington, *Papers*, vol. 3, *1889–1895*, 459.

32. Perdue, *Race and the Cotton States Exposition of 1895*, 45.

33. Washington, *Papers*, vol. 3, 583–87.

34. Hickey, *Hope and Danger in the New South City*, 17.

35. Ibid., 17.

36. Perdue, *Race and the Cotton States Exposition of 1895*, 47–48.

37. Eltzroth, "Woman Suffrage"; Blee, *Women of the Klan*, 24–75.

38. Godshalk, *Veiled Visions*, 216.

39. On southern anti-suffrage, see Elna Green, *Southern Women and the Woman Suffrage Question*, chapter 2; Eltzroth, "Woman Suffrage." As support grew for woman suffrage, anti-suffrage activists sprang into action, forming a Georgia chapter of the National Association Opposed to Woman Suffrage, led by Mildred Lewis Rutherford, the president of the United Daughters of the Confederacy.

40. *Atlanta Constitution*, 12 March 1914, 1.

41. Ibid.

42. *Atlanta Constitution*, 17 November 1915, 1.

43. Ibid.

44. *Atlanta Constitution*, 4 February 1895, 5.

45. Scott, *Natural Allies*, 140.

46. Gilmore, *Gender and Jim Crow*, 200. Quotation from "What the Negro Woman Asks of the White Women of North Carolina," Charlotte Hawkins Brown Speeches, 1920–29, Reel 1, #14, in Charlotte Hawkins Brown Collection, Arthur and Elizabeth Schlesinger Library on the History of Women in America, Radcliffe College, Cambridge, Mass., cited in Gilmore, *Gender and Jim Crow*, 302n112.

47. Ibid., 200.

48. Ibid.

49. Ibid., 201.

50. Ibid., 201. Quotation from Brown address, Folder 1, Box 1, Jessie Daniel Ames Papers, Southern Historical Collection, University of North Carolina at Chapel Hill, as cited by Gilmore, 302n119. See also Hall, *Revolt Against Chivalry*, 93–94.

51. Mary Frederickson, "'Each One Is Dependent on the Other,'" in Hewitt and Lebsock, eds., *Visible Women*, 300–301.

52. *Proceedings of the Sixth National Convention of the Young Women's Christian Associations of the United States of America, Cleveland, Ohio, 12–20 April 1920*, 112; Louise Leonard, "Reports of the YWCA Industrial Department, 1922–1926," YWCA of the USA Records.

53. *Proceedings of the Sixth National Convention*, 112.

54. Elisabeth Christman, Letter to Members of the Executive Board, NWTUL, 29 June 1927, Reel 4, NWTUL Papers.

55. Pat Knight, interviewed by author, Greensboro, N.C., 19 March 1980; Louise Leonard, "Report of the YWCA Industrial Department, November 1924," YWCA Records, 3.

56. See Mary Frederickson, "Recognizing Regional Differences: The Southern Summer School for Women Workers" and "Citizens for Democracy: The Industrial Programs of the YWCA," in Kornbluh and Frederickson, eds., *Sisterhood and Solidarity*, 75–106 and 148–86.

57. For the history of the YWCA Industrial Department, see Grace L. Coyle, "A Historical Outline of the Work of the Industrial Department," November 1923, YWCA Records; "The Work of the Industrial Committee," pamphlet issued by Woman's Press, 1924, YWCA Records; "The Young Women's Christian Association and Industry," pamphlet issued by Industrial Department, National Board of the YWCA, 1927–1928, YWCA Records; and Stewart, *The Industrial Work of the YWCA*.

58. Louise Leonard, "Reports of the YWCA Industrial Department, 1922–1926," YWCA Records; Mary Frederickson, "Citizens for Democracy," in Kornbluh and Frederickson, eds., *Sisterhood and Solidarity*, 75–106; Robertson, *Christian Sisterhood, Race Relations, and the YWCA*; and Browder, "A 'Christian Solution of the Labor Situation.'"

59. Nasim Moalem, "An Army of Christian Soldiers: Black and White Women YWCA Activists in Baltimore, Maryland, 1900–1912," in Ackermann, ed., *African American Experience*, 42–43.

60. Eleanor Copenhaver, Report, 12 May 1925, YWCA Records; Louise Leonard, "Report of the Industrial Department," February 1925, YWCA Records, 5.

61. [Louise Leonard?], Typescript Report on Sweet Briar Summer School, n.d., Southern Summer School Records, 1–4.

62. See Mary Frederickson, "Recognizing Regional Differences: The Southern Summer School for Women Workers," in Kornbluh and Frederickson, eds., *Sisterhood and Solidarity*, 180–86.

63. Ibid.

64. "Southern Summer School Scrapbook, 1933," Southern Summer School Records.

65. Ibid.

66. Beulah Carter, "Southern Summer School Scrapbook, 1933," Southern Summer School Records.

67. Ibid.

68. Taylor and Rupp, "Loving Internationalism."

69. Mary Frederickson, "'I Know Which Side I'm On': Southern Women in the Labor Movement in the Twentieth Century," in Milkman, ed., *Women, Work and Protest*, 156–80; and Mary Frederickson, "Beyond Heroines and Girl Strikers: Gender and Organized Labor in the Twentieth Century South," in Zieger, ed., *Organized Labor in the Twentieth Century South*.

70. On the Ku Klux Klan and the women associated with the Knights of the White Camellias, see MacLean, *Behind the Mask of Chivalry*, and Blee, *Women of the Klan*.

71. Anne F. Scott, *Natural Allies*, 140.

72. Methodist Episcopal Church, South, *Report of the 18th Annual Meeting, Woman's Missionary Council*, 139.

73. Megan Rosenfeld, "Through the Mill with Crystal Lee and 'Norma Rae,'" *Washington Post*, 11 June 1980.

Chapter 4. Beyond Heroines and Girl Strikers

1. Gorn, *Mother Jones*, 42.

2. Ibid., 45. Elliott Gorn points out that "the Knights did not organize in Chicago until years after the fire, and they did not admit women until 1880." And yet, he argues, there "is a core of truth" in the chronology outlined in Jones's autobiography, which, Gorn contends, "must be treated less literally than metaphorically; its specific details are often incorrect, but the book is best thought of as akin to religious testimony, to bearing witness, to a pilgrim's story."

3. Jones, *Autobiography*, 58, 232. Gorn, *Mother Jones*, 45.

4. Feldman, "Ella Mae [sic] Wiggins, North Carolina Mother Who Gave Her Life to Build a Union"; Feldman, "Ella May Wiggins and the Gastonia Strike of 1929"; Vera Buch Weisbord, *A Radical Life*, 217–219, 258–260; quotations from Larkin, "Ella May's Songs," and Vera Buch Weisbord, 288. See also Larkin, "The Story of Ella May" and "Tragedy in North Carolina; Mary Frederickson, "Ella May Wiggins," in Powell, ed., *Dictionary of North Carolina Biography*, and Huber, "Mill Mother's Lament."

5. Salmond, *Miss Lucy of the CIO*, 1–14.

6. Fetherling, *Mother Jones*, 168; quotation from *Federation News*, 20 December 1930, as cited by Fetherling, 246n18.

7. Long, *Where the Sun Never Shines*, 156–157.

8. Lader, "The Lady and the Sheriff."

9. Fetherling, *Mother Jones*, 134–136; see also Long, *Where the Sun Never Shines*, 233, 370, and Gorn, *Mother Jones*, 107–112, 217.

10. Fetherling, *Mother Jones*, 209.

11. Ibid., 138. Michel, born the same year as Jones, fought in the 1871 Commune, and throughout her life as a radical condoned the use of violence.

12. Ella May Wiggins's daughter, seven years old in 1929, reported that her mother was about seven months pregnant at the time of her death. Mrs. Merritt Wandell (Wiggin's daughter, of Waverly, New York), telephone interview by author, September 1979.

13. *Charlotte Observer*, 16 September 1929, 10; Vera Buch Weisbord, *A Radical Life*, 288.

14. Brownie Lee Jones, interviewed by author, 20 April 1976.

15. Mother Jones was described as an angel, for instance, and Lucy Mason was frequently said to have magical powers. "What kind of magic did you use . . . ?" queried Francis P. Miller, Mason's friend and colleague, in 1937. Paul Kellogg of the *Survey* wrote about Mason in the same year, "Her name has magic below the Mason and Dixon line."

16. Fetherling, *Mother Jones*; Francis P. Miller to Lucy R. Mason, 18 May 1937, Lucy Randolph Mason Papers; Paul Kellogg to Sidney Hillman, 14 June 1937, copy of original letter in Lucy Randolph Mason Papers; Jones, *Autobiography*, 8, 155.

17. Jones, *Autobiography*, 65; *Charlotte Observer*, 15 September 1929, 1; Wandell interview, September 1979; Bernard Borah, Southern Director, ACWA, to Gladys Dickason, 12 June 1941, Lucy Randolph Mason Papers; Lader, "The Lady and the Sheriff."

18. Gorn, *Mother Jones*, 228–230, 272.

19. Lader, "The Lady and the Sheriff," 17.

20. Ibid.

21. No work better describes this phenomenon than Hall's study of Elizabethton, "Disorderly Women." See also Smith-Rosenberg, *Disorderly Conduct*. Philip Foner also emphasizes the role of militant young women in the southern textile industry in *Women and the American Labor Movement*, 225–240.

22. Dowd, "Strikes and Lockouts in North Carolina."

23. *CIO News*, 2 July 1938, 1.

24. Bessie Hillman, untitled article, *The Advance*, 15 March 1948, 6.

25. Sherwood Anderson, "Elizabethton, Tennessee."

26. Typescript of quotations from Whitman, *God's Valley*, Highlander Research and Education Center Papers.

27. Larkin, "Ella May Wiggins and Songs of the Gastonia Textile Strike."

28. Typewritten copy of article in *Memphis Press-Scimitar*, 22 June 1937, Highlander Research and Education Center Papers.

29. In addition to their strategy of taking advantage of cross-class alliances, there is solid evidence that women unionists used a distinctive leadership style, fundamentally different from that adopted by male unionists. Karen Sacks describes this style in her study of union organizing at the Duke University Medical Center, where she argues, "Women and men both took leadership, although in different ways." She discovers that while almost all the public speakers and confrontational negotiators were men, women

were what she called "centers and sustainers of workplace networks—centerwomen or centerpersons—as well as the large majority of the union organizing committee." By equating leading with speaking, Sacks had initially overlooked women's key leadership role as "centerwomen." Sacks, *Caring by the Hour*, 120–121.

30. Jennie Spencer, "My Transition," autobiography written at Highlander Folk School, 1937, Highlander Research and Education Center Papers.

31. In the recession of 1979–1983, more black workers than white were laid off, so that some workforces that had been predominantly black in the 1970s once again had a majority of white workers. Leadership positions within some unions started by black workers passed to white women, who were less successful in uniting the workforce across racial lines. In 1982, in a southern Alabama mill, for example, soon after a white slate of officers took office, the plant's six-year-old union was voted out. Black workers felt betrayed by white officers who, they argued, did not fight hard enough to keep the union. A further drain on the black leadership of biracial locals was the mobility of black women activists. As these women worked within the union, they sharpened their organizing abilities and developed new skills that put them into competition for better jobs. But occupational mobility has often meant leaving the union behind, and workers remaining in newly organized locals suffered from the lack of well-qualified leaders. On the Alabama mill election, see McLendon, "Time and Time Again"; for an overview of black women in the southern labor movement in the period after 1965, see Mary Frederickson, "I Know Which Side I'm On," in Milkman, ed., *Women, Work and Protest*, 173–175, and "Four Decades of Change: Black Workers in Southern Textiles, 1941–1981," in James Green, ed., *Workers' Struggles, Past and Present*, especially 77–80; Giddings, *When and Where I Enter*, 154–155.

32. "Minutes of the Central Committee," 15–16 August 1931, Southern Summer School Records. Louise Leonard McLaren, director of the Southern School, wrote to George L. Googe of the AFL about the case, explaining that she was "interested in this case . . . almost as much for the other locals in the south as for the one in Mobile. The one in Macon [Ga.], for instance, has excellent leadership and could become a powerful local if it were not held back by the New York leaders." Louise Leonard McLaren to George L. Googe, 16 April 1935, Box 6, Folder 3, Mary Cornelia Barker Papers.

33. Dowd to Mrs. Robins, [January?] 1942, Reel 1, NWTUL Papers; Louise L. McLaren to George L. Googe, 16 April 1935, Box 6, Folder 3, Mary Cornelia Barker Papers.

34. This bimodal pattern of active union participation was not followed during times of crisis, such as a strike, when all workers, male and female, young and old, become involved to whatever extent possible, regardless of personal concerns. See Sacks, *Caring by the Hour*, chapter 5, and Frankel, "Women, Paternalism, and Protest in a Southern Textile Community," 188–190.

35. Marshall, *Labor in the South*, 34. Thanks to Susan Levine for sharing her knowledge about southern women's auxiliaries and for her exploration of women in the Knights of Labor, *Labor's True Woman*.

36. See Marjorie Penn Lasky, "'Where I Was a Person': The Ladies' Auxiliary in the 1934 Minneapolis Teamsters' Strikes," in Milkman, ed., *Women, Work and Protest*, 181–205, and Chateauvert, *Marching Together*.

37. Evidence for CIO treatment of women organizers can be found on pages 1150–92, Series IV, Reel 55, Operation Dixie: The CIO Organizing Committee Papers, 1946–1953; see also Mary Frederickson, "I Know Which Side I'm On," in Milkman, ed., *Women, Work and Protest*, 173; Hillman quotation appears in Amalgamated Clothing Workers of America (ACWA), "Report of the General Executive Board and Proceedings of the Twelfth Biennial Convention, 9–17 May 1938," *Documentary History*, 413.

38. Spencer, "My Transition."

39. The AFL announced a campaign to organize women workers in 1914 with Samuel Gompers declaring that "women do not want charity or patronage any more than men do. They want justice." Quoted in *American Federationist* 20:8 (March 1914): 234. William Green similarly condemned discrimination against women; see Kessler-Harris, *Out to Work*, 268. The TWUA-CIO also targeted women workers in a post–World War II organizing campaign promising that "women get whatever men get." Textile Workers Union of America, "What Every Woman Should Know."

40. See Horstman, *Sing Your Heart Out, Country Boy*.

41. Cosby Totten, telephone interview by author, 26 January 1990. See Giardina, "The Pittston Strike."

42. *American Federationist* 7:6 (June 1900), front cover. This figure reappeared on the May 1901 cover, vol. 8:5.

Chapter 5. Labor Looks South

1. See English, *A Common Thread*, on capital flight to the South long before the 1920s.

2. Haywood, "We Propose to Unionize Labor In the South," 35; "The Awakening of the South," *American Federationist*, 8:2 (February 1901), 167.

3. See Lahne, *The Cotton Mill Worker*; Marshall, *Labor in the South*; Bernstein, *The Lean Years*, especially 1–43; Hall et al., *Like a Family*; Zieger, ed., *Organized Labor in the Twentieth Century South*.

4. On the difficulties of union organizing in the textile industry, see Lahne, *The Cotton Mill Worker*, 240–259. Solomon Barkin, "Figures on Progress," Manuscript 129A/4A, TWOC Organizing Data, Box 1, TWUA Papers.

5. See Lahne, *The Cotton Mill Worker*, 87–101; Marshall, *Labor in the South*, 101–120.

6. Lahne, *The Cotton Mill Worker*, 167–172.

7. Mitchell, *Textile Unionism in the South*; Marshall, *Labor in the South*, 182–201; Carolyn Ashbaugh and Dan McCurry, "On the Line at Oneita," in Miller, ed., *Working Lives*, 205–214; Leon Fink, "Union Power, Soul Power."

8. For the history of the Knights of Labor in the South, see U.S. Bureau of Labor Statistics, *Report on the Condition of Woman and Child Wage-Earners in the United States*, vol. 10; Andrews and Bliss, *History of Women in Trade Unions*, chapter 4; McLaurin, *Paternalism and Protest*, 68–119; and Leon Fink, *Workingmen's Democracy*, 149–177. The United Garment Workers (UGW) did organize in the South in the early twentieth century. Of its ninety-six locals with a female membership of 90 percent or greater, eighteen were located in the South. The UGW sold labels to manufacturers of readymade cloth-

ing. UGW women's locals included 3,200 women members in 1902; 600 of these women lived in the South. See Willett, *The Employment of Women in the Clothing Trade*, 168–189.

9. Edith Kowski to A. J. Muste, 8 September 1928, Box 70, Brookwood Labor College Record.

10. Marshall, *Labor in the South*, 102–105; Shields, "Organizing the South."

11. For details about the Amoskeag strike, see Hareven and Langenbach, *Amoskeag*.

12. The best discussion of the stretch-out/speed-up phenomenon is in Lahne, *The Cotton Mill Worker*, 154–155.

13. Details about the 1929 strikes are available in Marshall, *Labor in the South*; Bernstein, *The Lean Years*; and Lahne, *The Cotton Mill Worker*. For a contemporary account, see Tippett, *When Southern Labor Stirs*.

14. For material on the UTW, see Lahne, *The Cotton Mill Worker*, 200–235; for the CPLA strategy in the South, see Muste, "The Call of the South," *Labor Age*, 5–6; on the NWTUL southern campaign, see Boone, *The Women's Trade Union Leagues in Great Britain and the United States of America*; on the NTWU, see Albert Weisbord, "Passaic, New Bedford, North Carolina"; and Vera Buch Weisbord, *A Radical Life*, 169–219.

15. American Federation of Labor, *Report of the Proceedings of the 49th Annual Convention*, 265.

16. Muste, "The Call of the South," 5; organizer quotation from Box 70, Brookwood Labor College Record.

17. Elisabeth Christman to Members of the Executive Board, 29 June 1929, Reel 4, NWTUL Papers.

18. Sharon Smith, *Subterranean Fire*, 98.

19. Trepp, "Union-Management Co-operation and the Southern Organizing Campaign," 615.

20. Ibid., 614.

21. Ibid., 624.

22. See Tippett, *When Southern Labor Stirs*, 109–155; National Executive Committee of the Conference for Progressive Labor Action, "The Marion Murder," 1-17.

23. "The Marion Murder," 16–17.

24. Tom Tippett to A. J. Muste, October 1929, Box 53, Folder 18, Brookwood Labor College Record.

25. See Boone, *The Women's Trade Union Leagues in Great Britain and the United States of America*, 174–211.

26. Mary Anderson to Margaret Robins, 10 April 1929, Margaret Dreier Robins Collection.

27. "National Committee on Southern Work," Minutes of Planning Committee, n.d., Reel 4, NWTUL Papers.

28. See Albert Weisbord, "Passaic," 321; Lahne, *The Cotton Mill Worker*, 212–238; and Mitchell, *Textile Unionism in the South*, 71–74.

29. Trepp, "Union-Management Co-operation and the Southern Organizing Campaign," 624.

30. On the General Textile Strike of 1934, see Irons, *Testing the New Deal*, especially

1, 10–12, and Salmond, *The General Textile Strike of 1934.* "Minutes of the Executive Council," 18–19 June 1936, Manuscript 396, Box 674, TWUA Papers.

31. Barkin, "Figures on Progress."

32. Mason, "The C.I.O. in the South." Interviews by the author with: P. Knight, Greensboro, N.C., 19 March 1980; P. H. Robkin, New York, N.Y., 2 November 1974; J. Spencer Pedigo, Charlotte, N.C., 25 July 1975.

33. Ibid.

34. Ibid., percentages based on Barkin's figures; Marshall, *Labor in the South,* 169–172.

35. On Operation Dixie, see Griffith, *The Crisis of Labor;* "Labor Drives South," and Marshall, *Labor in the South,* 246–269.

36. Marshall, *Labor in the South,* 246–269; "Labor Drives South," 138.

37. Baldanzi, "The South Is 32 Million Americans," 43; "Report of the Southern Wage Conference," Atlanta, Ga., 21 September 1947, Manuscript 129A/10A, Box 21, TWUA Papers.

38. Marshall, *Labor in the South,* 260–261.

39. Ibid., 270–282. The Henderson strike is analyzed in Frankel, "Women, Paternalism, and Protest in a Southern Textile Community." The J. P. Stevens campaign in Roanoke Rapids is documented in Conway, *Rise Gonna Rise.*

40. Marshall, *Labor in the South,* 274–276.

41. William Pollock to Joint Boards, Local Unions and Staff, 28 October 1959, Manuscript 129A/1C, Box 3, TWUA Papers; Sol Stetin to TWUA Staff Members, 15 April 1959, Manuscript 129/IC, Box 3, TWUA Papers; Paul Krebs Correspondence, February 1960, Manuscript 129/1C, Box 3, Folder: Henderson Strike Correspondence, June 1960–July 1961, TWUA Papers.

42. See chapter 3 in this volume.

43. McLendon, "Time and Time Again."

44. Carolyn Ashbaugh and Dan McCurry, "On the Line at Oneita," in Miller, ed., *Working Lives,* 205–214; Steve Hoffius, "Charleston Hospital Workers' Strike, 1969," in Miller, ed., *Working Lives,* 244–258; Leon Fink, "Union Power, Soul Power."

Chapter 6. "Living in Two Worlds"

1. John Foster, interview by author, Shawmut, Ala., 20–21 April 1982.

2. U.S. Equal Employment Opportunity Commission, *Minorities and Women in Private Industry, 1978 Report,* 1-19. See Minchin, *Hiring the Black Worker;* MacLean, *Freedom Is Not Enough.*

3. Genovese, *Roll, Jordan, Roll,* 495; Starobin, *Industrial Slavery in the Old South,* 13, 167.

4. Hall et al., *Like a Family,* 132, 222, 361; Wiener, *Social Origins of the New South;* Paul Worthman and James Green, "Black Workers in the New South, 1865–1915," in Huggins, Kilson, and Fox, eds., *Key Issues in the Afro-American Experience,* 476–69.

5. Lahne, *The Cotton Mill Worker,* 81.

6. Ibid., 82.

7. State of Georgia, Department of Labor, *Second Annual Report* (1938), 24.

8. Lahne, *The Cotton Mill Worker*, 289; Foner and Lewis, eds., *The Black Worker*, vol. 4, 315.

9. U.S. Department of Labor, Women's Bureau, "Negro Women in Industry in 15 States," *Bulletin of the Women's Bureau*, 32.

10. Life and work history information for 115 African American textile workers obtained by author from Callaway Mills, *Callaway Beacon*, vols. 1–18 (1949–1969).

11. Dewey, "Negro Employment in Seventy Textile Mills, October 1950–August 1951," in National Planning Association, Committee of the South, *Selected Studies of Negro Employment in the South*, 184; Richard L. Rowan, "The Negro in the Textile Industry," in Northrup, et al., eds., *Negro Employment in Southern Industry*, 84.

12. The information and quotations that follow are from the author's interviews with Julian West and Minnie Brown in West Point, Ga., on 20 April 1982. The name of each individual interviewed has been changed to protect his or her privacy.

13. Mattie Ivey, interviewed by author, Fairfax, Ala., 21 April 1982.

14. Data about the Thomas family from Callaway Mills, *Callaway Beacon*, vol. 6, no. 35 (6 September 1954); West interview.

15. Quoted in Conway, *Rise Gonna Rise*, 122–124.

16. Newman, "Work and Community Life in a Southern Town," 222.

17. Richard L. Rowan, "The Negro in the Textile Industry," in Northrup, et al., eds., *Negro Employment in Southern Industry*, 54, 98–99, 141; U.S. Equal Employment Opportunity Commission, *Minorities and Women in Private Industry*, 1–19. In Georgia, 43 percent of white textile workers held operative positions; a higher percentage of white than black workers performed craft jobs (16% vs. 9%) and office work (10% vs. 2%).

18. West interview; Brown interview; Richard L. Rowan, "The Negro in the Textile Industry," in Northrup, et al., eds., *Negro Employment in Southern Industry*, 85; Finley Wickham, interviewed by author, Macon, Ga., September 1981; Callaway Mills, *Callaway Beacon*.

19. Foster interview.

20. Floyd Harris, interviewed by author, West Point, Ga., 20 April 1982.

21. Du Bois, *The Souls of Black Folk*, 3.

22. West and Foster interviews.

23. Harris interview.

24. West, Harris, and Foster interviews.

25. Foster interview.

26. Foster and Harris interviews.

27. West interview.

28. Marshall and Christian, eds., *Employment of Blacks in the South*, 143–146; Frank Guillory, "N.C. Textile Firm Finally Unionized," *Washington Post*, 2 September 1974, A1, A9; Bruce Raynor, "Unionism in the Southern Textile Industry," in Gary Fink and Reed, eds., *Essays in Southern Labor History*, 89.

29. Chip Hughes, "A New Twist for Textiles," in Miller, ed., *Working Lives*, 350–351; Doug McInnis, "A New Chill on Organizing Efforts," *New York Times*, 30 May 1982, 4F–5F.

30. Newman, "Work and Community Life in a Southern Town," 220–222.

31. Quoted in Carolyn Ashbaugh and Dan McCurry, "On the Line at Oneita," in Miller, ed., *Working Lives*, 210.

32. Debbie Newby, "Long Campaign Worth It, Say Those Who Worked for Union," *Macon Telegraph*, 21 March 1980, 1B, 8B; Laura Curry, interviewed by author, Macon, Ga., September 1981.

33. Quoted in Conway, *Rise Gonna Rise*, 91.

34. Harris, Brown, and Ivey interviews.

35. Newby, "Long Campaign," 1B.

36. U.S. Department of Labor, Bureau of Labor Statistics, Southeastern Regional Office, Atlanta, Ga., "Southeastern Textile Mills Employment Monthly Reports," October 1980; U.S. Equal Employment Opportunity Commission, *Minorities and Women in Private Industry, 1978 Report*, 19; U.S. Department of Labor, Bureau of Labor Statistics, Southeastern Regional Office, Atlanta, Ga., "Textile Products Industry Employment in the Southeast, 1947–1979."

37. "South's Textile Mill Closings Continue from '74 Recession," *New York Times*, 17 February 1982, A13.

Chapter 7. Transformation and Resistance in the Nueva New South

1. See Bayly, et al., "AHR Conversation: On Transnational History," where Patricia Seed refers to transnational history as a new field that offers a "world of comparative possibility."

2. North American Free Trade Agreement Implementation Act, H.R. 3450, Congressional Record, 1 February 1994; Dominican Republic-Central America-United States Free Trade Agreement Implementation Act, H.R. 3045, *Congressional Record*, 27 July 2005.

3. Henry Grady's speech to the New England Club in New York, 1886, in Harris, *Life of Henry W. Grady*. Reprinted in Escott, et al., *Major Problems in the History of the American South*, vol. 2, 71–73.

4. Kochhar, Suro, and Tafoya, "The New Latino South."

5. Rachel L. Swarns, "In Georgia, Newest Immigrants Unsettle Old Sense of Place," *New York Times*, 4 August 2006.

6. Odem and Lacy, eds., *Latino Immigrants and the Transformation of the U.S. South*; Murphy, Blanchard, and Hill, eds., *Latino Workers in the Contemporary South*; Smith and Cohn, eds., *Look Away! The U.S. South in New World Studies*; Cobb and Stueck, eds., *Globalization and the American South*; Peacock, Watson, and Matthews, eds., *The American South in a Global World*; Mantero, *Latinos and the U.S. South*; Ansley and Shefner, eds., *Global Connections and Local Receptions*.

7. Suro and Passel, "The Rise of the Second Generation," 2.

8. Leon Fink, *The Maya of Morganton*, 199–200.

9. Sassen, "The Repositioning of Citizenship and Alienage."

10. Tindall, *The Ethnic Southerners*; Hennie, "20-County Metro Atlanta Population to Reach 7 Million by 2030," Atlanta Regional Commission, 12 October 2006; U.S. Cen-

sus Bureau, Atlanta, Ga., Demographic and Housing Estimates, Georgia Population and Housing Narrative Profile: 2005–2007.

11. Bell, "Gateway Cities," 130.

12. Elise Zeiger, "Town Hits Economic Jackpot to Become 'Kia-ville,'" CNN, 9 July 2009.

13. "Profiles by Metro Area, Atlanta-Sandy Springs-Marietta, Ga.: Summary Profile," compiled by the Harvard School of Public Health from U.S. Census Bureau Annual Estimates of the Resident Population by Sex, Race, and Hispanic Origin for Counties (1 April 2000 to 1 July 2008). Available from http://diversitydata.sph.harvard.edu/Data/Profiles/Show.aspx?loc=124 [accessed 20 March 2010].

14. Pew Hispanic Center, "Statistical Portrait of Hispanics in the United States, 2007," Table 34: Poverty by Age, Race and Ethnicity: 2007; Camarota and Jensenius, "A Shifting Tide"; Pew Research Center, "A Statistical Portrait of Hispanic Women in the U.S.," 8 May 2008.

15. Becky Gillette, "Southern Auto Corridor 'The Rage' for U.S., World Automakers," *Mississippi Business Journal*, 31 May 2004.

16. Adam Crisp and Mike Pare, "Chattanooga: Wall Lift Sets VW Imprint," *Chattanooga Times Free Press*, 15 May 2009.

17. "Kia Coming to West Point, GA," WTVM 9, Developing News; KIA Motors News Release, "Kia Celebrates Grand Opening of $1 Billion State-of-the-Art Automobile Manufacturing Plant in Georgia," 26 February 2010, http://www.kmmgusa.com/news_02_26_10.aspx [accessed on 3-20-10].

18. "At Midyear, Georgia 6th in Foreclosures," *Atlanta Business Chronicle*, 16 July 2009; Jonathan Cox and Sue Stock, "N.C. Unemployment Hits a Record 11.1%," *Raleigh News & Observer*, 20 June 2009.

19. U.S. Citizenship and Immigration Services, "Cap Count for H-1B and H-2B Workers for Fiscal Year 2010," 3 September 2009.

20. Kochhar, Suro, and Tafoya, "The New Latino South," 1.

21. De León and Griswold del Castillo, *North to Aztlán*, 10–85, 222; Ruiz, "Nuestra América."

22. Santos, *Places Left Unfinished at the Time of Creation*, 5, 95. See also Flores, *Remembering the Alamo*.

23. Croucher, *The Other Side of the Fence*.

24. Stout, *Why Immigrants Come to America*, 1–25.

25. Kevin Johnson, "ATF Take Aim at Deep 'Iron River of Guns,'" *USA Today*, 18 March 2009; Bryan Walsh, "Mexico's Mystery: Why Is Swine Flu Deadlier There?" *Time*, 29 April 2009.

26. "DHS: Border, Interior, Services," *Migration News*; "New Mexico: A Mass for Border Crossers," *New York Times*, 3 November 2005.

27. The number of undocumented workers in the United States peaked at almost 12 million in 2007, after a rapid rise from 3.5 million in 1990. Passel and Cohn, "A Portrait of Unauthorized Immigrants in the United States." Seventy-five percent of this immigrant population is Latino, and sixty percent of those, or seven million people, originate from Mexico.

28. Schultz, "Inside the Gilded Cage," 212.

29. Gill and Drake, *Going to Carolina del Norte*, 32–34.

30. Mendoza, Ciscel, and Smith, "Latino Immigrants in Memphis."

31. Robert Joe Stout, *Why Immigrants Come to America*, 177; Tallman, "Hispanic Growth Means Opportunities," *Atlanta Business Chronicle*, 26 June 2009.

32. Siler City, N.C., Population July 2008, http://www.city-data.com/city/Siler-City-North-Carolina.html; Viglucci, "Hispanic Wave Forever Alters Small Town in North Carolina," *Miami Herald*, 2 January 2000.

33. "Georgia, Meat, Fish," *Rural Migration News*; Rachel L. Swarns, "A Racial Rift That Isn't Black and White," *New York Times*, 3 October 2006.

34. Ruben Navarrette, Jr., "Black-brown Friction Waste of Energy," CNN, 3 October 2007.

35. Matthew Benjamin, "Republicans Face South Carolina Immigration 'Frenzy,'" *Bloomberg News*, 30 November 2007.

36. Biewen and Watson, "Pueblo USA."

37. Rachel L. Swarns, "In Georgia, Newest Immigrants Unsettle an Old Sense of Place," *New York Times*, 4 August 2006.

38. Bauer and Reynolds, "Under Siege."

39. See definition of Permanent Resident Alien, United States Citizenship and Immigration Services at http://www.uscis.gov/portal/site/uscis; Passel and Cohn, "A Portrait of Unauthorized Immigrants in the United States"; Bauer and Reynolds, "Under Siege," 5.

40. Ibid., 5, 11.

41. Ibid., 14.

42. Sen. Bernie Sanders, "The Harvest of Shame," *Huffington Post*, 15 April 2008; Bauer and Reynolds, "Under Siege," 14.

43. Eleanor Roosevelt, "My Day" (syndicated column), 30 October 1958.

44. Friendly, Lowe, and Murrow, *Harvest of Shame*; Rosenbaum and Shin, "Migrant and Seasonal Farmworkers," 1.

45. Rick Jervis, "Hispanic Worker Deaths Up 76% Since 1992," *USA Today*, 20 July 2009.

46. "Hispanic On-the-job Death Toll Rising," *United Press International*, 20 July 2009; National Council of La Raza, "Latino Employment Status, March 2009," 2009. National Council of La Raza figures from U.S. Department of Labor, Bureau of Labor Statistics, "Fatal Occupational Injuries, Employment, and Rates of Fatal Occupational Injuries by Selected Worker Characteristics, Occupations, and Industries, 2006."

47. ACLU of North Carolina Legal Foundation, "The Policies and Politics of Local Immigration Enforcement Laws: 287(g) Program in North Carolina," 22–26.

48. Mock, "Immigration Backlash"; Adam Nossiter, "Day Laborers Are Easy Prey in New Orleans," *New York Times*, 15 February 2009.

49. Judith Martínez-Sadri, "Latino Activists Face Death Threats in Georgia," *Atlanta Latino*, 25 May 2008, translated by New America Media; Lovato, "Juan Crow Grows More Violent"; United White Knights of the Ku Klux Klan, "What the Klan Is."

50. Julia Preston, "Rules Collide with Reality in the Immigration Debate," *New York*

Times, 29 May 2006; Raymond A. Mohl, "Globalization and Latin American Immigration in Alabama," in Odem and Lacy, eds., *Latino Immigrants and the Transformation of the U.S. South*, 51–69.

51. Leon Fink, *The Maya of Morganton*, 2–4.

52. Croucher, *Globalization and Belonging*, 41.

53. Croxdale, "Pecan Shellers' Strike"; Kilday quotation from Shapiro, "The Pecan Shellers of San Antonio, Texas," 235. See also Ruíz, *From Out of the Shadows*, 80, 90–128.

54. Vargas, *Labor Rights are Civil Rights*, 144; ACLU of Texas Board of Directors, "History of the ACLU in Texas," 2008, available at: http://www.aclutx.org/files/History%20ACLU%20in%20Texas.pdf [accessed 3-26-10]; Ruíz and Sánchez-Korrol, eds., *Latinas in the United States*, vol. 1, 744.

55. Ibid., 368.

56. Abowd, "Victory for Smithfield Workers"; Slaughter, "Smithfield Workers to Vote on Union."

57. Manuel A. Vásquez, Chad E. Seales, and Marie Friedmann Marquardt, "New Latino Destinations," in Rodríguez, Sáenz, and Menjívar, eds., *Latinas/os in the United States*, 19; Biewen and Watson, "Pueblo USA"; "Rallies across U.S. Call For Illegal Immigrant Rights," CNN, 10 April 2006.

58. "Yearly Remittances to Mexico Drop For First Time," Associated Press, 27 January 2009; Tracy Wilkinson, "Remittances to Mexico Down Sharply," *Los Angeles Times*, 2 June 2009.

59. "Population Report," Department of Economic and Community Development, Town of Carrboro, N.C.; Emily Burns, "The Bigger Picture of the Day Laborer Issue," *Carrboro Commons*, 1 November 2007.

60. Suzy Firestone, interviewed by author, Cincinnati, Ohio, 23 August 2009; Inter-Faith Council for Social Services, "IFC History."

61. Davis, "Boundaries and Surveyors," *Southern Cultures*, 104–108.

62. Kochhar, Suro, and Tafoya, "New Latino South"; Tafoya, "Shades of Belonging."

63. Benjamin, "Republicans Face South Carolina Immigration 'Frenzy.'"

64. Kristeva, *Strangers to Ourselves*, 191; Leon Fink, "New People of the Newest South," 740; St. John, *Outcasts United*; Cuadros, *A Home on the Field*.

65. President Barack Obama, "Health Care Speech to Congress," *New York Times*, 9 September 2009; Nill, "Mark Krikorian and CIS Conflate 'Uninsured Crisis' With 'Immigration Crisis'"; Lovato, "'Send them (immigrants) home with a bullet in their head'"; Carl Hulse, "In Lawmaker's Outburst, a Rare Breach of Protocol," *New York Times*, 9 September 2009.

66. Emilio T. Gonzalez, "Director's Message" in U.S. Citizenship and Immigration Services, *USCIS Strategic Plan 2008–2012*.

Chapter 8. Back to the Future

1. Historians repeatedly argue that the globalization of markets, labor, and investment is anything but new, giving credence to the adage *plus ça change, plus c'est pareil*—the more things change, the more they stay the same. See Coclanis, "Back to the Future,"

and Gabaccia's review of recent works on women's labor from a global perspective in "Beyond 'Déjà vu All Over Again?'"

2. Kolchin, *Unfree Labor*.

3. Karimov has insisted that his photograph be prominently displayed in each classroom, public building, and factory across Uzbekistan. Excerpts from his publications containing advice and adages are posted on blue-and-white billboards throughout the country. The air base the United States leased from Uzbekistan is commonly referred to as "K2." See Robin Wright and Ann Scott Tyson, "U.S. Evicted From Air Base In Uzbekistan," *Washington Post*, 30 July 2005.

4. Dockery, "Southern Hospitality by Association."

5. Lillian Link, Secretary-Treasurer, Southern Textile Association, Belmont, N.C., telephone interview with author, 24 June 2008.

6. "Pictures of Poor Business," 16; Ayers, "Certain Aspects of the Export Trade," 22. See also Gregory Clark, "Why Isn't the Whole World Developed? Lessons from the Cotton Mills." On the long history of industrialization in Britain, see Dean and Cole, *British Economic Growth, 1688–1959*.

7. Ching Kwan Lee, "Rights Activism in China," *Contexts* 7, no. 3 (Summer 2008): 16.

8. Alexander Jung and Wieland Wagner, "Vietnam is the New China: Globalization's Victors Hunt for the Next Low-Wage Country," *Spiegel Online International*, 14 May 2008.

9. Wright, "Cheap Labor and Southern Textiles, 1880–1930," 611. See Mary E. Frederickson, "A Place to Speak Our Minds: Locating Women's Activism Where North Meets South" and "Historical Consciousness and Women's Activism"; Delfino and Gillespie, eds., *Global Perspectives on Industrial Transformation in the American South*; and Carlton and Coclanis, *The South, the Nation, and the World*.

10. Wright, "Cheap Labor and Southern Textiles, 1880–1930," 627.

11. China Labour Bulletin, "Falling through the Floor." See Collins, *Threads*, 157.

12. Mitra, "Chinese Textile Workers Face a Lose-Lose Situation as China Joins the WTO." See also Elson and Pearson, "'Nimble Fingers Make Cheap Workers: An Analysis of Women's Employment in Third World Export Manufacturing."

13. *China Labour Bulletin*, "Falling through the Floor." For an excellent overview of the major labor issues in contemporary China, see Cobble, Nolan, and Winn, eds., *International Labor and Working-Class History*.

14. Wage differential figures from Lahne, *The Cotton Mill Worker*, 165–66.

15. Judith Banister cited in McCormack, "Good Luck Competing Against Chinese Labor Costs."

16. Davidson, *Child Labor Legislation in the Southern Textile States*, 11. Figures on women workers from Lahne, *The Cotton Mill Worker*, 290, and U.S. Congress, Senate, *Report on the Condition of Woman and Child Wage-Earners in the United States*, vol. 1, *Cotton Textile Industry*, 29.

17. U.S. Bureau of Labor Statistics, *Report on the Condition of Woman and Child Wage-Earners in the United States*, 177.

18. Baldanzi, "The South Is 32 Million Americans," 43. Figures on women's contribu-

tion to family income available in Lahne, *The Cotton Mill Worker*, 134–35, and in Textile Workers Union of America, *Southern Textile Conference Notes*, 12.

19. International Labour Organization, "Facts on Child Labour."

20. Mary Frederickson, "Four Decades of Change: Black Workers in Southern Textiles, 1949–1981," in James Green, ed., *Workers' Struggles, Past and Present*; and Minchin, *Hiring the Black Worker*.

21. Dru C. Gladney, "China's Ethnic Divisions are Showing Up and Could Cause Trouble," *International Herald Tribune*, 22 February 1995.

22. Edith Kowski to A. J. Muste, 8 September 1928, Box 70, Brookwood Labor College Record. The other major type of southern industrialist was the absentee owner. Beginning in the last quarter of the nineteenth century, northern manufacturers invested heavily in southern industry to create a regional colonial economy, supplying raw materials and labor for businesses based in the North. Profits were skimmed and reinvested far from southern mill communities. This system of absentee ownership allowed manufacturers to intransigently oppose the demands of workers with whom they had no direct contact and in whose community they had only an economic interest. While absentee owners and paternalistic mill barons had very different philosophies of social organization and control, they were united in their opposition to all efforts to unionize "their people." For a discussion of northern investment in the South and its effects, see Woodward, *The Origins of the New South, 1877–1913*, 291–320, and Tindall, *The Emergence of the New South, 1913–1945*, 433–72.

23. Mei Fong, "A Chinese Puzzle: Surprising Shortage of Workers Forces Factories to Add Perks," *Wall Street Journal*, 16 August 2004.

24. "Georgia: Gene & Junior," *Time Magazine*.

25. Shapiro, *A New South Rebellion*, 13.

26. Collins, *Threads*, 4.

27. The estimate of 40 percent comes from conversations with Uzbek women in 2006. For a detailed study, see Minnesota Advocates for Human Rights, "Domestic Violence in Uzbekistan," December 2000. Available at: http://www.mnadvocates.org/uploads/Uzbekreport.pdf [accessed 3-26-10]. The Uzbek government maintains no official statistics on the problem.

28. "The Industrial South," *Fortune Magazine*.

29. Best, *Lost Time and Labor Turnover in Cotton Mills*, 16–17.

30. For an overview of southern organizing, see Hall et al., *Like A Family*; Hall, "Disorderly Women"; Daniel, *Culture of Misfortune*; Honey, *Southern Labor and Civil Rights*; Irons, *Testing the New Deal*; Korstad, *Civil Rights Unionism*; and Leon Fink, *The Maya of Morgantown*.

31. On Operation Dixie, see Griffith, *The Crisis of American Labor*; quote from Mary Frederickson, "'I know which side I'm on': Southern Women in the Labor Movement in the Twentieth Century," in Milkman, ed., *Women, Work and Protest*.

32. Mary Frederickson, "Heroines and Girl Strikers: Gender and Organized Labor in the Twentieth Century South," in Zieger, ed., *Organized Labor in the Twentieth Century South*. On the Southern Summer School, see Frederickson, "A Place to Speak Our Minds." On Highlander's history, see Glenn, *Highlander*.

33. The International Ladies' Garment Workers Union, AFL-CIO, Local 351, had already represented the primarily female workforce for a number of years when this violation of the National Labor Relations Act occurred. On the Stevens' campaign, see Minchin, *"Don't Sleep with Stevens!"*

34. On the migratory history of industrial corporations over the course of the twentieth century within and outside of the United States, see Cowie, *Capital Moves*.

35. David Barboza, "In Chinese Factories, Lost Fingers and Low Pay," *New York Times*, 5 January 2008.

36. For reports of child labor used by U.S. corporations, including Wal-Mart, Disney, and Hasbro, see ibid. For an extensive examination of the state of China's prison labor system (*laogai*) and how Chinese prison-made products enter the United States, see U.S.-China Economic and Security Review Commission, *Memoranda of Understanding Between the U.S. and China Regarding Prison Labor*, 110th Cong., 2d sess., 19 June 2008.

37. Lichtenstein, interviewed on *Frontline*, "Is Wal-mart Good For America?" PBS, 16 November 2004; and Lichtenstein, *Wal-Mart*.

38. Hollander, "Outlook"; Urquidi, "The Women of Ciudad Juárez"; STITCH, *Women Behind the Labels*; Hathaway, *Allies Across the Border*. For more information on the movement in Mexico, see La Botz, "Mexico's Labor Movement in Transition."

39. Ngai and Ling, "Community Based Labour Organizing."

40. Bodeen, "Two Women Arrested in Eastern China for Organizing Labor Protests."

41. Alexander and Gilmore, "A Strategic Organizing Alliance Across Borders." For information on the Highlander Research and Education Center's current transnational work, see Barbara Ellen Smith, "Across Races and Nations: Social Justice Organizing in the Transnational South," in Smith and Furuseth, eds., *Latinos in the New South*, 235–56.

42. The Binational Feminist Collective is an independent group that promotes the human rights of female workers in the maquiladora industry. The Binational is associated with the non-governmental organization CITTAC (Centro de Información para Trabajadoras y Trabajadores A.C) in Baja, California.

43. Mitra, "Chinese Textiles Workers Face a Lose-Lose Situation as China Joins the WTO."

44. Cheng, "Labor Unrest Is Growing In China."

45. China Labour Bulletin, "Trade Union Official Says China Is Just One Step Away From the Right to Strike."

46. Moyers, *Bill Moyers Journal*, 22 August 2008. Greenfield and Leong, "China's Communist Capitalism."

47. Thank you to Lawrence Gross, University of Massachusetts, Lowell, for his expertise in identifying the Margilan looms. For more on Draper looms, see Mass, "Mechanical and Organizational Innovation."

48. Kiplinger, "The Indian Head Connection III, Springs Industries—117 Years Young."

49. Ministry of Foreign Affairs of the Republic of Uzbekistan, "Uzbekistan in the Twentieth Century." On the shipment of American industrial equipment to the USSR, see Sivachev and Yakovlev, *Russia and the United States*, 85–89, and Foglesong, *The American Mission and the 'Evil Empire,'* 95–100.

50. Drye, "In U.S. South Textile Mills Gone But Not Forgotten"; Inskeep, "Former S.C. Textile Workers Look for Ways to Cope"; Minchin, "'It knocked this city to its knees.'"

51. See Tokhtakhokzhaeva, *The Re-Islamization of Society and the Position of Women in Post-Soviet Uzbekistan*. Tokhtakhokzhaeva, the co-founder of the Women's Resource Centre of Tashkent, emphasizes that "life in Uzbekistan has always seen a balance of good and bad in each era." For more on the relationship between the local and the global, see Naples and Desai, *Women's Activism and Globalization*.

52. "'Where Do Human Rights Begin?' Remarks at the United Nations, March 27, 1953," in Black, *Courage in a Dangerous World, 190.*

53. Tina Rosenberg, "Globalization," *New York Times Magazine*, 18 August 2002.

54. Cowie, *Capital Moves*, 11.

55. Patterson, "Textile Jobs in Decline."

56. STITCH, *Women Behind the Labels*; China Labour Bulletin, "Falling Through the Floor," 40.

Coda

1. George Pozzetta, "Migration to the Urban South," in Miller and Pozzetta, *Shades of the Sunbelt*, 194.

Bibliography

Manuscripts and Archival Sources

Duke University, Special Collections Library, Durham, N.C.

Congress of Industrial Organizations ("Operation Dixie")
Lucy Randolph Mason Papers

George A. Smathers Libraries, University of Florida, Gainesville, Fla.

Margaret Dreier Robins Collection

Library of Congress, Washington, D.C.

Manuscript Division

National Women's Trade Union League of America (NWTUL) Papers
Slave Narratives from the Federal Writers' Project, 1936–1938

Prints and Photographs Division

African American Photographs Assembled for the Paris Exposition of 1900
Nannie Helen Burroughs Papers

Manuscript, Archive, and Rare Book Library, Emory University, Atlanta, Ga.

Mary Cornelia Barker Papers

Martin P. Catherwood Library, Cornell University, Ithaca, N.Y.

Southern Summer School Records, American Labor Education Service (ALES) Papers
The Messenger. Jackson, Tenn.: Woman's Connectional Council of the Colored Methodist
    Episcopal Church, published monthly, 1940–1949
Methodist Episcopal Church, South, Nashville, Tenn. Annual reports, Woman's Home
    Mission Society and Woman's Missionary Council, 1901–1939

Southern Historical Collection, The Wilson Library, University of North Carolina at Chapel Hill.

Frank Porter Graham Papers #1819

State Historical Society of Wisconsin, Madison, Wis.

Highlander Research and Education Center Records, 1917–1999
Textile Workers Union of America Records, 1915–1990

Sophia Smith Collection, Smith College, Northampton, Mass.

YWCA of the USA Record, 1860–2002

Special Collections Department, McFarlin Library, University of Tulsa, Tulsa, Okla.

Tulsa Race Riot of 1921 Archive, Collection 1989-004-5

Troup County Archives, LaGrange, Ga.

Callaway Mills, LaGrange, Ga. *Callaway Beacon*, vols. 1–18 (1949–1969)

Walter P. Reuther Library, Wayne State University, Detroit, Mich.

Brookwood Labor College Records, 1921–1937

Published Sources

Abowd, Paul. "Victory for Smithfield Workers." *In These Times*, 28 January 2009.
Ackermann, Karen L. T., ed. *African American Experience: Personal and Social Activism in the 19th and 20th Centuries*. Bowie, Md.: Heritage Books, 2004.
ACLU of North Carolina Legal Foundation. "The Policies and Politics of Local Immigration Enforcement Laws: 287(g) Program in North Carolina." Raleigh, N.C.: February 2009.
ACLU of Texas. "History of the ACLU in Texas," 1 December 2006. http://www.aclutx.org/article.php?aid=387 (accessed 30 March 2010).
African Methodist Episcopal Church. *A.M.E. Year Book, 1918*. Philadelphia: A.M.E. Book Concern, 1918.
Alexander, Robin, and Peter Gilmore. "A Strategic Organizing Alliance Across Borders." In *The Transformation of U.S. Unions: Voices, Visions and Strategies from the Grassroots*, edited by Ray M. Tillman and Michael S. Cummings, 255–266. Boulder, Colo.: Lynne Rienner Publishers, 1999.
Amalgamated Clothing Workers of America (ACWA). *Documentary History, Amalgamated Clothing Workers of America, 1936–1938*. New York: ACWA, 1938.
American Federation of Labor. *Report of the Proceedings of the 49th Annual Convention of the American Federation of Labor*. Washington, D.C.: Law Reporter Printing Company, 1929.

Anderson, James D. *The Education of Blacks in the South, 1860–1935.* Chapel Hill: University of North Carolina Press, 1988.

Anderson, Sherwood. "Elizabethton, Tennessee," *Nation* 128 (1 May 1930): 527.

Ansley, Fran, and Jon Shefner, eds. *Global Connections and Local Receptions: New Latino Immigration to the Southeastern United States.* Knoxville: University of Tennessee Press, 2009.

Arnesen, Eric, ed. *Encyclopedia of U.S. Labor and Working-Class History.* New York: Routledge, 2006.

Ayers, Howard. "Certain Aspects of the Export Trade," *Textile American*, 13, no. 1 (January 1910): 22.

Bailey, Kenneth K. *Southern White Protestantism in the Twentieth Century.* New York: Harper and Row, 1964.

Baker, Ray Stannard. *The Atlanta Riot.* New York: Phillips Publishing, 1907.

———. "Following the Color Line." *American Magazine* 64, no. 1 (May 1907): 135.

———. *Following the Color Line: An Account of Negro Citizenship in the American Democracy.* New York: Doubleday, 1908.

Baldanzi, George. "The South Is 32 Million Americans." *Labor and Nation* 1 (April/May 1946): 43–44.

Bauer, Mary, and Sarah Reynolds. "Under Siege: Life for Low-Income Latinos in the South." Montgomery, Ala.: Southern Poverty Law Center, April 2009.

Bauerlein, Mark. *Negrophobia.* San Francisco: Encounter Books, 2001.

Bayly, C. A., Sven Beckert, Matthew Connelly, Isabel Hofmeyr, Wendy Kozol, and Patricia Seed. "AHR Conversation: On Transnational History." *American Historical Review* 111, no. 5 (December 2006): 1440–64.

Bell, John. "Gateway Cities." *Mortgage Banking Magazine*, 1 October 2008, 130–35.

Benjamin, Matthew. "Republicans Face South Carolina Immigration 'Frenzy.'" *Bloomberg News*, 30 November 2007.

Bennett, James B. *Religion and the Rise of Jim Crow in New Orleans.* Princeton, N.J.: Princeton University Press, 2005.

Berlin, Ira, Barbara J. Fields, and Steven F. Miller, Joseph P. Reidy, and Leslie S. Rowland. *Free at Last: A Documentary History of Slavery, Freedom, and the Civil War.* New York: New Press, 1992.

Bernstein, Irving. *The Lean Years: A History of the American Worker, 1920–1933.* Boston: Houghton Mifflin, 1969.

Best, Ethel L. *Lost Time and Labor Turnover in Cotton Mills.* Washington, D.C.: GPO, 1926.

Biewen, John, and Tennessee Watson. "Pueblo USA," Part 3. *American Radio Works.* American Public Media, 2009.

Bieze, Michael. *Booker T. Washington and the Art of Self-Representation.* New York: Peter Lang, 2008.

Black, Allida Mae Black. *Courage in a Dangerous World: The Political Writings of Eleanor Roosevelt.* New York: Columbia University Press, 1999.

Blair, Karen. *The Clubwoman as Feminist: True Womanhood Redefined, 1868–1914.* New York: Holmes and Meier, 1980.

Blassingame, John W. *Black New Orleans, 1860–1880.* Chicago: University of Chicago Press, 1973.

Blee, Kathleen. *Women of the Klan: Racism and Gender in the 1920s.* Berkeley: University of California Press, 1991.

Blight, David. *Race and Reunion: The Civil War in American Historical Memory.* Cambridge, Mass.: Harvard University Press, 2001.

Bodeen, Christopher. "Two Women Arrested in Eastern China for Organizing Labor Protests." AP Worldstream, 26 October 2004.

Boles, John B. *Black Southerners, 1619–1869.* Lexington: University of Kentucky Press, 1983.

Boone, Gladys. *The Women's Trade Union Leagues in Great Britain and the United States of America.* New York: Columbia University Press, 1942.

Boyer, Paul S. *Purity in Print: Censorship from the Gilded Age to the Computer Age.* Madison: University of Wisconsin Press, 2002.

Brophy, Alfred L., and Randall Kennedy. *Reconstructing the Dreamland: The Tulsa Riot of 1921.* New York: Oxford University Press, 2002.

Browder, Dorothea. "A 'Christian Solution of the Labor Situation': How Workingwomen Reshaped the YWCA's Religious Mission and Politics." *Journal of Women's History* 19, no. 2 (2007): 85–110.

Brown, Elsa Barkley. "Polyrhythms and Improvisation: Lessons for Women's History." Roundtable Presentation, American Historical Association, New York, 28 December 1990.

Brown, Joshua. "Presidential Ears." *Now and Then: An American Social History Project Blog.* New Media Lab, CUNY Graduate Center, 17 November 2008. http://ashp.cuny.edu/nowandthen/2008/11/presidential-ears/ (accessed 8 August 2010).

Brown, Leslie. *Upbuilding Black Durham: Gender, Class, and Black Community Development in the Jim Crow South.* Chapel Hill: University of North Carolina Press, 2008.

Brown, Oswald Eugene, and Anna Muse Brown. *Life and Letters of Laura Askew Haygood.* Nashville: Publishing House of the M.E. Church, South, 1904.

Bucke, Emory Stevens, ed. *The History of American Methodism,* vol. 2. New York: Abingdon Press, 1964.

Caldwell, Erskine. *Deep South: Memory and Observation.* New York: Weybright and Talley, 1968.

Camarota, Steven A., and Karen Jensenius. "A Shifting Tide: Recent Trends in the Illegal Immigrant Population." Washington, D.C.: Center for Immigration Studies, July 2009.

Carlton, David Lee, and Peter A. Coclanis. *The South, the Nation, and the World: Perspectives on Southern Economic Development.* Charlottesville: University of Virginia Press, 2003.

Cassedy, James Gilbert. "African Americans and the American Labor Movement." *Federal Records and African American History* 29, no. 2 (Summer 1997): 113–21.

Chateauvert, Melinda. *Marching Together: Women of the Brotherhood of Sleeping Car Porters.* Champaign: University of Illinois Press, 1998.

Cheng, Allen T. "Labor Unrest Is Growing In China." *Bloomberg News,* 27 October 2004.

China Labour Bulletin. "Falling through the Floor: Migrant Women Workers' Quest for Decent Work in Dongguan, China." *CLB Research Series* no. 2 (September 2006).

———. "Trade Union Official Says China Is Just One Step Away from the Right to Strike." *China Labour Bulletin*, 17 June 2008.

Cimbala, Paul, and Randall M. Miller, eds. *The Freedmen's Bureau and Reconstruction: Reconsiderations.* New York: Fordham University Press, 1999.

Clark, Gregory. "Why Isn't the Whole World Developed? Lessons from the Cotton Mills." *Journal of Economic History* 47, no. 1 (March 1987): 141–73.

Cobb, James, and William Stueck, eds. *Globalization and the American South.* Athens: University of Georgia Press, 2005.

Cobble, Dorothy Sue, Mary Nolan, and Peter Winn, eds. "Labor in a Changing China." Special issue, *International Labor and Working-Class History* 73, no. 1 (Spring 2008).

Coclanis, Peter A. "Back to the Future: The Globalization of Agriculture in Historical Context." *SAIS Review* 23, no. 1 (Winter–Spring 2003): 71–84.

Collins, Jane L. *Threads: Gender, Labor, and Power in the Global Apparel Industry.* Chicago: University of Chicago Press, 2003.

Conrad, Glenn R., ed. *Dictionary of Louisiana Biography*, vol. 2. New Orleans: Louisiana Historical Association, in cooperation with the Center for Louisiana Studies, University of Southwest Louisiana, 1988.

Conway, Mimi. *Rise Gonna Rise: A Portrait of Southern Textile Workers.* Garden City, N.Y.: Anchor Press/Doubleday, 1979.

Cowie, Jefferson. *Capital Moves: RCA's Seventy-Year Quest for Cheap Labor.* New York: New Press, 2001.

Cross, Coy F. *Justin Smith Morrill: Father of the Land-Grant Colleges.* East Lansing: Michigan State University Press, 1999.

Croucher, Sheila. *Globalization and Belonging: The Politics of Identity in a Changing World.* Lanham, Md.: Rowman and Littlefield, 2003.

———. *The Other Side of the Fence: American Migrants in Mexico.* Austin: University of Texas Press, 2009.

Croxdale, Richard. "Pecan Shellers' Strike." *Handbook of Texas Online.* http://www.tshaonline.org/handbook/online/articles/PP/oep1.html (accessed 15 February 2010).

Cuadros, Paul. *A Home on the Field: How One Championship Team Inspires Hope for the Revival of Small Town America.* New York: Harper Collins, 2007.

Dailey, Jane. *Before Jim Crow: The Politics of Race in Postemancipation Virginia.* Chapel Hill: University of North Carolina Press, 2000.

Daniel, Clete. *Culture of Misfortune.* Ithaca, N.Y.: ILR Press, 2001.

Davidson, Elizabeth H. *Child Labor Legislation in the Southern Textile States.* Chapel Hill: University of North Carolina Press, 1939.

Davis, David A. "Boundaries and Surveyors." Review essay of *Look Away! The U.S. South in New World Studies,* edited by Jon Smith and Deborah Cohn; *The American South in a Global World,* edited by James L. Peacock, Harry L. Watson, and Carrie R. Matthews; and *Globalization and the American South,* edited by James C. Cobb and William W. Stueck, Jr. *Southern Cultures* 11:3 (Fall 2005): 104–08.

Deane, Phyllis, and W. A. Cole. *British Economic Growth, 1688–1959: Trends and Structure*. Cambridge: Cambridge University Press, 1967.

De León, Arnold, and Richard Griswold del Castillo. *North to Aztlán: A History of Mexican Americans in the United States*. Wheeling, Ill.: Harlan Davidson, 2006.

Delfino, Susanna, and Michele Gillespie, eds. *Global Perspectives on Industrial Transformation in the American South*. Columbia: University of Missouri Press, 2005.

Delgado, Richard, and Jean Stefancic, eds. *Critical White Studies: Looking Behind the Mirror*. Philadelphia: Temple University Press, 1997.

Docherty, Thomas. *Postmodernism: A Reader*. New York: Harvester Wheatsheaf, 1993.

Dockery, Alfred. "Southern Hospitality By Association." *Textile World* 28, no. 5 (May 1999): 112–17.

Dorsey, Allison. *To Build Our Lives Together: Community Formation in Black Atlanta, 1875–1906*. Athens: University of Georgia Press, 2004.

D'Orso, Michael. *Like Judgment Day: The Ruin and Redemption of a Town Called Rosewood*. New York: G. P. Putnam's Sons, 1996.

Dossett, Kate. *Bridging Race Divides: Black Nationalism, Feminism, and Integration in the United States, 1896–1935*. Gainesville: University Press of Florida, 2008.

Dowd, Jerome. "Strikes and Lockouts in North Carolina." *Gunton's Magazine* (February 1901): 136–41.

Dresser, Tom. *African Americans on Martha's Vineyard*. Charleston, S.C.: History Press, 2010.

Drye, Willie. "In U.S. South Textile Mills Gone But Not Forgotten." *National Geographic News,* 19 October 2004.

Du Bois, W. E. B. "The American Negro at Paris." *American Monthly Review of Reviews* 22, no. 5 (November 1900).

———. *The Autobiography of W. E. B. Dubois: A Soliloquy on Viewing My Life from the Last Decade of Its First Century*. New York: International Publishers, 1968.

———. *The Crisis Writings*. New York: Fawcett, 1972.

———. *Darkwater*. New York: Simon and Schuster, 2004.

———. "The Riot-Mill," *Crisis* 18, no. 6 (October 1919).

———. *The Souls of Black Folk*. Chicago: A. C. McClurg, 1903.

———. *W. E. B. Du Bois: A Reader*. Edited by David L. Lewis. New York: Macmillan, 1995.

Du Bois, W. E. B., ed. *Economic Co-Operation among Negro Americans*. Atlanta, Ga.: Atlanta University Press, 1907.

duCille, Ann. *The Coupling Convention*. New York: Oxford University Press, 1993.

Ellsworth, Scott. *Death in a Promised Land: The Tulsa Race Riot of 1921*. Baton Rouge: Louisiana State University Press, 1992.

Elson, Diane, and Ruth Pearson. "'Nimble Fingers Make Cheap Workers': An Analysis of Women's Employment in Third World Export Manufacturing." *Feminist Review* 7, no. 1 (Spring 1981): 87–107.

Eltzroth, E. Lee. "Woman Suffrage." *New Georgia Encyclopedia*. Athens: University of Georgia Press, 2002.

English, Beth. *A Common Thread: Labor, Politics, and Capital Mobility in the Textile Industry*. Athens: University of Georgia Press, 2006.

Escott, Paul, David R. Goldfield, Sally Gregory Mcmillen, and Elizabeth Hayes Turner, eds. *Major Problems in the History of the American South: Documents and Essays,* vol. 2, *The New South.* New York: Houghton Mifflin, 1999.

Evans, Peter, and Sarah Staveteig. "21st Century Industrialization and Development in the Global South: The Chinese Case in Comparative-Historical Perspective." Paper presented at the meeting of the American Sociological Association, Montreal Convention Center, Montreal, Quebec, Canada, 11 August 2006.

Fedo, Michael W. *The Lynchings in Duluth.* St. Paul: Minnesota Historical Society, 2000.

Feldman, Eugene. "Ella Mae [sic] Wiggins, North Carolina Mother Who Gave Her Life to Build a Union." *Southern Newsletter* 2 (March–April 1957): 15–17.

———. "Ella May Wiggins and the Gastonia Strike of 1929." *Southern Newsletter* 4 (August–September 1956): 8–11.

Fetherling, Dale. *Mother Jones: The Miners' Angel: A Portrait.* Carbondale: Southern Illinois University Press, 1974.

Fink, Gary M., and Merl E. Reed, eds. *Essays in Southern Labor History: Selected Papers, Southern Labor History Conference, 1976.* Westport, Conn.: Greenwood, 1977.

Fink, Leon. *The Maya of Morgantown: Work and Community in the Nueva New South.* Chapel Hill: University of North Carolina Press, 2003.

———. "New People of the Newest South: Prospects for the Post-1980 Immigrants." *Journal of Southern History* 75, no. 3 (August 2009): 739–50.

———. "Union Power, Soul Power: The Story of 1199B and Labor's Search for a Southern Strategy." *Southern Changes* 5 (1983): 9–20.

———. *Workingmen's Democracy: The Knights of Labor and American Politics.* Urbana: University of Illinois Press, 1983.

Fischer, Diane P., and Linda Jones Docherty, eds. *Paris 1900: The "American School" at the Universal Exposition.* New Brunswick, N.J.: Rutgers University Press, 1999.

Flores, Richard R. *Remembering the Alamo: Memory, Modernity, and the Master Symbol.* Austin: University of Texas Press, 2002.

Foglesong, David S. *The American Mission and the 'Evil Empire': The Crusade for a 'Free Russia' Since 1881.* Cambridge: Cambridge University Press, 2007.

Foner, Eric. *Reconstruction: America's Unfinished Revolution.* New York: Harper and Row, 1998.

Foner, Philip S. *History of the Labor Movement in the United States,* vol 2. New York: International Publishers, 1975.

———. *Women and the American Labor Movement: From World War I to the Present.* New York: Free Press, 1980.

Foner, Philip S., and Ronald L. Lewis, eds. *The Black Worker,* vol. 4. Philadelphia: Temple University Press, 1979.

Frankel, Linda. "Women, Paternalism, and Protest in a Southern Textile Community: Henderson, North Carolina, 1900–1960," Ph.D. diss., Harvard University, 1986.

Franklin, John Hope. "W. E. B. Du Bois: A Personal Memoir," *Massachusetts Review* 31, no. 3 (Autumn 1990), 409–29.

Frederickson, Mary E. "A Place to Speak Our Minds." Ph.D. diss., University of North Carolina at Chapel Hill, 1981.

———. "A Place to Speak Our Minds: Locating Women's Activism Where North Meets South." *Journal of Developing Societies* 23, no. 1–2 (2007): 59–70.

———. "Historical Consciousness and Women's Activism: Finding Women's Resistance Where North Meets South." In *Gender and Globalization: Patterns of Women's Resistance*, edited by Ligaya Lindio-McGovern and Erica Polakoff. Willowdale, Ontario: de Sitter Publications, 2010.

Friendly, Fred W., David Lowe, and Edward R. Murrow. *Harvest of Shame*. CBS Documentary, 1960.

Gabaccia, Donna R. "Beyond 'Déjà vu All Over Again?' Women's Work in the Global Economy." *Journal of Women's History* 19, no. 3 (October 2007), 222–31.

Garraty, John. *Quarrels That Have Shaped the Constitution*. New York: Harper and Row, 1987.

Gates, E. Nathaniel, ed. *Cultural and Literary Critiques of the Concepts of "Race."* New York: Routledge, 1997.

Genovese, Eugene D. *Roll, Jordan, Roll: The World the Slaves Made*. New York: Vintage, 1974.

"Georgia: Gene & Junior," *Time Magazine*, 7 September 1936, 10–11.

"Georgia, Meat, Fish." *Rural Migration News* 12, no. 4 (October 2006).

Gere, Anne Ruggles. *Intimate Practices: Literacy and Cultural Work in U.S. Women's Clubs, 1880–1920*. Urbana: University of Illinois Press, 1997.

Giardina, Denise. "The Pittston Strike: Solidarity in Appalachia." *Nation*, 3 July 1989, 12–14.

Giddings, Paula. *A Sword Among Lions: Ida B. Wells and the Campaign Against Lynching*. New York: Harper Collins, 2008.

———. *When and Where I Enter: The Impact of Black Women on Race and Sex in America*. New York: William Morrow, 1984.

Gilkes, Cheryl Townsend. "'Together and in Harness': Women's Traditions in the Sanctified Church." *Signs: Journal of Women in Culture and Society* 10, no. 4 (Summer 1985), 678–700.

Gill, Hannah, and Todd Drake. *Going to Carolina del Norte: Narrating Mexican Migrant Experiences*. Chapel Hill, N.C.: University Center for International Studies, 2006.

Gilmore, Glenda. *Gender and Jim Crow: Women and the Politics of White Supremacy in North Carolina*. Chapel Hill: University of North Carolina Press, 1996.

Glenn, John. *Highlander: No Ordinary School*. Knoxville: University of Tennessee Press, 1996.

Godshalk, David Fort. *Veiled Visions: The 1906 Atlanta Race Riot and the Reshaping of American Race Relations*. Chapel Hill: University of North Carolina, 2005.

Goodstein, Anita Shafer. "A Rare Alliance: African American and White Women in the Tennessee Elections of 1919 and 1920." *Journal of Southern History* 64, no. 2 (May 1998): 219–46.

Gordon-Reed, Annette, ed. *Race on Trial: Law and Justice in American History*. New York: Oxford University Press, 2002.

Gorn, Elliott J. *Mother Jones: The Most Dangerous Woman in America*. New York: Hill and Wang, 2002.

Green, Archie. *Only a Miner: Studies in Recorded Coal-Mining Songs*. Urbana: University of Illinois Press, 1972.

Green, Elna C. *Southern Women and the Woman Suffrage Question*. Chapel Hill: University of North Carolina Press, 1997.

Green, James, ed. *Workers' Struggles, Past and Present*. Philadelphia: Temple University Press, 1983.

Greenfield, Gerard, and Apo Leong. "China's Communist Capitalism: The Real World of Market Socialism." *Socialist Register* 33 (1997): 96–122.

Griffith, Barbara. *The Crisis of American Labor: Operation Dixie and the Defeat of the CIO*. Philadelphia: Temple University Press, 1988.

Hall, Jacquelyn D. "Disorderly Women: Gender and Labor Militancy in the Appalachian South." *Journal of American History* 73 (September 1986): 354–82.

———. *Revolt Against Chivalry: Jessie Daniel Ames and the Women's Campaign Against Lynching*. New York: Columbia University Press, 1979.

Hall, Jacquelyn D., James Leloudis, Robert Kornstad, Mary Murphy, Lu Ann Jones, and Christopher B. Daly. *Like A Family: The Making of a Southern Cotton Mill World*. Chapel Hill: University of North Carolina Press, 1987.

Handbook for Adult Missionary Societies. Nashville: Woman's Connectional Council of the Colored Methodist Episcopal Church, 1930.

Hareven, Tamara K., and Randolph Langenbach. *Amoskeag: Life and Work in An American Factory City*. New York: Pantheon, 1978.

Harris, Joel Chandler. *Life of Henry W. Grady Including His Writings and Speeches*. New York: Cassell Publishing, 1890.

Hathaway, Dale. *Allies Across the Border: Mexico's "Authentic Labor Front" and Global Solidarity*. Cambridge, Mass.: South End Press, 2000.

Haywood, A. S. "We Propose to Unionize Labor In the South," *Labor and Nation* 1 (1946): 35–37.

Hennie, Matt. "20-County Metro Atlanta Population to Reach 7 Million by 2030." Atlanta Regional Commission, 12 October 2006.

Hewitt, Nancy A., and Suzanne Lebsock, eds. *Visible Women: New Essays on American Activism*. Urbana: University of Illinois Press, 1993.

Hickey, Georgina. *Hope and Danger in the New South City*. Athens: University of Georgia Press, 2003.

Higginbotham, Elizabeth. *Righteous Discontent: The Women's Movement in the Black Baptist Church*. Cambridge, Mass.: Harvard University Press, 2006.

Hill, Samuel S., ed. *Religion and the Solid South*. Nashville: Abingdon Press, 1972.

Hine, Darlene Clark. "Some Preliminary Thoughts on Rape, the Threat of Rape, and the Culture of Dissemblance." *Signs: Journal of Women in Culture and Society* 14, no. 4 (Summer 1989): 912–20.

———. *When Truth Is Told: A History of Black Women's Culture and Community in Indiana, 1875–1950*. Indianapolis: National Council of Negro Women, Indianapolis Section, 1981.

Hirsch, James S. *Riot and Remembrance: America's Worst Race Riot and Its Legacy*. New York: Houghton Mifflin, 2003.

Hollander, Elizabeth. "Outlook: 'Hellraiser Martha Ojeda.'" *Mother Jones* (November/December 1999), 21.

Honey, Michael. *Southern Labor and Civil Rights*. Urbana: University of Illinois Press, 1993.

Horstman, Dorothy. *Sing Your Heart Out, Country Boy*. Nashville, Tenn.: Country Music Foundation Press, 1975.

Huber, Patrick. "Mill Mother's Lament: Ella May Wiggins and the Gastonia Textile Strike of 1929." *Southern Cultures* 15, no. 3 (2009): 81–110.

Huggins, Nathan, Martin Kilson, and Daniel M. Fox, eds. *Key Issues in the Afro-American Experience*, vol. 2. New York: Houghton Mifflin Harcourt, 1971.

Hunter, Tera. *To 'Joy My Freedom: Southern Black Women's Lives and Labors After the Civil War*. Cambridge, Mass.: Harvard University Press, 1997.

"The Industrial South." *Fortune Magazine*, 18 (November 1938), 44–55.

Inskeep, Steve. "Former S.C. Textile Workers Look for Ways to Cope." National Public Radio, 13 August 2008.

Inter-Faith Council for Social Services. "IFC History." Chapel Hill, N.C. http://www.ifcweb.org/history.html (accessed 15 March 2009).

International Labour Organization (ILO). "Facts on Child Labour." Geneva: ILO Department of Communication and Public Information, 2006.

Irons, Janet. *Testing the New Deal: The General Textile Strike of 1934 in the American South*. Urbana: University of Illinois Press, 2000.

Jackson, Cynthia L., and Eleanor F. Nunn. *Historically Black Colleges and Universities: A Reference Handbook*. Santa Barbara, Calif.: ABC-CLIO, 2003.

Jacobson, Matthew. *Whiteness of a Different Color*. Cambridge, Mass.: Harvard University Press, 1998.

Janiewski, Delores. *Sisterhood Denied: Race, Gender and Class in a New South Community*. Philadelphia: Temple University Press, 1984.

Jimoh, A Yemisi. "Playing in the Dark: Whiteness and the Literary Imagination." *The Literary Encyclopedia*, 2 July 2004. http://www.litencyc.com/php/sworks.php?rec=true&UID=2769 (accessed 29 March 2010).

Jones, Jacqueline. *Saving Savannah: The City and the Civil War*. New York: Knopf, 2008.

Jones, Mother. *Autobiography of Mother Jones*. Edited by Mary Field Parton. Chicago: Charles H. Kerr and Co., 1925; New York: Arno Press, 1969.

Kessler-Harris, Alice. *Out to Work: A History of Wage-Earning Women in the United States*. New York: Oxford University Press, 1982.

Kiplinger, Joan. "The Indian Head Connection III, Springs Industries—117 Years Young: The Springs Story, 1827–1935." *Vintage Fabrics* (January/February 2004). http://www.fabrics.net/joan204.asp (accessed 9 August 2010).

Klarman, Michael J. *Brown v. Board of Education and the Civil Rights Movement*. Oxford: Oxford University Press, 2007.

Kochhar, Rakesh, Roberto Suro, and Sonya Tafoya. "The New Latino South: The Context and Consequences of Rapid Population Growth." Washington, D.C.: Pew Hispanic Center, 26 July 2005.

Kolchin, Peter. *Unfree Labor: American Slavery and Russian Serfdom.* Cambridge, Mass.: Harvard University Press, 1987.

Kornbluh, Joyce L., and Mary Frederickson. *Sisterhood and Solidarity: Workers' Education for Women, 1914–1984.* Philadelphia: Temple University Press, 1984.

Korstad, Robert. *Civil Rights Unionism: Tobacco Workers and the Struggle for Democracy in the Mid-Twentieth Century South.* Chapel Hill: University of North Carolina Press, 2003.

Kristeva, Julia. *Strangers to Ourselves.* New York: Columbia University Press, 1994.

"Labor Drives South," *Fortune* 34 (November 1946): 134–40.

La Botz, Dan. "Mexico's Labor Movement in Transition." *Monthly Review* 57, no. 2 (2005): 62–72.

Lader, Lawrence. "The Lady and the Sheriff." *New Republic,* 5 January 1948, 17–19.

Lahne, H. J. *The Cotton Mill Worker.* New York: Farrar and Rinehart, 1944.

Larkin, Margaret. "Ella May's Songs." *Nation* 129 (9 October 1929): 382–83.

———. "Ella May Wiggins and Songs of the Gastonia Textile Strike." *Sing Out!* 5, no. 4 (Autumn 1955): 8.

———. "The Story of Ella May." *New Masses* 5, no. 6 (November 1929): 3–4.

———. "Tragedy in North Carolina." *North American Review* 208 (1929): 686–90.

Lee, Ching Kwan. "Rights Activism in China." *Contexts* 7, no. 3 (Summer 2008): 14–19.

Letwin, Daniel. *The Challenge of Interracial Unionism: Alabama Coal Miners, 1878–1921.* Chapel Hill: University of North Carolina Press, 1997.

Levine, Susan. *Degrees of Equality: The American Association of University Women and the Challenge of Twentieth-Century Feminism.* Philadelphia: Temple University Press, 1995.

———. *Labor's True Woman: Carpet Weavers, Industrialization and Labor Reform in the Gilded Age.* Philadelphia: Temple University Press, 1984.

Lewis, David Levering. *W. E. B. Du Bois: Biography of a Race.* New York: Holt and Company, 1993.

Lichtenstein, Nelson. Interviewed on *Frontline,* "Is Wal-mart Good For America?" PBS, 16 November 2004.

———. *Wal-Mart: The Face of 21st Century Capitalism.* New York: New Press, 2006.

Lieberson, Stanley. *A Piece of the Pie: Black and White Immigrants since 1880.* Berkeley: University of California Press, 1981.

Lincoln, C. Eric, and Lawrence H. Mamiya. *The Black Church in the African American Experience.* Durham, N.C.: Duke University Press, 1990.

Long, Priscilla. *Where the Sun Never Shines: A History of America's Bloody Coal Industry.* New York: Paragon House, 1989.

Lovato, Roberto. "Juan Crow Grows More Violent: Latino Activists Face Death Threats in Georgia." *Of América Blog,* 27 May 2008. http://ofamerica.wordpress.com/2008/05/27/juan-crow-grows-more-violent-latino-activists-face-death-threats-in-georgia/ (accessed 10 March 2010).

MacLean, Nancy. *Behind the Mask of Chivalry: The Making of the Second Ku Klux Klan.* New York: Oxford University Press, 1994.

———. *Freedom Is Not Enough: The Opening of the American Workplace.* Cambridge, Mass.: Harvard University Press, 2008.

Madigan, Tim. *The Burning: Massacre, Destruction, and the Tulsa Race Riot of 1921.* New York: St. Martin's Press, 2001.

Mantero, José María. *Latinos and the U.S. South.* Westport, Conn.: Praeger, 2008.

Marshall, F. Ray. *Labor in the South.* Cambridge, Mass.: Harvard University Press, 1967.

Marshall, F. Ray, and Virgil L. Christian, eds. *Employment of Blacks in the South: A Perspective on the 1960s.* Austin: University of Texas Press, 1978.

Martin, Waldo E., ed. *Brown v. Board of Education.* Boston: Bedford/St. Martins, 1998.

Mashburn, J. L. *Black Americana: A Century of History Preserved on Postcards.* Enka, N.C.: Colonial House, 1996.

Mason, Lucy R. "The C.I.O. in the South." *The South and World Affairs* 6 (1944).

Mass, William. "Mechanical and Organizational Innovation: The Drapers and the Automatic Loom." *Business History Review* 63, no. 4 (Winter, 1989): 876–929.

McAfee, L. D. [Sara]. *History of the Woman's Missionary Society in the Colored Methodist Episcopal Church.* Jackson, Tenn.: Publishing House, C.M.E. Church, 1934.

McCormack, Richard. "Good Luck Competing Against Chinese Labor Costs." *Manufacturing & Technology News* 13, no. 9 (2 May 2006).

McDowell, John Patrick. *The Social Gospel in the South: The Woman's Home Mission Movement in the Methodist Episcopal Church, South, 1886–1939.* Baton Rouge: Louisiana State University Press, 1982.

McLaurin, M. A. *Paternalism and Protest: Southern Cotton Mill Workers and Organized Labor, 1875–1905.* Westport, Conn.: Greenwood, 1971.

McLendon, Paula. "Time and Time Again: The Women, the Union and the Vanity Factory." *Southern Changes* 6, no. 5 (1984): 8–17.

Medley, Keith Weldon. *We as Freemen: Plessy v. Ferguson.* New Orleans: Pelican, 2003.

Mendoza, Marcela, David H. Ciscel, and Barbara Ellen Smith. "Latino Immigrants in Memphis: Assessing the Economic Impact." *Southern Changes* 23, no. 3–4 (2001): 24–26.

Milkman, Ruth, ed. *Women, Work and Protest: A Century of U.S. Women's Labor History.* London: Routledge and Kegan Paul, 1985.

Miller, Marc S., ed. *Working Lives: The Southern Exposure History of Labor in the South.* New York: Pantheon, 1980.

Miller, Randall M., and George E. Pozzetta. *Shades of the Sunbelt: Essays on Ethnicity, Race, and the Urban South.* New York: Greenwood Press, 1998.

Minchin, Timothy J. *"Don't Sleep with Stevens!" The J. P. Stevens Campaign and the Struggle to Organize the South, 1963–1980.* Gainesville: University Press of Florida, 2005.

———. *Hiring the Black Worker: The Racial Integration of the Southern Textile Industry, 1969–1980.* Chapel Hill: University of North Carolina Press, 1999.

———. "'It knocked this city to its knees': The Closure of Pillowtex Mills in Kannapolis, North Carolina and the Decline of the US Textile Industry." *Labor History* 50 (2009): 287–311.

Ministry of Foreign Affairs of the Republic of Uzbekistan. "Uzbekistan in the 20th Century: Uzbekistan during the World War II." http://mfa.uz/eng/about_uzb/history/uzb_20th-90th/ (accessed 8 August 2010).

Mitchell, George Sinclair. *Textile Unionism in the South*. Chapel Hill: University of North Carolina Press, 1931.

Mitra, Sabyasachi. "Chinese Textile Workers Face a Lose-Lose Situation As China Joins the WTO." *China Report* 39, no. 1 (2003): 81–86.

Mixon, Gregory. *The Atlanta Riot: Race, Class, and Violence in a New South City*. Gainesville: University Press of Florida, 2005.

Mock, Brentin. "Immigration Backlash: Hate Crimes against Latinos Flourish." *Southern Poverty Law Center Intelligence Report* 128 (Winter 2007).

Montgomery, William E. *Under Their Own Vine and Fig Tree: The African-American Church in the South, 1865–1900*. Baton Rouge: Louisiana State University Press, 1993.

Morrison, Toni. *Playing in the Dark: Whiteness and the Literary Imagination*. Cambridge, Mass.: Harvard University Press, 1992.

Moyers, Bill. *Bill Moyers Journal*. PBS, 22 August 2008.

Murphy, Arthur, Colleen Blanchard, and Jennifer Hill, eds. *Latino Workers in the Contemporary South*. Athens: University of Georgia Press, 2001.

Murray, Gail S. *Throwing Off the Cloak of Privilege: White Southern Women Activists in the Civil Rights Era*. Gainesville: University Press of Florida, 2008.

Muste, A. J. "The Call of South." *Labor Age* 17, no. 8 (August 1928): 5–6.

Naples, Nancy A., and Manisha Desai. *Women's Activism and Globalization: Linking Local Struggles and Transnational Politics*. London: Routledge, 2002.

National Council of La Raza. "Latino Employment Status, March 2009." Washington, D.C.: NCLR, 2009.

National Executive Committee of the Conference for Progressive Labor Action. "The Marion Murder" (pamphlet no. 2). New York: Progressive Labor Library, 1929.

National Planning Association, Committee of the South. *Selected Studies of Negro Employment in the South*. Washington, D.C.: National Planning Association, 1955.

National Railroad Passenger Corporation. *Amtrak Crescent Route Guide*, 2009.

Newman, Dale. "Work and Community Life in a Southern Town." *Labor History* 19, no. 2 (Spring 1978): 204–25.

Ngai, Pun, and Chan Wai Ling. "Community Based Labour Organizing." *International Union Rights* 11, no. 4 (2004): 10–11.

Nicholson, Philip Yale. *Labor's Story in the United States*. Philadelphia: Temple University Press, 2004.

Nill, Andrea. "Mark Krikorian and CIS Conflate 'Uninsured Crisis' With 'Immigration Crisis.'" *The Wonk Room Blog*, Center for American Progress, 29 June 2009. http://wonkroom.thinkprogress.org/2009/06/29/health-care-immigration/ (accessed 10 August 2010).

Northrup, H. R., Richard L. Rowan, Darold T. Barnum, and John C. Howard, eds. *Negro Employment in Southern Industry*. Philadelphia: University of Pennsylvania Press, 1970.

Odem, Mary, and Elaine Lacy, eds. *Latino Immigrants and the Transformation of the U.S. South*. Athens: University of Georgia Press, 2009.

Olsen, Otto H. *The Thin Disguise*. New York: Humanities Press, 1967.

Passel, Jeffrey S., and D'Vera Cohn. "A Portrait of Unauthorized Immigrants in the United States." Washington, D.C.: Pew Hispanic Center, 14 April 2009.

Patterson, Janet. "Textile Jobs in Decline." Interview by Betty Ann Bowser. *News Hour*. PBS, 23 September 2008.

Payne, Elizabeth Ann. "The Lady Was a Sharecropper: Myrtle Lawrence and the Southern Tenant Farmers' Union." *Southern Cultures* 4, no. 2 (1998): 5–27.

———. *Reform, Labor, and Feminism: Margaret Dreier Robins and the Women's Trade Union League*. Urbana: University of Illinois Press, 1988.

Peacock, James L., Harry L. Watson, and Carrie R. Matthews, eds. *The American South in a Global World*. Chapel Hill: University of North Carolina Press, 2005.

Perdue, Theda. *Race and the Cotton States Exposition of 1895*. Athens: University of Georgia Press, 2010.

Pew Hispanic Center. "Statistical Portrait of Hispanics in the United States, 2007." Washington, D.C.: Pew Hispanic Center, 5 March 2009.

———. "A Statistical Portrait of Hispanic Women in the U.S." Washington, D.C.: Pew Hispanic Center, 8 May 2008.

"Pictures of Poor Business." *Textile American* 13, no. 4 (April 1910): 16.

Powell, William, ed. *Dictionary of North Carolina Biography*, vol. 6. Chapel Hill: University of North Carolina Press, 1996.

Proceedings of the Sixth National Convention of the Young Women's Christian Associations of the United States of America, Cleveland, Ohio, 12–20 April 1920. New York: National Board, Young Women's Christian Associations, 1920.

Reed, Christopher Robert. *All the World is Here! The Black Presence at the White City*. Bloomington: Indiana University Press, 2000.

Robertson, Nancy Marie. *Christian Sisterhood, Race Relations, and the YWCA, 1906–46*. Urbana: University of Illinois Press, 2007.

Rodríguez, Havidán, Rogelio Sáenz, and Cecilia Menjívar. *Latinas/os in the United States: Changing the Face of América*. New York: Springer, 2008.

Roosevelt, Eleanor. "In Your Hands." Remarks to the United Nations Commission on Human Rights. United Nations, New York, 27 March 1958.

Rosenbaum, Sara, and Peter Shin. "Migrant and Seasonal Farmworkers: Health Coverage and Access to Care," Washington, D.C.: Kaiser Family Foundation, 2005.

Rosenberg, Daniel. *New Orleans Dockworkers: Race, Labor, and Unionism*. Albany, N.Y.: SUNY Press, 1988.

Rouse, Jacqueline Anne. *Lugenia Burns Hope, Black Southern Reformer*. Athens: University of Georgia Press, 1989.

Roydhouse, Marion Winifred. "The 'Universal Sisterhood of Women': Women and Labor Reform in North Carolina, 1900–1932." Ph.D. diss., Duke University, 1980.

Rucker, Walter C., and James N. Upton, eds. *Encyclopedia of America Race Riots*. Westport, Conn.: Greenwood, 2007.

Ruether, Rosemary R., and Rosemary S. Keller, eds. *Women and Religion in America, 1900–68*, vol. 3. San Francisco: Harper and Row, 1986.

Ruíz, Vicki L. *From Out of the Shadows: Mexican Women in Twentieth Century America.* New York: Oxford University Press, 1998, 2008.

———. "Nuestra América: Latino History as United States History." *Journal of American History* 93, no. 3 (December 2006): 655–72.

Ruíz, Vicki, and Viginia Sánchez-Korrol, eds. *Latinas in the United States: A Historical Encyclopedia*, vol. 1. Bloomington: Indiana University Press, 2006.

Sacks, Karen. *Caring by the Hour: Women, Work and Organizing at Duke Medical Center.* Urbana: University of Illinois Press, 1988.

Salmond, John A. *The General Textile Strike of 1934: From Maine to Alabama.* Columbia: University of Missouri Press, 2002.

———. *Miss Lucy of the CIO: The Life and Times of Lucy Randolph Mason, 1882–1959.* Athens: University of Georgia Press, 1988.

Santos, John Phillip. *Places Left Unfinished at the Time of Creation.* Friday Harbor, Wash.: Turtleback Books, 2000.

Sassen, Saskia. "The Repositioning of Citizenship and Alienage: Emergent Subjects and Spaces for Politics." *Globalizations* 2, no. 1 (May 2005): 79–94.

Schultz, Benjamin J. "Inside the Gilded Cage: The Lives of Latino Immigrant Males in Rural Central Kentucky." *Southeastern Geographer* 48, no. 2 (August 2008): 201–18.

Scott, Anne F. *Natural Allies: Women's Associations in American History.* Urbana: University of Illinois Press, 1991.

———. *The Southern Lady: From Pedestal to Politics, 1830–1930.* Chicago: University of Chicago Press, 1970.

Scott, Rebecca J. "Public Rights, Social Equality, and the Conceptual Roots of the Plessy Challenge." *Michigan Law Review* 106, no. 5 (2008): 777–804.

Shapiro, Harold A. "The Pecan Shellers of San Antonio, Texas." *Southwestern Social Science Quarterly* 32 (March 1952): 229–45.

Shapiro, Karin A. *A New South Rebellion: The Battle Against Convict Labor in the Tennessee Coalfields, 1871–1896.* Chapel Hill: University of North Carolina Press, 1998.

Sharpe, Rhonda V. "All Land Grants Were Not Created Equal: The Benefits of White Privilege." *Review of Black Political Economy* 32, no. 3–4 (March 2005): 29–38.

Shaw, Stephanie. *What a Woman Ought to Be and To Do: Black Professional Women Workers during the Jim Crow Era.* Chicago: University of Chicago Press, 1995.

Shields, A. "Organizing the South: How Labor Movement Can Do This Job." *Labor Age* 17 (1928): 4–7.

Sims, Anastasia. *The Power of Femininity in the New South: Women's Organizations and Politics in North Carolina, 1880–1930.* Columbia: University of South Carolina Press, 1997.

Sivachev, Nikolai V., and Nikolai N. Yakovlev. *Russia and the United States.* Chicago: University of Chicago Press, 1980.

Slaughter, Jane. "Smithfield Workers to Vote on Union." *Labor Notes* 357 (December 2008).

Smith, Heather A., and Owen J. Furuseth, eds. *Latinos in the New South: Transformations of Place.* Burlington, Vt.: Ashgate Publishing, 2006.

Smith, Jon, and Deborah Cohn, eds. *Look Away! The U.S. South in New World Studies.* Durham, N.C.: Duke University Press, 2004.

Smith, Lillian. *Killers of the Dream.* New York: Norton, 1949, 1994.

Smith, Sharon. *Subterranean Fire: A History of Working-Class Radicalism in the United States.* Chicago: Haymarket Books, 2006.

Smith, Shawn Michelle. "'Looking at One's Self through the Eyes of Others': W. E. B. Du Bois' Photographs for the 1900 Paris Exposition." *African American Review* 34, no. 4 (Winter 2000): 581–99.

———. *Photography on the Color Line: W. E. B. Du Bois, Race, and Visual Culture.* Durham, N.C.: Duke University Press, 2004.

Smith-Rosenberg, Carroll. *Disorderly Conduct: Visions of Gender in Victorian America.* New York: Knopf, 1985.

Smyth, William D. "Blacks and the South Carolina Interstate and West Indian Exposition." *South Carolina Historical Magazine* 88, no. 4 (October 1987): 211–19.

Starobin, Robert S. *Industrial Slavery in the Old South.* New York: Oxford University Press, 1970.

State of Georgia, Department of Labor. *Second Annual Report* (1938).

Stewart, Annabel M. *The Industrial Work of the YWCA.* New York: Woman's Press, 1937.

STITCH. *Women Behind the Labels: Worker Testimonies from Central America.* Toronto: Maquila Solidarity Network and STITCH, 2000.

St. John, Warren. *Outcasts United: A Refugee Soccer Team, an American Town.* New York: Random House, 2009.

Stout, Robert Joe. *Why Immigrants Come to America: Braceros, Indocumentados, and the Migra.* Westport, Conn.: Greenwood, 2008.

Sullivan, Patricia. *Lift Every Voice: The NAACP and the Making of the Civil Rights Movement.* New York: New Press, 2009.

Suro, Roberto, and Jeffrey S. Passel. "The Rise of the Second Generation: Changing Patterns in Hispanic Population Growth." Washington, D.C.: Pew Hispanic Center, 14 October 2003.

Tafoya, Sonya. "Shades of Belonging." Washington, D.C.: Pew Hispanic Center, 6 December 2004.

Tatum, Noreen Dunn. *A Crown of Service: A Story of Woman's Work in the Methodist Episcopal Church, South from 1878–1940.* Nashville: Board of Missions, Women's Division of Christian Service, 1960.

Taylor, Verta, and Leila Rupp. "Loving Internationalism: The Emotion Culture of Transnational Women's Organizations, 1888–1945." *Mobilization* 7, no. 2 (Summer 2002): 141–58.

Terborg-Penn, Rosalyn. *African American Women in the Struggle for the Vote, 1850–1920.* Bloomington: Indiana University Press, 1998.

Textile Workers Union of America (TWUA). *Southern Textile Conference Notes.* Atlanta, 25 January 1941.

———. "What Every Woman Should Know" (pamphlet). New York, 1946.

Thomas, Hilah F., and Rosemary Skinner Keller, eds. *Women in New Worlds: Historical Perspectives on the Wesleyan Tradition*, vol. 1. Nashville, Tenn.: Abington Press, 1981.

Tindall, George Brown. *The Emergence of the New South, 1913–1945*. Baton Rouge: Louisiana State University Press, 1967.

———. *The Ethnic Southerners*. Baton Rouge: Louisiana State University Press, 1979.

Tippett, Tom. *When Southern Labor Stirs*. New York: Jonathan Cape and Harrison Smith, 1931.

Tokhtakhokzhaeva, Marfua. *The Re-Islamization of Society and the Position of Women in Post-Soviet Uzbekistan*. Kent, UK: Global Oriental Publishers, 2008.

Trepp, Jean Carol. "Union-Management Co-operation and the Southern Organizing Campaign." *Journal of Political Economy* 41 (1933): 602–24.

Trotter, Joe William. *The Great Migration in Historical Perspective: New Dimensions of Race, Class, and Gender*. Bloomington: Indiana University Press, 1991.

Umfleet, LeRae. *1898 Wilmington Race Riot Report*. Wilmington, N.C.: Wilmington Race Riot Commission, 2006, http://www.history.ncdcr.gov/1898-wrrc/report/report.htm (accessed 9 August 2010).

United White Knights of the Ku Klux Klan. "What the Klan Is." http://www.uwkkkk.com/what.html (accessed 25 March 2010).

Urquidi, Mariclaire Acosta. "The Women of Ciudad Juárez." Center for Latin American Studies, UC Berkeley Working Papers Series, no. 3 (May 2005).

U.S. Bureau of Labor Statistics. *Report on the Condition of Woman and Child Wage-Earners in the United States*, vol. 10, *History of Women in Trade Unions*. Senate Document no. 645, 61st Cong., 2nd sess. Prepared by John B. Andrews and W.D.P. Bliss. Washington, D.C.: Government Printing Office, 1911.

U.S. Census Bureau. Georgia Population and Housing Narrative Profile. 2005–2007 American Community Survey 3-Year Estimates.

U.S. Citizenship and Immigration Services. "Cap Count for H-1B and H-2B Workers for Fiscal Year 2010," 3 September 2009.

———. *USCIS Strategic Plan 2008–2012*. Washington, D.C.: USCIS, 2007.

U.S.-China Economic and Security Review Commission. *The Memoranda of Understanding Between the U.S. and China Regarding Prison Labor*. 110th Cong., 2nd sess., 19 June 2008. Washington, D.C.: Government Printing Office, 2008.

U.S. Congress. Senate. *Report on the Condition of Woman and Child Wage-Earners in the United States*, vol. 1, *Cotton Textile Industry*, Senate Document no. 645, 61st Cong., 2nd sess. Washington, D.C.: Government Printing Office, 1910.

U.S. Department of Labor. Bureau of Labor Statistics. Southeastern Regional Office. Atlanta, Ga. "Southeastern Textile Mills Employment Monthly Reports," October, 1980.

———. "Textile Products Industry Employment in the Southeast, 1947–1979."

U.S. Department of Labor. Women's Bureau. "Negro Women in Industry in 15 States." *Bulletin of the Women's Bureau* 20 (1922).

U.S. Equal Employment Opportunity Commission. *Minorities and Women in Private Industry, 1978 Report*, vol. 1. Washington D.C.: Government Printing Office, 1980.

Vargas, Zaragosa. *Labor Rights are Civil Rights: Mexican American Workers in Twentieth-Century America*. Princeton, N.J.: Princeton University Press, 2007.

Waligora-Davis, Nicole. "W. E. B. Du Bois and the Fourth Dimension." *CR: The New Centennial Review* 6, no. 3 (Winter 2006): 57–90.

Wallinger, Hanna. *Pauline E. Hopkins: A Literary Biography*. Athens: University of Georgia Press, 2005.

Wallis, Brian. "Black Bodies, White Science: Louis Agassiz's Slave Daguerreotypes." *American Art* 9, no. 2 (Summer 1995): 39–61.

Washington, Booker T. *The Booker T. Washington Papers, Volume 3: 1889–1895*. Edited by Louis R. Harlan. Champaign: University of Illinois Press, 1974.

———. *Up From Slavery: An Autobiography*. New York: Doubleday & Co., 1901.

Washington, Booker T., and W. E. B. Du Bois. *The Negro in the South: His Economic Progress in Relation to His Moral and Religious Development*. Philadelphia: George W. Jacobs and Co., 1907.

Weisbord, Albert. "Passaic, New Bedford, North Carolina," *The Communist* 8, no. 6 (June 1929): 319–23.

Weisbord, Vera Buch. *A Radical Life*. Bloomington: Indiana University Press, 1977.

Wheeler, Marjorie Spruill. *New Women of the New South: The Leaders of the Woman Suffrage Movement in the Southern States*. New York: Oxford University Press, 1993.

Whitman, Willson. *God's Valley*. New York: Viking Press, 1939.

Wiener, Jonathan M. *Social Origins of the New South: Alabama, 1860–1885*. Baton Rouge: Louisiana State University Press, 1978.

Willett, Mabel Hurd. *The Employment of Women in the Clothing Trade*. New York: Columbia University Press, 1902.

Williams, Lillian Serece. *Strangers in the Land of Paradise: Creation of an African American Community*. Bloomington: Indiana University Press, 2000.

Williams, T. Harry. "The Louisiana Unification Movement of 1873." *Journal of Southern History* 11, no. 3 (1943): 349–69.

Williamson, Joel. *The Crucible of Race: Black-White Relations in the American South Since Emancipation*. New York: Oxford University Press, 1984.

Wilmore, Gayraund S., ed. *African American Religious Studies: An Interdisciplinary Anthology*. Durham, N.C.: Duke University Press, 1989.

Winik, Jay. *April 1865: The Month that Saved America*. New York: Harper Collins, 2001.

Wishart, David J., ed. *Encyclopedia of the Great Plains*. Lincoln: University of Nebraska Press, 2004.

Wood, Amy Louise. *Lynching and Spectacle: Witnessing Racial Violence in America, 1890–1940*. Chapel Hill: University of North Carolina Press, 2009.

Woodward, C. Vann. *The Origins of the New South, 1877–1913*. Baton Rouge: Louisiana State University Press, 1971.

Wright, Gavin. "Cheap Labor and Southern Textiles, 1880–1930." *Quarterly Journal of Economics* 96, no. 4 (November 1981): 605–29.

Zeiger, Elise. "Town Hits Economic Jackpot to Become 'Kia-ville,'" CNN, 9 July 2009.

Zieger, Robert, ed. *Organized Labor in the Twentieth Century South*. Knoxville: University of Tennessee Press, 1991.

Index

Page numbers in *italic* refer to illustrations.

Mary E. Frederickson is a professor of history at Miami University, Oxford, Ohio. She is the editor (with Joyce L. Kornbluh) of *Sisterhood and Solidarity*.

SOUTHERN DISSENT

Edited by Stanley Harrold and Randall M. Miller

The Other South: Southern Dissenters in the Nineteenth Century, by Carl N. Degler, with a new preface (2000)

Crowds and Soldiers in Revolutionary North Carolina: The Culture of Violence in Riot and War, by Wayne E. Lee (2001)

"Lord, We're Just Trying to Save Your Water": Environmental Activism and Dissent in the Appalachian South, by Suzanne Marshall (2002)

The Changing South of Gene Patterson: Journalism and Civil Rights, 1960–1968, edited by Roy Peter Clark and Raymond Arsenault (2002)

Gendered Freedoms: Race, Rights, and the Politics of Household in the Delta, 1861–1875, by Nancy Bercaw (2003)

Civil War on Race Street: The Civil Rights Movement in Cambridge, Maryland, by Peter B. Levy (2003)

South of the South: Jewish Activists and the Civil Rights Movement in Miami, 1945–1960, by Raymond A. Mohl, with contributions by Matilda "Bobbi" Graff and Shirley M. Zoloth (2004)

Throwing Off the Cloak of Privilege: White Southern Female Activists in the Civil Rights Era, edited by Gail S. Murray (2004)

The Atlanta Riot: Race, Class, and Violence in a New South City, by Gregory Mixon (2004)

Slavery and the Peculiar Solution: A History of the American Colonization Society, by Eric Burin (2005), first paperback edition, 2008

"I Tremble for My Country": Thomas Jefferson and the Virginia Gentry, by Ronald L. Hatzenbuehler (2006)

From Saint-Domingue to New Orleans: Migration and Influences, by Nathalie Dessens (2007)

Higher Education and the Civil Rights Movement: White Supremacy, Black Southerners, and College Campuses, edited by Peter Wallenstein (2007)

Burning Faith: Church Arson in the American South, by Christopher B. Strain (2008)

Black Power in Dixie: A Political History of African Americans in Atlanta, by Alton Hornsby Jr. (2009)

Looking South: Race, Gender, and the Transformation of Labor from Reconstruction to Globalization, by Mary E. Frederickson (2011)